T0388244

"Combining fascinating historical analysis with refreshing sociological insights, this book fills a vital gap in political thinking. Thoroughly researched and fiercely defended, Tichelar draws on geography, race and class to answer one of politics' unanswered questions."

— Rt. Hon. David Lammy, Labour Party Member of Parliament for Tottenham, 2000–present, UK

"This wide-ranging book sheds light on a vital political question: why has London become such a bastion of Labour Party support and radical politics, at the same time that it has become such a central site of global capitalism? In placing London's profile in long term wide ranging historical perspective, Michael Tichelar offers a valuable account which will interest everyone concerned with the future of left politics in the UK."

— Mike Savage, London School of Economics and Political Science, UK

Why London Is Labour

This book answers the question why London has been a stronghold for the Labour Party for relatively long periods of the last century and continues to be so to this day to an extent that surprises contemporaries.

The book draws on evidence from history and political sociology as well as the personal experience of the author in London local government during the 1980s. It argues that while changes in the London economy, plus the ability of the party to forge cross-class alliances, can go some way to explain the success of the Labour Party in London, a range of other demographic and social factors need to be taken into account, especially after the year 2000. These include the size of London's growing black and ethnic minority communities; higher concentrations of well-educated younger people with socially liberal values; the increasing support of the middle-classes; the impact of austerity after 2008; and the degree of poverty in London compared to non-metropolitan areas.

This book will be of key interest to readers interested in the history of the Labour Party, the politics of London, Socialist politics/history, British politics/history, government, political sociology, and urban studies.

Michael Tichelar is a Visiting Fellow in History at the University of the West of England, UK.

Routledge Studies in British Politics
Series editors: Patrick Diamond and Tim Bale of Queen Mary University, London, UK.

This series aims to promote research excellence in political science, political history and public-policy making, whilst addressing a wide array of political dynamics, contexts, histories and ideas. It will retain a particular focus on British government, British Politics and public policy, while locating those issues within a European and global context.

Centralisation, Devolution and the Future of Local Government in England
Steve Leach, John Stewart and George Jones

The Struggle for Labour's Soul
Understanding Labour's Political Thought since 1945, second edition
Edited by Matt Beech, Kevin Hickson and Raymond Plant

British Public Opinion on Foreign and Defence Policy
1945–2017
Ben Clements

Neoliberalisms in British Politics
Christopher Byrne

The Making of the Conservative Party's Immigration Policy
Rebecca Partos

Inequality in Britain
Alan Ware

Why London Is Labour
A History of Metropolitan Politics, 1900–2020
Michael Tichelar

For more information about this series, please visit: https://www.routledge.com

Why London Is Labour
A History of Metropolitan Politics, 1900–2020

Michael Tichelar

LONDON AND NEW YORK

First published 2021
by Routledge
2 Park Square, Milton Park, Abingdon, Oxon OX14 4RN

and by Routledge
52 Vanderbilt Avenue, New York, NY 10017

Routledge is an imprint of the Taylor & Francis Group, an informa business

© 2021 Michael Tichelar

The right of Michael Tichelar to be identified as author of this work
has been asserted by him in accordance with sections 77 and 78 of
the Copyright, Designs and Patents Act 1988.

All rights reserved. No part of this book may be reprinted or
reproduced or utilised in any form or by any electronic, mechanical,
or other means, now known or hereafter invented, including
photocopying and recording, or in any information storage or
retrieval system, without permission in writing from the publishers.

Trademark notice: Product or corporate names may be trademarks
or registered trademarks, and are used only for identification and
explanation without intent to infringe.

British Library Cataloguing in Publication Data
A catalogue record for this book is available from the British Library

Library of Congress Cataloging in Publication Data
A catalog record has been requested for this book

ISBN: 978-0-367-17523-8 (hbk)
ISBN: 978-0-429-05730-4 (ebk)

Typeset in Times New Roman
by codeMantra

Contents

List of tables	xi
About the author	xiii
Foreword	xv
Acknowledgements	xvii
List of abbreviations	xix

Introduction 1
The scope and outline of the book 6

PART I
Chronological – from an imperial metropolis to a City of
Rampant Capitalism 15

1 Labour in an imperial metropolis 17
Introduction 17
Labour contained within the Progressive Alliance (1900–1918) 18
Three-way party competition (1918–1929) 29
Conclusion 42

2 'Labour in a Municipal Social Democracy' 44
Introduction 44
Rise of a municipal social democracy (1929–1968) 45
'The Forward March of Labour Halted' (1968–1997) 54
Conclusion 65

3 Labour in a 'City of Rampant Capitalism' 67
Introduction 67
'Then the suburbs turned Red' (1997–2015) 70
Labour consolidated (2015–2020) 78
Conclusion 86

viii *Contents*

PART II
Thematic – localities, workplaces, trade unions, class, socialism, personal identity　　　　91

4　Localities, workplaces and trade union organisation　　　　93
Introduction 93
Inner-city dispersal and overspill – the case of Lambeth
　(1900–1968) 98
Suburban expansion – the case of Croydon (1900–2020) 107
De-industrialisation, gentrification and regeneration
　(1968–2020) 114
Working Capital & London Voices. London Lives
　(2000–2020) 118
Conclusion 124

5　Voting and social class　　　　127
Introduction 127
Class suppressed (1900–1918) 133
'Labourism' (1918–1968) 138
Dealignment (1968–1997) 145
Working-class remade (1997–2020) 147
Conclusion 155

6　Party organisation, membership and the influence of socialism　　　　167
Introduction 167
Socialists, Progressives and Labour (1900–1918) 172
Growth and decline of a mass party (1918–1968) 180
Rise and fall of the New Left (1968–1997) 194
Momentum – the Old Left Reborn (1997–2020) 200
Conclusion 203

7　The politics of personal identity – gender, race and religion　　　　206
Introduction 206
The role of women (1900–2020) 208
Black sections – the case of Lambeth (1970–1990) 219
Religious decline and then a religious revival (1900–2020) 232
Anti-Semitism (1917–2020) 239
Conclusion 242

Contents ix

Conclusion   245

Summary and historical review 245
The changing definition of social class 251
Future prospects for the Labour Party in London 256

Appendix – Demographic and election statistics   263
Bibliography   279
Index   303

Tables

2.1	Changing socio-economic classification of London constituencies 1978–1997	65
5.1	Croydon electorate 1915 and 1918 compared	141
5.2	Social and economic characteristics of Croydon in the 1950s	144
5.3	Differences in voting between areas where immigration was an important factor (1959 & 1964)	145
5.4	Labour vote (%) by social class (general elections 1945–1966)	153
5.5	Labour vote (%) by social class (general elections 1964–1997)	153
5.6	1910 (December) general election result for Greater London	157
5.7	1918 general election result for Greater London	158
5.8	1929 general election result for Greater London	159
5.9	1935 general election result for Greater London	160
5.10	1945 general election result for Greater London	161
5.11	1966 general election result for Greater London	162
5.12	1974 (February) general election result for Greater London	163
5.13	1979 general election result for Greater London	164
5.14	1997 general election result for Greater London	165
5.15	2017 general election result for Greater London	166
6.1	Party membership figures and affiliations – London Labour Party 1894–1929	182
6.2	Organisations affiliated to the London Labour Party in 1933	184
A1	Population for inner, outer and greater London 1901–2041	265
A2	Changes in ethnicity in London 1991–2011	266
A3	Current ethnicity in London compared to England & Wales (%)	266
A4	Population of London's sub-regions (2006–2016) compared to England	266
A5	Current demographics of London (race; religion and languages)	267
A6	Inner London 1889–1964 electorate, turnout and number of seats	268
A7	Inner London: percentage of parliamentary electorate to population in 1901 and 1911	269
A8	Growth of the suburban electorates before 1914	271
A9	Comparison of electorate between 1915 and 1918	272
A10	Inner London: Size of parliamentary electorate (male and female) 1918–1945	273

xii   *Tables*

A11	Greater London 1964–2018 – electorate and turnout	273
A12	Labour results in parliamentary elections in London compared to the UK 1900–1970	274
A13	Labour results in parliamentary elections in London compared to the UK 1974–2017	274
A14	Results London County Council (LCC) 1889–1961	275
A15	GLC Election results 1964–1981	275
A16	Percentage share of vote London Assembly elections 2000–2020	276
A17	Percentage share of the vote London Mayoral elections 2000–2020	276
A18	Metropolitan Borough elections 1919–1937	276
A19	Share of votes and seats in the London Boroughs 1900–1962	277
A20	Percentage share of vote London Borough elections 1964–2018	277
A21	Referendum on Europe 2016; results for Greater London	278

About the author

Michael Tichelar is a visiting fellow in History at the University of the West of England, UK. He is retired from academic life and a career in local government and managing voluntary organisations. He is the author of *The History of Opposition to Blood Sports in Twentieth Century England – Hunting at Bay* (2017) and *The Failure of Land Reform in Twentieth Century England: The Triumph of Private Property* (2019). His interest in London politics stems from research he started and did not finish in the 1970s and from working for the London Borough of Lambeth in the 1980s as Head of Policy. He was a tutor organiser for the Workers Educational Association in Bristol before training as a psychotherapist. He was born in Croydon and now lives in Bath.

Foreword

Why do Londoners have such a marked allegiance to the Labour Party, both in local and national politics? That there is such loyalty is plain to see and it has been especially notable in the twenty-first century. But the reasons for it are obscure and need to be teased out with skill and care, for on the face of it London is not a natural Labour heartland. It is overwhelmingly the richest part of the nation, with a population that is on the average far better-off than the general run of the people of England's provinces or Britain's smaller nations. Just why, apparently against all the odds, have the citizens of this wealthy metropolis generally favoured so strongly the British political party that has mostly been identified with the unprivileged and the 'under-dog'?

Perhaps the answer lies in class? Well, London is a very unequal city, sure enough, but there is much evidence to show that it is by no means only the poorer of London's localities that vote Labour when the opportunity arises to do so. Take Islington, a borough which has seen immense changes in fortune since the end of the First World War, including an extraordinary class make-over since the 1960s. Yet, Islington and Labour have now been essentially synonymous for the best part of a century, a link cemented in the past twenty years or so by the extraordinary fact that the Labour Party has chosen three of its five most recent leaders from among the borough's residents, with one more living just over the border in Kentish Town. The connections between Islington and Labour have remained stable despite the growth there of a huge middle-class and generally wealthy population that far outnumbers in voting power those Islingtonians who continue to live in the remaining council (or ex-council) estates, and despite the borough having become one of the great multicultural melting-pots of the UK.

The same point could be made for most of the boroughs making up the area of the old London County Council or today's inner London, where allegiance to Labour has been generally remarkably solid in local and national politics since the early 1930s. But it is not just the 'inner city' that has helped Labour to power in London. The metropolitan suburbs famously launched the first Attlee government to power in 1945 and were essential building blocks in Tony Blair's three successful election victories from 1997. The comparisons with other parts of the country have become more, not

xvi *Foreword*

less, stark in recent years. The astonishing loss of Labour's heartlands in Scotland in the 2010s, or in the territories of the fabled 'red wall' across northern England at the General Election of 2019, makes the stolidity of London's support for Labour remarkable by contrast. And, though nothing is permanent in politics – or in the changing composition of the Londoner – that loyalty seems unlikely to change any time soon.

So 'Why is London Labour?' asks an important question, indeed the most salient question in British political geography. It's astonishing that no one has bothered to ask it till Michael Tichelar did so here. Perhaps, though, it's not quite so surprising when we consider the difficulties of providing an answer: Karl Marx once wrote that (I paraphrase) humanity only asks itself questions it can solve, and this undoubtedly is a tough conundrum to unlock. Tichelar approaches it with subtlety, intelligence and great experience. He has both a background in twentieth-century political history (especially the history of the Labour Party) and a deep understanding of how local government (especially London government) has actually worked over the past forty years. This is a unique combination, and it helps him dissect the answers to 'Why is London Labour' on many levels.

Tichelar shows that we need to answer this question historically but that in doing so we need to use history in new and surprising ways. So, he examines the deep roots of Labour in London by taking us back to 1919 when Labour first had unexpected victories in the local elections of that year, and then moving through the many ups and downs of the Party's slow consolidation of the metropolis as the most reliable Labour constituency in the country. But he also reminds us that there are many Londons: that Kensington is very different indeed from Newham, and that Bexley is a world away from Brent. So, Tichelar takes us into the microhistories of London's localities. He explores the differences and changes in their economies, their class and ethnic make-up, and their voting patterns over time. He opens out the significance of pan-London questions of identity (race, religion, age) that cut across notions of class and locality. Nor is he afraid to confront problematic issues like the Party's relationship with Jewish Londoners, causing bitter factionalism within the Party in the 1980s and again after 2015 and which loosened its grip on some traditional Labour loyalties. All of this shows that Labour's hold on London is not immutable but is contingent on politics, identity and the shifting patterns of population movements in this, the most dynamic city in the country, over time.

In all, this is a sophisticated and enlightening examination of a question that is not only important to London but of vital significance to the future of the Labour Party in the UK. Tichelar's book deserves to be read by anyone interested in the history of London, and by everyone concerned with the place and prospects of Labour in British politics.

Jerry White
Professor of Modern London History,
Birkbeck, University of London

Acknowledgements

I am very grateful for the help provided by the archivists, librarians and staff of the Bishopsgate Institute, London; the Black Cultural Archives, Brixton; the British Library; the British Library of Political and Economic Science, London; the Croydon Archives and Local Studies Centre; the Lambeth Archives and Local Studies Centre; the London Metropolitan Archives; the People's History Museum, Manchester; the Modern Records Centre, University of Warwick; and the University of the West of England.

I have benefited enormously from the expertise, knowledge and patience of a wide range of friends and colleagues, including Nick Abercrombie, Duncan Bowie, Sean Creighton, Andrew Graham, Dr Barbara Humphries, Professor Emeritus June Hannam, University West of England, Harry Harmer, Cath Tate and my wife Dr Linda Watts, who read either drafts or chapters of the whole book and provided invaluable feedback. I remain responsible for any errors or opinions expressed in the book.

A number of people responded to a questionnaire relating to the period in the book after 1970, including Janet Daby MP, John Grigg, Geoff Gill, David Lammy MP, Stan Newens, Reg Race, Peter Rowlands, Joan Twelves and the secretary of London Labour Heritage who kindly circulated a questionnaire to members of that Society.

I would also like to thank the editorial staff at Routledge who provided sound and timely advice.

Abbreviations

BME	Black and Ethnic Minority
BNP	British National Party (fascist)
BSP	British Socialist Party
BUF	British Union of Fascists
CARD	Campaign Against Racial Discrimination
CLP	Constituency Labour Party
CLT	Community Land Trust
CND	Campaign for Nuclear Disarmament
CPGB	Communist Party of Great Britain
GLC	Greater London Council
ILEA	Inner London Education Authority
ILP	Independent Labour Party
LCC	London County Council
LLP	London Labour Party
LRC	Labour Representation Committee
LSC	London Society of Compositors
LMA	London Metropolitan Archives
LSE	London School of Economics
LTC	London Trades Council.
MRP	Municipal Reform Party
NEC	National Executive Committee (Labour Party)
NFWW	National Federation of Women Workers
NSP	National Socialist Party
NSLL	New Survey of London Life and Labour
NUF	National Union of Fascists
NUR	National Union of Railwaymen
OMOV	One Member One Vote
RACS	Royal Arsenal Cooperative Society
RCP	Revolutionary Communist Party (Trotskyist)
SDF	Social Democratic Federation
SDP	Social Democratic Party
SPD	Social Democratic Party of Germany

xx *Abbreviations*

TUC	Trades Union Congress
T&GWU	Transport and General Workers Union
WCG	Women's Cooperative Guild
WLL	Women's Labour League
WLM	Women's Liberation Movement

Introduction

On 5 May 2016, London elected Sadiq Khan the Labour MP for Tooting to be the first Muslim Mayor of any major city in the West, following a controversial campaign during which the Conservatives branded him a terrorist and after Labour had lost the 2015 general election. Brought up on a council estate and son of a taxi driver, he said in his victory speech that 'I never dreamt someone like me could be elected mayor of London.' One hundred years earlier, George Lansbury, the future leader of the Labour Party following the defection of Ramsay MacDonald in 1931, was elected Mayor of Poplar in the East End in 1919 when Labour unexpectedly and spectacularly won majority control for the first time of 13 borough councils in the capital. In his victory speech, he declared that 'I thought I should always be in opposition and fighting a forlorn hope. But something like a miracle has happened, and here I am!'[1]

This book will seek to answer why has London been a stronghold for the Labour Party for relatively long periods of the last century and especially in the new century. Through a historical analysis of the reasons for Labour's success in the capital, it will help to address the question of how far London (the paramount 'World City') is unique or different from the rest of the country in the way that it votes. The extraordinary growth of London since 1980, both as a world financial centre and as a multi-ethnic melting pot, where a quarter of its households live below the poverty line,[2] raises a number of important questions relating to the governance of the UK as a whole in an age of growing nationalism and populism. One of these questions is how far London has become almost a separate country, where the UK is now talked about as made up of five parts: Scotland, Northern Ireland, Wales, London and 'England-without-London,' and where London is referred to as 'the Alpha City' amongst world cities, outperforming New York and Tokyo as centres of concentrated private wealth and gross inequality.[3] Is the gap

---

1 *East London Advertiser*, 14 November 1919.
2 Greater London Authority, *Poverty in London 2019*.
3 Barnett, *The Lure of Greatness*, p. 101; Atkinson, *Alpha City*.

2 *Introduction*

so wide that it is now threatening to tear apart the way the country is governed? Is the future of Labour as a historic national Party damaged by its strength in London (and other big metropolitan cities), based on the support of a combination of its extensive precariat of exploited workers and large sections of the middle class, while it loses support of the white working class in the rest of England, Scotland and Wales?

In the early twentieth century, Labour's strength in the capital was as a party of local government in clearly defined working-class communities, in what the historian Eric Hobsbawn described as the 'red belt' of inner London boroughs, similar to those working-class areas in Paris and Vienna.[4] Its performance in parliamentary elections was, however, less strong and intermittent, more influenced by national events such as war and economic crises. In London, Labour peaked in the general elections of 1929, 1945, 1997, with bigger swings than elsewhere in the UK. It then strengthened after 1997 and even more so after 2015, following the election of Jeremy Corbyn as a leader, while its position in non-metropolitan areas of England (and most notably Scotland but less so in Wales) has weakened quite considerably during the recent past. Labour is now dominant in both local and parliamentary elections in the capital, which along with other big cities like Liverpool and Manchester are now strongholds for the party, in contrast to the party's traditional heartlands in the smaller towns and urban districts of the north of England (the so-called 'Red Wall' of previous relatively safe working-class seats). It looks likely to stay that way for the foreseeable future as its young, well-educated and multi-ethnic population continues to grow, although demographically the BME population will age and its voting behaviour may change from supporting Labour to voting for other parties.

Labour is now perceived by many as a 'London-centric' party, particularly after the election of Jeremy Corbyn as a leader in 2015. It is not clear at this stage how far the new leadership of Keir Starmer, another London-based MP, but less radical than Corbyn, will reverse this perception or indeed how far the perception is in fact an accurate forecast of how politics will evolve in the longer term. The demographic changes which have led to Labour's now dominant position in the capital, namely its increasingly young, better-educated and above all multi-ethnic electorate, are not present to anywhere near the same scale in non-metropolitan areas of the country. Fifty per cent of Labour's constituency in London is working class and multi-ethnic (C2DE) and has been adversely affected by austerity after the financial crash of 2008, perhaps more so than in other parts of the country. The other 50% is middle class and (to a lesser extent) multi-ethnic (ABC1). It votes Labour for reasons linked to what might be best described as a metropolitan or socially liberal outlook. As a 'World City,' London is certainly unique in this combination of social structure. However, it is not clear if

---

4 Hobsbawn, 'Labour in the Great City.'

Introduction 3

there is a specific London effect separate from the demography of the capital. If Labour continues to adopt policies opposed to austerity in the future, and is perceived by the BME electorate as the party best opposed to racial discrimination, it is likely to remain dominant in London unless such policies are expropriated (and actually implemented) by other parties. Whether it can appeal to other areas of the country in the same way remains one of the key issues facing the party today. This book will argue that the history of the Labour Party in London, from its origins during the Edwardian period, suggests that its success depends on its ability to forge cross-class alliances bringing together a variety of different interests (class, race, gender, religion, socialism), and this might help us think about where the party is going in the future.

Before the First World War, London was regarded as a weak area for Labour politics, restricted above all by the narrowness of the franchise. There were only three MPs and very few elected councillors in working-class areas like Poplar and in some outlying areas like Croydon, West Ham and Woolwich, where it had achieved some limited but sometimes short-lived success. This was built mainly on trade union organisation and some evidence of religious non-conformity. But during the 1920s and up to the 1960s, London (mainly inner but also in some parts of the eastern and northern outer industrial suburbs) became a strong Labour area making a significant contribution to its national success as a governing party. It had by 1929 replaced the Liberals in London as the main opposition to the Conservatives, both in local elections to the London County Council (LCC) and borough councils, and slightly later in parliamentary contests. The party was stronger at a local level during the interwar period, and it took much longer to break through in the number of its MPs, culminating in its dominant performance in the 1945 general election, when it took 48 seats in inner London and 37 in outer London, making it the strongest region in the country.[5]

By 1950, the capital had developed into a 'municipal social democracy,' in which the LCC and the local boroughs, together with the support of the Labour government of 1945, 'had significantly improved the quality of life and had to a significant extent reversed the overcrowding, poverty and social disorganisation which had been characteristic of the East End before 1914.'[6] The *New Survey of London Life and Labour* undertaken during the 1920s attributed these improvements to rehousing the population in healthier conditions, better maternity care, the medical inspection of school children, the introduction of old age pensions and steps to deal with venereal disease.[7] A reduction in the size of families was also a contributory factor. The Labour-controlled LCC after 1934 made long-lasting and significant

5 See Table 12 in Appendix A and Table 5.6 in Chapter 5.
6 Butler and Rustin, *Rising in the East*, pp. 3–4.
7 Smith, *The New Survey of London Life and Labour,* Vol. 1, pp. 200, 204.

4   Introduction

reforms to health and public housing, transport, parks and open spaces, and was a driving force in creating the Green Belt. The party sought 'to create a new social life and a more educated democracy.'[8] Its grip on inner London up to 1968 has been described by the historian Roy Porter as a 'Fabian dream of municipal socialism run by experts for Londoners' good.'[9]

But after 1970, Labour's share of the vote declined in line with national trends, such as de-industrialisation, the slow and sporadic dealignment of class and voting, and the dispersal and turnover of population to the suburbs and beyond. The economy of London was restructured from one based on manufacturing to one dominated by finance, services and the creative industries, becoming, according to the urban historian Sir Peter Hall, a 'City of Rampant Capitalism' by the turn of the twenty-first century.[10] This coincided in the 1980s with the emergence of the 'New Left' on the Greater London Council (GLC) and many Labour-controlled councils in inner London. The growth of student radicalism and community activism in the 1960s challenged the old guard which had controlled many constituency labour parties and council labour groups since the 1940s. Ageing membership and poor political organisation, born of complacency and alleged voter apathy, created the circumstances for a revival of the left and a new type of politics no longer based on strong community or neighbourhood identities.[11] The rediscovery of poverty, always present in London, particularly in relation to housing (*Cathy Come Home*), rejuvenated the party at a local level attracting a new, younger and more left-wing membership. However, the scale of de-industrialisation in London and the beginnings of inner-city gentrification, taken together with a revival in the fortunes of the Liberal Party and the formation of the breakaway Social Democratic Party in 1981 (in many ways a direct response to the growth of the New Left), combined to badly reduce the national swing back to Labour in London in the 1987 general election. Contemporaries regarded these changes as marking the beginning of the death of the party not only in London but perhaps nationwide. *Must Labour lose?* and *Farewell to the Working Class* were just two of several books published at the time forecasting the death of the party.[12]

But after the 1997 general election, Labour regained its dominant position in the capital, and this was consolidated in the general elections which followed in 2001, 2005 and especially in 2017 and then again in 2019. The psephologist Ivor Crewe described the 1997 landslide in terms of the suburbs unexpectedly 'turning red!'[13] London continues to be a stronghold for the Party to this day. It now has an electorate that votes Labour by clear and in-

---

8 White, *London in the Twentieth Century*, pp. 373–86; Jackson, *A Short History of the LCC*.
9 Porter, *London*, p. 407.
10 Hall, *Cities in Civilization*.
11 Davies, 'Community and the Labour Left in 1970s London,' 207–13.
12 Abrams and Rose, *Must Labour Lose?*; Gorz, *Farewell to the Working Class*.
13 *New Statesman*, 4 June 2001, pp. 19–20.

Introduction 5

creasing majorities. Its population has become 'socially liberal, multi-racial and cross-class,' made up of a significant proportion of students and ethnic minorities (35% of the population is non-white, 54% of which votes Labour). It has been estimated that a quarter of the membership of Momentum, the left-wing pressure group which supported Jeremy Corbyn, lives in London.[14] In the 2019 general election, dominated by the issue of Europe, the Conservative share of the vote dropped in London unlike in some other areas of the country where it increased by nearly 10%, although this masked some important trends in certain constituencies which saw increased support for the Greens and the Liberal-Democrats. Labour's support in London amongst the BME electorate and people aged under 35 was consolidated.

A book on 'Why London is Labour?' is intended to fill a serious gap in the history of the capital, the Labour Party and national politics. It will be the first to attempt to explain the strength of the Party in London from its creation in 1914 up to the present day using a mixture of historical research and electoral sociology. It is deliberately ambitious in its scope. The scale of the Greater London Area and the problem of defining its boundaries, together with the extraordinary pace of economic and social change during the twentieth century, have discouraged historians from embarking on what many might see as a foolhardy and over-ambitious project. This has left a 'politics-shaped' hole in the history of London and a 'London-shaped hole' in the history of politics.[15] The renowned urban historian H. J. Dyos agreed with such a conclusion. He argued that 'far from there having been too much emphasis by historians on the metropolitan centre of national life there may have been in some respects too little.'[16] He pointed out that historians have given more attention to the growth of civic consciousness in the provinces, where radical politics, for example, had deeper routes in local communities. This was in contrast to London where gentrification and rapid population dispersal and turnover, combined with very high levels of immigration, undermined a strong sense of local community identity in which a stable political culture could develop. Explanations based on class and traditional labour history are therefore not enough by themselves to explain why London has been a Labour stronghold for most of the twentieth century.

The size and heterogeneous nature of London raises the interesting question of whether it is unique in terms of its political history. Perhaps it has more in common with other capital cities such Paris, Berlin or New York.[17] London has always been regarded as a problem, seen in the nineteenth

---

14 Bailey and Baston, *For the Many*; Beckett, 'How London became a Labour City?' *Guardian,* 11 May 2016.
15 Cragoe and Taylor, *London Politics*, p. 1.
16 Dyos, 'Greater and Greater London,' 89 112.
17 Hobsbawn, 'Labour in the Great City'; Hall, *London Voices, London Lives*; King, *Global Cities;* Massey, *World City*; Sutcliffe, *Metropolis 1890–1940.*

6 *Introduction*

century as a centre of crime and disease; by William Cobbett as 'The Infernal Wren'; as a source of 'old corruption'; and as the cause of physical and national degeneration at the time of the Boer War. The situation has not changed significantly in the twentieth century. Barlow's Royal Commission on Industrial Distribution, published in 1940 just after the outbreak of war, warned against the dangers of the over-concentration of economic and political power in London, and of course population, making it the unfortunate target of enemy bombing. Robert Colls, in his exploration of the *Identity of England*, has drawn useful attention to the way the provinces could offer no countervailing force to the ongoing problem and dominating presence of the capital.[18] 'It brooks no rivals,' according to the historian of Britain's decline as a world power.[19] The sociologist Ruth Glass, who coined the term 'gentrification' in the 1960s in relation to London, recognised the complexity and uniqueness of the metropolis when she concluded that 'the city is too vast, too complex, too contrary and too moody to become entirely familiar... and that London can never be taken for granted.'[20]

The scope and outline of the book

London is geographically defined as the area of the current London Assembly and the 32 borough councils and the City Corporation.[21] As a region, it has become almost a country within a country. It exercises a very powerful economic, social and political position within the UK, too powerful for many citizens both past and present. The gulf between London and the provinces is also a pressing contemporary political issue for all political parties, not least for the Labour Party and its current dilemma of the way that support is dividing between the big cities and its so-called northern working-class heartlands. Labour's post-mortem into its defeat in the general election of 2019 acknowledged the way it lost support across the North and Midlands, Scotland and North Wales, posing profound questions about the future prospects of the Party. It concluded that

> Labour's electoral coalition had been fracturing for a long time and was broken in 2019. We were rejected by many of the communities we were founded to represent. We lost all types of voters everywhere compared with 2017, except in London. Age, education and place are the new electoral divides even more than traditional conceptions of class. We have seen dramatic changes in relation to older voters, those with lower levels of education and qualifications. Labour lost votes across every region and country in the UK; Labour's vote share declined most in small,

18 Colls, *Identity of England*, pp. 329–33.
19 Rubinstein, *Capitalism, Culture and Decline in Britain*, p. 156.
20 Glass, 'Introduction to *London: Aspects of Change*,' p. xiii.
21 See the Appendix for a definition and historical background.

Introduction 7

medium, and large towns, but consolidated in cities. Labour lost support amongst all classes but amongst working class communities the most. The swing away from Labour in our heartland seats in the 2017 election, masked by the much better than expected result, foreshadowed our 2019 defeat. The Conservatives made significant gains in 2017 in seats they would go on to win in 2019.[22]

This geographical division has been characterised as one between a middle-class metropolitan elite, socially liberal and pro-Europe, and a working class living in smaller towns and cities, socially authoritarian and opposed to Europe, a split it is argued between 'winners' and 'losers' in their response to globalisation.[23] This book, however, does not fully accept this characterisation, and it rejects the idea that class has now been displaced by culture and identity. It seeks to combine historical analysis and political sociology (hopefully without causing too much offence to either discipline), in accounting for why London has been a stronghold for the Labour Party. It argues that social class continues to determine the way Londoners vote Labour in the present as it did in the past. The only difference is that the definition of what it means to be working class has changed, but not fundamentally it is suggested, in either historical or sociological terms. Definitions of class now reflect a shift away from occupational classifications to the influence of culture, identities and lifestyles.[24] But when polled, the proportion of the public that identify themselves as working class has remained stable over time at about 60%, despite the long-term decline in the actual size of the manual working class.[25]

There is, however, one very important difference between the working class of interwar London and the new working class of modern London. It is now much younger, better-educated (given the enormous expansion of higher education) and far more multi-ethnic to an extent that makes London unique in the UK. The BME electorate vote Labour in the capital by a large and increasing margin as they do across the country.[26] Younger people also vote Labour by a similar margin, but they are less likely to turnout to vote than their parents, although this changed in 2017, but only a little after the election of Jeremy Corbyn as a leader in 2015. London is also a more racially integrated city in comparison to other more polarised conurbations, in, for example, the USA or South America. The proportion of BME electors in any of its large number of electoral wards does not exceed 50%.[27] Moreover, London is also growing far more rapidly than any other cities in the

22 Labour Together, *Election Review 2019.*
23 Wheatley, *The Changing Shape of Politics.*
24 Devine et al., *Rethinking Class.*
25 Evans and Mellon, 'Identity, Awareness and Political Attitudes.'
26 Heath, 'Why Ethnic Minorities Vote Labour: Group Norms.'
27 Khan, 'One Nation Boris? Not for Black or Asian Londoners.'

8 *Introduction*

UK, adding to its demographic uniqueness and raising previous concerns about how to control its remorseless spread, despite the Green Belt.[28] In contrast, support for Labour during the earlier part of the twentieth century was based on a type of working-class consciousness defined by historians as 'labourism,' which derived its strength in large part from stable homogeneous and white working-class neighbourhoods in the capital's 'Red Belt,' although inner London was at this time starting to experience population dispersal and the beginnings of de-industrialisation. 'Labourism' was a general feeling of 'them and us' expressed in class terms. In the modern period, it has not so much disappeared but has become more hidden from view, less explicit and expressed in terms of 'ordinariness.'[29] It is still driven by poverty and relative deprivation, and London is the most economically polarised region of the country.[30]

The theory of relative deprivation developed by the sociologist Walter Runciman, in a groundbreaking book published in 1966, and by Peter Townsend in his study of poverty in the UK published in 1979, thus continues to be relevant in understanding the way social class has been remade rather than displaced in contemporary London and elsewhere. It is defined as the lack of resources to sustain the diet, lifestyle, activities and amenities that an individual or group are accustomed to or that are widely encouraged or approved in the society to which they belong.[31] This concept applies as much to London today as it did in the age of a municipal social democracy (1929–1968). The majority of Londoners, apart from those upper-middle-class elites living in gentrified neighbourhoods (about 50% of whom vote Labour), and those living in a declining number of very middle-class suburban areas who still vote Conservative, form part of an enlarged lower-middle- and working-class population which commentators refer to as the precariat. It is a class that maybe culturally rich, but it is impoverished by the lack of property wealth, low wages generated by a very insecure labour market and the very high cost of living.[32] Its upward social mobility has been blocked by gross inequality, especially since the financial crash of 2008, in a new gilded age of extreme disparity between rich and poor, similar to Edwardian London or late nineteenth-century New York.[33] Since the turn of the millennium, its experience of relative deprivation and racial discrimination has, it will be argued, resulted in increasing majorities for Labour as the historic party of the working class. Such deprivation has also generated political disengagement and violence at times

---

28 Hall, *London Voices. London Lives*; Saint, '"Spread the People": The LCC's Dispersal Policy, 1889–1965.'
29 Savage, *Social Class in the Twenty First Century.*
30 Dorling, *Peak Inequality.*
31 Runciman, *Relative Deprivation and Social Justice*; Townsend, *Poverty in the UK.*
32 Standing, *Precariat.*
33 Schneer, *London 1900.*

Introduction 9

of acute social crises, as demonstrated, for example, by the history of rioting in the capital during the 1980s and then again in 2011, when certain suburbs such as Croydon and Ealing went up in flames as a consequence of police methods perceived by many as institutionally racist. There is a strong case to be made that there is a difference between *measured* inequality and *felt* inequality in London which is not present to the same extent in non-metropolitan areas. London condenses the experience of felt inequality because it is so deep and polarised in comparison to other areas of the country (a detailed discussion which is outside the scope of this book but worthy of further research).[34]

It is not possible in just a chronological approach to do justice to the way the politics of the capital have been transformed since 1900. For this reason, the book is divided into two parts, combining both history and political sociology, more historical for the earlier period and more sociological for the later period. Part I is a chronological outline of the way Labour politics ebbed and flowed over the course of the century. Part II focuses on a number of themes (empirical and theoretical) identified in Part I, which require more in-depth consideration, such as the influence of localities, workplaces and trade union organisation, social class, socialism, gender, race and religion. These themes will be illustrated by examples taken from specific areas such as suburban Croydon and inner-city Hackney and Lambeth, allowing for different areas of the capital to be compared and contrasted in terms of the growth and development of Labour politics. The chronological chapters will indicate where issues are dealt with in more depth in the thematic chapters. In different ways, both chronology and themes contributed to a metropolitan political culture that either benefited or hindered the growth and development of Labour politics in London and marked it out from other areas of the country.

Part I is made up of three chronological chapters outlining the development of Labour politics from 1900 to 2020. The first chapter ('Labour in an Imperial Metropolis) covers the period 1900–1929. It describes the way independent Labour representation was contained before 1914 within an alliance of socialists, Progressives and Labour politicians, restricted above all by the narrowness of the franchise. After 1918, Labour competed with the Conservatives in a three-way contest with a declining and badly divided Liberal Party, to represent the new enlarged electorate, made up of many first-time working-class voters. By 1929, it had replaced the Liberals as the main opposition to the Conservatives, the result primarily, it will be argued, of the extension of the vote in 1918 and 1928, the domestic impact of the First World War and the particular social geography of the capital, with its 'red belt' of predominantly working-class inner-city neighbourhoods in both inner and outer London.

34 Dorking, *Peak Inequality.*

10 *Introduction*

The second chapter ('Labour in a Municipal Social Democracy) covers the period 1929–1997. It describes the way Labour came to dominate the capital, particularly at a municipal level, supported by a working-class electorate of a particular of type, the beliefs and values of which have been best described as 'labourism.' But Labour also attracted the support of important elements of the capitals growing middle class, advocating socialism for the 'black coated proletariat.' This very much contributed to its success in the 1945 general election, when Greater London as a whole became a regional stronghold of the party on a much bigger swing than elsewhere. But by 1968, Labour in the capital started to lose support, as it was doing country-wide, finding it difficult to adjust to a period of increasing post-war affluence and a weakening of class identity. The historian Eric Hobsbawn characterised the period as one of 'the Forward March of Labour Halted,' to describe the way a process of class dealignment undermined Labour's support after the Second World War. It will be argued that Labour's decline in London was largely the result of a massive loss of manufacturing jobs. By the 1980s, many commentators identified a 'London Effect' marking a decline (for some fatal), either delaying or preventing a revival in Labour's political fortunes.

The third chapter ('Labour in a City of Rampant Capitalism') covers the period leading up to 1997 and thereafter. The 1980s and early 1990s witnessed a continuing decline in the party's fortunes, more pronounced in London than in its northern heartlands. In London, the New Left experienced a series of defeats, the most serious being the abolition of the GLC in 1986 and then the Inner London Education Authority (ILEA) in 1990. However, in the period after 1997 up to the present day, support for the party revived and then consolidated. In 1997, while inner-city constituencies continued to vote Labour, the 'Suburbs of London unexpectedly turned red,' and continued to vote Labour thereafter, although this did not apply to the few solidly middle-class suburbs that remain Conservative strongholds to this day in what might be best described as what remains of the 'Stockbroker Belt.' (Highly paid executives now tend to live in the gentrified areas of inner London rather than the suburbs.) Support for Labour in London was consolidated after 2015, the result it will be argued of the way the precariat was increasingly pushed out to the suburbs and the growth of the capitals young, multi-ethnic and socially liberal electorate, combined with elements of what was left of the traditional white working class that had not been decanted or escaped to the outer suburbs and beyond (known colloquially as 'white flight').

Part II is made up of four chapters which discuss (in both empirical and theoretical terms) important themes identified in the party's chronological development outlined in Part I. Chapter 4 assesses the influence of localities, workplaces and trade union organisation, arguing that neighbourhood identities played a more important role than trade union militancy in mobilising support for Labour. Chapter 5 discusses the question of voting and social class, arguing that social class (now redefined in terms of culture and identity rather than by just occupation) is still an important determinant of voting behaviour. Chapter 6 explores the influence of party organisation, membership and socialism and paints a picture of local political activity in London that belies some of the more critical, polemical and static accounts of Labour Party history. Finally, Chapter 7 looks at the role of 'the politics of personal identity,' (gender, race and religion), arguing that it played a significant role in differentiating London from other non-metropolitan areas of the country, helping in some respects to widen the gulf between the capital and Labour's so-called traditional heartlands in the north, harshly exposed by the 2016 referendum on Europe and in the general election of 2019. Conversely, such politics strengthened Labour support from within the new, younger and multi-racial electorate of the capital. The conclusion reviews and summarises the chronological outlines, integrating evidence from the thematic chapters; discusses the way the meaning of social class may have changed in London after the year 2000; and speculates on the future prospects of the Labour Party, not only in London, in the context of demographic change and the election of Keir Starmer as the new leader to replace Jeremy Corbyn.

The role of personality also cannot be ignored, but there is no scope to do it full justice in this book. London has produced a range of politicians that have attracted controversy and an unusual level of public attention. For example, in the early twentieth century, there were figures such as Lord Rosebery, a future Liberal Prime Minister; John Burns, the Progressive MP for Battersea; Will Crooks, the first Labour Mayor of Poplar and MP for Woolwich; and Jack Jones, the witty and left-wing socialist who was elected MP for Silvertown in 1919 for the National Socialist Party. He defeated the official Labour Party candidate who was a conscientious objector and an anti-war supporter of the Independent Labour Party (ILP). After 1918, London produced Herbert Morrison, the secretary of the regional party, and MP for Hackney, who became Home Secretary in the wartime coalition in 1940; George Lansbury, the pacifist leader of the party after the defection of Ramsay MacDonald; and Doctor Alfred Salter, MP for Bermondsey West. Together with his wife Ada, a campaigner for the beautification of the capital, they set up a clinic to treat children with TB, laying the foundations of the NHS. In the period after 1950, London also provided a platform for Boris Johnson as the second Mayor of London before his election as the leader of the Conservative Party and Prime Minister in 2019. The GLC and local government in London was also the base for the careers of several national Labour Party figures, such as Jeremy Corbyn, Ken Livingstone, Sadiq Khan and John McDonnell.

Why therefore has London been a stronghold for Labour for lengthy periods in the twentieth century? How do we begin to account for this success? What explanatory factors and theoretical perspectives need to be considered operating at a local, regional and national level? The book will argue that

12   *Introduction*

support for Labour was not entirely dependent on the particular strength of local trade unionism, given its historic general weakness in the capital. De-industrialisation after 1960 further destroyed its influence. The politics of local communities and neighbourhood identities played a more important role. Moreover, the policies the party adopted in an age of mass-democracy to appeal to a new electorate of men and women after 1918, largely non-unionised, especially housing, education and welfare reform (chasing 'the slum vote' according to its critics), and rate-equalisation across the capital to pay for them, were just as influential in determining the way Londoners voted. London is still a city where younger people come to live or study and to make their fortunes, leaving their parents in rural areas or smaller towns. Age and education are now two factors which influence voting intentions over social class and religion in the modern era.[35] The book will also argue that suburbanisation does not always lead to people voting Conservative, as argued by some electoral sociologists.[36] This is certainly not the case in modern London. Indeed, Labour's success in London in 1945 and after 1997 was based on its ability to reverse the Conservative domination of the suburbs, which had been such a significant and important feature of the political geography of the interwar period.[37]

There are, of course, other competing explanations for why people vote in the way that they do. For example, before 1914, it was thought that religion played a more important role than class, while after 1918, class assumed a much greater role, at least up until the 1970s when a process of dealignment created new types of voting behaviour.[38] More recently, the psychology of voting has added a new dimension to electoral sociology, where human intuition is thought to be more important than rational decision making.[39] Others have suggested that British politics is now more influenced by tribal loyalties than traditional class allegiances.[40] There are those who believe that political alignment has shifted away from social class towards a geographical divide which is 'emerging between citizens residing in locations strongly connected to global growth and those who are not?'[41] This argument may have particular relevance for understanding why London increasingly voted Labour after 1997 and to remain within the European Union by very large margins, where age, level of educational qualifications and regional differences were clearly important factors. The policies of New Labour in promoting globalisation and the social market may also have

---

35 Evan and Tilley, *The New Politics of Class.*
36 Clapson, *Suburban Century*, pp. 169–90; Silverstone, *Visions of Suburbia.*
37 Huq, *On the Edge.*
38 Wald, *Crosses on the Ballot*; Alderman, *British Elections.*
39 Haidt, *The Righteous Mind.*
40 Goodhart, *The Road to Somewhere.*
41 Jennings and Stoker, 'Tilting towards the Cosmopolitan Axis?'; Wheately, *The Changing Shape of Politics.*

Introduction   13

played a role in attracting Labour support, or paradoxically they may have had the opposite effect as demonstrated by support for the anti-austerity policies of Jeremy Corbyn. For the modern period, there are approaches based on rational choice theory, such as valence or performance politics.[42] But while this book may refer to these theories in passing, it is above all a work of history, using concepts such as relative deprivation and the Marxist understanding of class, to account for the way people vote, based on a historical combination of local social structure and national politics.

Finally, the book also raises the very contemporary as well as historical issue of London's relationship to the rest of the UK. Is the Labour Party now in danger of betraying its traditional working-class supporters in those areas of the country left behind by London's dominating economic, political and social influence? The result of the general election in 2019 may support this conclusion. But has the contrast between affluent London (and a few other affluent or more cosmopolitan cities with their so-called metropolitan elites) and the deprived working-class areas of the country (described as Labour's heartlands or 'Northern Wall') been exaggerated? Does it also underestimate the level of deprivation and poverty in the capital? Although 'inner London is now one of the richest parts of both the UK and Europe,' this, it has been argued, was due

> to the short-term effects of the 1990s financial boom, which ushered in gentrification that, in practice, brought about social cleansing – as there was no longer space for new middle-income English hopefuls to arrive, apart from those prepared to accept Rachman-type rented housing.[43]

The left-wing architectural critic, Owen Hatherley, despairing of the destruction to the capitals' architectural heritage and skyline inflicted by large-scale redevelopment schemes (approved by all three mayors) has recently argued, in line with the conclusion to this book, that on

> a classical definition, of people who have to sell their labour power to survive and do not own property, London is the most proletarian city in the country...Londoners have the lowest disposable income in the country, because of its immense cost of living. This is a strange elite.[44]

When given the opportunity, this new working class voted, on a bigger turnout, for a radical if not social democratic manifesto ('For the Many Not the Few') in the general election of 2017.[45] In London, the party attracted 54.5% of the vote, while in the UK, it was 40%, one of its best results in a generation

---

42 Whiteley, *Affluence, Austerity and Electoral Change in Britain.*
43 Dorling and Tomlinson, *Rule Britannia*, p. 283.
44 Hatherley, 'The Government of London,' p. 112.
45 Pantich and Leys, *Searching for Socialism*, pp. 201–55.

14   *Introduction*

attracting a higher turnout of younger voters, but this was not repeated in 2019. In the changed, if perhaps one-off, circumstances of the 2019 general election, the party still polled a record 48% in London on a reduced turnout, losing 6% to the Liberal-Democrats over the issue of Europe and questions over the leadership of Jeremy Corbyn on Brexit and anti-Semitism. The Conservative vote dropped by 1% in 2019, whereas it increased by nearly 10% in non-metropolitan areas, including many previously safe working-class seats in the north of England.[46] Recent analysis of the 2019 general election shows that the Conservatives are now more popular with people on low incomes than those on higher incomes, 'while Labour is as popular with the wealthy as with those on low incomes.'[47] Labour may in the future recover these lost votes in its so-called 'Northern Heartlands,' if it can forge cross-class alliances and develop a coherent national programme of reforms which address the economic and social decline of such areas, including policies which acknowledge the concerns of low income voters about 'Britain's place in the world, immigration, and law and order.'[48] The history of the Labour Party in London demonstrates that it only achieves power on the basis of cross-alliances which bring together different interests (class, race, gender and religion). But the demographic trends which are driving London and the regions apart pose a very particular challenge. Other areas of the country may catch up London economically, which may then have positive outcomes for Labour. In these circumstances, those areas of the country which had been left behind by London's remarkable economic dynamism, and which as a consequence resulted in many people voting to leave Europe, may return to previous patterns of voting.

46 House of Commons Briefing Paper, *General Election 2019* (CBP 8749 – 28 January 2020), 32.
47 Goodwin and Heath, *Low Income Voters, the 2019 General Election and the Future of British Politics*, p. 3.
48 Ibid., p. 21.

Part I

Chronological – from an imperial metropolis to a City of Rampant Capitalism

1 Labour in an imperial metropolis

Introduction

This opening chapter will explore the growth of the Labour Party in London from 1900 to the late 1920s, a period when the capital was the centre of an enormous overseas world empire, influencing its everyday life and politics. Today, it is no longer an imperial metropolis with very different social and political traditions. The chapter is divided into two sections. Section I, 'Labour contained within a Progressive Alliance (1900–1918),' discusses the way independent Labour representation was unable to forge a political identity of its own before 1914, restricted above all by the narrowness of the franchise and the strength of a Progressive Alliance of Liberals, radicals, socialists and trade unionists, which politically controlled the London County Council (LCC) up to 1907. It also summarises how historians have accounted for Labour's weakness before the Representation of the People's Act in 1918 tripled or quadrupled the size of the electoral registers in London's 57 parliamentary constituencies (not including the 14 suburban seats in outer London).[1] Section II, 'Three Way Party Competition (1918–1929),' describes the period after the war when all three parties, Labour, Liberal and Conservative, competed for the support of the enlarged electorate, made up of many first-time working-class voters. By 1929, Labour had replaced the Liberals as the main opposition to the Conservatives in London, resulting from two developments – the extension of the vote in 1918 and 1928 and the party's success in representing the interests of working-class communities living in relatively close-knit homogeneous neighbourhoods. Labour was above all a party of local government after 1918. It did not really break through in parliamentary elections until 1945, although it did well enough in 1929 when it won most seats for the first time (287 of which 44 were in London), but not enough to outvote the combined strength of the opposition parties (328). It lasted only until the financial crisis of 1931 badly split the party with the defection of Ramsay MacDonald to form a National Government. This was a shock from which Labour did not really recover

---

1 See charts of election results in Chapter 5 on voting and social class.

18 *Chronological*

in parliamentary elections until after the Second World War, although its progress in local elections in London was confirmed when it won control of the LCC in 1934 for the first time.

Labour contained within the Progressive Alliance (1900–1918)

In 1891, Sidney Low, a journalist and Alderman representing the Municipal Reform Party (Conservatives) on the newly created LCC, hoped that the growth of the suburbs would make the capital, if not the country, safe for the Conservative Party. His party needed to appeal to the more socially mixed and respectable voters who had escaped inner-city overcrowding and poverty to live in the more salubrious areas of outer London, such as Croydon and Walthamstow. Like many politicians and social reformers at the time, he advocated the separation of the respectable working class from the 'residuum' of 'Outcast London.'[2] Politicians and settlement workers alike, influenced by eugenics, sought to rescue this under-class from an environment of crime and disease, overcrowding and endemic poverty. Low predicted that 'the son and grandson of the man from the fields will neither be a dweller in the country nor a dweller in the town. He will be a suburb dweller. The majority of the people of this island,' he hoped, 'will live in the suburbs; and the suburban type will be the most widespread and characteristic of them all, as the rural has been in the past.'[3] He had to wait until 1907 before the Municipal Reform Party, opposed to what it saw as the 'extravagance' and excessive spending of ratepayers money, captured the LCC from a Progressive Alliance of Liberals, radicals, socialists and trade unionists, committed to various schemes of state intervention, such as slum clearance and land reform. His long-term forecast proved to be accurate in some respects but disappointing in others. In the long term, suburbanisation did not necessarily make London safe for the Conservative Party, although it guaranteed a good deal of success for the party during the interwar and in the immediate post-war periods. Although most people now live in what we might call suburbs ('close to the city but distinct from it and boasting the benefits of general salubriousness, cleanliness, greenery and proximity to the country'), they are the locations of ethnic and religious diversity, and 'are now attracting interest as sites of political transformation, targeted by all the political parties as key territories to unlock if they are to win power.'[4]

Charles Masterman, the radical Liberal MP elected for the working-class constituency of West Ham North in the Liberal landslide of 1906, also identified the suburbs as the reason why the Conservatives captured the LCC

---

2 Jones, *Outcast London.*
3 Lowe, *Contemporary Review*, October 1891.
4 Huq, *On the Edge*, p. 175; Silverstone, *Visions of Suburbia*; Gilbert, 'Ethnic and Religious Diversity in the Politics of Suburban London.'

Labour in an imperial metropolis 19

in 1907, ending nearly 20 years of Progressive rule. The Liberals, he complained, had

> forgotten the dimensions and power of these enormous suburban peoples which are practically the product of the last century and have so greatly increased, even within the last decade. They are the creations not of the industrial, but of the commercial and business activities of London. They form a homogeneous civilisation, – detached, self-centred, unostentatious, – covering the hills along the northern and southern boundaries of the city and spreading their conquests over the quiet fields beyond.[5]

Certainly, by the end of the twentieth century, the Conservative Party had come to dominate the South East region. It is now a regional stronghold of the party, apart that is from Greater London and its diversifying suburbs. The Progressives and then the Labour Party, which had replaced the Liberals after 1918 as the main opposition to the Conservatives, had not been contained by the spread of the suburbs as predicted by Sidney Low. But Labour had by the end of the twentieth century consolidated its political control of the Greater London area, including its expanding suburbs, with the exception of pockets of high-status middle-class neighbourhoods such as Chelsea and parts of Kensington and in the stock broker belt of Kent and Surrey.

By the end of the twentieth century, suburban development had not fulfilled the predictions of either Sidney Low or Charles Masterman. By the mid-century, critics of the suburbs, of which there were many, suggested that they would become the 'slums of the future,' while by the year 2000, they no longer represented a particular image of English national identity, having become pivotal sites in social and cultural changes and hotly contested by political parties.[6] In some respects however, the social geography of London elections has not changed fundamentally since 1900. The historian Henry Pelling concluded that 'if London itself was on the whole inclined to Conservatism,' in the period before 1914, 'the South East Region as a whole, with its great weighting of class, of wealth, and of rank, was the real strength of Conservatism in Britain and in the Empire which, to a large extent, it controlled.'[7] The only major difference 100 years later is the absence of an overseas territorial Empire. Imperial wealth and influence have now been replaced by a different kind of imperialism, the enormous international financial power of the City of London.[8] In the space of a century, London has been transformed from an 'Imperial Metropolis' to a centre of

5 Masterman, *The Condition of England*, p. 65.
6 Gilbert and Preston, 'Stop Being So English,' 220.
7 Pelling, *Social Origins of British Elections*, pp. 85–6; Scheer, *London 1900*.
8 Massey, *World City*; Ackroyd, *London – The Biography*.

20 *Chronological*

international finance, described by the urban historian Sir Peter Hall as a 'City of Rampant Capitalism.'[9]

Henry Pelling was less conclusive about the social geography of inner London before 1914. He argued that 'class counted for more than any other factor in London elections,' but that this leaves the historian 'with two remaining problems to solve. One is to account for Conservative voting in some sections of the working class. The other is to explain the comparative weakness of the independent labour movement in a situation of class-dominated politics.'[10] In seeking to answer these questions, the historian Paul Thompson provided what became until quite recently the orthodox explanation for the origins of the Labour Party in London (and nationally), when he argued that:

> The politics of the provinces were those of the smaller, stabler communities of the past, still to a large extent centred on church and chapel. London was already a conurbation, a vast built-up region without stable local communities, with a huge shifting population, notorious for religious apathy, frequently travelling long distances to work, and clearly separated by classes into socially distinct residential districts. Here, rather than in the provinces, can be seen the political setting of the future.[11]

But as a long-term forecast, this conclusion proved to be unduly pessimistic. The experience of Labour politics in the capital developed along more complex lines where class played an important role, but where other factors need to be considered in the light of the electoral record of the Labour Party in London. In 1900, one of the most important of these factors was London's role as the capital of Britain's overseas empire. It was 'the imperial metropolis of the world' – its 'public spaces, monuments and cultural preferences as well as its inhabitants – was closely defined and reshaped by its imperial character.'[12]

London was 'the hub of the nation's road, rail and port networks, and the centre of the country's armaments production.'[13] It 'dwarfed the great provincial centres, ...adding over 60,000 people every single year between 1901 and 1911, with a growing middle class of clerks and shop assistants, men and women both, driving suburban expansion, and absorbing waves of mass immigration from Russia and Poland, mainly Jews, Italians as well as Germans from the Austro-Hungarian Empire'.[14] Most of its trade came

---

9 Hall, *Cities in Civilisation.*
10 Pelling, *Social Origins*, p. 57.
11 Thompson, *Socialists, Liberals and Labour.*
12 Schneer, *London 1900*, pp. 3–14.
13 White, *London in the Twentieth Century*, p. 185.
14 Goebel and White, 'London and the First World War.'

Labour in an imperial metropolis 21

through the docks and these links influenced the way many working-class Londoners saw their capital city. Streets in the East End were named after the ports and cities of the Empire, in the same way that the public houses were named after royalty, reflecting the depth of patriotic working-class support for the monarchy. The relief of Mafeking in 1900 was celebrated across London in a 'frenzy of jingoism,' when the verb 'mafficking' entered the English language.[15] The capital had a domesticated relationship with the Empire and royalty, and annual events like Empire Day were a feature of its everyday culture.[16] London's growth was built above all on its overseas connections, and it had reached an enormous size by 1900, stretching from 6 to 15 miles in every direction from Charing Cross. It encompassed the rapidly expanding suburban districts opened up by the railways and the introduction of workmen's fares, creating a series of speculative house-building booms along the lines of communication with the centre, a boom which had started to slow down by 1900. By this date, it contained a significant proportion of the country's manufacturing and service industries, satisfying a highly concentrated and sophisticated consumer market.

In the East End, the gas works, railways and the extensive network of docks, which was the main gateway for the country's imperial trade, employed thousands of workers in massive factories and goods yards.[17] The Victorian manufacturing belt formed a great crescent which ran around the north and east sides of central London,

> from the western edge of the City and the West End, through the southern parts of St Marylebone and St Pancras, through Islington, Finsbury, Holborn, Bethnal Green and Stepney. It extended to Southwark on the south bank of the river; to the north it throws out two great projections, one north and north-west to Camden Town, Kentish Town and Holloway, one north-east to south Hackney and Stoke Newington.[18]

It was around these concentrations that working-class neighbourhoods or quarters developed with specific identities, sometimes around a football club, such as Tottenham Hotspur or West Ham ('The Hammers'), or a food market, like Petticoat Lane and Portobello Road. This gave London its unique heterogeneous character as a series of urban villages with strong neighbourhood identities.[19] The suburbs also became a site of industrial development especially to the north east along the Lea Valley, the north west in central and west Middlesex and east along the Thames to Silvertown, Woolwich and Dagenham.

15 Morgan, 'The Boer War and the Media (1899–1902).'
16 Samuel, 'Empire Stories: The Imperial and the Domestic,' 94.
17 Porter, *London*, pp. 327–9.
18 Hall, 'Industrial London,' 262; Hall, *The Industries of London since 1861*.
19 Hobsbawn, 'Labour in the Great City.'

22 *Chronological*

The nature of the mid-Victorian labour market helped create distinct working-class areas defined by the distance the worker had to walk, at most three to four miles, from home to work. The development of cheap public transport such as workmen's fares from the 1890s widened the geographical limits of these districts and encouraged suburban expansion with much longer distances of travel to work.[20] One such area was south of the river, which saw the strongest concentration of trade unionists, working in engineering and river trades in the larger factories that characterised this part of London. It was radical, with a non-conformist tradition, and districts like Walworth, Newington West, Bermondsey and Southwark regularly returned Progressives to the LCC after 1888. In fact, there was a wide distribution of radical clubs in London in the 1870s and 1880s. The Metropolitan Radical Federation collaborated with socialists in the Social Democratic Federation (SDF) and the Socialist League. It also ensured that the Liberal Party selected working-class radicals as candidates in vestry and borough elections.[21] But by the turn of the century, these clubs had declined, their political tradition replaced by an altogether less radical set of political concerns. It has been argued that they were sites of a growing conflict between political and recreational objectives. Historians have suggested that, while their membership numbered no more than 16,000 in 1875, they had increased to over 45,000 by 1900, and had become depoliticised as a result of the growth of commercial recreations such as the music hall and the public house, encouraging it has been argued 'a culture of consolation' and political apathy.[22]

In terms of trade unionism, London was a weak area and continued to be so for most of the twentieth century. In 1892, the Fabians Sidney and Beatrice Webb estimated that 'the vast agglomeration of the London District, in which we must reckon Middlesex, the subsidiary boroughs of West Ham, Croydon, Richmond and Kingston, as well as Bromley in Kent, yields not more than 194,000 Trade Unionists,' amounting to only 3.52% of the population.[23] Historians of Victorian and Edwardian London have identified several factors in the East End that were not conducive to the growth of strong trade unions and Labour Party politics. These included high levels of abject and endemic poverty, small-scale workshop production which employed sweated labour, an absence of larger-scale manufacturing industry, an over-supply of unskilled casual labour, polarisation between skilled workers and the casual poor and significant levels of ethnic conflict. It has been argued that Irish and Jewish immigration in the early part of the

---

20 Hobsbawm, 'The Nineteenth Century London Labour Market.'
21 Davis, 'Radical Clubs and London Politics, 1870–1900'; German and Rees, *A People's History of London*; Rosenberg, *Rebel Footprints*; Shipley, *Club Life and Socialism in Victorian London*.
22 Stedman-Jones, *Outcast London*.
23 Webb, *History of Trade Unionism*, p. 412.

Labour in an imperial metropolis 23

century, followed by later waves of migrants from the new commonwealth, generated a tradition of racism and right-wing political behaviour in parts of the East End antithetical to the Labour Party.[24] Others have argued that area like Tower Hamlets, where the organised labour movement had weak foundations, given the casual nature of its labour market, was a good recruiting ground for fascism. Such a negative culture, it has been argued, was based on feelings of consolation and fatalism, allowing support for xenophobic, pro-imperialist and protectionist policies.[25] In contrast, West Ham (now the London Borough of Newham) had a tradition of stronger trade union organisation and social democracy, where the unionised dock and gas workers provided the social foundation for a more vibrant working-class political culture which sought independent Labour representation.[26]

From the 1880s onwards, the poverty of the East End was considered by both contemporaries (and by later historians) as a breeding ground of despair, misery and political apathy.[27] Such conditions gave rise, amongst other things, to the Settlement Movement and inspired patriotic politicians like Clement Atlee, an Anglican and future leader of the party, to press for state intervention to address the poverty that confronted him as a social worker in the East End before 1914. He had helped Beatrice Webb produce the famous minority report on the Poor Law in 1909, based on research in the East End, which prefigured the welfare state. Like several of his contemporaries, such as George Lansbury, another Anglican, his involvement in such work in 'Darkest London' provided the platform for his election as a Labour MP for Stepney after the First World War.[28] Some historians have stated that the weakness of trade unionism in London and the political volatility of the casual poor, 'who sung Rule Britannia when they rioted over unemployment in 1886 – ruled out any class conscious alternative to the radicalism of the artisans.'[29] Others have suggested that it was a culture that was inward looking and apolitical, more influenced by the music hall, sport and betting than socialism.[30] More recent studies have noted, however, that such a view underestimates the influence and vibrancy of popular Conservatism and the way Labour had to adapt its electoral strategy to reflect the patriotic and imperialist allegiances of the electorate, not only but especially in areas like London.[31] The characterisation of the working class in London as apathetic and non-political has been until quite recently the

24 Husbands, 'East End Racism 1900–1980.'
25 Jones, *Outcast London.*
26 Marriott, 'The Political Modernism of East London,' 108–22.
27 Mearns, *The Bitter Cry of Outcast London*; Booth, *Inquiry into Life and Labour of the People of London*; London, *People of the Abyss*; Masterman, *From the Abyss*; Jones, *Outcast London.*
28 Bew, *Citizen Clem*; Shepherd, *George Lansbury.*
29 Hinton, *Labour and Socialism,* p. 55.
30 Jones, 'Working-Culture and Working-Class Politics in London, 1870–1900.'
31 Pugh, 'The Rise of Labour and the political culture of Conservatism 1890–1945.'

24 *Chronological*

orthodox explanation for the weakness of Labour in the capital before 1914 and conversely its strength in its northern heartlands. However, it is now accepted that the economic conditions in the East End were not as uniformly bleak as previously thought and that the Conservative Party did not have a political monopoly over patriotism and imperialism.[32]

There were small pockets of Labour support in the outer suburbs, such as Croydon, Woolwich, West Ham and Battersea, reflecting a degree of trade union organisation and some limited evidence of religious non-conformity. In West Ham South, which had undergone extraordinarily rapid industrialisation and population growth in the 1870s and 1880s, Keir Hardie was returned as the first independent Labour MP in 1892, albeit without Liberal opposition, but with the support of dockers and labourers, and the Irish, all recently radicalised by the unionisation of unskilled workers during the 'New Unionist' upsurge of the late 1880s.[33] In 1890, West Ham became the first Labour Council elected in the UK, where the Labour group was an alliance of ILP members and Progressives. In working-class Battersea, John Burns forged an alliance of Progressive interests around the Battersea Labour League.[34] But the move towards independent working-class representation in many areas of London tended to be sporadic or short-lived before 1914. Some socialists regarded London as 'Godless' and a difficult area for organising independent Labour politics. It was an environment with 'a generally weak trade unionism and an absence of community structures that would generate a range of voluntary institutions and solidarity able to provide a basis for working-class political initiatives.'[35]

The move towards independent Labour representation was thus contained within a relationship with radical liberalism from which it found difficult to escape. Differences between socialist groups held back the creation of a London-wide party before 1914, although there was an independent Labour group of councillors on the LCC from 1898 working in collaboration with the Progressives and Fabians. There were relatively high levels of voter registration for parliamentary elections, especially amongst working-class householders after 1885 who could demonstrate continuity of residence, unlike those younger families or single people moving regularly to avoid paying high rents, as well as young middle- and working-class lodgers who did not meet the strict residency and household requirements to qualify for the vote. After 1885, most heads of households in the capital, who had been living in their borough for at least a year, had been enfranchised, making the working class 'a majority of the electorate in thirty eight of the fifty-eight

---

32 August 'A Culture of Consolation?'; Brodie, *The Politics of the Poor, 1880–1914*; Roberts, 'Popular Conservatism in Britain, 1832–1914.'

33 Marriott, *East of the Tower.*

34 Brown, 'London and the Historical Reputation of John Burns.'

35 Howell, *British Workers and the Independent Labour Party*, pp. 264–5.

Labour in an imperial metropolis   25

constituencies within the county of London.'[36] For Greater London, 'the proportion of men on the electoral register aged over 21 rose from just under half in 1885 (594,000) to about 55% (1,016,000) in 1910'.[37] The capital was outgrowing its boundaries even before the LCC was established in 1889. The electorate in the constituencies outside of the LCC area expanded more rapidly than in inner London where the size of the electorate was restricted by population decline and the limitations of the franchise.[38]

The capital also contained a very high number of transient lodgers and families who moved around on a regular basis, to find cheaper rents in the slums or to escape landlords altogether ('moonlight flitting'), making registration to vote a hit or miss affair. The same might be said of many parts of London today. The percentage of the population moving each year was estimated at over 30%. Detailed research into the electoral registers before 1914 'shows that age and housing patterns (not class) were the primary factors in determining enfranchisement.' There were many East End areas 'where the only middle-class residents were likely to be clergymen or Settlement house workers, and where the male electorate came overwhelmingly from the slums.'[39] In those constituencies where the working class had deeper roots in local communities and qualified for the vote (and were more likely to be members of a trade union), they did not necessarily vote Liberal or Labour. Harry Gosling, the leader of the Amalgamated Society of Watermen and Progressive member of the LCC for St Georges-in-the-East from 1898 to 1919, complained that even members of his own union did not vote for him 'because the exercise of their craft had made them Tory in outlook, or at best politically apathetic.'[40]

Before 1914, Labour's share of the vote for all elections was under 5%. In the general election of 1910, it contested only three seats in inner London (Bow & Bromley, Deptford and Woolwich) and polled just 2.7% and in outer London it contested only one seat (West Ham). Following the December 1910 general election, London remained a metropolis dominated by the Conservatives and Liberals, with the Progressives very much on the defensive against a revival of popular Conservatism, especially suburban ratepayer interests which had mobilised in 1907 to end Progressive control of the LCC. For local elections, the record of independent Labour representation was almost non-existent before 1914. In the 1912 council elections, Labour won 11 seats in Deptford, only 1 in Islington, 6 in Kensington and 15 in Woolwich (33 counsellors out of a total 1,362) or just 3% of the vote, while Poplar saw the election of 9 independent socialists and 4 in Shoreditch, mainly from the

---

36 Thompson, 'Liberals, Radicals and Labour in London,' 74; Tanner, *Political Change and the Labour Party*, pp. 102–11, 388–91, 441–2.
37 Thompson, *Socialists, Liberals and Labour*, p. 69.
38 See Table 2 in the Appendix for growth of suburban electorates before 1914.
39 Tanner, *Political Change and the Labour Party*, pp. 102–5.
40 Gosling, *Up and Down Stream*, p. 81.

26 Chronological

Marxist SDF.[41] In the last LCC election before the war, Labour captured only 2 seats and polled under 1% of the vote. London was moving to become a Conservative city during the Edwardian period. Indeed, it could be argued that it was only the growth of Labour after 1918 that provided an effective opposition. But to get elected in such circumstances, Labour had to tailor its strategy to the counter the appeal of popular Conservatism amongst the working-class electorate. For example, Charles Bowerman 'held on to Deptford, an impoverished constituency with naval and military traditions... he was linked to the Club and Institute Union and defended working-class recreations such as gambling.'[42] It also had to acknowledge the continuing strength of working-class liberalism in parliamentary elections in areas like Bethnal Green, Camberwell, Southwark and Tower Hamlets. The Conservatives dominated middle-class constituencies, such as Brixton, Clapham, Norwood, Paddington and Wandsworth, some working-class constituencies, such as Finsbury Central and Lambeth North, and nearly all of the suburban constituencies. This was apart from Woolwich which was unique to London (and the UK) in having a Labour Party covering both parliamentary divisions made up of a large number of individual members, many affiliated through the Royal Arsenal Cooperative Society (RACS). It also contained a high number of trade union members active in the large and well-organised munitions factories which dominated the area.[43]

Thus before 1914, the Labour movement in London was made up of a complex range of parties, associations, trades and labour councils, trades councils and the London Trades Council itself, covering inner London, but not the growing suburbs. The few Labour councillors on the LCC had left the Progressives in 1898 to form an independent group but still worked closely with their Liberal allies. The socialists in the Independent Labour Party (ILP), which was stronger in northern and more industrial areas of the country, supported the creation of a regional Labour Party, while the British Socialist Party (previously the SDF), which was stronger in the capital, tended to be suspicious of the trade unions and their allegiance to the Liberal Party, an employers party. Socialists stood as independents in elections rather than forming a political relationship with organised Labour. Where independent Labour candidates did stand, the Progressives tended to regard the party as a semi-independent group, which occasionally threatened its electoral base but not seriously enough to cause it too much concern. Moreover, it was difficult to distinguish between the political programmes of the different organisations seeking to represent the trade unions, which in many areas of policy were similar to the more radical policies of the New Liberals led by Lloyd George and Winston Churchill, such as old age pensions and

---

41 *Times,* 4 November 1912.
42 Pugh, *Speak for Britain,* p. 73; Pugh, 'The rise of Labour and the Political Culture of Conservatism.'
43 Weinbren, 'Labour Representation in Woolwich.'

Labour in an imperial metropolis 27

radical land reform. Rather than facing any serious political challenge from Labour, both Labour and the Progressives in the capital were losing out to the Conservatives before 1914, especially in local elections and to a lesser extent in parliamentary contests. The Labour Party in London did not pose a real threat before 1914, restricted in the main by the narrowness of the franchise, the general weakness of the trade unions and the reluctance of socialists in the Marxist SDF, which was stronger in the capital than the more reformist ILP, to create independent labour parties free from Liberal Party influence. As a result, a regional party for London was not established until as late as 1914.[44]

The First World War changed everything. The economic and geographic consequences of the conflict provided the stimulus for the growth of the Labour Party in the post-war period. 'Geographically, and perhaps most importantly, the war caused a long-term westward shift in the economic balance of power, with entirely new industrial areas established on the borders of Wembley and Acton.'[45] The war transformed the capital's labour market. Government armament factories filled vacant sites in many suburban areas, such as in Wembley and Willesden (now the London Borough of Brent) and in Croydon around the aerodrome, which became London's main commercial airport after the war. The demand for Labour outstripped supply. Wages rose accordingly, although living standards did not keep pace with wartime inflation and profiteering caused acute distress in the early years of the war. However, the living standards of the unskilled increased significantly. The number of semi-skilled workers in factory employment grew at the expense of sweated workshop trades. The static poverty of low wages replaced the endemic poverty of unemployment which had been such a major feature of the pre-war London economy.[46] As a result, trade union membership in London increased from 103,000 in 1913 to a peak of over 300,000 in 1920.[47] Growth was particularly pronounced in transport and munitions.

> For probably the first time in London's history, the casual labour fringe of under-employed men in building, road transport and the docks entirely disappeared... The docks were so short of men that...dockers had to be drafted in from Southampton... When casual labour supply was exhausted, then demand ate into the so-called 'residuum' of 'unemployables.[48]

The estimated loss of 600,000 births due to the separation of married couples during the war caused a rapid fall between 1914 and the early 1920s in

---

44 Thompson, *Socialists, Liberals and Labour.*
45 Goebel and White, 'London and the First World War,' 214.
46 Llewellyn-Smith, *The New Survey of London Life and Labour,* Vol. 1, pp. 115–17.
47 Clinton, *The Trade Union Rank and File,* pp. 192–4.
48 White, *London in the Twentieth Century,* pp. 186–7.

28   *Chronological*

the number of children under 5 in working-class families. This combined with the secular trend towards smaller families contributed to a decline in poverty in London.[49] The workhouse population fell, child labour rose to over 600,000 and thousands of working-class women were recruited into the armaments factories (28,000 alone in the Woolwich Arsenal by 1917) as well as into transport and office work, many of them leaving domestic service to become bus conductors and factory workers, all jobs previously reserved for men.[50] Moreover, after the war Labour undoubtedly benefited from the movement of working-class families from those areas of the country experiencing industrial depression to work in the industrialising suburbs of London. The motor-car industry at Dagenham, for example, proved a particularly strong magnet, especially skilled workers from Manchester factories. 'Of the total number of migrants 24% came from the North East, 19% from the South-West, 18% from Wales and 15% from the midlands.'[51] Migrants from Wales made an important contribution to the growth and development of the Labour movement in West London and in Croydon after 1918, bringing a degree of political consciousness and organisation to the party in areas where it had been almost non-existent before 1918.[52]

Politically, although the labour movement was badly split into pro- and anti-war factions, it remained surprisingly united throughout the course of the war and its prestige and profile were raised by its campaigning on local class-based issues. In many instances, 'Anti-War' agitation was dropped after pressure from the national leadership for local activists to concentrate on unemployment and the relief of distress caused by rising prices. There was conflict over the reluctance of some local authorities to co-opt working-class representatives onto local committees responsible for dispensing relief.[53] Trades councils, socialist groups and women's cooperative guilds campaigned on the issues of war pensions, profiteering, food prices and rents, sometimes initiating and supporting rent strikes.[54] The militant suffragette Sylvia Pankhurst was a consistent thorn in the side of the government over wage rates for women munition workers and inadequate pensions for soldiers' wives. She attracted the support of working-class women, many of them unmarried, as well as key members of the Labour Party in London such as George Lansbury.[55] Charitable organisations complained about the increasing role of the state in undermining their independence in

---

49 Waites, *A Class Society at War 1914–1918*, p. 121.

50 White, *Zeppelin Nights*, pp. 93–114.

51 Thomas, 'The Movement of Labour into South-East England, 1920–32,' 220–41.

52 Humphries, 'The origins and development of the Labour Movement in West London, 1918–1970,' (Ph.D., Reading University, 2019).

53 MLA: LLP Archives: Report of 4th Annual Conference November 1917.

54 Hunt, 'The Politics of Food and Women's Neighbourhood Activism in First World War Britain,' 8–26.

55 Pankhurst, *Home Front*; Jackson and Taylor, *East London Suffragettes*, pp. 109–25.

the provision of outdoor relief to the so-called deserving poor. Their role came to be questioned during the war as the state intervened on a range of domestic issues to support the war effort. As a consequence, working-class deference towards middle-class charity was replaced by a more assertive class-consciousness and a growing faith in the potential of local government and direct action to meet the needs of working people. Such trends gave legitimacy to a new party of Labour after 1918 based on a more assertive class-consciousness.

By the end of the war, the London Labour Party (LLP) had prioritised local government intervention as the best means of defending working-class interests (see Chapter 3). The party's success after 1918 was not therefore based just on the extension of the vote, but it can be attributed to 'the ability of its members to link everyday life with the conventions of political parties. Support for the party grew where its activists ensured that it was associated with the redistribution of resources, particularly the provision of housing and the payment of outdoor relief, and where it provided a route to power for working-class men, migrants and women.'[56] For some like Beatrice Webb, the Labour Party in Poplar after the war developed into what she rather patronisingly described as 'a working-class benefit society.'[57] For the LCC elections in 1922, the TUC, the Parliamentary Labour Party and the LLP issued a joint manifesto which declared that

> Labour candidates put the interest of the community first and foremost, and regard the municipality as one of the instruments by which the lot of the working and middle classes can be improved, and by which the mass of consumers can be materially benefited.[58]

Labour was above all a party of local government during the interwar period. Herbert Morrison, its new secretary, did his best to distance the party from industrial militancy and the influence of the newly formed Communist Party (CPGB) – see Chapter 6 for more details.

Three-way party competition (1918–1929)

The period after 1918 was one when all three parties, Labour, Liberal and Conservative, competed for the votes of the much-enlarged and considerably new electorate. Establishment politicians were nervous of the potential threat of the newly enfranchised working class. After the extension of the franchise in 1918, London's large working-class population voted Labour on an increasing and consistent basis, but did not turn out in sufficient

---

56 Weinbren, 'Building Communities, Constructing Identities,' 41.
57 Cole, *Diaries of Beatrice Webb*, 25 October 1928 – quoted in Weinbren, op cit., p. 45.
58 Labour Party NEC Minutes, 1 March 1922.

30   *Chronological*

numbers in the hastily called general election in December 1918 to make its difference felt. Before 1914, Labour failed to win the allegiance of many of the enfranchised male heads of households in predominantly working-class constituencies in both local and parliamentary contests, fought on different electoral registers. They either continued to vote Liberal as they had done since winning the vote in 1867 or they voted for a programme of popular Conservatism influenced by support for tariff reform, empire and immigration controls.[59] But this radically changed after 1918. Labour's electoral fortunes were transformed by the extension of the franchise and the domestic experience of the Great War. This was especially the case in local elections, such as to the boards of guardians and the new borough councils, fought on larger registers but with more plural voters. Labour councillors pursued a strategy of municipal intervention, paying generous poor relief to the new working-class electorate ('chasing the pauper vote' according to its critics). A consistent feature of the party's objectives throughout the twentieth century was to use a London-wide authority, like the LCC and then the GLC, 'to equalise resources and improve the position of people in poorer communities.'[60] To maintain high levels of payments to the unemployed, the newly elected labour councillors in Poplar were sent to prison for refusing to levy the precepts for the LCC, undermining the respectability which the party's new secretary Herbert Morrison was so keen to establish.[61] However, Labour's progress in parliamentary elections was more limited, fought on smaller registers, held back by pockets of entrenched working-class liberalism as well as the continuing influence of popular Conservatism.

Support for the party after 1918 was confined to the predominantly working-class areas of the traditional East End such as Poplar and Bermondsey, the docks (Deptford, Millwall and Silvertown), Woolwich, an independent town dominated by the Arsenal, the manufacturing areas of the Lea Valley (Leyton, Tottenham and Edmonton) and in some parts of the outer western suburbs, such as Acton, Wembley and Willesden, which experienced significant industrial development and in-migration from economically depressed areas such as the North East and South Wales. It was not until the 1930s that Labour started to break through into the inner residential areas of metropolitan London, such as Hackney, some of the western suburbs and south of the river, when it began to attract lower-middle-class voters (what Labour liked to call 'the black-coated proletariat') on a significant scale in mixed social-class areas like Lambeth and Lewisham. It was in this period that the foundation of Labour's political domination of London was laid, culminating in the general election of 1945. But in local elections,

---

59 Windscheffel, *Popular Conservatism in Imperial London*; Readman, 'The Conservative Party, Patriotism and British Politics.'
60 Ward, *Municipal Socialism.*
61 Booth, *Guilty and Proud of it*; Branson, *Poplarism*; Gillespie, 'Poplarism and Proletarianism.'

Labour in an imperial metropolis 31

it had achieved this much sooner based on its particular strength in close-knit working-class neighbourhoods; its policy of rate equalisation across the capital to fund welfare relief; higher wages for municipal workers; and above all its programmes of slum clearance and municipal housing.

After 1918, Labour Party organisation in London, meticulously encouraged by its newly appointed regional secretary Herbert Morrison (following the death of Fred Knee, the radical housing reformer and member of the SDF), was a difficult task in challenging circumstances. But it was certainly more successful in the long term and in sharp contrast to the debilitated state of the Liberal Party.[62] Only a handful of Liberal Associations, such as Deptford and Greenwich, that had relied on the support of local trades councils before the war supported Labour after 1918.[63] But many others were too disorganised to oppose Labour. The Fulham Liberal Association, for example, had to admit that its weakness prevented it from putting up candidates in 1924.[64] Labour's organisation steadily improved and by the end of the 1920s, it was able to contest over 95% of seats in local and national elections in the Greater London area.[65] Its new constitution adopted in 1918 led, albeit tentatively, to the creation of many borough or divisional Labour parties, some merging with already established trades councils (made up of affiliated unions), with a notional individual membership. Trade union branches provided most of the finances and the personnel to fight elections, although the Fabians and the ILP also supported some candidates. Individual membership started to pick up by the end of the decade and reached a peak in the 1950s.[66] The party decided very quickly after the war to reject the idea of a Progressive Alliance between Labour and the Liberals, which had been a political strategy of MacDonald before 1914 and had formed the basis of a secret electoral pact with the Liberal Party in 1903 to give Labour candidates a free run in two-member constituencies.[67] This dream died after 1918 when Labour, no longer constrained by the limited franchise, embraced a strategy of complete political independence. In contrast, the Liberals could not always decide whether to enter anti-socialist pacts with the Conservatives or to continue to entertain the prospect of a Progressive settlement with Labour, an outcome which still has some traction today.[68]

Strategically, the Liberal Party in London made the mistake of allowing the Conservatives and Coalition Liberals after 1918 to be perceived as the party best placed to withstand the threat of socialism. In London, it continued to do well in some of their pre-war working-class strongholds like North

---

62 Searle, *The Liberal Party.*
63 *Kentish Independent*, 15 November 1918.
64 *West London Observer*, 17 October 1924.
65 See election statistics in the Appendix.
66 Seyd and Whiteley, *Labour's Grass Roots.* See Chapter 4 for more details.
67 Bealey and Pelling, *Labour and Politics.*
68 Marquand, *The Progressive Dilemma.*

32 Chronological

Lambeth, Tower Hamlets, Bethnal Green and Southwark, but failed to appreciate that public opinion increasingly saw them as a party 'of the right' rather than 'of the left,' unable to decide whether they were still part of a Progressive Alliance with Labour, as was the case before the war, especially in London, or as part of an anti-socialist alliance with the Conservatives after it.[69] The major exception was in Greenwich, 'where former Liberals formed the basis of the Labour Party which was formed in 1918...and in 1922 the Progressives formed an alliance with Labour in Camberwell North and Lambeth Kennington.'[70] But on the whole, the Liberals negotiated anti-socialist alliances with the Conservatives and in so doing lost recruits and votes to Labour. The eminent anatomist Dr Christopher Addison, who was the Liberal MP for the working-class constituency of Hoxton (Shoreditch) from 1910 to 1922, and Housing Minister in Lloyd George's coalition government, converted to the Labour Party in 1923 disillusioned by the cuts to his housing programme in a period of post-war austerity (the 'Geddes Axe').[71] He was one of several Liberal, as well as Conservative recruits to Labour after the war, influenced by the polarisation of politics between capital and labour, leaving the Liberal Party (and the Progressives in London) bereft of leadership and organisation.[72]

By 1926, it was too late for the Liberal Party to change direction, having allowed the Labour Party to take power nationally and locally, and achieve a degree of constitutional respectability. The decline of the Liberal Party was particularly marked in London. It never really recovered from the disruption of the war time split between Lloyd George and Asquith and the disaster of the 1918 and 1922 general elections, when they were almost destroyed as a viable opposition to the Conservatives. They revived a little after 1924 under the restored leadership of Lloyd George and did well enough in 1929, contesting more seats and splitting the anti-socialist vote to allow Labour to win a sizeable number of seats in inner and outer London. But after the election of a National Government in 1931, they split three ways and collapsed as a serious political force.[73] It was not until the 1960s and the formation of the Social Democratic Party (SDP) in 1981, that liberalism again posed a political threat to Labour, albeit short-lived, in parliamentary seats like Bermondsey and Greenwich, and in elections in some of the western suburbs. They revived again after New Labour lost some of its initial radical credentials in the general elections of 2001 and 2005, but were badly damaged by their participation in the coalition government of 2010–2015.

---

69 Hart, 'The Liberals, the War and the Franchise.'
70 Weinbren, 'Building Communities, Constructing Identities,' p. 42 and fn. 5.
71 Morgan and Morgan, *Portrait of a Progressive.*
72 Cline, *Recruits to Labour*; Pugh, '"Class Traitors": Conservative Recruits to Labour 1900–1930.'
73 Cook, *The Age of Alignment*; Morgan, *Consensus and Disunity*; Searle, *The Liberal Party.*

Labour in an imperial metropolis   33

The period after 1918 witnessed the spectacular growth of the Labour Party in London. From a position of limited representation, the party gained control of 13 councils (with 573 counsellors) in November 1919, with 39% of the vote and 41% of the 1,370 seats, on a relatively low turnout of 28%.[74] It contested a thousand seats, in contrast to the Progressives, who could only muster about 700, and won Battersea, Bethnal Green, Camberwell, Deptford, Fulham, Greenwich, Hackney, Islington, Poplar, Shoreditch, Southwark, Stepney and Woolwich. Lambeth was no overall control, with Labour holding some key committees, such as housing. Labour also won seats in outer London, in East Ham, Wimbledon, Richmond and Hornsey, gaining a majority in West Ham for the second time in a generation. Labour mayors were elected in Poplar (George Lansbury), Stepney (Clem Attlee), Southwark (George Isaacs) and Hackney (Herbert Morrison). The elections for the LCC in March 1919 were also affected by very low turnout, at just 16%, and a more restricted franchise, provoking complaints from the Conservative press about the political apathy of new working-class voters. Widespread abstention in 1919 by middle-class men, as well as women, might explain both the low turnout and Labour gains of that year. Anti-Labour alliances may also have contributed directly to low turnout, suggesting that the higher the turnout, the lower the support for Labour tended to be.[75] *The Manchester Guardian* put Labour's success in London down to its campaigning over profiteering, which enabled it to 'win a large share of that unknown quantity (dreaded a little by all...) the votes of the working woman.'[76] Labour did particularly well in elections to the local Boards of Guardians, which administered the Poor Law. After 1925, Labour gained seats on many boards in London, 'strengthening their existing majorities in Poplar, Shoreditch and Greenwich, and gaining new ones in Stepney, Bermondsey and Woolwich...Over a third of Labour gains were in South London, an area previously dominated by a Conservative-Liberal Coalition.'[77]

Labour's reversals in the LCC and borough elections in 1922, when it lost majority control of seven councils, was mainly due to the way their opponents combined to reduce Labour's impact. By this date, the unrest and revolutionary fervour of the immediate post-war years had been blunted by the onset of economic depression and dramatic increases in unemployment. The subsequent drop in trade union membership, never that high in London as a whole, turned the labour movement away from industrial militancy towards political activism, particularly after the failure of the General Strike in 1926. But by the end of the 1920s, Labour's electoral record at a local level had recovered from the reverses of 1922 and it controlled 8 councils in London with 458 counsellors. But after the split of 1931, this was reduced

74 Young, *Local Politics and the Rise of Party*, pp. 224–5.
75 Davies and Morley, 'Electoral Turnout in County Borough Elections,' 167–86.
76 *Manchester Guardian*, 3 November 1919.
77 Deacon and Briggs, 'Local Democracy and Central Policy,' 347–64.

34 Chronological

to 3 councils with only 257 counsellors, although it had recovered its 1919 position by 1934 with majorities on 15 borough councils.[78] Labour captured the LCC for the first time in that year, doubling its representation to 69 seats at the expense of the Progressives. As a result, its regional and national prestige increased enormously. By 1937, it won over 60% of the seats on the LCC and controlled 17 of the 28 borough councils with nearly 800 councillors. On the eve of the Second World War, Herbert Morrison claimed that this could not have happened without the support of the trade unions (135,000 affiliates), the cooperative movement (55,800 affiliates), which had started to affiliate to Labour after 1918, and local Labour parties (63,225 members).[79]

Many local parties developed a close relationship with the cooperative movement, which was strong in London during the interwar period, especially in Woolwich although less so in areas like Brent and Harrow.[80] The movement was based on the principles established by the Rochdale Pioneers Shop, established in 1844 to protect the interests of working-class people as consumers rather than as producers. Like the Women's Cooperative Guild (WCG), it proved to be attractive to many women who were not organised in trade unions. Membership of the movement was in fact higher than that of the trade unions reaching a peak of 10 million in 1945.[81] Although ostensibly non-political, the RACS, formed in 1896, and the London Cooperative Society (LCS), formed in 1920, both played a critical (and sometimes underrated) role in encouraging support for the Labour Party during the interwar period, in terms of candidates, finance and the ideology of cooperation, although the LCS was very wary of developing a close relationship with the LLP.[82] The Cooperative Party was established in 1917 to promote cooperation in parliament, and it formed an electoral pact with the Labour Party not to stand candidates against each other. However, it is not clear how far the party in London after 1918 gained votes from the large paper-affiliation of the RACS that it would not otherwise have won. But it did provide financial and practical support, such as meeting halls where the trade union movement was weak.[83] One of the few working-class women elected to parliament for Labour in 1945 (South Battersea) was Caroline Ganley,

---

78 Young, *Local Politics and the Rise of Party,* pp. 223–5.
79 LMA: LLP – The Work of the London Labour Party 1938–1939, p. 4; Barker, *Labour in London.*
80 Rhodes, *An Arsenal for Labour*; Snow, *Signs of Co-operation in Brent and Harrow.*
81 Cole, *The Coops and Labour.*
82 Wilson, Webster, and Vorberg-Rugh, *Building Co-operation*; see also the Archives of the London Cooperative Society, Bishopsgate Institute (GB372). See also Bowie, *Reform and Revolt in the City of Dreaming Spires,* for the important role the cooperative movement played in the establishment of the Labour Party in Oxford. See Chapter 6 for a difficult relationship between the LCS and the LLP.
83 Roberston, 'A Union of Forces Marching in the Same Direction'; Humphries, 'The Origins and Development of the Labour Movement in West London, 1918–1970' (Reading: University of Reading, Ph.D., 2019), pp. 240–71.

Labour in an imperial metropolis 35

a leading light in the WCG and the LCS, the membership of which had increased from 141,000 in 1925 to over 860,000 by 1945.[84]

Of less influence were the campaigns organised by the Communist Party (CPGB) on unemployment, leading to the disaffiliation of several local constituency parties enforced by the regional and national parties. The TUC played a similar role in disaffiliating and reorganising local trades councils which had been infiltrated by the CPGB. Local constituency parties forged effective alliances around state interventionist policies, such as housing, slum clearance and welfare reform, based on a policy of rate equalisation across London.[85] The party assiduously courted the female vote by developing policies that it considered would appeal to women directly as consumers. Many constituency parties had set up women's sections by the end of the 1920s (see Chapter 7 for the role of women in the party). One of the few historians to have researched the success of Labour in the East End after 1918 concluded that it was the result of advances in local government elections rather than the strength of trade union organisation or industrial action, such as the General Strike in 1926:

> The politics of social class which dominated the East End of the 1920s was founded on a series of alliances between groups sharing a common political interest in the control of the institutions of local government. The use of borough councils and boards of guardians to advance the interests of Labour's constituency provided the basis of political unity, not any sense of class unity engendered by the workplace.[86]

However, Labour's record in the East End was not consistent. In West Ham, for example, the war had increased the size of Labour's industrial base and there were high levels of unionisation of gas and transport workers, on which a strong labour and cooperative movement developed after 1918. But this was not always matched in other East London boroughs, such as Tower Hamlets where the mood of the largely unskilled working-class electorate was described as 'one of profound apathy,' where support for the Labour Party was patchy, pockets of liberalism survived and where there was some support for the fascist movement of Oswald Mosely.[87]

The development of 'Poplarism' in the East End during the 1920s, when Labour-controlled councils refused to pay the precepts to the LCC in protest against the rising cost of supporting the unemployed, cannot be understood other than in the context of this changing political attitude to the local state. While before the war, the labour movement was suspicious of

---

84 Chapman, *Caroline Ganley*, pp. 12–49.
85 *The London Labour Party's Municipal Handbook*, 1931.
86 Gillespie, 'Poplarism and Proletarianism: Unemployment and Labour Politics in London,' 164.
87 Marriott, 'The Political Modernism of East London,' 117.

36 Chronological

state intervention, especially legislation such as national insurance which threatened the independent role of trade unions to protect their members, after the war in the East End in particular, radical politics was based much more on state intervention in local government rather than on industrial militancy, given the weakness of trade union organisation. A study of Poplar, for example, has shown that

> it was the institutions and sensibilities of Poplar's civil society outside of the factory, dock or workshop which provided the basis of the borough's politics, through the local Labour Party's intimacy with local people and community activists: the riotous conviviality of neighbourhood life, the democratic commitment of local feminist activists such as Sylvia Pankhurst and Muriel Lester, the moral fervour of local churches (Poplar seems to have had unusually high levels of church attendance in the 1920s) and the socialism of political parties based on mutual aid practices of Poplar neighbourhoods.[88]

In the absence of effective Liberal organisation, Labour also attracted middle-class support as a Progressive political party during the 1930s, especially on issues such as peace and disarmament, which galvanised opinion on a large scale across the country and all social classes, such as support for the 'Peace Pledge,' and the League of Nations.[89]

But Labour's record in parliamentary elections was not nearly as successful during the interwar period. The party was not prepared, and its organisation was minimal when Lloyd George called a khaki 'cut and run' election immediately after the end of the war in December 1918, seeking to capitalise on his record as a successful wartime coalition leader. Coalition propaganda identified Labour with the spread of revolution. Industrial militancy in 'Red Clyde side' and in other areas of the country, including the creation of embryonic shop stewards' committees in the East End, mutinies in the army and a police strike in London, created a feverish atmosphere of ruling-class panic in the immediate post-war period, made more uncertain by the unpredictable way the new enlarged electorate might vote.[90] In the jingoistic atmosphere of post-war euphoria, only four Labour MPs were elected, no different from its pre-war performance. Will Crooks in Woolwich was unopposed; Charles Bowerman in Deptford also did not face Liberal opposition, as did Will Thorne in West Ham Plaistow, while Jack Jones, who was one of several National Socialist Party candidates, defeated the official Labour Party candidate, who was anti-war member of the ILP, in the new constituency

---

88 Rose, 'Locality, Politics and Culture,' 151–68; Rose, 'Locality Studies and Waged Labour,' 317–28.

89 Taylor and Young, *Campaigns for Peace*.

90 Bush, *Behind the Lines*, p. 198; Ramsden, *An Appetite for Power*, pp. 237–40; Cronin, 'Coping with Labour,' 113–45; Pankhurst, *Home Front*; Winter, *Socialism and the Challenge of War*.

of West Ham Silvertown. (Jones took the Labour Whip on entering parliament to the disappointment of the recently constituted local party.)[91] He and Will Thorne were both members of the National Socialist Party, which had broken away from the British Socialist Party (the successor to the SDF) in 1915 over its opposition to the war and conscription. They fought on a pro-war platform of 'Victory Abroad; Welfare at Home.'[92] The only other official Labour Party candidates who got close to being elected were George Lansbury, who was very narrowly defeated in Bow and Bromley, and Doctor Robert Ambrose, previously the Irish nationalist MP for West Mayo, who was within 500 votes in Whitechapel St Georges, but on a very low turnout of only 37%. He attracted the votes of the large Irish and Jewish communities. The Party's national wartime leader Arthur Henderson was beaten into third place in the industrial constituency of East Ham, following a scurrilous campaign where he was accused of being a pacifist and a Bolshevik, 'friend of Lenin and Trotsky, and a German under an assumed name.'[93]

The turnout in London in December 1918 was only 45%, which was over 10% lower than the rest of the UK. In 1910 on a more limited franchise, it had been 85%. However, it could not be regarded as a real test of Labour's potential strength as the party contested less than half the seats and polled only 13% of the vote in inner London. 'Even the victors knew that the distribution of seats was not an accurate reflection of the underlying mood of the country.'[94] One of the reasons for the high level of abstentions was that the registered service vote (predominantly working-class men over 19 years of age, amounting to just under 700,000 in Greater London) failed to turn out, despite the introduction of postal voting. *The Times* reported that Labour agents had great difficulty in getting from registration officers the addresses of the newly enfranchised servicemen.[95] This undoubtedly helped minimise Labour's share of the vote.[96] Moreover, it is not clear how many of the newly enfranchised voters in London actually cast their vote for the first time. It has been estimated that nationally 20% of the electorate in 1918 were men who would probably not have been enfranchised under the old system.[97] This figure was higher in London, given the extent of disenfranchisement before 1914.[98] Women over the age of 30 were newly enfranchised, but the evidence suggests that these new voters were Conservative rather than Liberal or Labour.[99]

---

91 Labour Party Archives: Minutes of the NEC (January 1919).
92 Marriott, *The Culture of Labourism*, p. 31.
93 Bush, *Behind the Lines*, pp. 96–7.
94 Cronin, 'Coping with Labour,' 115.
95 *Times*, 24 October 1918.
96 McKibbin, *Parties and People*, p. 34, n.1.
97 Turner, 'The Labour Vote and the franchise after 1918,' 138.
98 Tanner, 'Elections, Statistics, and the Rise of the Labour Party.'
99 Turner, 'Sex, Age and the Labour Vote in the 1920s.'

38 *Chronological*

Up to 70% of the adult male population of the UK was disqualified from voting before 1914.[100] The electoral registers automatically excluded paupers; any son living with his parents who could not claim exclusive use at any time of his own room; and lodgers in rooms whose unfurnished rental was less than £10 (as well as peers, lunatics and, of course, women).[101] This was further restricted by a length of residence qualification: a year for a male head of household and six months for a male occupier paying a minimum of £10 in rent.[102] Many of these social groups were over-represented in London, such as students and lodgers, whose regular movements around the capital disqualified them from voting. Inner London thus had the lowest levels of enfranchisement in the country, with Tower Hamlets (35.7%), Bethnal Green (42.6%), Southwark (49.4%) and Islington (49.4%) topping the list. Before 1914, probably one-fifth of the middle classes were electors but only one-tenth of the working class were registered in many areas of Inner London.[103] Regularity of work was one of the most important factors in determining who would or would not gain the vote in the East End, rather than class.[104]

Despite its relatively poor showing in the 1918 general election, Labour in London benefited in the long term, firstly from the extension of the franchise, which gave the vote to a new generation of younger middle- and working-class people who had never voted before; secondly from the re-drawing of electoral boundaries to create new constituencies in the suburbs to take account of the enormous increases in population, some of which were working-class areas, such as Edmonton, West Ham and Tottenham; and thirdly from the normal turn-over of population (including war deaths). While this new electoral environment worked to the advantage of both the Labour and Conservative parties, the Liberals struggled to adapt either organisationally or politically.[105] When the Conservatives withdrew from the coalition in 1922, Labour's organisation in London was therefore in much better shape to fight the subsequent election following the resignation of Lloyd George. In 1918, the party's National Executive Committee (NEC) had identified only 4 seats it stood a chance of winning in the capital, 14 where there was a reasonable chance of success and 14 where it stood no chance.[106] In the event, the party contested 42 seats in inner London (out of 61) winning 9, and 26 seats in outer London (out of 37), winning 7. It did relatively well again in 1923 contesting 48 seats (out of 61), all-in three-way contests and increasing its share of the vote to 38% in inner London (winning 22),

---

100 Blewett, 'The Franchise in the United Kingdom 1885–1918.'
101 McKibbin, 'The Franchise Factor in the Rise of Labour.'
102 Thompson, *Socialists, Liberals and Labour*, pp. 68–72.
103 See Table 7 in the Appendix.
104 Brodie, 'Voting in the Victorian and Edwardian East End of London.'
105 Taylor, 'The Effect of Electoral Pacts on the Decline of the Liberal Party.'
106 Labour Party Archives: Minutes of the NEC, 7 May 1919.

Labour in an imperial metropolis 39

while in outer London, it contested 35 seats (out of 37), although with fewer Liberal opponents, increasing its share to 35% and winning 15 seats. Its success in London enabled the party to form a minority government, significantly increasing its respectability and advantage over the Liberals, a constitutional image which Herbert Morrison carefully cultivated with the London press. It suffered a setback in 1924 following the collapse of the minority Labour government, but in the circumstances only lost 2 seats in inner London and 8 in outer London. In 1924, the Liberals again failed to contest many seats allowing Labour to maintain their profile and propaganda as a viable opposition to the Conservatives.

In 1929, Labour recorded their best result before the landslide of 1945, winning most seats (34 out of 60) in inner London and 18 (out of 37) in outer London. This was a remarkable result in so short a time. The Liberals contested many more seats this time (85 instead of 60 in 1924) following a revival in their fortunes under the resumed leadership of Lloyd George. More three-way contests therefore split the anti-socialist vote and gave Labour a significant advantage. The strategy of Herbert Morrison to attract the large and fluid lower-middle-class vote in the socially mixed and residential constituencies of south and west London saw Labour 'winning for the first time in such inner suburban seats as Hackney Central, Hammersmith South, Battersea South and Fulham West.'[107] But this proved to be a 'false dawn.' The defection of MacDonald and Snowden to form a National Government with the Conservatives in 1931 wiped out Labour in the capital for reasons relating solely to national politics and the economic crisis rather than to any fundamental weaknesses in its organisation. It did not really recover in parliamentary contests until the Second World War transformed its national fortunes, although contemporary public opinion believed it to be stronger than it was.[108] In 1933, Labour won a remarkable by-election in East Fulham, on a swing over 25% against the National Government. The constituency, redrawn to reflect population changes, was a mixed lower-middle-class and working-class division with a high level of private rented housing. The Conservative-controlled council had a very poor record of house building. The Liberals did not stand and in the event their middle-class vote went to Labour, influenced by the issue of peace and disarmament, while Labour's working-class vote was boosted by the issue of housing, attracting a high level of support from female voters protesting against high rents in the private sector.[109]

It is not possible to accurately estimate the proportion of the newly enfranchised electorate who voted Labour in parliamentary elections after 1918 when three-way competition between the parties provided new voters

---

107 Jeffery, 'The Suburban Nation. Politics and Class in Lewisham,' 189.
108 Beers, 'Education or manipulation?,' 149; Worley, *Labour Inside the Gate,* pp. 38, 60.
109 Stannage, 'The East Fulham By-election,' 165–200.

40   *Chronological*

with a range of different political choices. Did Labour advance by mobilising formerly uncommitted electors than by converting Liberals and Conservatives? Did more Liberals become Conservatives as had become Labour voters, given the tendency of the Liberals to form anti-Labour alliances?[110] In 1928, the vote was extended to the so-called Flapper vote, women aged under 30. In London, the size of the female electorate grew from just over 800,000 in 1918 to nearly 1,300,000 in 1937 and was over 250,000 larger than the male electorate.[111] All parties recognised the importance of the female vote during the interwar period, with the Conservatives gaining most.[112] What research has been carried out tends to suggest that new voters, and especially women over 30, might not have voted Labour in the way suggested by some historians, particularly in London and the South East. Labour's success after 1918 lay with male working-class voters, whose unionisation, respectability and economic security were probably the key to their political allegiance.[113]

Moreover, it is equally difficult to gauge the extent to which the non-unionised working class, the casual poor or what was left of 'the residuum' voted, if at all. It was this under-class that respectable society accused of political apathy and was seen as beyond reach by those more politically active Londoners, but not perhaps settlement workers.[114] Estimating is made more difficult by what must have been a vast turn-over in the population, geographic mobility, war deaths and generational change. In terms of mobility between residences, characteristic of the large number of lodgers and boarders in London, it was estimated that before the war over 30% moved every year in contrast to only 5% in provincial cities and towns. This resulted in a high proportion of both middle- and working-class men losing the right to vote.[115] Improved housing conditions after 1918, when the LCC embarked on a major programme of house building, such as the Becontree Estate near Dagenham, may well have reduced this mobility, but tended to concentrate the working-class vote in specific neighbourhoods. In terms of generational change, the

> coming of age of workers born in the late Victorian and Edwardian period helps explain in part the coming of age of Labour...and was the result of growing up into adulthood of successive cohorts of workers with different ways of translating social experiences into political choices.[116]

110 Taylor, 'The Effect of Electoral Pacts.'
111 See Table 5 in the Appendix.
112 Jarvis, 'Mrs Maggs and Betty,' 129–52.
113 Turner, 'The Labour Vote and the Franchise.'
114 White, *Campbell Bunk.*
115 Tanner, 'The Parliamentary Electoral System.'
116 Childs, 'Labour Grows Up.'

Labour in an imperial metropolis   41

It is not clear how far trade union membership was a factor in voting behaviour in London as it was in other Labour strongholds outside of metropolitan areas. After 1918, support for Labour extended well beyond the limits of union influence. There had been a dramatic increase in trade union membership during the war reaching a peak of over 8 million in 1920. But this had declined to 4.8 million by 1928, and there were no more than about 2 million affiliated to the party. The vast majority were men and a majority of the growing industrial labour force of unskilled female and male workers did not belong to a union, especially in London, where the working-class 'remained remarkably backward in trade union organisation, with the limited exception of the docks and sections of the clothing trades.'[117] Yet, a sizeable proportion of these newly enfranchised voters, especially after the vote was extended to all women over 21 in 1928, must have voted Labour in the 1929 general election, which saw the party win a large number of seats in both inner and outer London.[118]

Voting intentions in London may also be influenced by the nature of the working environment and travel to work patterns unique to the metropolis. These were very different to Labour strongholds in the provinces where the Labour vote was based on a closer relationship between residence and place of work in more stable and homogeneous working-class communities, such as, for example, Preston.[119] After the war, the census started to record for the first time the extent of the gap between residence and workplace in London. A census report acknowledged that the resident population of any locality is no longer the sole matter of concern to that locality, and

> that it should not be forgotten that a full half of the working day – even, it may be said, a full half of the active life – of the worker is often spent in an entirely different environment which cannot fail to leave its mark upon him.[120]

In London, this divorce between residence and place of work made trade union organisation difficult. The London Trades Council complained in 1935 that it was unable to cope with the dispersal of trade union membership over the rapidly expanding metropolitan area.[121]

Given the nature of the capital's changing housing and labour markets, travel to work patterns and the extension of the vote to probably about a quarter of the electorate who were new voters, it is not possible therefore to

---

117 Gillespie, 'Economic and Political Change in the East End of London during the 1920s,' (Ph.D. Cambridge 1984), p. 368.
118 Phillips, *The Rise of the Labour Party,* pp. 39–45.
119 Savage, *Dynamics of Working-Class Politics.*
120 Census of England & Wales, County of London, Tables, Part III (supplementary), 1923, p. iii.
121 London Trades Council, Annual Report 1935.

42 *Chronological*

identify with any degree of certainty the link between social class and voting in the general elections after the war or to discern the political motivation of those voting Labour for the first time (see Chapter 4). It was certainly not reliant to a very high degree on trade union organisation, apart from where there was a stronger tradition of trade unionism amongst both skilled and unskilled workers stretching back before 1914.[122] Neither is it possible to compare constituencies pre- and post-war, given the extensive redrawing of boundaries to account for the growth of suburban populations. After the First World War, the number of constituencies outside of the LCC area (but within Greater London) more than doubled from 14 to 37. For example, Wandsworth was a single seat before 1914 but became five new constituencies after 1918. The number of seats in Kent, Surrey, Essex and Middlesex increased from 15 to 40.[123]

Conclusion

Historians have recently expressed some doubt about the extent to which London can be characterised solely in terms of stable and homogeneous working-class communities before 1939, given the degree of occupational and social mobility in the labour market, questioning whether such communities had ever 'been the norm in Britain.'[124] Certainly, the new demand for unskilled and semi-skilled labour (and especially female workers) in the rapidly industrialising suburbs after 1918 provided employment opportunities, for example, in the new electrical engineering plants in Acton and Willesden, and the expanding furniture factories in Edmonton, Tottenham and Walthamstow, creating, in turn, a 'floating workforce,' largely ununionised, with loyalty to the area rather than to the individual factory.[125] These improved economic conditions were partly responsible for reducing the extreme levels of poverty and political apathy which had characterised the East End before 1914.

However, while the existence of closely knit working-class neighbourhoods might have been over-romanticised, it is difficult to account for support for the Labour Party other than to recognise the importance of social class (see Chapter 5).[126] But Herbert Morrison also stressed the need to appeal to both working- and middle-class electors after 1918. As the Editor of the *London Labour Chronicle*, he ran a series of articles in the early 1920s on the imperative of securing 'the political attachment of the social

---

122 Marriott, *Beyond the Tower.*
123 Tanner, *Political change and the Labour Party*, p. 391.
124 Baines and Johnson, 'In search of the "Traditional" Working Class.'
125 Scott and Walsh, 'Patterns and Determinants of Manufacturing Plant Location in Interwar London,' 109–41.
126 Kynaston, *Modernity Britain*, pp. 19–30; Lawrence, *Me, Me, Me*; Wilmott and Young, *Family and Class in a London Suburb.*

strata known as the Middle Class.'[127] In October 1923, he wrote an article on 'Brain Workers and the Census,' directly appealing to the political strength of London's 'Black Coated Workers,' which made up a growing proportion of office employees in the capital, urging them to join the white-collar National Union of Clerks, an important affiliate to the regional party.[128] He appealed to such workers on a class basis ('Socialism for Mr Blackcoat'), pointing out their similarity with manual workers, often their parents.

Chapter 5 will discuss the importance of social class in more depth. But the link needs to be qualified and correctly interpreted. The sociologist Michael Savage has argued that the social structure of a locality, whether it be London or Preston, is 'an extremely important determinant of voting patterns.' He went on to emphasise that it should be related to the specific way local labour and housing markets developed over time, avoiding just seeing social structure only as a single snap shot in time. It is important to consider the pace of social change. 'People's perceptions of their locality,' he argued, 'are closely linked to perceptions of what their locality "used to be like." This point holds, to some extent, regardless of the precise socio-structural characteristics of that place.'[129] It certainly can help account for identifying local influences on voting behaviour, although national politics were also beginning to exercise more influence during the interwar period. These changes will be explored in more depth in Chapter 4 on the influence of localities, workplaces and trade union organisation.

---

127 *London Labour Chronicle*, August 1922; February 1923; March 1923.
128 Ibid., October 1923.
129 Savage, 'Understanding Political Alignments in Contemporary Britain: Do Localities Matter?' 76.

2 'Labour in a Municipal Social Democracy'

Introduction

This chapter explores the rise and fall of Labour Party politics in London from 1929 to 1997. The national swing to Labour in the UK during the 1990s was held back in the capital by what commentators called a 'London Effect.'[1] They argued that the party had been fatally damaged (not just 'halted') by a combination of demographic change, gentrification and a revival in a social democratic tradition, in the form of the breakaway Social Democratic Party (SDP) and then the formation of the Liberal Democrats. But as we will see in Chapter 3, dealing with the later period, the swing to Labour in London in 1997 was higher than elsewhere, similar to the result in 1945 when Labour did so well in the suburbs. This chapter is in two parts using the examples from suburban Croydon and inner-city Lambeth to illustrate the argument. The first part covers the period 1929–1968, when the capital had developed into what the historian Roy Porter described as a 'Municipal Social Democracy.'[2] The period between the general elections of 1945 and 1966 represented in many respects the highpoint of the party's fortunes both in local and parliamentary contests. In 1945, Labour swept the board in inner and outer London, attracting a large tranche of middle-class votes in the suburbs, as well as its traditional working-class support in the area covered by the LCC and in many working-class constituencies in suburban outer London, such East and West Ham, Tottenham, Leyton and Hayes and Harlington. It went on to consolidate and increase its control of the LCC and the borough councils in the local elections of 1945 and 1946. It continued to maintain this position until 1966.[3]

The second part of the chapter covers the period 1968–1997, or what Eric Hobsbawn called 'the Forward March of Labour Halted.' It focuses on the economic and social changes which were undermining support for Labour. The local elections in 1968 saw the near total elimination of the party in

---

1 Hamnett, 'London's Turning: The 'London Effect,' *Marxism Today*, July 1990.
2 Porter, *London: A Social History*, p. 407.
3 See Table 12 in the Appendix and Chapter 5 for full election results.

'*Labour in a Municipal Social Democracy*'   45

municipal government, a disastrous year across the country at the height of the unpopularity of Harold Wilson's economic policies (wage freeze and 'the pound in your pocket' devaluation) and only a few weeks after Enoch Powell's notorious 'Rivers of Blood' speech. It recovered in 1971 but in many respects, 1968 marked the beginning of Labour's decline in the capital, a situation not reversed until the advent of New Labour in 1997. After the reorganisation of London government in 1965, which created the GLC and 32 London boroughs, Labour continued to do reasonably well in local, regional and parliamentary elections, but it was not as dominant as it had been during the period 1929–68. A massive loss in manufacturing jobs undermined its support from within a declining manual working class. After the New Left took control of the GLC in 1981, it suffered a series of defeats culminating in the collapse of opposition to ratecapping in 1985 and the abolition of the GLC in 1986 and then ILEA in 1990 (see Chapter 6 on party organisation and the influence of socialism). The Liberals and the newly formed SDP threatened the middle-class base of Labour's support and Labour lost a series of crucial by-elections during the 1980s. As a result, the swing against an increasingly unpopular series of Conservative governments during the late 1980s and early to mid-1990s was less in the capital than other areas of the country.

Rise of a municipal social democracy (1929–1968)

By the eve of the Second World War, Labour in London had not broken the hold of the Conservative Party in parliamentary elections, but it had achieved a dominating position in elections for the LCC and the borough councils. It had taken control of the LCC in 1934, completing replacing and eliminating the Liberals. It remained in office until the creation of the Greater London Council in 1965, and then for a further four years thereafter until the electoral disaster of 1968. During the interwar period, it controlled the predominantly working-class boroughs of Deptford, Poplar, Walthamstow and West Ham for 20 years; Battersea, Bermondsey and Enfield for 17 years; Hayes and Harlington and Woolwich for 16; and Edmonton, Bethnal Green, Shoreditch, Stepney, Dagenham, East Ham and Greenwich for over ten years. In the elections after 1933, it took control for the first time of Camberwell, Finsbury, Fulham, Hackney, Tottenham, Islington, Southwark, Barking, Epson and Ewell, Willesden, Hammersmith, Southall, Chingford and Mitcham.[4] In 1937, it took all the seats in Bermondsey and Bethnal Green, and took control for the first time of Lambeth, Southwark and Stepney (where it lost one seat to the Communist Party), but it failed to win any seats at all in Chelsea, Hampstead and Westminster. There were, however, increasing Labour majorities in a few socially mixed areas such as

4 Weinbren, 'Building Communities, Constructing Identities,' 54.

46 *Chronological*

Battersea, Hammersmith and Islington.[5] By 1939, London was a city polarised at a local level between rich and poor boroughs and between the Municipal Reform Party (Conservatives) and Labour Party.

Labour's record on the LCC was impressive. In 1934, it inherited an authority with an excellent housing record. The Municipal Reformers had provided over 75,000 new dwellings, mostly built on vast new suburban housing estates in Becontree, St Helier, Watling, Downham, Bellingham and Mottingham. The LCC represented a population of 4,500,000 and was responsible for an enormous range of public services – 966 elementary schools, 67 secondary schools, 259 technical and evening schools. It employed 23,500 teachers, ran 160 miles of tramways, maintained 66 fire stations, 10 mental hospitals, all on a budget of £23 million of which 'nearly £12 million came from the rates and over £7 million from government grants.'[6] The new Labour regime 'behaved in a slow-and-steady way, despite widespread expectations of socialist radicalism.' Herbert Morrison, its new leader, 'recognised he had to appeal to the middle-class as well as working class voters' and was fearful of 'left-wing firebrands in the boroughs, in trade unions and on trades councils.' His first priority 'was to uphold discipline and unity and create confidence.'[7] Labour secured a bigger majority in 1937, gaining a further six seats and increasing their popular vote from 341,000 to 446,100. By 1948 and after five years of war had wreaked enormous destruction on the capitals infrastructure, the LCC boasted that it had rehoused 83,000 slum dwellers, built 7 new schools, bought 700 acres of playing fields, abolished the 'Spirit of the Poor Law' in London's hospitals ('designed to help not humiliate – but no extravagance'), re-built Waterloo Bridge, a particular initiative of Morrison, and took credit for the creation of the Green Belt 'to ring London with a perpetual breathing space,' not fully established until after the war.[8] The Labour Party had turned London into what the historian Roy Porter called 'a Fabian dream of municipal socialism run by experts for Londoners' good.'[9]

Social democracy has been defined as a political ideology that originally advocated a peaceful evolutionary transition of society from capitalism to socialism using established political processes. In the second half of the twentieth century, as demonstrated by internal disputes within the Labour Party over nationalisation, there emerged a more moderate version of the doctrine, which generally espoused state regulation, rather than state ownership of the means of production and extensive social welfare. Eric Hobsbawn described social democracy in terms of a Golden Age.[10] In

---

5 Hadfield and MacColl, *Pilot Guide to Political London*, pp. 159–96.
6 Porter, *London*, pp. 408–11.
7 Ibid., p. 409; Worley, *Labour Inside the Gate*, pp. 198–9.
8 LMA: Labour Keeps Faith with London: The Work of the Labour LCC 1946–1948.
9 Porter, *London*, p. 407.
10 Hobsbawn, *Age of Extremes*, pp. 225–401.

'Labour in a Municipal Social Democracy' 47

London, Herbert Morrison, its powerful regional secretary, and Minister of Transport in the 1921–1939 Labour Government, developed a model of state control during the 1930s (e.g. London Transport Passenger Board, Port of London Authority) that went on to influence the nationalisation programme of the 1945 Labour government (e.g. Coal Board, NHS).[11] Such forms of state regulation provide a practical working definition of social democracy in a British context. It was in London that these models were introduced by the Labour Party, and Herbert Morrison, in particular. His vision of socialism and state control did not win him many left-wing friends within the party advocating a more radical approach.

Labour's rise to power at a local level in London coincided with the period when local government was responsible for providing a wide range of services funded from locally raised taxes rather than central grants. 'Gas and Water Socialism' included utilities like gas and electricity, transport, social security (until nationalised in 1930), further education, all schools, ambulances and the fire service (although not the police which in London had always remained a responsibility of the Home Office, much to the chagrin of Morrison). The decline of local government after 1950 (not ironically lamented that much by Herbert Morrison after he achieved cabinet rank) gathered apace as the control of services became increasingly centralised in Whitehall, and as funding by government grants replaced the rates as the primary source of revenue. This, it might be argued, coincided with the slow decline of support for Labour after the Second World War. Such a coincidence supports the view that Labour was above all a party of local government in London during the interwar period, carrying on the tradition of the Progressives before 1914, who, in line with New Liberal thinking of the time as pursued by Lloyd George, had strongly advocated municipal intervention to address social questions, including the creation of direct works departments and improved transport.[12]

The Second World War accelerated Labour's growing dominance in London. But unlike the First, the Second did serious damage to London's economy. The blitz destroyed more property than people and dispersed population to the suburbs and beyond, with many not returning after the war, leading to an acceleration of population loss from the centre. Whole areas of the city and the East End had been destroyed, especially the docks.[13] But like the First, the Second also transformed the fortunes of the Labour Party in London (this time more permanently) and strengthened its hold on both working- and middle-class areas of the capital, apart from a few safe and predominantly upper-class Conservative seats in central London, such as Chelsea, Hampstead, St Marylebone and Westminster, and a handful of

11 Donoghue and Jones, *Herbert Morrison*; Morgan, *Labour in Power*.
12 Saint, *Politics and the People of London*.
13 White, *London in the Twentieth Century*, pp. 197–8.

48   *Chronological*

solidly middle-class suburban areas such as Finchley, Harrow and Rich-mond. On a national level, its role in the coalition government demonstrated above all its patriotic fitness for office. On a local level, although criticised in the early part of the war over inadequate civil defence, by 1945 the rep-utation of the Labour-controlled LCC had been enhanced by its record on running services such as the fire brigade and ambulances, as well as the publication of an ambitious reconstruction plan (Abercrombie), promising further extensive slum clearance and municipal housing.

The Second World War also 'deepened a sense of class identity and re-shaped class relations in important ways – ways that could not have been predicted in, say, 1925 or 1931.'[14] The reputation of London, particularly the Blitz spirit demonstrated by the East End, enhanced Labour as a party of government. Before the war, Conservative domination in many areas of London, especially the suburbs, relied on a coalition of middle-class voters and a sizeable proportion of working-class electors, especially newly enfran-chised women. This coalition was united by the primary objective of keep-ing down the rates, but was also based on the cultural politics of a revived version of popular Conservatism emphasising morality and respectability.[15] The trade union movement had been weakened by economic depression and high unemployment. But the war enhanced the power and prestige of organised labour through the creation of production committees in many engineering factories manufacturing munitions (see Chapter 4 for the exam-ple of Croydon). It created a new framework of industrial relations and full employment. 'The war experience nationalised workers, both in a patriotic sense and in forging closer class unity and the sense of a common political agenda. Distinctive regional class identities remained and continued to be important, but the war had increased the sense of belonging to a national class, superimposed upon more parochial loyalties.'[16] The war 'had poured new life' into many working-class communities, in areas previously domi-nated by urban Toryism in provincial cities such as Liverpool and Manches-ter, and in the suburbs of London, as well as traditional Labour-supporting areas in the country's industrial heartlands and the East End of London. It gave birth to a more homogeneous working-class culture which became the subject of post-war eulogies by writers like Richard Hoggart and the sociol-ogists Wilmott and Young, in their study of family and Kinship in the East End.[17] Recent research suggests that this picture of tight-knit working-class communities has been over-romanticised.[18]

---

14 Field, *Blood, Sweat and Toil*, p. 6.
15 Nott, 'The Plague Spots of London.'
16 Field, *Blood, Sweat and Toil*, p. 7; see also Edgerton, *The Rise and Fall of the British Nation*, pp. 215–7.
17 Jones, *The Working-Class in Mid-Century England*; Hoggart, *The Uses of Literacy*; Will-mott and Young, *Family and Kinship in East London*.
18 Lawrence, *Me, Me, Me*.

'*Labour in a Municipal Social Democracy*'   49

Thus, in the general election of 1945, Labour's share of the vote was over 10% higher than in the rest of the country. The swing to Labour in London was 17% since 1935 in comparison to 12% nationally.[19] Popular opinion on the home front during the war also witnessed a radical shift in public opinion away from the Conservatives, although it is not clear if this was over appeasement or the issue of post-war reconstruction, especially after the publication of the Beveridge Report in 1942, combined with a strong desire not to return to the poverty, poor housing and unemployment of the interwar years.[20] Either way, Labour swept the board across both inner and outer London, ushering in a period of two-party domination for the next 25 years, and reducing the Liberals to the status of a very minor and divided party. In local elections, it took control of 23 boroughs (out of 28). In the general election, 48 MPs were elected in the County of London and 41 in the Greater London area, making it the most successful region in the country.[21] It attracted the vote of large numbers of the middle classes. However, while its 'lead over the Conservatives stood at almost 20% among men, it shrank to 2% among female voters,'[22] confirming the extent to which the Conservative Party still continued to get the support of the majority of women.

In 1946, Labour increased its majority on the LCC, a position it held until the end of the 1960s, when its share of the vote fell below 40% for the first time in a generation. After 1945, Labour had developed into a clearly defined a social democratic party on a platform of reforms to improve the economic and social position of a working class no longer experiencing the extreme poverty of the Edwardian period and living in relatively stable and homogeneous communities, like Bermondsey, for example, with strong community and sporting identities.[23] It still controlled 21 boroughs in 1962. This geographical pattern of political control matches the social geography of London in terms of class and the location of industry.[24] There was a direct correlation between working-class areas of London, the location of industry and support for Labour.[25] For most electoral sociologists, social class has been the primary influence in British politics from 1945 to the 1970s, with British society divided into two monolithic groups: a homogeneous unionised working class and a somewhat more heterogeneous middle class (see Chapter 5 for further discussion of the relationship between class and voting). Labour and Conservative parties dominated the political landscape contesting and winning

---

19 Donoughue and Jones, *Herbert Morrison,* p. 339.
20 Addison, *Road to 1945*; Mason and Thompson, 'Reflections on a Revolution?' 54–70; Fielding, 'What Did the People Want? The Meaning of the 1945 General Election.'
21 Cole, *A History of the Labour Party since 1914*, p. 439.
22 Pugh, *Making of Modern British Politics*, p. 256.
23 Alexander, 'A New Civilisation? London Surveyed 1928–1940s.'
24 Wilmott and Young, 'Social Class and Geography,' in Donnison and Eversley (eds.), *London: Urban Patterns, Problems and Policies.*
25 Rowley, 'The GLC Elections of 1964 and 1867,' 118.

50   *Chronological*

98% of all seats in the House of Commons.[26] The socialist historian Raphael Samuel described this polarisation of opinion between Right and Left as overwhelming in 1945, stating that it 'grew even more dominant in the subsequent years...Two great parties, with huge memberships rising to an all-time peak in the early 1950s, confronted each other in two class blocs.'[27] However for London, this conclusion certainly under-estimates the cross-class support which the party received from public sector professionals after 1945. Several post-war surveys of voting behaviour in London confirm the importance of a settled and stable electorate dominated by two mass parties. But such surveys also began to identify the way voting started to be influenced by other trends that in the longer term started to undermine the social base of Labour Party support.

The best example was the Greenwich Election Survey carried out by academics at the London School of Economics (LSE) in 1949. It was a study of the sociology of politics in a socially mixed inner London constituency, the London Borough of Greenwich. Its main conclusion was that 'social class, in one or other of its protean manifestations, is the chief determinant of political behaviour.' It assessed the class structure of local political organisations and found that voting was more closely related to the class image of the parties than to any of the detailed policies they advocated. The authors found that

> The classes vote for themselves to an unequal extent, both in fact and by admission. Data on the voting intentions of family, friends and co-workers suggest that the more politically homogeneous the individual's social environment, the more likely he is to vote according to the predispositions of his class; and conversely, where an individual finds himself in political disharmony with his social environment, he is likely to betray the fact in his indecisions and vacillations.[28]

In a similar vein, a similar study conducted into the GLC elections of 1961, including a detailed survey of the socially mixed and politically marginal seat of Clapham, found a strong association of social class, age and to a lesser extent sex, with party choice:

> In broad terms, the working class, the young and men tended to vote Labour and the middle-class, the old and women tended to vote Conservative. In so far as a comparison is possible, these findings are similar to those previous studies of voting at Parliamentary elections...So, too

---

26 Norris, *Electoral Change since 1945*, p. 26.
27 Samuel, 'The Lost World of British Communism,' 8–9.
28 Benny and Geiss, 'Social Class and Politics in Greenwich,' 310–27; Benney, Gray and Pear, *How People Vote*.

'Labour in a Municipal Social Democracy' 51

is the almost even division of the lower middle-class between the two parties.[29]

This study also found that there was little to differentiate the manifestos of the two main parties; that there was a general tendency for the London electorate to vote on national rather than local issues and that only a third of those interviewed in Clapham could 'correctly attribute a series of party policy statements to their respective party. Even the party members interviewed showed little familiarity with either their own or the opposing party's policies.'[30] Such findings go some way to confirm that the motivation for voting was not based on any specific ideology so much as the self-perception of the voter as to their social position in the class hierarchy and their identity with particular neighbourhoods. Labour's success in interwar London was founded on the growth of such a localised class-consciousness, built around those areas which had or were industrialising, and where control of boards of guardians and local councils created 'a sense of civic identity.'[31] However, in the decade or so after 1945, this type of municipal politics began to decline in the face of demographic and social change.

Other slightly later electoral studies present a more complex picture, where factors such as age, gender and race start to play a greater role. A comprehensive analysis of three contrasting inner London constituencies (the very safe Labour seat of working-class Bermondsey; the marginal Labour seat of mixed-class Fulham; and the safe Conservative seat of middle- and upper-class South Kensington), carried out by an American political sociologist in the early 1960s, takes into account not only occupational categories, but age, education and housing tenure and links them to voting patterns.[32] Bermondsey was described as an isolated socially homogeneous riverside community, with strong family linkages, shared experiences of hardship during the depression and the blitz, with very little social or geographic mobility, and with most mainly male wage earners having jobs within a short distance from their homes. The Conservatives failed to contest many wards because the Labour vote was consistently over 80% in parliamentary elections. Fulham was described as working class, with many clerical workers, but with a small number of 'aristocratic' areas which contain some of the costliest housing in London, and with a higher level of geographic mobility than Bermondsey. South Kensington was described as an area of high rental property, with many retired business executives and professional people, and intermediate office workers, with over 25% of the inhabitants, including single people and young women, who have recently moved into the constituency. The study demonstrated a clear and unmistakable relationship

29 Sharpe, *A Metropolis Votes*, p. 87.
30 Ibid., p. 7.
31 Weinbren, 'Sociable Capital: London's Labour Parties, 1918–1945,' 194–215.
32 Turner, *Labour's Doorstep Politics in London*, pp. 99–119.

52 *Chronological*

between voting, occupation, education and housing tenure, supporting a strong general correlation between politics and social class.

In other areas of London, Labour held on to the gains it made in 1945 in socially mixed and marginal constituencies, like Hammersmith South and Baron's Court, which were predominantly residential areas with little locally based industry, and where a large part of the working population commuted to other areas of London for work. In Hammersmith South, for example, which had been a Conservative stronghold in the interwar period, Labour increased its majority in 1951. It was socially mixed (23% professional and middle class, 36% lower middle class and skilled working class, and 41% semi-skilled and unskilled) with several thousand migrant workers, mainly Irish and Poles. It contained 'large Council estates, a deteriorating area of once pretentious middle-class dwellings and a number of large blocks of privately-owned flats. Both the slums and the prosperous areas suffered heavy damage from bombing.'[33] In the neighbouring, socially mixed and very marginal seat of Baron's Court, Labour defeated Sir Keith Joseph, the future Thatcherite minister, by only 125 votes in 1955. It was estimated that the large Catholic population of over 5,000 voted Labour over the party's support for Irish unification. Housing was identified as a key political issue.[34]

Race started to feature in London towards the end of the 1950s. It was dramatically highlighted during the Notting Hill Gate riots of 1958, marking the resurgence of fascism when Oswald Mosely contested the seat of North Kensington in the general election of 1959. Labour held on to this marginal seat, but only just in a constituency characterised by class polarisation and slum housing conditions. According to one observer, half the population, mainly Afro-Caribbean, lived in dilapidated mansions, grim tenements and slums, a third lived in posh houses and flats in the south of the area, and the rest lived in Council flats and semi-detached houses. The Labour candidate (George Rogers MP) was regarded as 'a good constituency man' by Herbert Morrison. But he was not liked by the intellectual and CND faction in his party, demonstrating the beginnings of radical community and youth movements starting to challenge the old guard which controlled the London Labour Party up to the 1960s. It was reported that Oswald Mosely took more Labour votes than Conservative and set a precedent for a revival of fascism in the form of the National Front in certain working-class areas of the capital.[35] Along with James Harrison, the Labour MP for Nottingham North, which also experienced a race riot in 1958, George Rogers lobbied the party leadership to legislate for tighter immigration controls, arguing that this did not imply 'colour discrimination,' although this was not a

---

33 Butler, *British General Election of 1951*, pp. 160–73.
34 Butler, *British General Election of 1955*, pp. 117–30.
35 Kullmann, 'Notting Hill Hustings.'

'Labour in a Municipal Social Democracy' 53

view shared by the General Secretary of the party who pointed out that net migration had fallen between 1931 and 1947.[36] Fascist politics had not returned to London since the defeat of Mosley in the 'Battle of Cable Street' in 1936. The British Union of Fascists contested the LCC elections in 1937, polling 23% in Bethnal Green North East, 19% in Limehouse and 14% in Shoreditch, when William Joyce, subsequently known as 'Lord Haw-Haw,' stood unsuccessfully as a candidate.[37]

The London Labour Party and the blue-collar trade unions, which dominated its executive, did little to counter the upsurge of racism in the docks and in the car factory in Dagenham, for example, as immigration from the New Commonwealth and Pakistan led to the growth of deprived black and ethnic minority communities (ghettos) in the East End, in Brixton and in some of the western suburbs.[38] The old guard of the party was perceived as representing the interests of a declining white working-class electorate, which felt that they were losing out to such communities in terms of housing and welfare, although the evidence indicated that the new comers experienced overt discrimination in terms of employment and housing (see Chapter 7 for a discussion of race). In April 1968, London dockers and Smithfield Market porters marched in support of Enoch Powell after his dismissal from the shadow cabinet over his 'Rivers of Blood' speech. A few weeks later, Labour was heavily defeated in the local elections across London. By the 1970s, the National Front, founded in 1968, started to gain support in some working-class constituencies in inner London. A study into the 1977 GLC elections showed that Hackney Central and Hackney South, Bethnal Green and Bow, Stepney and Poplar, Newham South and Newham North East were areas where votes for the National Front were higher than in the adjacent seats of Hackney North and Islington Central, which contained higher percentages of New Commonwealth immigrants. It concluded that the former six areas were part of an old East End political culture characterised by the casual labour system in dockland, stretching northwards along the Lea Valley. 'This finding fits the historical evidence of population migration outwards from the East End,' which 'was primarily in a northward and north east direction rather than eastwards.'[39]

However, by the 1981 GLC elections, the National Front had suffered a dramatic decline in support, undergoing factional splits and fielding only four candidates describing themselves as 'Enoch Powell was Right.'[40] This decline was the result of a number of demographic trends. These included further outward migration of the white working class to the suburbs of Redbridge, Barking and Dagenham; further waves of immigration

36 LP Archives: GS/RAC/49-50.
37 Porter, *London*, p. 412.
38 Marriott, *Beyond the Tower*, pp. 335–42.
39 Whitely, 'The National Front Vote in the 1977 GLC Elections,' 370–80.
40 Bartley and Gordon, 'London at the Polls,' 39–62.

54   *Chronological*

after 1980; the birth of second and third generations of ethnic minorities, under-recorded in the census figures; the continuing effects of the loss of manufacturing jobs; the redevelopment of the docklands and the start of the gentrification of the East End. These were all developments which in the long term undermined the social basis of the old east end political culture of labourism which had remained loyal to Labour since the 1920s.[41] The emergence of the far-right from the 1960s and a revival in the fortunes of the Liberal Party in London were perhaps the first signs that the period of two-party domination was beginning to break down, replaced by one of class dealignment and a growth in working-class support for far-right parties. In London, such developments represented the beginning of the demise of the municipal social democracy epitomised by Labour's political domination of the LCC.[42]

'The Forward March of Labour Halted' (1968–1997)

In 1987, one year after the abolition of the GLC, its leader Ken Livingstone published an unapologetic book ironically called, *If Voting Changed Anything, they'd abolish it*, expressing his dismay in democracy and listing the achievements of the council which he led so controversially from 1981.[43] His use of the phrase is perhaps a little different from the way Mark Twain originally used it or how electoral sociologists have analysed trends in voting behaviour such as low turnout, uncontested seats and the role, for example, of apathy in elections.[44] Not all voters in London had signed up to the vision of socialism as advocated by the GLC and some of the London boroughs controlled by the 'New Left' in the 1980s. But many of the GLC policies were popular, such as transport ('Fares Fair') and training schemes to address de-industrialisation ('Alternative Economic Strategy'). Labour also benefited from the support of grant-aided voluntary groups delivering a range of services from childcare to law centres, part of the 'rainbow alliance' of interests which supported the New Left. Up to the late 1960s and early 1970s, the working class in London had voted Labour in the same way it had done since 1945, broadly reflecting a culture of 'labourism.' But such a tradition was being slowly displaced as the size of the manual working class shrank following the loss of manufacturing jobs. At the same time, the party was struggling to adapt in

---

41 Marriott, *Beyond the Tower*, pp. 335–54.

42 Field, *Regional Dynamics*; Shaw, *The Labour Party since 1945*.

43 Livingstone, *If Voting Changed Anything, they'd Abolish It*. The phrase was originally attributable to Mark Twain – 'If voting made any difference, they wouldn't let us do it.'

44 Denver and Hands, *Issues and Controversies in British Electoral Behaviour*. The term apathy can have a number of different political meanings, either disenfranchisement (as for many electors before 1918), disinterest in politics altogether or a conscious decision to abstain.

'Labour in a Municipal Social Democracy'   55

terms of organisation or policies. It has been argued that the record of the Attlee government had 'locked Labour into a particular kind of political identity,' based on austerity, rationing and nationalisation; the party then failed to respond to the new economic and social conditions of affluence after 1951; and it was perceived by many voters as only representing the interests of male trade unionists as producers; and as a result, it could not relate to the demands or needs of voters as consumers, especially women in an age of increasing affluence.[45]

However, the party did in fact recognise that its policies and organisation had not kept pace with the economic and social changes transforming the country during the 1950s. It carried out two major enquiries into party organisation, the first in 1955.[46] It began to develop policies which appealed, for example, to female voters, although progress was slow (see Chapter 7). However, revisionists in the party like Anthony Crosland failed to reverse a commitment to nationalisation as part of a process of modernisation.[47] In many respects, the left in the party also struggled to adjust. While many party members regarded the success of 1945 as the first step towards a socialist society,[48] the slow decline in the Labour vote in both national and local elections after 1968, combined with a continuing drop in party membership after the high point of 1951, represented a severe disappointment. It tended to reinforce their negative view about the apathy and alleged backwardness of the working-class electorate.[49] The New Left, which emerged in London during the 1970s and in other metropolitan areas like Sheffield, developed an agenda, merging traditional class politics with an emphasis of the politics of personal identity. This was quite a different agenda from that which had defended the interests of a previous generation of white working-class voters.[50] After the defeat of the left during the 1980s, London took longer to return to voting Labour than other areas of the UK. It had to wait until the advent of 'New Labour' in 1997 for its fortunes to be restored to the levels it had achieved in the immediate post-war period. London elected Ken Livingstone when he stood as an independent for the mayor in 2000, and then again in 2004 when he was readmitted to the Labour Party. But this was not necessarily a vote for a return to the politics of the GLC, or for socialism for that matter.[51] It had more to do perhaps with personality, specific policies like congestion charging and the failed attempt by Tony Blair to control and

---

45 Brooke, 'Labour and "The Nation" after 1945,' 163; Tiratsoo, 'Popular Politics, Affluence and the Labour Party in the 1950s,' 44–61.
46 Interim Report of the Sub-Committee on Party Organisation (1955).
47 Crossland, *The Future of Socialism*.
48 Fielding, 'Labourism in the 1940s.'
49 Tanner, 'Labour and Its Membership,' 286–301.
50 Body and Fudge, *Local Socialism?* Pailing, 'Socialist Republic of South Yorkshire,' 602–27.
51 McNeil, 'Livingstone's London,' 75–91.

56   *Chronological*

impose his own 'New Labour' candidate, although the official candidate Frank Dobson was not 'New Labour.'

By the 1970s, a mixture of class dealignment, the loss of manufacturing jobs, the impact of immigration and the migration of many working-class voters to the suburbs and new towns, some to escape the growing immigrant communities in certain areas of inner London ('white flight'), created a crisis for the party in London. Many constituency parties' lost members and became moribund. A new generation of activists took them over in the early 1970s, not necessarily with the same roots in local working-class communities, who were made up in the main of public sector professionals such as teachers and social workers and a declining number of blue-collar trade union members. They challenged the old guard which controlled the machinery of the party at a regional level. They pursued a more left-wing agenda, still influenced albeit by traditional workerist issues. At the same time, the Labour vote continued to decline in national elections, from an average of over 45% between 1945 and 1970, to under 35% between 1974 and 1992. In London, it fell from 44% in 1974 to 31% in 1987, recovering to only 37% of the vote in 1992. By this date, the debate on 'The Forward March of Labour Halted' had been initiated by Eric Hobsbawm. Commentators started to forecast the death of the working class and the party on which it was based, especially in London. Following the heavy defeat in the general election of 1983, the regional party despaired that it only had 26 MPs out of 84. 'Labour faces a bleak period in Greater London,' it concluded. 'The GLC is threatened. We have to fight even in Tory strongholds to prevent the Social Democratic Party (SDP) from becoming the main alternative to the Tories.'[52]

Several factors may have been responsible for the delayed revival in Labour's fortunes in London. They include the extent of gentrification of parts of inner London; the very severe loss of manufacturing jobs, more so than elsewhere; the effectiveness of the vitriolic attacks by the right-wing press on the record of the GLC ('loony left') and the surge in support for the SDP during the early 1980s, the social base of which was particularly concentrated amongst public sector professionals in London. But at the time, this influential element of London's middle class was not large enough to challenge the historic hold which Labour had in the capital. Ironically only when the size of the middle class had grown by the turn of the millennium, and was driving out lower income households from central London, did this tradition of social democracy revive. But it expressed itself in terms of support for New Labour, rather than for the SDP, which by that time had merged with the Liberals to become the Liberal Democrats. Its moment had passed, destroyed by the way the electoral system works against the interests

---

52 Records of the Greater London Labour Party, Report on the 1983 General Election, June 1983.

'Labour in a Municipal Social Democracy' 57

of smaller parties. Thus, although the formation of the SDP in 1981, established at the height of left-wing influence, posed a political threat to Labour, in parliamentary seats like Greenwich and Croydon North West, and in local elections in some of the western suburbs, it was short-lived. The dream of a Progressive alliance between the radical wing of the Liberal Party and the Labour Party, which had been influential in London before 1914, briefly flourished again during the 1980s. However, the defeat of the Bennite left by the end the 1980s (see Chapter 6) saw this strand of social democracy restored and the fortunes of the Liberal Democrats declined.

At a deeper level, political sociologists argued that the slow collapse of the Labour vote after the war was the result of the increasing affluence of the working class, and the fact that its traditional 'cloth-cap' image and support for public ownership were losing appeal.[53] With some justification, they concluded that the outlook for social democracy was not encouraging. Social democracy had been founded on 25 years of near full employment, strong trade unions, rising living standards, the safety net of a comprehensive welfare state and some upward but probably limited social mobility achieved through expanding secondary and higher education. During the 1950s, contemporaries started to believe that support for Labour as a class party was being undermined and that the party needed to modernise.[54] By the 1970s, many predicted the death of class politics, subsumed but not destroyed by a new politics of individualism and personal identity. Post-war affluence had given rise to a search for more personal autonomy and self-determination. This unsettled the outlook of many in the generation that had lived through the depression of the 1930s and had made enormous personal sacrifices during the Second World War. The implementation of race relations and sex equality legislation in the 1960s was both a reflection and in part responsible for the birth of 'second wave feminism' and the growth of popular individualism (see Chapter 7 for a discussion of the politics of personal identity). The period before the election of Mrs Thatcher has been described as the beginning of a complex transition from 'social democracy to neo-liberalism.'[55]

In the case of London, the social and political consequences of these trends were profound and more extensive than in other regions of the country. In terms of industrial relations, for example, trade unions were weakened and collective bargaining diminished by the expansion of individual employment law which emphasised rights and justice at work rather than pay.[56] The link between the organised labour movement and the political party which represented the trade unions was undermined as industrial

---

53 Crewe, 'The Labour Party and the Electorate,' 9–10; Goldthorpe, *The Affluent Worker in the Class Structure.*
54 Crossland, *The Future of Socialism.*
55 Robinson, 'Telling Stories about Post-war Britain,' 263–304.
56 Whiting, 'Affluence and Industrial Relations in Post-War Britain,' 519–36.

58 *Chronological*

action came into conflict with the interests of more affluent consumers. This is perhaps best illustrated by the 'Winter of Discontent' which helped bring down the Labour government of James Callaghan in 1979. While the majority of the labour force in 1960 was made up of manual workers, they had as voters the electoral power to

> pursue collective goods. As producers they were able to disrupt production. The majority left school with no qualifications. Their human capital consisted of skills specific to particular production processes. These became obsolete with de-industrialisation, and with the large rise in secondary and higher education. Educated workers relied more on individual bargaining power, and less on collective goods. Casting workers as consumers rather than citizens or producers punished those with low purchasing power, de-legitimised producer collective action and justified low wages...The majority continued to identify as working-class, but their culture was discredited by market liberalism and consumerism.[57]

De-industrialisation changed the social base of politics in London. After 1960, London experienced an enormous contraction in manufacturing jobs and the slow disappearance of the white working class as a significant presence in many inner London constituencies. The capital lost over 800,000 manufacturing jobs in the period 1961–1985, especially in the docks.[58] Between 1963 and 1973, the male membership of the T&GWU in London reduced by nearly 20% although its female membership increased by 7%, reflecting the growth of married women in the workforce, but with many not joining a union.[59] De-industrialisation and its impact on the labour market have been defined in terms of a number of inter-related trends:

> It has meant the radical decline in activities that offered large amounts of regular, relatively well-paid employment to working-class people with relatively limited educational qualifications (but often with high level job-specific skills). The now dominant service sector, in contrast, is characterised by a much more polarised range of jobs, with formal educational qualifications much more important in determining who gets the 'lousy or lovely jobs.' This polarisation is associated not just with great divergencies in wage levels, but also less security for those at the bottom end; work for many has become much more uncertain and precarious.[60]

57 Offer, 'British Manual Workers,' 537–71.
58 Hall, *Cities in Civilisation,* p. 889.
59 Undy, *Change in the Trade Unions,* p. 137.
60 Tomlinson, 'De-industrialisation,' 1–21.

'Labour in a Municipal Social Democracy' 59

The data for London is stark and quite different to other conurbations, small towns and rural areas in the period 1960–1978. During this period, manufacturing employment reduced by 42.5% in London in comparison to 26% in other conurbations, while it increased by nearly 16% in small towns and by 38% in rural areas.[61] This contraction in the economy was matched by changes in the demography and physical geography of the capital. The speed of physical redevelopment, driven by speculative house and office development, privatisation and unprecedented rises in the price of land, broke up many working-class neighbourhoods, dispersing their populations to adjacent high-rise blocks of flats or the outer suburbs. The impact of the Right to Buy policy after 1980 also undermined labour's electoral support in many parts of inner London. As the proportion of council housing reduced, it was replaced by a private rented sector with much higher rents, whose tenants no longer automatically voted Labour in the way they had done in previous generations, identifying with Labour as a party of slum clearance and municipal housing.

The beginnings of the expansion of higher education in London, which was the largest centre of universities, polytechnics and colleges, stimulated the growth of community activism and the New Left. Young people who had been radicalised in the 1960s started to involve themselves in local constituency parties.[62] The campaign for nuclear disarmament (CND), opposition to the Vietnam War and the feminist demand for abortion rights, rejuvenated the capital's socialist groups and parties. Socialist groups had always been well represented in the capital but they were no longer constrained by the influence of Stalinism following the splits in the Communist Party in the 1950s, and the Soviet invasion of Hungary in 1956 and then Czechoslovakia in 1968. Squatting movements and community activism, such as law centres, provided a new radical agenda of policy issues, especially the ever-present housing crisis and the rediscovery of homelessness and poverty following the screening of, for example, Ken Loach's *Cathy Come Home* in 1966.[63] This more issue-based and middle-class approach to politics was markedly different from the tradition of labourism, which, for example, prioritised the family needs of the white working class over the equal treatment of immigrants, especially in the area of housing and welfare allocations. The politics of identity slowly displaced (but did not replace) the politics of class, epitomised by the way the GLC under the leadership of Ken Livingstone championed equal opportunities (see Chapter 7). At the same time, the GLC pursued an economic strategy of encouraging workers cooperatives to counter the worse effects of de-industrialisation, funded by rate equalisation across the capital. This was a strategy established by Herbert

61 Martin and Rowthorn, *The Geography of De-Industrialisation*, p. 231.
62 Lent, *British Social Movements since 1945*, pp. 7–30.
63 Davis, 'Community and the Labour left in 1970s London'; Wainwright, *Labour. A Tale of Two Parties*.

60   *Chronological*

Morrison in the 1930s after he took control of the LCC, but which started to generate more opposition from ratepayer interests in the outer suburbs during the 1980s, which took legal action against GLC attempts to subsidise public transport (Fares Fair) from a London-wide tax base.[64]

The membership of many inner-city Labour parties declined from the 1950s as a result of population dispersal and turnover. Political apathy, however defined, was in part the result of a sense of powerlessness in the face of the centralisation of state-run services previously run by local authorities. Party organisation stagnated. Many inner-city constituencies became unrepresentative fiefdoms controlled by narrow caucuses which resisted enrolling new members and reselected candidates for election automatically without opposition. The Herbert Commission into the government of Greater London, 'which reported in 1960, had attributed much of this stagnation to institutional causes: the local borough councils too often encapsulated socially homogeneous areas, with the result that they had become single-party monopolies.'[65] The heavy losses in the local elections in 1968 'swept away many senior Labour councillors...and they were replaced by younger, more assertive, and more left-wing councillors.'[66] It was in such circumstances that the New Left, made up but not exclusively of young college-educated professionals and public sector workers, took over constituency parties and the machinery of the London Labour Party during the 1970s and 1980s. They challenged the old guard of older and more working-class party members with roots in the declining blue-collar trade unions. There was a fight back by the traditional right after the left experienced a series of political defeats of the 1980s, such as the miners' strike and the collapse of opposition to ratecapping. Lambeth councillors were surcharged and disqualified from office for refusing to set a rate, having modelled themselves on the similar stand that councillors in Poplar had taken in the 1920s in refusing to levy the precept to the LCC. Similar stands were taken by labour councils over the 1972 Housing Finance Act, such as in Clay Cross in Derbyshire, but less so in the capital where opposition to government-enforced rent rises was more muted.[67] However, such attempts to oppose central government attacks on local labour councils could not necessarily rely on the support of the political culture of 'labourism' that derived its strength from homogeneous working-class communities a generation earlier (see Chapter 6 for more details on the influence of socialism).

Gentrification after 1980 led to a further contraction of the manual working class and a massive expansion of lower professional and non-manual

---

64 Seyd, *The Rise and Fall of the Labour Left*; Michael Ward, *Municipal Socialism?*

65 Davis, 'From GLC to GLA: London Politics from Then to Now,' in Joe Kerr and Andrew Gibson (eds.), *London from Punk to Blair*, 109.

66 Kavanagh, *The Reordering of British Politics*, p. 177.

67 Passmore, The Responses of Labour-controlled London Local Authorities to Major Changes in Housing Policy (Ph.D London University, 2015).

'Labour in a Municipal Social Democracy' 61

groups and a general social upgrading in inner London.[68] There was a high degree of class polarisation where the migration of population to the suburbs and new towns after 1950 left only the very rich and the very poor living side by side in some inner London constituencies, although London has remained to a large extent a fairly well integrated city in comparison to some American conurbations. After 1980, the process of gentrification started to accelerate in certain parts of inner London, transforming the social make-up of previously homogeneous working-class neighbourhoods and putting further pressure on the Labour vote, at least in the short term as it appeared to contemporaries. The term gentrification was first coined by the sociologist Ruth Glass in 1964 to describe the changes she observed in the social structure and housing market in inner London:

> One by one, many of the working-class quarters of London have been invaded by the middle-classes – upper and lower...Once this process of 'gentrification' starts in a district it goes on rapidly until all or most of the original working class occupiers are displaced and the whole social character of the district is changed.[69]

Academics started thereafter to draw attention to the way gentrification was changing the social structure of inner London, undermining traditional politics and creating a new wave of inequality.[70] For many commentators, the decline in support for the Labour Party after 1979 was particularly pronounced in the capital, where the newly formed SDP and a rejuvenated Liberal Party started to capture safe Labour seats in by-elections. For example, in Bermondsey in 1981, the Liberal Simon Hughes defeated the Labour candidate and gay activist Peter Tatchell after the right-wing Labour MP for the constituency Bob Mellish fell out with his local party eventually joining the SDP.[71] In a similar fashion in Greenwich in 1987, the official Labour candidate, the left-wing GLC councillor Diedre Woods, was defeated by the SDP at the height of its popularity following the defection of the 'Gang of Three' from the Labour Party in 1981.[72] The journal *Marxism Today* identified a 'London Effect' which threatened to undermine Labour's performance 'caused by the vast demographic changes that have taken place during the last twenty years.'[73]

---

68 Butler, Hamnett and Ramsden, 'Inward and Upward'; Butler and Robson, *London Calling*; Hamnett, *Unequal City.*
69 Glass, Introduction to *London: Aspects of Change.*
70 Hammett, 'Gentrification and the Middle-class Remaking of Inner London,' 2401–26; Hammett and Butler, 'Reclassifying London,' 197–208.
71 Tatchell, *The Battle for Bermondsey.*
72 Norris, *British By-Elections*, pp. 89–107.
73 *Marxism Today*, July 1990, pp. 26–31.

62   *Chronological*

Gentrification in London speeded up even further after the deregulation of the City of London in the mid-1980s and the growing colonisation of adjacent inner-city areas by highly paid financial executives in boroughs like Hackney and Islington. By this time, waves of asylum seekers and immigrants from outside the EEC had really started to radically transform labour markets across London, providing a cheap source of sweated workers. By the turn of the century, London's economy had polarised between a metropolitan elite of well-paid executives and an underclass of low paid migrant workers, with an expanding lower middle class sandwiched between them. The very high turnover of labour was such that it made trade union organisation even more difficult to sustain.[74] Trade unionism in London, at under 25% of all employees in 2007, was concentrated in the public sector with over 50% occupying positions of managers and foremen.[75] Population turnover increased, outstripping the 30% of annual removals which had characterised Edwardian London, with 10 of the 32 London boroughs experiencing rates in excess of 50% every five years. 'In the most mobile areas a typical resident would say goodbye to more than half of their neighbours every five years (and) as many as a third of London's population were born abroad, a rate that has increased from 18% in 1986.'[76]

These demographic pressures placed enormous stress on community cohesion and political organisation, with large reductions in party membership. Social surveys recorded that it was the 'poorest wards that are the most diverse and which also tend to have the highest rates of population mobility, making it particularly difficult to foster the strong social relationships that can underpin the community-based organisation that might also facilitate political voice.'[77] Recent studies of the way the class structure of London was being remade showed that new political and social movements or identities were being forged in different neighbourhoods based on a middle-class search for values, structure and security. The new middle class in these areas sought to enhance and protect local schools for their children and support local shops and farmers markets selling specialised niche products, quite unlike the traditional street markets, for example, Covent Garden and Portobello Road, before they were gentrified, which had been a feature of working-class community life up to that time.[78]

In some respects, by the year 2000, the economic and social characteristics of London in 1900 had to a significant extent returned. Growing inequality reversed the progress made in the period after 1918. A casual labour

---

74 Buck, *Working Capital.*
75 Labour Force Survey, 2007.
76 Wills, 'The Geography of Community and Political Organisation in London Today,' 114–26.
77 Ibid., p. 119.
78 Butler and Robson, *London Calling.*

'Labour in a Municipal Social Democracy'   63

market made up of exploited and non-unionised migrant workers had replaced a workforce which had enjoyed a high degree of job security and incomes which could support a family and purchase a home.[79] Immigration had created ethnically distinct areas with their own shops, social networks and places of worship, similar in some respects to the Jewish ghetto in Whitechapel during the Edwardian period. Economic insecurity had become a significant feature of the London labour market impoverishing both working- and middle-class individuals to an extent that shocked many think tanks and political commentators. Flexible working, such as short-term contracts in the expanding service industries, spread this insecurity to the lower middle classes in the suburbs, making the housing crisis one of the most urgent political issues in the capital. Sociologists now refer to this new class as 'the precarious precariat.'[80]

One feature of this new underclass is that they are unlikely to belong to a trade union that might defend their interests. Membership of the public sector unions in London began to shrink after 1980 in line with the financial cuts to the civil service and local government and the privatisation of services. Trade union density of employees in public administration fell from 57% in 2003 to 53% in 2007.[81] London continues to be the weakest area for trade union organisation in the country, as it was before 1914. It might be safe to conclude that membership of a trade union has probably been of only marginal influence in the way some Londoners might or might not have voted Labour. In 1996, the London Labour Party calculated that on average, there were about 6,000 trade unionists in each constituency but only 1% were members of the party; and that in the country as a whole, up to a quarter of a million party members did not belong to a trade union at all.[82]

The physical regeneration of London since the 1980s was also responsible for driving many of these demographic and social changes, especially in the dockland areas of North Southwark, Tower Hamlets and Newham, the traditional East End. The Local Government, Planning and Land Act in 1980 had encouraged local authorities to sell off areas of derelict and vacant land in London and other metropolitan areas, such as Liverpool. Such areas had extensive disused docks following their relocation to container ports like Tilbury. The Conservatives finally accomplished their aim of abolishing the Dock Labour Scheme in 1986, breaking the hold of organised labour and of the Labour Party in the East End. The Act created the London Docklands Development Corporation, where local planning powers did not apply, preventing Labour-run local councils from controlling urban development in the interest of their working-class communities. The

79 Cockburn, *Looking to London*; Judah, *This is London*.
80 Savage, *Social Class in the Twenty First Century*, pp. 331–58; Standing, *The Precariat*.
81 Labour Force Survey (2003 and 2007).
82 London Labour Party Executive Committee minutes 23 January 1996.

64 *Chronological*

subsequent financialisation of housing and development set in train the continuous physical regeneration of the capital, based on private finance generating enormous increases in the value of land on the granting of planning permission. This precipitated yet further rounds of regeneration that now affect many parts of the capital. This has transformed not only the skyline, but has significantly reduced the amount of affordable local authority housing, further undermining traditional support for Labour as the party of municipal housing.[83]

Less than 10% of new jobs created by the redevelopment of the docks went to local people. 'In 1989, only 3% of the employees of the twelve biggest office firms in the Isle of Dogs were local residents.' Furthermore

> between 1971 and 1981, employment loss in Greater London was 10.5%, in East London 16%, and in Docklands 32.5%. Then, between 1981 and 1990 Docklands lost 20,532 jobs; however it gained 41,421 jobs, three-fifths of which were transfers from other places – chiefly other parts of London...Between 1981 and 1987 employment in transport showed a loss of 56%, manufacturing a gain of 4%, services a gain of 74%, ...hotels and catering 91%, banking insurance and finance a gain of 495%.[84]

The Labour-controlled GLC and the borough councils in the East End were in the forefront of opposition to the redevelopment of the docks. But their power and influence were reduced during the 1980s, further compounded by the abolition of the Labour-controlled GLC in 1986.[85] The attempt by New Labour to forge 'a third way' to address what was seen as 'London in Crisis' did little to change the speed or prevent the damage to working-class neighbourhoods caused by redevelopment.[86]

The remarkable demographic and social changes that took place in London in the last quarter of the twentieth century had an uneven and unpredictable impact on the politics of the capital. However, one very clear trend was the way the growth of the black population in London was redefining the way electoral sociologists were classifying parliamentary constituencies in terms of their social and economic composition. Table 2.1 shows a comparison between 1978 and 1997 in the way, for example, that the constituencies in Brent, Croydon, Hackney and Lambeth were clustered into different social categories based on status, race and deprivation.

These changes in classification represented a clear move away from class to race. But it would be a mistake to conclude that social class no longer counted (see Chapter 5 for further discussion).

---

83 Minton, *Big Capital.*
84 Hall, *Cities in Civilisation*, p. 926.
85 Barnes, Colnutt and Malone, 'London: Docklands and the State,' 15–36.
86 Rogers and Fisher, *A New London.*

Table 2.1 Changing socio-economic classification of London constituencies
1978–1997

Constituency	1978 Classification	1997 Classification
Brent Central		North London immigrant deprived
Brent North		North London immigrant deprived
Brent East	Metropolitan Centre – low status	Abolished
Brent South	Metropolitan Centre – low status	Abolished
Croydon Central	Outer ring mixed class suburbs	Middle Britain
Croydon North +		Outer London immigrant concentration
Croydon North East	Outer ring mixed class suburbs	Abolished
Croydon North West	Outer ring mixed class suburbs	Abolished
Croydon South	Middle-class suburbs	Middle-class suburban
Hackney North	Metropolitan Centre – low status	Inner London immigrant concentration
Hackney South	Metropolitan Centre – low status	Inner London immigrant concentration
Dulwich and West Norwood	Metropolitan Centre – low status	Mixed inner-city area
Streatham	Metropolitan Centre – low status	Mixed inner-city area
Vauxhall	Metropolitan Centre – low status	Inner London immigrant concentration

Source: Compiled from Webber, *Parliamentary Constituencies: a socio-economic classification*; Johnston, Rossiter and Pattie, *Three Classifications of Great Britain's New Parliamentary Constituencies.*

Conclusion

At a local level in elections to the borough councils and the LCC, the party's hold on the working-class areas of inner London and in the industrial suburbs had been consolidated by the eve of the Second World War. As Eric Hobsbawm has argued, the real strength of labour in London, as in other giant cities, 'lay entirely in those urban villages which actually constituted so much of the megalopolis,' like the 'Red Belt' in Paris, 'and around which Abercrombie tried to structure his London Development Plan in 1944: places like Poplar and Clerkenwell.' He cited the example of Woolwich, which was one of the few parties in the country with a mass individual membership (over 5,000 in 1939) as a 'town within a city, a defined community whose working class was based on the great Arsenal, which generated both the football club and the Royal Arsenal Cooperative Society

66 *Chronological*

which eventually colonised other parts of London.'[87] But unlike Paris, for example, where working-class suburbs were to be found concentrated in the outer-ring of its metropolis (a red doughnut around a blue centre), or Vienna (a red island in a blue sea), working-class suburbs in London did not start to develop until new industries were founded in areas like Southall and Hayes, which became local bastions of Labour during the interwar period and after 1945.[88] In contrast, the suburb of Croydon experienced some industrial development after 1918, but not on a sufficiently large enough scale to provide the growth of a more powerful labour movement (see Chapter 4).

The Second World War accentuated these trends through rearmament and the expansion of light engineering factories in suburban areas, such as Croydon and Willesden, which became growth hotspots after the war, providing the foundation for the further growth of Labour politics. Labour in Croydon, for example, failed to take control of the Council in 1945, but narrowly won Croydon South for the first time in the general election, but this was not to be repeated until the 1990s. Labour did better in the western suburbs where industry and in-migration from the depressed areas of the country, such as South Wales and the midlands, were more extensive. Labour held on to the predominantly working-class areas of the East End and the Lea Valley, secured in the support of the working-class vote, identified in the social surveys of the time. But all these areas started to experience large-scale de-industrialisation after the 1960s (see Chapter 4 on localities and workplaces), and the size of the manual working-class contracted together with the influence of the blue-collar trade unions. By the late 1970s, the 'Forward March of Labour' had been 'halted' in London, more so than in other areas of the country where the loss of manufacturing jobs was less extreme.

---

87 Hobsbawm, 'Labour in the Great City.'

88 Humphries, 'The Origins and Development of the Labour Movement in West London, 1918–1970' (Reading: University of Reading, Ph.D, 2019).

3 Labour in a 'City of Rampant Capitalism'

Introduction

This chapter covers the period from 1997 to 2020, when the performance of the Labour Party in London improved, quite dramatically in the general election of 1997, very similar to that of 1945. London continued to vote Labour in the general elections of 2001 and 2005, although its vote was marginally lower following the decline in popularity of Tony Blair and the government's decision to go to war in Iraq.[1] It suffered a further but not disastrous set-back in 2010 following the financial crash of 2008, recovering a little by 2015, but it was restored to dominance after 2015. The general elections of 2017 and 2019 consolidated Labour's strength in Greater London, despite a swing of 6% in 2019 to the Liberal Democrats as a result of the party's confused policy on Brexit, while support for the Conservatives dropped to 32%, a historic low. Since 2015, the record of the Labour Party in local, regional and parliamentary elections has been impressive (see Appendix A and Chapter 5 for full results). It remains on average about 10% ahead of the Conservatives in terms of voting intentions for parliamentary elections. In 2020, this figure was even higher for Labour's Sadiq Khan when 49% of Londoners said that they would vote Labour in the mayoral election in May 2020 (before the election for Mayor was postponed as a result of the Coronavirus pandemic).[2]

This chapter will argue that Labour's dominance after 1997 was based on the unique social composition of the capital. Commentators recognised that by 2015 London had become 'socially liberal, multi-racial and cross-class,' made up of a significant proportion of students and ethnic minorities (35% of the population is non-white, 54% of which votes Labour). It has been estimated that a quarter of the membership of Momentum, the left-wing pressure group supporting Jeremy Corbyn, lives in London.[3] Moreover, London's politics was influenced by the extent to which the capital had

---

1 Whiteley et al., *Affluence, Austerity and Electoral Change in Britain*, pp. 46–51.
2 YouGov/QMUL Survey results 30 Oct–4 Nov 2019 & 2–8 March 2020.
3 Beckett, 'How London became a Labour City?' *Guardian Newspaper*, 11 May 2016.

68   *Chronological*

developed into a relatively integrated and tolerant city, despite its transformation into a 'City of Rampant Capitalism,' and the presence of extreme levels of inequality.[4] When the Mayor of London in 2007, Ken Livingstone, told the Marxist geographer Doreen Massey that the big advantage that London had over other cities 'is that the races and places mix much better here...people can preserve their identity whilst participating in the city.'[5]

London is now one of the strongest, if not the strongest region for Labour. But at the same time, the party is also experiencing a significant loss of support in other areas of the country, especially in its traditional northern heartlands (the so-called 'Red Wall'), where the Conservatives have made inroads into Labour's white working-class base. But it has also been severely damaged in Scotland by the rise of the Scottish National Party (SNP). Its hold in Wales has also slipped to the benefit of Plaid Cymru, another nationalist party. In Northern Ireland, it does not exist as a separate party, given historic nationalist divisions. Thus, there is nothing new about working-class support for parties other than Labour. For example, before 1914, parts of the north such as Lancashire had been centres of working-class Toryism, until the progressive policies of Lloyd George (New Liberalism) helped the Liberal Party capture working-class votes in what was a former Conservative stronghold.[6] A significant proportion of working-class voters have to varying degrees always voted Conservative, ever since a Conservative Prime Minister, Benjamin Disraeli, gave male heads of working-class households in urban areas the vote in 1867. After 1918, a large proportion of newly enfranchised working-class women also voted Conservative. The gender gap between Labour and Conservative did not close until the 1970s. Such working-class voters have been described by historians as 'Angels in Marble,' posing the interesting (and largely unresolved) sociological question why electors do not vote in line with their class interests.[7] Working-class support for the Conservative Party in the general election of 2019 is not therefore unusual in historical terms, and it remains to be seen if the Tories can hold on to these votes in the future, or whether Labour can broaden its appeal to include the white working class outside of the big cities.

Conversely, Labour has always attracted the support of elements of the upper and middle classes, including aristocratic socialists such as Tony Benn (previously Viscount Stansgate), especially so in London. In Croydon, for example, during the 1920s, the Labour Party was a predominantly middle-class party, attracting 'many black-coated workers' after the introduction of individual membership in 1918, making it possible (at least for its party agent) 'for those few and exceptional persons, who strictly speaking, belong – from an economic point of view – to the capitalist class, but who

---

4 Massey, *World City*.
5 Massey, 'The World We're In: An Interview with Ken Livingstone,' 13–14.
6 Clarke, *Lancashire and the New Liberalism*.
7 McKenzie and Silver, *Angels in Marble*; Walsh, *Making Angels in Marble*.

Labour in a 'City of Rampant Capitalism' 69

find sympathy with the workers stronger than their economic self-interest.'[8] In modern-day London, members of the party in Hounslow, for example, the previous home of the middle-class socialist William Morris in the 1880s, include 'a retired senior army officer, a former head of HM Custom and Excise, a successful West-End theatre playwright, and a number of well-known actors.'[9] Indeed by 2019, 37% of ABC1 social grades said that they intended to vote Labour in London, only slightly less than social C2DE grades – an even split between the middle and working classes.[10]

The chapter is in two parts. Part I ('Then the Suburbs turned Red') describes the remarkable result for the party in 1997, when it captured many suburban constituencies as well as retained its support in inner London. It explains Labour's success in terms of the continuing economic and social transformation of the capital, following the massive loss of manufacturing jobs and the beginnings of gentrification (see the previous chapter). Many of the previously working-class areas of London now have high concentrations of middle-class professionals and managers working in the city and in the bohemian quarters of inner London. They have been joined by an enlarged 'middle-mass' of lower professionals and other non-manual workers (the precariat), made of a significantly growing proportion of BME citizens. These social strata have 'now displaced the manual working classes as the single largest group in most areas of London.'[11] At the same time, the precariat, and what remains of the traditional white working class, unable to afford inflated housing costs in the centre, have been increasingly pushed to the outskirts of London or beyond, reinforcing feelings of social distance and a sense of heightened working-class consciousness.[12] Part I also briefly looks at the policies pursued by the party in London after the year 2000 to address this severe housing shortage, which is now (as it always has been) one of the most pressing and unresolved political issues in the capital. Part II ('Labour consolidated') seeks to account for the party's success in London after 2015. It argues that the capital's expanding precariat (increasingly young, better educated and multi-ethnic) now votes Labour as the historic party of the working class, in contrast to non-metropolitan areas (with an older population, less educated and less multi-ethnic, but with greater property wealth) where Labour is losing support. Increasing inequality in London, now one of the most polarised regions of the country in terms of deprivation, has created the circumstances for a revival of a new form of working-class consciousness similar in many respects to the 'labourism' of any earlier generation, but now self-identified in different terms as 'ordinary' or 'just about managing.'

---

8 *Croydon Labour Outlook*, September 1924.
9 Written evidence from a constituency ward secretary in Hounslow.
10 YouGov/QMUL Survey results 30 October to 4 November 2019.
11 Butler, Hamnett and Ramsden, 'Inward and Upward,' 72.
12 Cunningham and Savage, 'An Intensifying and Elite City,' 25–46.

70   *Chronological*

'Then the suburbs turned Red' (1997–2015)

London voted Labour in 1997 on a bigger swing than other areas of the UK. It attracted the support of not only its traditional base in the inner cities, parts of which were gentrifying, but a sizeable proportion of voters in the suburbs. Areas like Brent South, Croydon North and Croydon Central were taking on the characteristics of the inner city, becoming the sites of immigrant concentrations and an expanding lower middle class (see Chapter 4). Political sociologists lost no time in noting that the swing to Labour was higher in London than elsewhere and was particularly pronounced in the suburbs. New Labour's victory was deeper in those areas where the Conservative Party had been remarkably strong in the Thatcher decade. London cabbies, for example, living in areas like Ilford South ('a constituency containing 1,000 cabbie voters'), and 'epitomised as 'Essex Man' of the 1908s, switched from supporting cultural elements of Thatcherism (English nationalism and a hard-line approach to crime and punishment), to voting New Labour.[13] London experienced a swing of over 14% to Labour in 1997. It won an extra 25 seats in Greater London, while the Liberal Democrats picked up five seats in the middle-class suburbs of south west London. The Conservatives were reduced to 11 seats 'clustered in the stock-broker commuter belt on the Kent borders as well as the affluent City, and Kensington and Chelsea.'[14] There was no more talk of the 'Forward March of Labour Halted.'

London voted Labour after 1997 in a way that surprised many commentators. Psephologists drew attention to the way the social basis of voting had been transformed. They argued that at the constituency level before the 1990s, the Labour heartland had been inner-city working-class areas, with all the multiple social problems associated with council estates, high unemployment and urban deprivation, a high concentration of Asian and black residents, and industrial decline. But on the contrary, the evidence from the 1997 election showed that:

> New Labour has managed to widen its appeal beyond its core, like the Social Democrats in Sweden, yet also hold onto its traditional working-class vote... Blair did better in constituencies with a high concentration of professional and managerial workers. While seats with many skilled non-manuals (C1s) swung sharply towards Thatcher in 1979, these areas shifted most strongly towards Labour. From 1979 weakening Labour support in working-class seats indicates dealignment, particularly among the skilled working class (the C2s). In a similar trend, from 1966–79 Labour support strengthened in seats with high levels of council housing, but this association subsequently weakened

13 Davis, 'The London Cabbie and the Rise of Essex Man.'
14 Norris and Gavin, *Britain Votes* 1997, pp. 11–12.

in the 1990s...Labour's support among council tenants remained solid and unchanged, but the swing to Labour was marked among owner-occupiers, especially those with a mortgage...The modest gender gap in 1992 closed in 1997, as more women (+11%) than men (+8%) shifted into the Blair camp...The strongest swing to Labour was monitored among the younger generation (+18%), while Labour made no gains among the over 65s.[15]

The result in 1997 has also been attributed to the adoption by New Labour of policies that proved 'attractive to university-educated public sector professionals as well as the shrinking Labour base of skilled and unskilled blue-collar workers in manufacturing industry.'[16]

Labour consolidated its support in the suburbs in the general election of 2001. 'How the suburbs turned red' was the view of Ivor Crewe in an article for the *New Statesman*. 'The drum beat of Labour gains in 1997 was a roll-call of the suburban home counties: Braintree, Harrow, Hendon, Putney, Enfield Southgate – Southgate! – Watford. Only Surrey stayed solidly blue. The rest of John Betjeman country turned red.'[17] 'Why,' he asked, 'were the professionals, managers and small business people won-over in such unprecedented numbers?' After 2002, Labour experienced a drop in voting share, culminating in the election of Boris Johnson as Mayor in 2008, based to some extent on a higher turnout in the outer London suburbs. Membership also dropped as elements of the middle class deserted the party after the Iraq War and who were opposed to New Labour's more neo-liberal policies. It did relatively badly in 2010 and in 2015, but it still maintained its lead over the Conservatives. By this time, it was becoming clearer that the residents of smaller towns or rural areas were more likely to vote Conservative (up 40% since 2010), while the opposite has happened for Labour. Between 2010 and 2017 the party's share of city voters increased from 35% to 49%.[18] In the general election of 2019, Labour lost support in those smaller cities and towns in the north which have been described as having slower population growth; as being more middle-aged; as more likely to be owner-occupiers; as having less demographic and social mobility (with less desertion by the young). These were areas that had much lower economic dynamism than that found in larger metropolitan cities like London, and especially London. They voted to leave Europe in the 2016 referendum. These areas are poor, but are not the poorest, if measured by property wealth and income.[19]

15 Ibid., pp. 16–17.
16 Norris, 'Elections and Public Opinion,' 55.
17 *New Statesman*, 4 June 2001, pp. 19–20.
18 Bailey and Baston, *'For the Many.'*
19 Gardiner et al., 'Painting the Towns Blue.'

72   *Chronological*

In 2018, the Fabian Society undertook a survey to explore the reasons for Labour's success in metropolitan areas. It identified a group of 24 constituencies in London other than in

> the Docklands, the East End and a parallel group of seats in West and Central London that have generally been Conservative inclined and have their own historical pattern. They include the remainder of the London County Council area plus the close-in boroughs of Willesden, Leyton, Hornsey, Tottenham, Edmonton, Leyton, Walthamstow and East Ham, all of which were 'London' in administrative terms long before they became part of Greater London in 1964. Broadly, this is the metropolis without the concentrated extremes of wealth and poverty of the East and West Ends.[20]

It was in these areas that Labour outperformed the rest of England and Wales by 25 points with a swing of over 9% since 1997. For example, in the three constituencies in Lambeth (Dulwich & West Norwood, Streatham and Vauxhall), the percentage share of the Labour vote increased from 48% to 67% between 2005 and 2017. The same goes for constituencies which have high proportions of black and ethnic minority voters, like Croydon North, now one of the most diverse seats in the country. The survey found that there had been a swing to Labour in these seats of 7% since 2005 and that Labour won 44 of the 50 most diversifying seats in 2017. One sociological survey cited showed that 'Ethnic minorities tend to support Labour in much the way that the traditional working class used to support Labour back in the 1950s and 1960s, providing Labour with its safest seats.'[21] The survey placed the two most northern constituencies in Croydon (Central and North) in the category of seats which were diversifying in terms of ethnic composition. (Croydon South was excluded from the survey as a safe, largely white Conservative seat, although it contained an upwardly mobile Asian population.) The two northern Croydon seats were in a group of 50 where there had been the largest fall in the white British population between 2001 and 2011 and where Labour had enjoyed a 20% advantage in terms of vote share. The Fabian report quoted a black voter in London as saying

> London, as a city, is not dominated by one thing... we're gay, we're straight, we're this, we're that, we're tall, we're short, you can find one of everything in London and we live next door to each other – London is a country within a country.[22]

---

20 Bailey and Baston, *'For the Many.'*
21 Heath, 'Ethnic Minority Voters at the Ballot Box'; Martin and Khan, 'Ethnic Minorities at the 2017 British General Election.'
22 Bailey and Baston, *'For the Many,'* p. 12.

The growing size of the ethnic vote is thus one of the primary reasons for increasing support for the Labour Party in London after the year 2000. The relationship between race and class is complex as demonstrated by the *Great British Class Survey* published in 2015. This showed that ethnic minorities are under-represented among the elite, especially in London, but well represented in the established middle class beneath the extraordinary concentration of elite social groups in the gentrified neighbourhoods of the capital. They are, however, also

> well represented among the emerging service workers, the group of well-educated young people who have not yet procured large amounts of economic capital... They have considerable amounts of cultural capital but have not been able to translate this into economic capital in the same way that white Britons have.[23]

Such a social position may well reinforce feelings of anti-elitism and anti-snobbery that defines a modern understanding of what it means to be working class. It goes someway to account for the way the black electorate in London votes Labour. Labour's record in government of enacting race equality legislation, in sharp contrast to other parties, is likely to be another reason for their support.

After the year 2000, London continued to experience a transforming process of capital accumulation and related demographic and social change. 'London's contribution to the nation's economic value is almost seven times that of its closest "rival" in Greater Manchester. (This is) an economic imbalance that has rarely existed in other nations or at other times in history. (Moreover), the financial crash (of 2008) caused the rest of the country to fall further behind.'[24] One of the many consequences of this has been to undermine to varying degrees a strong sense of identity with place, creating feelings of alienation and dislocation. The rapidly evolving neighbourhoods in the capital, described so eloquently in Peter Halls' *London Voices. London Lives*, published in 2007, contain populations seeking to forge and sustain community cohesion in the face of enormous economic and social changes (see Chapter 4 for a review of these neighbourhoods). But within London, the extraordinary wealth and geographical separation of its powerful elites, living in increasingly segregated areas close to the City of London, such as Islington and Hackney, have intensified a growing class divide between inner and outer London. Disadvantaged social groups are forced out to the suburbs or chose to live in less expensive adjacent neighbourhoods.[25]

---

23 Savage et al., *Social Class in the Twenty First Century*, p. 173.
24 Savage, *Social Class in the Twenty First Century*, p. 267; Dorling, *Peak Inequality*; Massey, *World City.*
25 Cunningham and Savage, 'An Intensifying and Elite City,' 25–46.

74 *Chronological*

Research into middle-class colonisation of certain London districts, like Brixton, for example, suggests that many of these areas are 'fragile' in terms of the ability of residents to sink roots in or to identify with local communities. In these 'fragile' communities, many residents consider relocating to more stable areas with better education facilities for their children (or even paying for private education), particularly when their children reach secondary age when street life becomes more fraught with growing knife crime and drug dealing. The research concluded that these demographic changes had created 'social distance' between different social groups, undermining a sense of place.[26] In turn, such changes, it could be argued, reinforced a sense of exclusion and resentment towards cultural or financial elites, accentuated by a growing sense of geographic separation. This separation has been driven in large part by the scale of physical regeneration spreading across the capital, driven by enormous increases in the value of land.

A sense of place in London has thus been severely affected by the extent of the continuing physical redevelopment of the capital, or regeneration (a more neutral term employed by property developers and their partners in local government). There is a remarkable similarity between the 'regeneration areas' identified in the *2011 London Plan* and the 'opportunity areas' in the *1943 County of London Plan*. While the latter remained an unfulfilled blue print, when the local state (town planning authorities) was constrained from planning and rebuilding those parts of London destroyed by the blitz (opposed in the main by the interests of private property), the former has been implemented with a degree of ruthlessness and speed overriding the objections of local communities unable to defend their neighbourhoods from large-scale financially driven redevelopment. The failure of Land Reform has allowed a bonanza of regeneration to take place, not only in the East End, but in other areas where land on which there is public housing has been sold off to private developers in order to realise planning gain, with the hope of obtaining a limited amount of affordable housing, often unrealised following post-contractual renegotiation to maximise profits.[27] A film produced by the London Borough of Newham in 2012, promoting the area as a site of inward private investment, described the process as 'a regeneration supernova ...exploding across Newham.'[28] This has been replicated across London transforming the social make-up of areas like the Isle of Dogs. In many East End boroughs, where in the past council housing sometimes constituted over 75% of all tenures (and to a large extent formed the social basis of support for municipal socialism), there has been, as a result, a dramatic drop in the proportion of social housing, replaced by private tenancies

---

26 Robson and Butler, 'Coming to Terms with London,' 70–86; Butler and Robson, *London Calling*.
27 Tichelar, *The Failure of Land Reform*; Minton, *Big Capital*.
28 Quoted in Campkin, *Remaking London*, p. 163.

charging unregulated market rents. This has become one of the primary causes of poverty in the capital.

A good example of the way regeneration can change the social character of a working-class area, and generate political opposition, was the controversial proposal in 2012 to redevelop Cressingham Gardens in Lambeth, as part of a deal between the council and a private developer. It was opposed by a group of local residents who took the council to the High Court. Cressingham Gardens was an award-winning council garden estate comprising 306 dwellings, a mixture of four, three- and two-bedroom houses, and one-bedroom apartments. It was designed at the end of the 1960s by the communist architect Edward Hollamby, owner of William Morris's Red House in Walthamstow, and employed by Lambeth Council as its Director of Development. Forty years later, in 2012, Lambeth Council proposed to demolish the terraced houses and replace them by apartment blocks in a deal with a private developer. Most of the apartments would then be for sale to the private sector. The existing council tenants, and those in Lambeth who wished to prevent the gentrification of the borough, combined with those who wanted to conserve what they believed to be important architectural heritage, to prevent its demolition. The majority of the new apartments were intended for those who can afford to buy them at market prices, way beyond the means of most of Lambeth's population. In July 2015, the residents were granted permission to seek judicial review of the Council's decision to demolish the estate and not to consider the option of repair and refurbishment, supported by the tenants. In November 2015, the High Court ruled that it was unlawful for Lambeth Council not to consider this option and in 2016 residents were granted permission to seek judicial review of the second demolition decision.

A minority of Labour councillors were opposed to this redevelopment along with other schemes such as the council's 'hugely contentious library closure programme which plans to turn libraries into gyms, alongside unstaffed book sections. After questioning the council's policy towards estate demolition and library closures, a Labour councillor was suspended for six months.'[29] It had been maintained that the majority Labour Group in Lambeth was dominated at this time by *Progress*, an internal party pressure group founded in 1996 to support the New Labour leadership of Tony Blair. These councillors believed 'that the market mechanisms and private financing behind the current approach to increasing private renting and home ownership are the best way – perhaps the only way – of providing public goods such as housing.'[30] Such state-led gentrification, however, is reducing working-class residential space in London, particularly in East London, a process described by the Marxist geographer David Harvey

29 Minton, *Big Capital*, p. 74.
30 Ibid., p. 75.

76 *Chronological*

as 'accumulation by dispossession.'[31] The regeneration associated with the 2012 Olympic Games, for example, displaced large numbers of lower-income East Londoners and according to one study 'is producing increasingly antagonistic class relations and resentment against corporate wealth and power.'[32]

The priorities of Ken Livingstone, during his second term as mayor (2004–2008, this time representing Labour rather than as an independent), included a commitment to build more affordable housing, as part of an ambitious policy of strategic planning, similar to the alternative economic strategy he perused while leader of the GLC in the early 1980s. But as a strategy it remained largely unrealised, given the severe constraints on public expenditure imposed by central government. The strategy was reversed by Boris Johnson after 2008, who redefined affordable housing as 80% of market rents, a level way beyond the reach of most Londoners.[33] But Livingstone's other priorities came into conflict with his target for affordable housing, such as seeking to promote London's position as a major world city, edging ahead of New York. This was an approach which got him into trouble with his critics over the close relationship he developed with architects and developers in building new skyscrapers.[34] He sought to improve public services, particularly transport, such as the introduction of the all-purpose Oyster Card, after failing to prevent the part-privatisation of the underground network, a hard fought but unsuccessful battle with Gordon Brown, Labour's Chancellor of the Exchequer at the time.[35] While prioritising measures to combat climate change, he also developed a philosophical approach of fostering the city as 'a multi-racial, multi-cultural metropolis, where people would be allowed to live their lives as they liked provided they did no harm to others.'[36] The relationship between the party and the BME electorate, culturally rich but economically poor, was probably strengthened in London as a result, further cementing its loyalty to the party. The commitment to build affordable housing was an attempt to relieve the pressure on the capital's low-wage population unable to afford market rents let alone become owner-occupiers. Without being able to build in the Green Belt, or gain the cooperation of Conservative-controlled local authorities outside of the Greater London area, which housed about a third of the capital's labour force which commuted everyday into the centre, Livingstone adopted a strategy of increasing housing densities within London, while at

31 Harvey, 'The Right to the City,' 23–40.
32 Watt, '"It's Not For Us," 99–118.
33 Bowie, *Politics, Planning and Homes in a World City*; Holman and Thornley, 'The Reversal of Strategic Planning in London.'
34 McNeill, 'The Mayor and the World City Skyline.'
35 Livingstone, *You Can't Say That*, pp. 439–1, 551–2.
36 Johnson, 'Perfect Political Storm.'; see also interview with Ken Livingstone by Doreen Massey, 'The World We're In.'

Labour in a 'City of Rampant Capitalism' 77

the same time trying to come to deals with private developers to provide affordable housing (through section 106 planning agreements). While this was partly successful, such deals were generating growing opposition from within constituency Labour parties opposed to developing what were seen as toxic relationships with private capital. Livingstone was accused of working in the interests of the City of London, not helped by his policy on allowing developers to build skyscrapers. Failure, it should be added, was also the result of substantial public spending cuts to central government grants for social housing, a problem which the current Mayor Sadiq Khan is facing with increasing frustration.[37]

While physical regeneration has created new neighbourhood identities for those incomers who can afford to purchase or rent a desirable and expensive place to live in gentrified neighbourhoods, it has undermined community cohesion and created social alienation for London's growing precariat. What did such demographic and social changes do to class relationships in London? Before the turn of the millennium, the *Great British Class Survey* found that people had no longer simplistically accepted the old divisions of 'us and them' 'around which notions of the working and middle classes were constructed, finding it hard to adapt to multicultural capitalism. Britain may remain a class society,' it concluded, 'but it is not one that most of its citizens see as defining their lives.'[38] However after the year 2000, the economic transformation of London has severely restricted social mobility driven by gross inequality.[39] The precariat (made up of an increasing majority of working- and lower-middle-class residents, both black and white) has been excluded from secure employment and affordable housing. Research by the Centre for Labour and Social Studies found that 11% of white households in the UK, 29% of Black households and 27% of Asian households lived in persistent poverty over the period 2012–2016. Moreover, class disadvantages intersected

> with racial and gender disadvantage, with white men more likely to have better outcomes in the labour market than women and BME people of similar class backgrounds'...It concluded that class remains a 'significant determinant of disadvantage, with the main factors for "success" in life being the wealth of your parents and your place of birth.[40]

Such disadvantage only increased after the financial crash of 2008. These developments go some way to account for Labour's growing political hold on the capital as a party of the historic working class (see Chapter 5 on voting and social class).

37 Bowie, *Politics, Planning and Homes in a World City.*
38 Savage, *Social Class in the Twenty First Century.*
39 Hamnett, *Unequal City*; Massey, *World City.*
40 Centre for Labour and Social Studies, *The Facts and Fixes*; Dorling, *Peak Inequality.*

78 *Chronological*

Labour consolidated (2015–2020)

Support for Labour fluctuated after 1997, but it has remained ahead of the Conservatives by a margin of about 10% (in terms of voting intentions) for parliamentary elections.[41] In the general election of 2017 (broadly repeated in 2019), the Labour Party won 49 out of 71 seats in the Greater London area on a swing of over 10%. Like 1945, this was a bigger swing than in other areas of the country. The party currently controls 21 out of 32 London boroughs with over 1,000 elected councillors. It has 12 elected London Assembly members and four MEPs before the UK left the EEC in 2020. In 2016, the party obtained 57% of the vote in the election for the Mayor of London (see Appendix A and Chapter 5 for all election results). National membership had reached over 500,000 by the beginning of 2016, not seen since the high point of 1951 when membership was over a million, with a large proportion drawn from the capital and other metropolitan areas.[42]

The Labour Party is now by far the most dominant political force in London, the home of the 'precariat' of lower-middle- and working-class voters, an increasing proportion of which is made up of third- and fourth-generation migrants from the New Commonwealth and now fresh waves of new migrants from many other parts of the world. The population is growing at a faster rate than many other cities in the UK, making London unique.[43] In contrast, the Conservatives remain the party of some of the outer suburbs, smaller towns and the countryside. The Centre for Towns, an independent non-partisan organisation dedicated to providing research and analysis of smaller non-metropolitan towns, has shown that between 1981 and 2011, core cities like London and larger towns 'saw large increases in the numbers of 25 to 44-year olds,' and a corresponding steep decline in the number of older age groups. While London has got younger, villages, small communities and smaller towns have grown older. In local elections, Labour's share of the vote between 2014 and 2018 in core cities increased from about 40% to just under 48%, while the Conservative share in villages increased by over 12% in the same period.[44]

It is the size of the black and ethnic minority population in London (or now majority in many areas), and its class composition and much younger age structure, that accounts for Labour's growing dominance in the capital during the first two decades of the twenty-first century. Since 2001, the white population of London has declined by 4%. The Asian or Asian British population has increased by nearly 60%. The Black or Black British population

---

41 YouGov poll November 2019 and March 2020.
42 Audickas, 'Membership of UK Political Parties'; Bale, Webb and Poletti, 'Grass Roots. Britain's Party Members.'
43 Hall, *London Voices. London Lives*; see also Tables 1–5 in the Appendix for demographic statistics.
44 Centre for Towns, *The Aging of Our Towns*.

Labour in a 'City of Rampant Capitalism' 79

has increased by nearly 40%. The mixed ethnic group has grown by 80%, demonstrating the degree to which London is a racially integrated city.[45] All the national evidence points to a sizeable percentage of the ethnic minority electorate voting Labour. In the 2010 general election, 68% of ethnic minority voters gave their support to Labour and only 16% supported the Conservatives – a whopping lead of 52 points.[46] There is some evidence that this support might have lessened in the general election of 2015, although in London support for Labour from BME voters seems to be consolidating.[47] However, while the BME population vote Labour, especially in London, they do not join the party (see Chapter 7 on the politics of race). National figures for party membership suggest a figure of only 5%.[48] However, this undoubtedly under-estimates BME party membership in London, or more accurately in certain parts of London with very high concentrations of Asian or Caribbean communities. Anecdotally, certain wards, for example, in West London where there is a large Asian population, have estimated current BME membership running at about 40%. A ward secretary in Hounslow, for example, stated that recently safe Conservative wards have now been captured by Labour, and that their ward parties contain a younger BME membership drawn to the party by policies on housing and employment. Conversely, second- and third-generation Hindu or Sikh families, who in the past had been 'solidly Labour,' have gravitated towards the Conservatives, embracing traditional Tory values of enterprise, self-reliance, low-taxation and the small-state.[49]

In Tower Hamlets, to take another example of a high concentration BME area (predominantly Asian), the party has acquired (perhaps undeservedly) a reputation on social media and in the pages of *Private Eye*, as one dominated by 'Islamic separatists' and a so-called 'cynical and dangerous left.'[50] In 2006, George Galloway's Respect Party won 17 seats amid accusations of electoral fraud, especially the misuse of postal votes.[51] In 2014, when it was estimated that the borough contained over 65,000 Muslims, an independent (Lutfur Rahman) faced similar accusations of fraud when he defeated Labour's candidate for Mayor (John Biggs).[52] Despite these scandals, the current council has a large number of Asian Labour councillors and its two

---

45 See Table 2 on ethnicity in the Appendix.
46 Heath, 'Why Ethnic Minorities Vote Labour: Group Norms'; Heath, *The Political Integration of Ethnic Minorities in Britain.*
47 Khan, 'One Nation Boris? Not for Black or Asian Londoners'; Martin, 'Ethnic Minority Voters in the UK 2015 General Election: A Breakthrough for the Conservative Party?'; Sobolewska, 'Is Labour Losing the Ethnic Minority Vote?'
48 Audickas, '*Membership of UK Political Parties*'; Bale, Webb and Poletti, *Grass Roots. Britain's Party Members.*
49 Written evidence from a Labour Party ward secretary in Hounslow.
50 *Private Eye*, 29 April 2020 (issue 1520) – 'Faulty Towers.'
51 *Times*, 6 May 2006.
52 *Times*, 20 August 2014 – 'Muslim's Ordered to Vote for Mayor or be Damned.'

80   *Chronological*

constituencies have Labour MPs from an Islamic background (Rushanara Ali in Bethnal Green and Bow with a current majority of over 40,000 and Apsana Begum in Poplar & Limehouse with a majority of over 35,000). This suggests that the party has a significant BME membership. Limehouse and Poplar Party have published membership figures of 2,400. Allegations of entryism by ethnic interests have been part of a tradition of racism within the party that reflect tensions over questions of race and class (also present in wider society), similar to the negative reactions to working-class Irish involvement in constituency labour parties in London during the interwar period.[53]

If we take growing inequality in London, exacerbated by the financial crash of 2008, together with the demographic trends described earlier relating to age and race, then it is clear that the issue of equality has now resurfaced to politically question the legitimacy of meritocracy and its promise of social advancement. Both Thatcher and Blair promoted the benefits of progress as a natural right, if individuals could take advantage of the opportunities presented by either private enterprise and/or globalisation. However, for many younger Londoners, such advancement is no longer a realistic possibility. They have been excluded from housing and labour markets, paying ever increasing rents, interest charges on their student loans and priced out of certain cultural and leisure activities by further rental charges. 'Generation rent' covers more than just what is owed to a landlord.[54] They remain powerless to change their circumstances apart from moving to other places to find accommodation or work. This is similar in some respects to the way that the disenfranchised working class in Edwardian London moved to avoid the rent collector or the bailiff. Such powerlessness may have, in turn, reinforced feelings of anti-elitism or anti-snobbery which has helped change the meaning of social class. After 1970, meritocracy and popular individualism had displaced a collective sense that the state could intervene to improve people's lives, a belief which, as we have seen in Chapter 2, underpinned growing support for Labour after 1918 as part of a social democratic settlement. For Mrs Thatcher, 'there (was) no such thing as society. There are individual men and women, and there are families.'[55] This belief had a powerful influence in slowly recasting the way individuals saw themselves within the class structure. Working class was no longer a term which many people felt comfortable with despite their family backgrounds and objective position within the class hierarchy. It promoted

---

53 Fielding and Geddes, 'The British Labour Party and 'ethnic entryism': Participation, Integration and the Party Context.'

54 Milburn, *Generation Left.*

55 The full quote by Mrs Thatcher is as follows: 'And no government can do anything except through people, and people must look to themselves first. It's our duty to look after ourselves and then, also to look after our neighbour. People have got the entitlements too much in mind, without the obligations.'

a belief in social mobility while at the same time demonising the poor as 'chavs' or 'benefit scroungers.'[56]

However, in a recent survey into race and class by the Runnymede Trust, it was noted that the term working class

> has mutated from being a term used to foster solidarity and to describe those working in industrial jobs, to being a divisive concept within which the 'white working-class' are pitted against immigrants and the minority ethnic population. A caricature of the working-class – as male, white, racist, Brexit voting and residing only in the North of the country – has seeped into the public psyche, creating a phase of class politics that is both toxic and wholly divorced from reality.[57]

This survey went on to point out, however, that growing inequality and the brake on social mobility have increasingly undermined this caricature. The question of political equality, and perhaps a renewed faith in state intervention to address disadvantage, has returned to the political agenda, albeit expressed differently than in the past. Confidence in meritocracy is now being displaced by more muted feelings of 'ordinariness' or anti-elitism. For those who vote, this may account in part for the revival in the fortunes of the Labour Party in London after 1997, and perhaps in other metropolitan areas experiencing similar but less intense demographic and social changes. For those who are not politically active, the third of the mainly working-class population who now do not vote, this may account for their disengagement from politics and their political exclusion. Recent analysis has concluded that such alienation played a significant role in the outcome of the referendum to leave Europe.[58]

During the last 20 years, most areas of London have seen increasing cross-class support for the Labour Party for all types of elections, apart from when Boris Johnson was elected the Mayor of London in 2008, when his populist political appeal managed to maximise the vote of outer London against his metropolitan rival (Ken Livingstone) whose strength was more concentrated in middle-class inner-city boroughs. Sadiq Khan reversed this result in 2016 as the first Muslim mayor elected in any western city, picking up the votes of the growing number of black and ethnic minority voters in the suburbs displaced by gentrification from the centre. As we have seen, speculative regeneration of many parts of central London, based on extraordinary increases in the value of land, has 'driven low – or even moderate-income households' out of the centre 'with catastrophic effects on class disparities and the well-being of underprivileged populations.'[59]

56 Jones, *Chavs*; Standing, *The Precariat.*
57 Snoussi and Mompelat, *'We Are Ghosts.'*
58 Evans and Tilley, *The New Politics of Class.*
59 Harvey, *The Ways of the World*, p. 273.

82 *Chronological*

These trends are confirmed by census data for socio-economic structure, ethnicity, housing tenure and level of educational qualification.[60] Between 2001 and 2011, the increase in the proportion of higher managerial groups in the inner London constituencies, such as in Hackney and Lambeth, was much more marked than in the constituencies further out, like in Brent and Croydon. In Croydon North, for example, it rose from 7.9% to 16.3%, while in Hackney South, it rose from 8.65% to 23%. The figures for the London region as a whole were 12%–26%. The smaller increases in the proportion of semi-skilled and unskilled socio-economic groups are more evenly spread across both inner and outer areas, indicating that there is probably a higher degree of polarisation between rich and poor in inner-city districts undergoing gentrification than in middle-class suburban areas like Croydon South, which are relatively more stable. In terms of ethnicity, the difference between inner and outer London was less marked but more concentrated. In Brent Central, the white population declined from 47% to 39% and in Croydon North from 51% to only 35%, while in Hackney North it dropped from 61% to 58% and in Streatham from 64% to 58%, while the figures for London as a whole were 71% to 60%. Within the ethnic communities, there are, however, clear class differences identified in the 1991 census and which have continued to this day.

> The Indians and Chinese are among the groups of high performers, well-educated, property owning and professional. The Bangladeshis are at the other end of the scale, found in manual labour, with high rates of unemployment and exceptionally high levels of overcrowding... (There is a) high proportion of mixed Black and White households ... one of the most integrated groups...The Black social group is ...divided between the more professional Black-Africans and the more manual Black-Caribbean's.[61]

These first- and second-generation immigrant communities have been joined by a diverse and extraordinarily mixed population of immigrants from across the world, making London today one of the most multi-racial cities on earth.[62]

Other key indicators show similar trends in these constituencies. In terms of council housing, outer London did not experience the same dramatic drop in publicly rented housing as occurred in some inner London constituencies. There was no change in Croydon Central (13.5%) and in Brent North it dropped from 6.5% to 5.4%. In contrast, Vauxhall dropped from 36% to 23% as its riverside areas became the sites of gentrified high-rise apartments,

---

60 Census reports for parliamentary constituencies 2001 and 2011.
61 Peach, *Ethnicity in the 1991 Census*, pp. 23–4.
62 Judah, *This is London*.

Labour in a 'City of Rampant Capitalism' 83

many remaining empty, purchased by overseas buyers as a safe investment. The rise in the number of residents with higher qualifications across London in this period rose from 31% to 37%, while the increases in inner London experiencing gentrification were much higher rising from 35% to 42% in Hackney North and 41% to 49% in Vauxhall. A common feature of all these inner and outer London constituencies was the decline in the proportion of elderly residents. Like in London as a whole, these were areas where young people formed an increasing majority.[63] By 2019, all the seats in Brent, Hackney, Lambeth and in the northern and central parts of Croydon were increasingly safe for the Labour Party. The Conservative Party in these areas have been reduced to a relatively small opposition group on most councils, apart from areas further out, such as South Croydon, originally part of Surrey, or Dartford, part of North West Kent on the Thames Estuary (see Chapter 4 for the influence of localities and workplaces).

One clear political trend, which can be identified from the changing patchwork of neighbourhood development in London, is the way their socially mixed, multi-racial and younger electorates increasingly support the Labour Party after the turn of the century. This includes both inner and outer London. The suburbs of London are no longer the preserve of the Conservative Party. As early as the 1960s, commentators noted how identification with left-wing political parties had spread outwards from central London.[64] In most areas of the capital after 1997, the Labour vote increased, such as in the 'The New Melting Pots' like gentrified Battersea; the 'Proletarian Islands Under pressure,' like Bermondsey; the up and coming boroughs, 'with potential,' like Newham; the more settled but 'challenged suburbs,' like Eltham; and the more traditional and homogeneous suburbs like Gants Hill in Ilford; and in 'Edge Cities,' like Croydon. The 'Dynamic Edge suburbs,' like Dartford, do not conform to this trend as their more segregated working- and middle-class areas, with their more middle-aged and elderly populations, conform to a pattern of voting similar to less metropolitan and industrially declining areas of the country (see Chapter 4 for further details).

As the middle class grew as a proportion of the electorate in London, the Labour Party under Blair presented itself as one to appeal to all classes, similar to the strategy adopted by Herbert Morrison during the interwar period. In 1999 at the party conference, Tony Blair declared that 'the class war is over,' re-emphasising his pitch to the middle class, a claim made by other prime ministers from Baldwin to MacMillan and John Major. Recent political analysis has argued that

> the transition from a big working-class to a big middle class was the engine of this political change. Politics in Britain today involves middle

63 Census for Parliamentary Constituencies, 2002 and 2011.
64 Cox, 'Suburbia and Voting Behaviour,' 126.

84 *Chronological*

class parties fighting it out for middle class votes. The working class are bystanders, no longer represented within the political mainstream.[65]

Moreover, the middle classes can be relied on to vote, while the working class tend to abstain. In 2015, it was estimated that 85% of the middle classes voted, while for 'people with a working-class job and low education,' it was under 50%.[66] In London, like in other large towns and cities, turnout was lower than in smaller towns and rural areas. In 2017, it was 67% in big cities, and even lower in 2019. Low turnout is compounded by non-registration, recently estimated at 17% of those eligible to vote, or nearly 10 million potential voters country-wide.

It has been argued that the result of the referendum on Europe in 2016 and the subsequent general election of December 2019 confirmed rather than cut across these national trends. However, while commentary on the results focused on the difference between metropolitan remain and non-metropolitan leave, it tended to ignore the differences *within* London and the way the capital had developed into

> a complex patchwork of different kinds of place, made up of overlapping geographies of class, commuting patterns, housing tenure, education, migration, ethnicity and religious identity. Right across outer London for example, 'wards with relatively poor white working-class populations, such as the Cray Valley wards in Bromley and the New Addington and Fieldway wards in Croydon, voted strongly leave. Data for Hounslow and Ealing indicate a pattern where affluent, well-educated, majority white areas voted very strongly for remain, while working-class areas with lower educational attainment voted strongly for leave, and wards with higher a proportion of Asian voters tended to be more evenly split.[67]

Thus, economic inequality continues to determine voting outcomes (see Chapter 5 on voting and social class). There is in fact a remarkable similarity between the social geography of Labour support in London during the 1960s and support for Labour in the 2010s. Surveys by Wilmott and Young in the 1970s suggested that the working-class pattern of distribution in the capital formed the shape of a cross rather than conventional concentric zones.[68] This pattern continued into the period after the year 2000. Although the middle class now forms a much larger proportion of the overall class structure of London, if class is measured by economic deprivation,

65 Evans and Tilley, *The New Politics of Class*, p. 200.
66 Ibid., p. 174.
67 Gilbert et al., 'Ethnic and Religious Diversity in the Politics of Suburban London,' 73–4.
68 Wilmott and Young, 'Social Class and Geography,' 190.

the pattern of the cross remains a continuing feature of the capital's social structure and the distribution of political control within it.

This economic and social polarisation of London was dramatically exposed by the Grenfell Tower fire on 14 June 2017, just a week after the general election called by Theresa May to try and increase her majority in parliament to secure a Brexit deal. Seventy-three residents lost their lives in a dangerously (i.e. non-fire-resistant) clad tower block, the majority of whom were from poor families, including many from migrant and asylum backgrounds, typical of London's growing precariat. When the first public enquiry into the disaster was reported in the summer of 2019, Jeremy Corbyn berated the government by stating that 'Grenfell Tower would not have happened to wealthy Londoners. It happened to poor and mainly migrant Londoners.' The disaster brought home the political nature of austerity, when crucial decisions made by 'business-friendly' politicians of both main parties 'meant that tower blocks could be wrapped in combustible cladding that the market was only too happy to supply.'[69] Kensington contained some of the most exclusive and expensive real estate in the world, and up-market shopping epitomised by Harrods in Kensington High Street, while its deprived northern parts in areas like Ladbrook Grove (scenes of race riots in 1958) were made up of dense social housing, and where extremely high rankings of social deprivation were recorded. Labour had captured this marginal seat in 2017, when it obtained 54% of the vote across London on a relatively high turnout of 70%, boosted by more young people supporting the anti-austerity policies of a party led by the newly elected Jeremy Corbyn, on a manifesto which was markedly different from the one Labour went to the country with in 2015. The size of the vote represented a high point of Labour's fortunes in the capital as well as helped to secure Corbyn's leadership against any further challenges by his enemies in the parliamentary party. It was not, however, as high as the 59% recorded for Labour in inner London in1945, but it matched the 54% recorded for the party in outer London in that year.[70] The Conservatives had held on to their majority in the local elections of 2018, with Labour only picking up one extra seat. Labour's growing strength in London was demonstrated by its performance in neighbouring Westminster, 'where it gained four new council seats and far more votes than it has in living memory. It even, for the first time, gained a seat in the ward containing the superrich areas of Mayfair, Soho and Fitzrovia.'[71]

But Labour lost the seat of Kensington to the Conservatives in the general election of December 2019, called when the new Conservative leader, Boris Johnson, previous Mayor of London (2008–2016), managed to persuade a badly divided House of Commons to agree to a third election in four years

---

69 *Guardian*, 26 June 2017 'Grenfell Is Political'; *New Statesman*, 16 June 2017 'Grenfell Tower Is the Latest Sign that Britain Is an Undeveloping Country.'

70 See Table 12 in the Appendix.

71 Beckett and Seddon, *Jeremy Corbyn*, p. 306.

86 *Chronological*

(unwisely for Labour in the event), to resolve the issue of Europe, or as he put it to 'Get Brexit Done.' The election was dominated by Brexit, a national issue on which the Labour Party was seriously divided, unable to come to a clear decision either for or against. The controversy over Anti-Semitism also contributed to its unpopularity (see Chapter 7), compounded by growing factionalism within constituency labour parties, many of which were coming out more strongly against the regeneration policies of Labour-led councils in the capital.[72] Across the UK, Labour lost support (on a swing of nearly 8%), from those voters, mainly working class (C2DE) that had voted to leave Europe in the referendum of 2016. As a result, its share of the vote in December 2019 was reduced from 40% to only 32%. It lost 60 seats, all of them outside of London. In London itself however, where C2DE made up about 40% of the electorate, the swing against Labour was lower at 6.4% (from 54.5% to 48.1%), while support for the Liberal Democrats, which had a much clearer pro-European policy, increased by roughly the same amount (6.1%). The Conservative share of the vote dropped by 1.1% to 32%, a historic low.[73] This result highlighted (for strategists at least) the growing dilemma for Labour between its undoubted support in metropolitan areas from younger voters and its declining support in smaller towns and cities. In contrast, Labour's more traditional working-class voters in non-metropolitan areas (older, less educated, more likely to own their home and predominantly white) felt that they had been left-behind by a type of politics perceived as too middle class, metropolitan and no longer representing their interests, a view not necessarily shared by London's new working class.

Conclusion

Gentrification and suburbanisation, as well as class and ethnicity have created a new political culture in London during the last 20 years.[74] It is clear that an element of the lower social grades in the UK (comprising the unemployed, state pensioners, and semi-skilled and unskilled workers) opted for the Conservatives over Labour in the 2019 general election. But this represents a declining fraction of the working class in London. In contrast, that growing proportion of London's relatively young and cross-class population (who are politically engaged) now vote Labour for perhaps a variety of different reasons, including support for European integration, reflecting a particular set of metropolitan values, influenced above all by age, race and education. These are by and large the same electors who voted to remain in Europe in the 2016 referendum, motivated in large part by values identified as socially liberal, 'whether in impoverished mutli-ethnic Hackney (78.5%)

---

72 Bowie, *Politics, Planning and Homes in a World City.*
73 House of Commons Briefing Paper, *General Election 2019: Results and Analysis* (28 January 2020).
74 Butler and Hamnett, *Ethnicity, Class and Aspiration.*

Labour in a 'City of Rampant Capitalism' 87

or affluent Kensington and Chelsea (68.7%).'[75] The smaller more traditional and white working class in London, less educated and more elderly, and which is now more geographically concentrated in certain outer suburbs, voted to leave, motivated in large part, according to most opinion polls, by the values identified as socially authoritarian (although some probably remain economically left-wing). However, the former social group, while forming a majority in London and other big cities, like Liverpool and Manchester, was not numerically strong enough to affect the overall outcome of the referendum, or the general election of 2019, as their turnout was lower than the more elderly electorate living in non-metropolitan areas.[76]

Low turnout is a feature of the working-class vote in London and its younger electorate. It increases when there are few policy differences between the two main parties and where the result is largely anticipated, like in 1997.[77] In the 2015 general election, where it could be argued that these factors were also present, only 43% of 18–24-year-olds went to the polls compared with 79% aged 65 or over, although this percentage increased after the election of Jeremy Corbyn as the Labour leader, when stronger policy differences emerged between the two parties. *The British Election Survey* found in 2015 that 57% of millennials (who came of age politically at the turn of the millennium) reported voting, compared with an average of 79% of older generations. Pollsters have drawn attention to the growing trend of political non-participation by young people, and it was not necessarily reversed in 2017, when young voters overwhelmingly supported the Labour Party:

> When many millennials first voted in 2005, around 49% cast a ballot, compared with an average of 74% of their elders. The equivalent figures for the 90's generation in 1997 were 64% and 82%; for the 80s generation in 1987, 71% and 82%; for the 60s/70s generation in 1974, 80% and 89%.[78]

But in London, when low turnout is combined with high levels of non-registration, it results in a sizeable segment of the capitals population being politically disengaged. Some have argued that this segment makes up a fraction of the less respectable and rougher sections of the working class in London, characterised by poverty and insecurity, working in the 'black economy,' perhaps a new 'under-class,' harking back to earlier notions of 'the residuum' in late Victorian and Edwardian periods.[79] A flavour of some elements of this under-class can be found in Ben Judah's recent and dramatic exposure of life and death in the world city.[80]

---

75 Evans and Menon, *Brexit and British Politics*, p. 87.
76 Ibid., pp. 83–124.
77 Pattie and Johnston, 'A Low Turnout Landslide.'
78 Fox, 'Youthquake? The Mystery of the Missing Young Voters.'
79 Watt, 'Respectability, Roughness and "Race,"' 776–97; Bourdieu, *Distinction*, 1984.
80 Judah, *This is London*.

88 *Chronological*

But other more settled elements of the traditional white working class in London are a declining social group. It is under pressure, fearful in many respects of an uncertain future and having little confidence in party politics, and a Labour Party in particular, which is increasingly perceived or portrayed as no longer representing its class interests. A recent article on the social effects of gentrification in London pointed out that 'the largest occupational grouping, by some distance, is the middle class and that the next largest group is often the economically inactive.'[81] However, for some commentators, this enlarged lower middle class is in fact a 'new' working class,

> made up of people living on low to middle incomes employed as cleaners, shop workers, bar tenders, teaching assistants, cooks, carers and so on. It is multi-ethnic and much more diverse than the traditional working class. It makes up nearly half the population. Labour's future as a serious political force is dependent on these votes.[82]

In London, these social strata (a combination of the precariat and large sections of the middle class who have been adversely affected by austerity and thwarted social mobility) represent a growing constituency which (while maybe cynical of politics) exercises its right to vote and votes Labour. The extraordinary concentrated wealth of the capital, taken together with the growth of extreme inequality, where over a quarter of the capitals households live below the poverty line, generates 'a sense of deepening social injustice, compounded by gender and class pay gaps, unequal health and education outcomes, rising street violence, revelations of banker bonuses, tax evasion and political corruption, and planning decisions that favour the wealthy.'[83] The rising anger generated by this sense of injustice either expresses itself in voting against a political party that represents the wealthy, or voting for a political party that represents the opposite, or for a minority of the young, it expresses itself in the suburban riots of 2011 in areas like Croydon and Ealing, when property and wealth were targeted with arson and looting.

The values and beliefs of these different social groups, some politically engaged others not, will be explored in a little more detail in the conclusion. This seeks to draw together the various strands explored in the book (both chronological and thematic) to help identify the way the class-basis of Labour politics in London has been reformulated in the period after 1997 in terms of race, age and culture. The meaning of class has been modified but class itself has not disappeared. The dream of meritocracy promised by Margaret Thatcher and Tony Blair has been undermined by gross

---

81 Butler and Hamnett, 'Walking Backwards to the Future,' 217–28; Watt, 'It's Not for Us.'
82 Ainsley, 'Winning Back the Working Class,' 197; Ainsley, *The New Working Class.*
83 Atkinson, *Alpha City*, p. 226.

inequality, accentuated by the financial crash of 2008.[84] Across the UK, 'the pace of growth in young people's educational attainment has more than halved since the start of the 21st Century.'[85] While the result of the 2017 general election suggested a return of two-party domination, opposed to each other on clearer ideological grounds (reminiscent in some ways of the period of two-party domination discussed in Chapter 2)

> the social and geographical distribution of Remain and Leave voters cut across the traditional class basis of Britain's old two-party system. We are left with a realigned two-party system, based not so much on class, but on other demographic markers of values: education and age.[86]

Although not to be exaggerated, London is perhaps a living proof of this change in class outlook where its growing multi-ethnic communities aspire to improve their life chances, unlike what remains of the declining traditional white working class, which votes to restore something which has been lost. The result of the 2019 general election confirmed and consolidated Labour's dominance in the capital, despite a swing of over 6% to the Liberal Democrats over the question of Europe, an issue however, which is not likely to be repeated.

84 Littler, *Against Meritocracy.*
85 Henehan, 'Pick Up the Pace: The Slowdown in Educational Attainment Growth.'
86 Evans and Menon, *Brexit and British Politics*, p. 105.

Part II

Thematic – localities, workplaces, trade unions, class, socialism, personal identity

4 Localities, workplaces and trade union organisation

Introduction

This chapter will explore the themes of locality, workplaces and trade union organisation in relation to the growth and development of Labour Party politics in London. This will allow for a more in-depth discussion of some of the themes identified in the chronological chapters (1–3). The chapter will argue that the unprecedented and rapidly changing geographical and social landscapes of London since 1900 played a more important role in determining the nature of Labour Party growth and development than the influence of workplaces and trade union organisation. For the earlier part of the century, the labour movement developed more strongly in those relatively homogeneous and stable working-class communities characterised by a single or particular type of industry, such as textiles in Preston or the coal mines in Yorkshire.[1] Although London contained examples of these types of industrial areas in particular localities, such as Woolwich, it experienced a very different type of residential and urban development. This chapter will look at the way London's neighbourhoods underwent a series of urban changes unique to large metropolitan areas, such as inner-city dispersal and overspill, suburban expansion, de-industrialisation, gentrification and large-scale regeneration. By the beginning of this century, these urban processes had created a new type of working class (or precariat) unlike that produced by more stable but declining industrial areas of the country, such as Labour's 'northern heartlands.' The chapter is in three parts – 'dispersal and overspill,' 'suburban expansion,' and 'de-industrialisation and gentrification.' It will use examples from the inner London boroughs of Lambeth and Hackney and, the outer and suburban areas of Croydon to illustrate the argument covering the whole of twentieth century. It will then use examples from the neighbourhoods described in *Working Capital*, published in 2002 and the follow-up survey, *London Voices. London Lives*, published in 2007, covering the period after the year 2000.[2] The chapter will start with a

---

1 Savage, *Dynamics of Working-Class Politics*; Reynolds and Laybourn, *Labour Heartland.*
2 Buck, *Working Capital*; Hall, *London Voices. London Lives.*

94 *Thematic*

theoretical discussion about locality studies and their relevance for the study of labour history.

What does the social geography of London tell us about the origins and development of the labour movement over the course of the twentieth century? Quite clearly, the pronounced separation of place of work and residence has been a particular if not a unique feature of London's social and economic history. The degree of this separation distinguishes London from other towns and cities where in many cases the social classes lived and worked more closely together, albeit in segregated neighbourhoods divided in the main by housing tenure (owner-occupation or municipal housing). After the Second World War, when the close ties of family and kinship identified by Willmott and Young began to break down, new relationships were forged by de-industrialisation, gentrification and immigration.[3] In London however, very high levels of population turnover, waves of immigration and rapidly changing housing and labour markets affected community cohesiveness from the beginning of the century, posing a particular challenge to party workers trying to canvass for support. Activists from all parties despaired of the political apathy shown by the capital's voters, as electors either did not register to vote, or were prevented from registering due to population turnover and numerous changes of address, or abstained from politics altogether feeling that no party represented their interests.

But in the face of such reality, what accounted for the way in which the electorate did vote? For working-class Labour voters, did the strength of neighbourhood allegiances and identities outweigh the influence of the trade unions in defending working-class interests? Were municipal politics more important in London in achieving reforms that benefited working people than the reforms which the trade unions could achieve through industrial action? The examples of Croydon and Lambeth (supplemented by shorter references to other neighbourhoods) will be used to compare and contrast the experience of each area in the broader context of the history of the labour movement in London. Inner London boroughs like Lambeth and Hackney, for example, underwent over the course of the twentieth century an initial process of population increase and then decline; then an enormous loss of manufacturing jobs; then inner-city decay; followed by gentrification and population growth. They experienced waves of outward and inward migration, both becoming two of the most ethnically diverse boroughs in the country. In contrast, outer London boroughs, like Croydon and some of the outer western suburbs, witnessed a process of suburban and industrial expansion after 1918, absorbing significant levels of outward migration from central London and the distressed areas of the country, such as South Wales. They became the sites of new manufacturing industries, a process

---

3 Hall, *London Voices, London Lives*; Willmott and Young, *Family and Kinship in East London*; Dench, Gavron and Young, *The New East End*.

accelerated by the domestic impact of both world wars, such as rearmament. Gentrification in these outer London areas was less pronounced after 1980 than it was in the inner city. By the turn of the twenty-first century, parts of these suburban areas had taken on some of the characteristics of the inner-city areas from a generation earlier, also becoming centres of ethnic concentrations. What type of Labour politics did the combination of social geography, patterns of industry and level of trade union organisation give rise to?

The trade union wing of the labour movement often came into conflict with the political wing over the best way to achieve political reform. This tension has existed throughout the history of the Labour Party. The ebb and flow of this relationship changed the way the state was viewed by party members and influenced the development of democratic socialist ideas.[4] At times, for example, when industrial militancy could not defend working-class living standards, such as after the defeat of the General Strike in 1926, more importance was attached by the London Labour Party (LLP) to state intervention to defend working-class interests. After 1979, the trade unions were viewed as having exercised too much power during the long economic boom which followed the Second World War, and their influence and status declined as a result.[5] In such periods, the labour movement saw local government as a higher priority than industrial militancy. The party in London placed far more emphasis on achieving power through local government. This was very much the strategy of Herbert Morrison in trying to win cross-class support from the much-enlarged electorate in London after 1918. He sought to reduce the influence of local trades councils (the representative bodies of trade unions in local areas and often dominated by the Communist Party), in order to present the party as a respectable and constitutional political force appealing to all classes, especially the expanding population of 'black coated' workers. Although Herbert Morrison appealed to white-collar workers in class terms ('Socialism for the Blackcoats'), for many members, their party represented the nation, in patriotic contrast to the Conservatives who they accused of being a class party.

Moreover, allegiances to family networks and neighbourhood loyalties, such as working men's clubs, football teams, local street markets and schools, in predominantly white homogeneous working-class communities (what the historian Eric Hobsbawn described as 'red belts' in the big cities) were certainly more important than trade union action in defending working-class living standards. Trade union organisation and membership in the capital had always been weak in comparison to other regions of the country. Although there were pockets of trade union strength in areas like furniture manufacturing, public transport (T&GWU) and light engineering

4 Minkin, *The Contentious Alliance*; Dell, *A Strange Eventful History.*
5 Reid, 'Labour and the Trade Unions,' 221.

96 *Thematic*

(AEU), effective organisation was undermined by rapid changes in labour and housing markets, and the separation of home and work by long travelling distances. London had a labour market which for long periods of the twentieth century contained a mass of unskilled workers, boosted by high numbers of immigrants. The scale of this immigration depressed wages apart from during both world wars when labour scarcity increased trade union influence and organisation, helped by state intervention in the economy. By the end of the twentieth century, the trade unions in London had declined to a historic low, on a par with the weakness of the industrial and political movement before 1914. It was only during the period of municipal social democracy in London (1920s–1960s) that it exercised any significant influence. But even then, industrial militancy took second place to winning political control of local authorities and then central government. By the 1960s, the party came to represent the ideology of a centralised state, having moved away from its roots in local neighbourhoods. Before this, the party's reputation was built above all on programmes of slum clearance and municipal housing during the interwar period. However, the deterioration of the municipal housing stock after the 1950s, combined with a poor record of housing repairs and government-imposed rent increases, was one of the factors which contributed to the party's declining political fortunes in London.

Locality studies now compete with traditional labour history in seeking to account for the growth of the Labour Party in different parts of the UK. Up until the 1970s, Marxist historians emphasised the conflict between capital and labour, seeing the party as a political expression of the struggle of organised labour (predominantly male skilled workers) in the workplace. These struggles took place in the mines and factories of the country's industrial heartlands of the North, Wales and Scotland. From this perspective, an interpretation emerged which saw the Labour Party as primarily a vehicle for representing the trade unions in parliament in order to repeal anti-trade union legislation. Certainly, this argument is an important and undisputed aspect of the party's early history. The party was formed in 1900 as an alliance of trade unions and socialist groups to reverse anti-trade union legislation (Taff Vale Judgement). Socialists were faced with the difficult choice of either joining this alliance or fighting outside the party to win the working class for socialism. The ILP was instrumental in forging the alliance with the unions, recognising the existence of 'the class struggle,' while the Marxist SDF disaffiliated in 1901 after only a year, adhering more closely to the revolutionary concept of 'the class war.'[6] The frustration of socialists operating within these constraints is best represented by Ralph Miliband's critique of 'Parliamentary Socialism' and other historians who have explored the complex nature of 'Labourism.'[7] Historians have spent a

6 Bealey and Pelling, *Labour and Politics 1900–1906.*
7 Allender, *What's Wrong with Labour?*

Localities 97

great deal of effort in trying to understand the defensive qualities of a working class, many of whom voted Conservative before 1914 and continued to do so after 1918 following the extension of the franchise.

A new generation of historians have now moved away from, but not entirely abandoned Marxist interpretations. The old orthodoxy has now been replaced by a new one which argues that politics (either at a local or national level) is not just a reflection of the conflict between capital and labour. Support for the Labour Party in London, or in other similar metropolitan areas for that matter, such as Liverpool and Manchester, cannot be adequately explained by this traditional interpretation based on an over-emphasis on trade union organisation.[8] London was and remains a relatively weak area for trade union membership and solidarity. A 'New Political History' has developed, initially concerned with electoral sociology, popular politics and labour history, that argues that 'political values derive from local communities, where they are formed both by local workplace and neighbourhood experiences and by the political, social, economic, religious and recreational networks which underpin them.'[9] A number of studies of Labour Party history have now been published which explores the growth and development of Labour politics from this new perspective. One of the first and most influential was undertaken by Gillian Rose, a historical geographer who took the Poplar Labour Party in the 1920s as a case study. She argued that local studies 'still tend to conflate industrial, social and political geography by confining their analyses almost wholly to the sphere of waged labour.' She identified a range of non-class motivations for industrial unrest by local workers and suggested that waged labour was relatively unimportant in the lives of working-class people in Poplar. Neighbourhood solidarity and attempts to control local government for the benefit of women and the unskilled (not organised in trade unions) were far more important.[10]

At about the same time, the sociologist Michael Savage suggested a more complex relationship between social structure and support for the Labour Party in his study of the labour movement in Preston in the period 1880–1940. Using a theoretical model, based on an appreciation of working-class interests arising out of the need of workers to reduce the material insecurity inherent in capitalist society, he distinguished between the 'practical' politics of working-class people at a local level and the 'formal' politics of national political parties. He argued that political action is not solely determined by occupational or social structure or from cultural forms, like class consciousness. Instead, he maintained that in the case of Preston at least, the fortunes of the Labour Party were expressions of neighbourhood organisation and gender relations. He concluded that the success of the party in

8 McHugh, *Labour in the City*; Davies, *Liverpool Labour.*
9 Stevens, 'The Electoral Sociology of Modern Britain Reconsidered'; Lawrence, 'Political History'; Craig, 'High Politics and the New Political History.'
10 Rose, 'Locality-Studies and Waged Labour,' 317–28.

98   *Thematic*

Preston during the 1920s was not based on class consciousness or industrial conflict but on changes in neighbourhood solidarities and the political role of women, which, he argued, were more likely to vote Labour and support state intervention as consumers, such as welfare reform, rather than skilled men as producers, who looked not to the state, but to their trade union to defend their sectional interests. 'Labour's leaps forward,' he maintained, were correlated with the mobilisation of women, and later of the 'unskilled,' rather than with the great set piece labour disputes of the 1920s, such as the General Strike.[11]

Other aspects of the wider economic and social contexts have also been ignored or neglected, such as social and geographical mobility. Michael Savage went on to modify his views about social class and urban history, arguing that labour historians do not give sufficient emphasis to social mobility and what he described as 'spatial mobility,' a term borrowed from geographers and sociologists. 'Spatial mobility' is important, he maintained, in 'fixing people to specific places so that they become attached to neighbourhoods and acquaintances, and become familiar with the associational and informal cultural life of a specific place. In other words, place is a basis of class formation.'[12] In the Great British Class Survey, published in 2015, he wrote 'class is geographical' in his analysis of spatial inequality in the UK.[13] Other sociologists have suggested that people do not simply respond to economic or utilitarian issues but they have become more sensitised to matters concerning the quality of life as these affect their homes, locality and the natural environment.[14] This approach is particularly relevant to the study of politics in London, where place of work is separated by long distances from place of residence and where social mobility and population turnover takes place across geographical areas through transforming processes of economic and social changes. In the case of London, these changes include the growth of service industries, gentrification, polarisation of social classes and suburbanisation. The Marxist geographer David Harvey has argued that 'phenomena like post-war suburbanisation, deindustrialisation or the trend towards inner-city renewal' can only be fully understood in terms of the *geographical landscape* of capitalism.[15]

Inner-city dispersal and overspill – the case of Lambeth (1900–1968)

Lambeth was made up of a heterogenous mixture of social classes, housing tenures and industry, the combination of which was not conducive to strong

---

11 Savage, *The Dynamics of Working-Class Politics.*
12 Savage, 'Urban History and Social Class,' 70; Harvey, *The Urban Experience.*
13 Savage, *Social Class in the Twenty First Century,* p. 261.
14 Lash and Urry, *Economies of Signs and Space.*
15 Harvey, *The Urban Experience,* pp. 1–16.

trade union organisation or independent Labour representation. A Board of Trade Report in 1908 estimated that a considerable proportion of the population was working class occupying a range of different accommodation, including overcrowded slum tenements in the north of the borough. In the middle portion of the borough from Kennington Gate to Brockwell Park, which consisted of Brixton and Stockwell, the population was less dense and one-room tenements were less common than in the northern district. The more salubrious areas south of Brockwell Park, such as West Norwood, contained houses of the 'usual two-storey type' and were much more expensive to rent. They were occupied by a mixed class of relatively well-paid artisans and clerks and the middle classes who could afford to buy or rent in the more elevated and healthier areas south of the Thames, able to employ at least one domestic servant and commuting to well-paid employment in the city or Westminster.[16]

Hackney, to take another inner-city example, also contained a similar mix of housing and population, although it had a more stable working-class population engaged in manufacturing industry, such as clothing and furniture, concentrated in particular neighbourhoods to the south of the borough. Like Lambeth, it was predominantly a dormitory area where over 50% of its population worked outside of the borough mainly employed in the city. It was one of the larger metropolitan boroughs, extending from Tottenham and Walthamstow in the north to Shoreditch and Bethnal Green in the south, from Stoke Newington and Islington in the West to Leyton, West Ham and Poplar in the east. The working-class population lived in Homerton and the south-eastern part of Hackney, while the northern parts of the borough consisted of residential middle-class districts, where Herbert Morrison decided to live after he became the Mayor of Hackney in 1919.[17] Its population in 1901 was nearly 220,000 increasing to 222,000 in 1922 but then declining to 213,000 by 1931 as dwelling houses were displaced by factories and workshops. While the main concentration of Jewish immigrants was located in the areas to the east of the borough, Hackney contained a sizeable Jewish population employed mainly in sweat shops producing cheap consumer goods. The Jews lived in clearly demarcated residential areas, attending their own synagogues, shops, schools and recreational areas, and setting up own their labour movement and socialist organisations. Before 1914, and before moves towards integration, 'overcrowding increased, living conditions deteriorated, and rents soared,' instigating 'tremendous discontent among the East End's "original" inhabitants, who resented the new immigrants.'[18]

Lambeth had no sizeable Jewish population to speak of in comparison to the East End. The main industries were the printing and river trades

---

16 Cost of Living of the Working Classes, Board of Trade 1908, Cd.3864.
17 Donoghue and Jones, *Herbert Morrison*, p. 43.
18 Hofmeester, *Jewish Workers and the Labour Movement*, p. 107.

100   *Thematic*

concentrated along or near the southside of the Thames in Bermondsey and Camberwell and to a lesser extent in North Lambeth. For most of the nineteenth century, this side of the river had been a centre of waterside industries and engineering, such as the famous Maudslay's engineering workshop, considered to be the 'nursery of a dynasty of engineers.'[19] The area became well-known for glass making, pottery and boat building. Many printing workers lived immediately south of Waterloo Bridge, but worked in Southwark, where the trade was highly localised, providing urgent commissions for the newspaper and publishing houses in central London, and the advertising agencies in the West End.[20] In 1900, there were over 5,500 men living in North Lambeth employed in print, book and stationary trades and over 700 female bookbinders.[21] As a group of skilled workers, the compositors had undergone a significant deterioration in their working conditions before 1914

> as employers sought to cheapen and intensify their labour to meet rapidly rising demand for printed matter with traditional typesetting methods. The ensuing growth of casual, juvenile and female labour (had eroded) the printer's claim to regulate the conditions of trade and earnings fell behind those of other skilled crafts.[22]

In 1902, in response to these pressures, the London Society of Compositors (LSC), a craft union which represented nearly 8,000 male print workers in the capital, set up a political levy, sponsored their general secretary Charles Bowerman to defend their interests in parliament. He was a Fabian and Progressive Alderman on the LCC, who was elected as the Lib-Lab MP for Deptford in the 1906 general election, holding the seat after 1918 for the Labour Party. The LSC went on to become an important affiliate to the LLP in 1914 and its secretary George Isaacs, a close ally of Herbert Morrison.[23] Before this another printer of a more radical disposition, the social democrat and housing reformer, Fred Knee, was influential in overcoming socialist (SDF) resistance to the creation of the LLP in 1914.[24] He became its first secretary before his untimely death in December of that year, creating a vacancy filled by Herbert Morrison, while he was living in Letchworth as a conscientious objector. The only industrial union associated with independent labour in Lambeth was a branch of the Amalgamated Society of Engineers (AEU), probably representing a relatively small number of skilled workers in the light engineering trades. All the other

19 Martin, *Greater London*, p. 15.
20 Hall, *Industries of London since 1861*, p. 141; Martin, *Greater London*, p. 192.
21 Census for the County of London, 1901, p. 129.
22 Zeitlin, 'Craft Control and the Division of Labour,' 264.
23 London Society of Compositors, Jubilee Souvenir 1848–1923.
24 Englander, *The Diary of Fred Knee*; Thompson, *Socialists, Liberals and Labour*.

Localities 101

affiliated unions represented service, municipal or building trades, such as cab drivers, gas workers, postmen, railway men, shop assistants, carpenters and joiners, French polishers, bakers and confectioners.[25]

But it is doubtful how far these relatively small groups of trade unionists in Lambeth were representative of wider working-class culture or politics in the borough. Some of the older members of the craft trade unions would have belonged to one of the many working men's clubs, the history of which stretched back to the mid-Victorian period, when they were centres of a highly radical political culture, influenced by Chartism.[26] But by the turn of the century, they had declined, their political tradition replaced by an altogether less radical set of political concerns, reflecting 'a culture of consolation' and political apathy.'[27]

Certainly, this description applied to the vast majority of unskilled workers in London. A Liberal newspaper, the *Daily Chronicle*, described the constituency of North Lambeth as containing the 'least hopeful, least ambitious and most depressed classes of London workers.'[28] A settlement worker proselytising on the southside of the Thames lamented that politics did not stir the unskilled working man with only his labour to sell, 'even at the time of elections. Very many have no vote because they are always moving; the majority of the more settled do not attend the party meetings, but profess great indifference.'[29] By 1900, ten years after the upsurge of 'New Unionism,' when large numbers of unskilled workers took industrial action for the 'Eight Hour Day' and higher wages, trade unionism in inner London had declined with the growth of unemployment and the impact of immigration. The majority of the few mainly skilled workers who were organised into trade unions looked to Progressivism rather than independent labour to make their voice heard. This was certainly the case in North Lambeth where pockets of working-class Liberalism persisted into the interwar period and where craft trade unionism only provided the organisational base for relatively weak independent Labour politics. Other industries were, however, much less organised. In 1900, there were over 11,000 building workers resident in Lambeth, and just under 6,000 in Hackney, a small number of whom may have been members of a trade union, such as skilled carpenters and joiners, but most of them (and the many thousands employed as general labourers) would not have been unionised.[30]

Their political views are probably best represented by some of the characters in Robert Tressell's semi-autobiographical book, *The Ragged-Trousers*

---

25 Lambeth Trades Council Annual Report 1904.
26 Shipley, *Club Life and Socialism in Mid-Victorian London.*
27 Stedman-Jones, *Outcast London.*
28 *Daily Chronicle*, 14 June 1892.
29 Patterson, *Across the Bridges or Life by the South Side Riverside*, p. 215.
30 Census 1901.

102   *Thematic*

Philanthropists.[31] Their working life, according to the author, was not about class struggle, but reflected a limited political culture that bred a generation of working-class Tories who knew their place in society. These bricklayers, painters and decorators were employed by the large number of relatively small speculative house builders responding to the demand for better housing in the expanding middle-class and residential areas of south London.[32] Indeed, most workers living in Hackney and Lambeth would have been employed by small employers, such as independent house builders, medium-scale engineering works, furniture workshops, the transport industry (coachmen, carmen and messengers), and the food, tobacco and drinks trade, which in Lambeth formed part of an industrial food 'quarter,' including Bermondsey and Camberwell. There were also a large number of self-employed women working at home as 'sweated' dressmakers and seamstresses. Hackney contained over 11,000 women engaged in the dress making trades by 1914, on a par with Islington (at 12,700) and Stepney (at 15,800).[33]

As a result of the demand created by a series of speculative house-building booms, Lambeth, for example, contained by the turn of the century 3,500 national and local government workers, over 7,500 commercial or business clerks, and nearly 1,000 law clerks, what Labour referred to as 'Black coated' workers. These middle- and lower-middle-class families were supported by over 11,000 in-door domestic female servants, although this figure had dropped to just over 9,000 by 1914. Hackney contained slightly fewer residents working in commercial occupations (at just over 9,000 in 1914 and the number of domestic servants was correspondingly lower at 6,500).[34] Community identity in these inner London boroughs was therefore based on affinities to quite narrowly defined residential neighbourhoods, street life, nonconformist churches for a minority, railway stations and tram stops, pubs and local markets. For one member of the working class, while politics at election times might 'have been great fun for everybody,' canvassing was regarded as a nuisance... 'too many people were too poor, and too many people were too rich. The wealth of the country was unevenly distributed.'[35] Such cynicism no doubt contributed to a political culture of apathy and consolation, although to what extent is not open to exact measurement.

During the First World War, the area of North Lambeth, especially around Waterloo Station, acquired a notorious reputation for crime and prostitution, promoted by the press as a national scandal posing a danger to

---

31 Tresell, *The Ragged Trouser Philanthropists.*
32 Dyos, *Victorian Suburb*, pp. 124–37.
33 *London Statistics 1914–1915* (LCC 1916), p. 51.
34 Census 1901; *London Statistics 1914–1915.*
35 Newton, *Years of Change*, p. 46.

the health of the troops embarking for the western front.[36] The Progressives on the LCC sought to regulate the music halls and theatres, as they had done before the war, driven by puritanical impulses and the demand for temperance reform. Lib-Lab MPs and members of the LCC, such as Will Crooks and John Burns, campaigned against vice, drink and the music halls. Burns believed that 'drink, betting and vulgar music-hall fare diverted workers from their quest to understand the source of their oppression,' reinforcing the gulf within the London working class between respectable artisans and the so-called 'residiuum.'[37] The reputation of the music halls, of which there were a number south of the river, such as the Borough Music Hall in Southwark and the Canterbury Hall in Lambeth, diminished after 1918 with the growth of more respectable variety entertainment and stronger licencing regulations enforced by the LCC.

The New Survey of London Life and Labour (NSLLL), published in the early 1930s, still identified North Lambeth, especially the area around Waterloo Station which had been finally rebuilt after the war, as a site of vice, crime and poverty.[38] It was these areas that were devastated by the blitz a generation later, evacuating the population to the suburbs or further afield, many of whom did not return after the war. This was unlike, for example, the residents of Campbell Bunk, 'the worst street in London between the wars,' whose semi-criminal culture survived untouched by respectable society until the eve of the Second World War.[39] The NSLLL recorded that of the 146,000 occupied persons who lived in Lambeth in the early 1930s, those who worked elsewhere numbered 85,000 or 58%, with the majority working in the city (18,500) and in Westminster (24,000), while 41,000 persons who worked in Lambeth dwelt in neighbouring boroughs.[40] This division between work and residence was therefore very marked amongst the middle and lower middle classes, and perhaps less so amongst the working classes, who would have worked closer to home and in the other manufacturing industries carried out in the borough. The NSLLL concluded that Lambeth did not have any particular industries of

> any significant magnitude. There are candle and toilet soap works, beer and vinegar breweries, printing works, laundries, a flour mill, a lead-smelting works, potteries, and factories for the production of boot polishes, sauces and meat essences, hydraulic packing, and emery paper and polishes. All of these industries are situated in North Lambeth. Of the occupied male residents in 1921 the largest occupational group was that of road, rail and river transport. In the case of women and girls

---

36 White, *Zepppelin Nights*, pp. 189–97.
37 Waters, 'Progressives, Puritans and the Cultural Politics of the Council, 1889–1914,' 67.
38 *New Survey of London Life and Labour*, Vol. 6 (1934), p. 394.
39 White, *Campbell Bunk*.
40 Census of England and Wales 1921. County of London (1923).

104   *Thematic*

> personal service (domestic servants, laundry workers, waitresses etc.) formed the largest group.[41]

After 1930, the number of people employed in all industries in Lambeth declined from just over 100,000 in 1931 to 70,000 in 1950, a drop of 30%, encouraged by the LCC policy of dispersal to out of town estates and new towns.[42] Those working in light industry fell from 72,000 in 1931 to just under 28,000 in 1951, while the number of professional employees fell even more dramatically from 195,000 to just over 74,000, a drop of over 60%. The number of economically active males declined from 100,000 to 75,000 in the same period (with only just over 8,000 unemployed in 1931 indicating the shallowness of the depression in London in comparison to the depressed areas of the north). It was not matched by a similar drop in economically active females, which was much less from only 53,000 to 45,000, or just under a half of all adult women.[43] These figures paint a picture of a borough undergoing a slow contraction of small-scale manufacturing. Like many other inner London areas, it became more working class as the middle classes moved further out. Moreover, a significant proportion of the working class was rehoused in the newly built LCC estates in Tulse Hill and Kennington and in the outer suburbs in Merton on the St Helier Estate, similar to the large Becontree Estate in Dagenham.

The effect of the blitz accentuated this trend by destroying a significant proportion of industrial capacity located in the central and northern parts of the borough. As a result, Lambeth became a largely residential district after 1945 with only small pockets of industry. A civil defence worker based in Lambeth, Stanley Rothwell, has given an accurate account of this destruction, describing the way the German bombers approaching from the south-east, targeted the loop of the Thames between London and Chelsea Bridge. 'One only need to look at the map,' he wrote,

> and the trail of bomb incidents recorded after the war, to see what they were aiming for and why we got most continuous bombing by plane, doodle bug and rocket. The trail is like an arrow head with the point right at the mother of Parliaments, just over the river from us, with the railway stations and power stations situated along the embankment. Due to the German bomb aimers getting nervous before reaching their targets, due to the gun fire, we got the backwash as they released their bombs too soon...Lambeth Walk was hit badly. Sail Street, Juxon Street, China Walk demolished...This once light-hearted and carefree thoroughfare and the gay Lambeth Walk traders were sad eyed... A

41 *New Survey of London Life and Labour*, Vol. 6, p. 394.
42 Saint, 'Spread the People.'
43 GB Historical GIS/University of Portsmouth, Lambeth MetB.

Localities 105

gloom set into that once happy place; it lost its cheeriness which some-
how it has never regained since.[44]

Lambeth was one of the inner London boroughs where between 10% and
14% of properties were destroyed by enemy bombing creating over 300 acres
of vacant land, war damaged and temporary buildings after the war.[45] It
was on such vacant sites that the South Bank was redeveloped after 1945,
starting with the Festival of Britain and followed by the National Theatre,
the Royal Festival Hall, the rebuilt part of St Thomas's Hospital, which had
been hit by a V2 rocket, and the Shell Building.[46] There are still some vacant
sites in existence today used as carparks, waiting for redevelopment.

After 1945, the population recovered a little but like other parts of inner London, it started to fall again after 1951. The famous Lambeth Walk,
which had contained 159 shops and 11 butchers before the war, never fully
recovered from the blitz and the evacuations. A common feature of large
European and American cities at this time was 'a pattern of centrifugal expansion,' with the old metropolitan centre (in the case of London the area
covered by the LCC), losing population at a fast rate, especially in the period
1931–1951, when wartime bombing and evacuation reinforced the continuous pre-war trend of depopulation. This was accompanied by a corresponding reduction in manufacturing industries and a growth in services, such as
distribution, finance, administration and professional and personal services
of all kinds. The total number of people in insured employment dropped in
London from about 2,000,000 in 1939 to 1,600,000 in 1948.[47] Brixton, for
example, lost over 15,000 jobs, while the figure for Lambeth as a whole was
over 35,000.[48] By 1951, services accounted for 50% of the daytime labour
force in Greater London, while only 31% were employed in manufacturing.
The figures for inner south London and including Lambeth were 48% and
26%.[49] After 1950, Lambeth was losing a significant part of its manufacturing industry as industry relocated to cheaper sites with better transport connections on the outskirts. Napiers, for example, had moved from Lambeth
to Acton as early as 1902, while the Doutlon Pottery Factory had moved to
Erith in 1924.

After the Second World War, Lambeth started to become a mainly residential area with a less-skilled but increasingly unionised workforce employed in delivering a wide range of services in the expanding public sector
across London, such as local government, education, health, postal services

---

44 Rothwell, *Lambeth at War*, pp. 15 and 24.
45 LCC, *Administrative County of London Development Plan* (1957), p. 28.
46 Ward, *London County Council Bomb Damage Maps* (2015).
47 LCC, *Statistical Abstract for London 1939–1948*, pp. 54–5, 78–9.
48 LCC, *Administrative County of London Development Plan* (1951), p. 63.
49 Westergaard, 'The Structure of Greater London,' 93–113; see www.visionofbritain.org.
uk/lambeth/occupations.

106 *Thematic*

and transport. These were all areas experiencing significant increases in trade union membership and density. The growth areas in the period 1948–1958 were finance (75%), local government (25%), education (23%) and business services (18%). There were relatively high levels of trade union density in the transport industry during this period (74%) and the membership of the T&GWU grew from 635,000 in 1938 to 1,224,000 by 1958.[50] It was by far the most dominant trade union represented on the executive committee of the LLP. In 1951, over 13,000 residents in Lambeth worked in transport.[51] The Stockwell Bus Garage, which was opened in 1952, built on a cleared residential site destroyed in the blitz, had a record of employing a good number of black bus conductors. The garage was capable of housing up to 200 buses which were required at the time when the last trams were being phased out. By the 1950s, shortages in these expanding labour markets were increasingly filled by citizens from the West Indies, some recruited directly to the NHS by the government in the Caribbean, but most of them taking jobs where there were severe post-war labour shortages.

Before 1945, the population of Lambeth had been predominantly white. But after 1960, the ethnic composition of London was transformed. Brixton was one of the chosen areas for migrants from the West Indies, building on the existing and relatively small Jamaican community which had lived there from before the war. The British Nationality Act of 1948 granted citizenship to all residents of the Commonwealth irrespective of race, colour or nationality, although the government had not anticipated the flow of migrants increasing from the West Indies. Taking advantage of the prospect of self-improvement (and able to say 'London is the Place for Me'), by the early 1960s, there were already some 100,000 West Indians in Brixton and Notting Hill.[52] Like previous concentrations of black people in Britain, such as the seafaring communities in interwar Cardiff and Liverpool, and in Midland cities like Nottingham, they experienced discrimination and violence. An early sociological study of West Indian workers in Brixton during the late 1950s identified hostility towards 'foreign' labour, both male and female, restricting job opportunities to unskilled work. A high level of discrimination was also endemic in the private housing market where migrants were excluded from many areas.[53] By 1971, the black population of London had increased to 170,000, constrained by the Commonwealth Immigration Act of 1962, but preceded by an upsurge before the Act came into force, especially children joining their parents. The proportion of residents in inner London whose both parents were born in the New Commonwealth was officially estimated at only 8% in 1961, but this was an under-estimate (see Chapter 7 for further details of the black population in Lambeth).

---

50 Hindell, 'Trade Union Membership.'
51 www.visionofbritain.org.uk/lambeth.
52 Perry, *London is the Place for Me.*
53 Patterson, *Dark Strangers*; Perry, *London*, p. 86.

Localities 107

Suburban expansion – the case of Croydon (1900–2020)

In contrast, neighbourhood identities in Croydon were forged by different patterns of migration. Many workers migrated to the expanding manufacturing industries developing along railway lines on new industrial estates, like the Waddon Estate, the future site of the Croydon Aerodrome, London's first commercial airport. The population of Willesden, for example, increased from 90,000 in the mid-1890s to over 150,000 by 1911, while the population of more rural Wembley, further out, was much smaller at only 3,500 in 1894.[54] After 1850, Croydon absorbed a new upper class of suburbanites escaping from the overcrowded and unhealthy conditions of inner London. They took advantage of the town's healthier prospects and the fast train services to well-paid jobs in Westminster or the City of London. But by 1900, Croydon was also attracting a class of skilled artisans either as residents or commuters (able to afford workmen's fares on the trams or railways) as industry started to relocate to the suburbs, searching for more spacious premises and cheaper and non-unionised labour. They joined an existing and relatively small working class of general labourers who worked in the building and clothing and boot and shoe trades.

In the suburbs, there was a strong correlation between transport links and housing developments. The railways were an important factor in driving urban development.[55] Before East Croydon Station became one of the busiest non-terminus stations in the UK, the area boasted seven other smaller stations, now forgotten, around which local neighbourhoods of housing and shops developed into distinct residential areas.[56] During the 1890s, Croydon experienced a mix of different types of housing schemes aimed at both middle- and working-class residents. In 1888, a local estate agent purchased 260 acres of downland in rural Purley to build an estate on garden-city principles, with rental levels attracting the middle classes.[57] At the same time, distinct working-class districts grew up in low-lying areas on the eastern side of the Brighton Road as urban development stratified along class lines, following the relocation of certain industries which had been based in central London, such as light engineering and printing, attracted by more spacious premises and cheaper rents as well as lower wages.[58] In 1906, the Corporation built an estate of 'workman's dwellings' to the east of Spring Lane in South Norwood close to Crystal Palace.[59] As a result of these developments, Croydon's status as a predominantly middle-class

54 Snow, *Willesden Past.*
55 Levinson, 'The Orderliness Hypothesis.'
56 *Croydon Advertiser*, 5 May 2017.
57 Gent, *Croydon Past*, pp. 90–1.
58 Cox, 'Across the Road,' 167–78.
59 Gent, *Croydon Past*, p. 98.

108   *Thematic*

constituency in 1901 had lapsed by 1911 'owing to the arrival of a considerable artisan population.'[60]

The rapid growth of these suburban neighbourhoods created the need for new wards and the regular redrawing of electoral boundaries to reflect increases in the population. Such revisions became a striking feature of London's suburbs. Croydon's urban growth after 1900 was very different to the relative stability of electoral arrangements in inner-city boroughs, which experienced population decline after 1918. The distance between work and home also created different political cultures based on an identity with residential neighbourhoods. The working-class population of Croydon either worked in the borough, such as local building workers, or travelled outside by tram or tramped on foot to neighbouring districts, or commuted into the area by tram or the railways, benefiting from cheap workmen's fares. Trade union organisation was as a result weak and fragmented. The main trade unions in Croydon were those representing the building trades, such as carpenters and joiners, house decorators, plasterers, bricklayers and stonemasons.[61] The branch of the Amalgamated Society of Railway Servants had only 296 members, quite small, given that Croydon had 14 railway stations, while the Paddington branch had 850 members and Crewe over 1,200.[62] The Amalgamated Society of Carpenters and Joiners also only had 120 members during the 1890s, representing just 11% of the total workforce.[63] By 1911, there were 7,500 building workers in the borough and just under 2,000 print workers, many of them commuters or migrants from central London.[64] Wage rates for compositors were well below those for skilled building trade workers and labourers. The number of print workers had increased from 350 in 1891 to nearly 1,300, and the number working in engineering from 635 to 2,738, with most employed in small-scale motor vehicle production. A branch of the LSC was not established in Croydon until after 1909. After this date, the printers were far more successful than the engineers in improving their conditions of work.[65]

The weak position of the trade unions in Croydon mirrored the situation across the capital. Before 1914, Ben Tillett regarded the trade union movement in London as 'the Sphinx of Labour.' The Woman's Trade Union League also characterised the capital as 'an impossible undertaking.' London had fewer than 2,000 of the 120,000 women unionists in Britain, although it contained 10% of the nation's working women.[66] There were examples of industrial militancy during the period of industrial unrest before

60 Pelling, *Social Geography of British Elections*, pp. 64–5.
61 Tichelar, *Labour Politics in Croydon, 1880–1914*.
62 *Daily Herald*, 5 March 1913.
63 *Croydon Times*, 25 March 1891.
64 Census, 1911.
65 Zeitlin, 'Craft Control and the Division of Labour,' 264.
66 Olcott, 'Dead Centre.'

Localities 109

1914 when, for example, thousands of female workers in Bermondsey came out on strike in jam and biscuit factories during the sweltering summer of 1911.[67] The experience of such sweated and exploited labour was part of labour movement demands (and the Progressives in London) at the time for state intervention to enforce minimum wages, legislation introduced by the Liberal Government in 1909.[68] The war provided further justification for state intervention to protect workers' rights. While trade union membership increased rapidly during the war, especially on the docks and the railways, in areas of mixed- and small-scale sweated industries and workshops, its growth was less marked. The wartime coalition found it necessary in the circumstances of total war to force employers to ensure minimum standards of pay and working conditions. It was only towards the end of the war that membership nationally started to increase by nearly 20% a year, especially in the transport unions, prior to the formation of the T&GWU in the early 1920s.[69] At this time, the labour movement entered a period of rapid expansion, not seen since 'New Unionism.' It 'reorganised itself from top to bottom, and was continually involved in bitter conflict with employers and government.'[70]

After 1918, the trades councils and new local labour parties in London, some merging to become borough Labour parties, were very much part of this expansion, militancy and rapid change. Although the figures for Lambeth are not available, it is safe to say that the borough was not an area of high trade union membership. A reporter on wartime distress in London described Lambeth as a weak area for trade union organisation, 'with the slums of North Lambeth in particular the home of casual waterside labourers, Covent Garden porters, street sellers, building labourers and other casual workers living on what their wives earn.'[71] Brixton and Kennington were more residential areas, 'with a sprinkling of casual builders' labourers and other general workers employed at Nine Elms railway station.' Norwood was described as largely residential with 'a number of boarding houses frequented by foreigners... but all through the borough there are scattered many folk in the various grades of the Music Hall professions, as well as many postmen and policemen.'[72] There was a significant increase in the number of women registering for relief during the first year of the war (from only 55 in 1913 to 420 by the end of 1915), many of them soldiers wives, often unmarried thrown into destitution in the absence of their husbands in

---

67 Taylor, *Ada Salter*, pp. 115–8.
68 Trade Board Act 1909.
69 Coates and Topham, *The Making of the Labour Movement*, p. 611.
70 Clinton, *Trade Union Rank and File*, pp. 114–37.
71 Pember-Reeves, *Around About a Pound a Week*.
72 LSE: Webb Papers – GB97 Coll Misc. 0242, Vol. 1 – Individual report on Lambeth by G. Moses 31 October 1914, pp. 80–2.

110   *Thematic*

the trenches and the late or non-payment of war pensions.[73] The War Emergency Committee of the LCC, on which the trade union leader and Progressive Harry Gosling was one of only two representatives, estimated that 16% of occupied males and 25% of occupied females in Lambeth were seriously affected by the war, particularly building workers and dressmakers caused by the requisitioning of building and clothing materials for the war effort.[74]

It was not so much an increase in trade union membership or militancy which improved the fortunes of independent Labour in London after 1918, but the fight to get representation on the local committees set up by the government to grant outdoor relief arising from the war emergency and to control food prices and rent levels. In practice, state intervention was more effective in defending working-class living standards than trade union militancy. In Lambeth, for example, the Conservative Mayor controversially put the whole membership of the borough council 'en-bloc' on the local relief committee, ensuring unwieldly and total control by the Municipal Reform Party, concerned above all to keep public expenditure down.[75] There was no trade union or Labour representation at first, although this had changed by the end of 1915 but only marginally. Towards the end of the war, it was further reported that conditions had improved, despite an increase of 25% in the cost of living. In fact, there was evidence that the 'the more well to do' class was applying for outdoor relief, as their savings began to run out. Smaller landlords could not let their properties at higher rent levels. It was noted with a degree of alarm that many able-bodied paupers had left the workhouse to get employment in the Woolwich Arsenal, many of them over 60 years of age, along with a considerable number of juveniles, eliminating pre-war levels of chronic poverty and unemployment.

Faith in state intervention to defend working-class living standards, rather than industrial militancy, was also a feature of working-class politics in Croydon during the war. The government intervened to protect the rights of female and unskilled workers, while the craft unions of male skilled workers fought a losing battle against dilution and the use of female labour in traditional engineering trades, especially in the munitions industries. In the short term, the war weakened the position of trade unionism in Croydon. The local labour movement was split between pro-war and pacifist wings. The patriot Will Crooks, the Labour MP for Woolwich, spoke at a recruiting rally in the borough in February 1915 'making one of his characteristically vigorous appeals to the patriotism of our young men.'[76] In such circumstances, the trade unions could not defend their members from wartime inflation when the price of food outstripped wages during the first two years of the war. A local protest meeting in 1915 attended by the pacifist

73 Ibid., Appendix E.
74 LMA: LCC Emergency Committee 1914–1915.
75 LSE: GB97 Coll Misc. 0242, Vol. 2, p. 687.
76 Moore, *Croydon and the Great War*, p. 26.

Localities 111

Labour MP for Sheffield Attercliffe, W C Anderson, led to pressure for state intervention. The Croydon Corporation started to grant war-bonuses in 1915 to its workmen as a contribution towards the increased cost of living. As the war progressed, state intervention increased to unprecedented levels. In May 1916, the Military Services Act introduced conscription for all men between 18 and 21 (badly splitting the Liberal Party in the process), and the Corporation started to administer a state pension scheme for soldiers and their dependents. In 1917, the council took over the control of all allotments to increase the production of home-grown food and a local Food Committee was appointed to implement a national scheme of rationing.[77] The Women's Labour League in Croydon succeeded in getting established wartime canteens to provide cheap meals at subsidised prices.[78] Labour shortages in munitions and transport led to the increasing use of female workers.

Industrial relations on the trams run by the Croydon Corporation boiled over in the spring of 1916. The membership of the London Cab Drivers Union had grown to 20,000 in 1913 following a successful strike which forced the employers to pay for petrol used by the cab drivers. As the tramway system extended into the suburbs, it was renamed the London and Provincial Union of Licensed Vehicle Workers and it started to recruit members who drove public vehicles as well as private cabs. In 1916, it achieved arbitration over a dispute about the use of women drivers. But the Croydon Corporation, which ran the trams as a municipal service, voted against the decision.[79] However, as the war progressed, the level of industrial militancy increased. Disputes broke out in the new National Aircraft Factory built by the Ministry of Munitions at Waddon in 1917 to manufacture the De Havilland By-plane. The factory employed nearly 3,000 staff, of which 50% were women. The factory was beset with labour issues over new working methods, dilution and bonus payments, described in the local press as being 'in a state of perpetual agitation, which frequently resulted in strikes.'[80] By this stage in the war, industrial action started to succeed to a certain extent in defending working-class living conditions in those heavily industrialised parts of the country, but not so much in London. The unofficial Shop Stewards Movement was capable by 1917 of leading mass strike action in defiance of trade union officials, but its main strength was to be found in areas like Glasgow, Sheffield and Manchester, apart from a short-lived West London Workers Committee, formed by the engineer and Syndicalist Jack Tanner.[81] Militancy spread to those industries, like transport and munitions, where

77 Ibid., pp. 26–46.
78 *The Labour Woman*, July 1917.
79 *Times*, 13, 18 & 24 April 1916.
80 *Wallington Advertiser*, 17 January 1919 – quoted in McInnes and Sparkes, *Croydon at Work*, p. 55.
81 Clegg, Fox and Thompson, *History of British Trade Unions*, Vol. 2, p. 181; Hinton, *The First Shop Stewards Movement*.

112   *Thematic*

traditional craft skills were threatened with dilution from female workers. In August 1918, there was a rerun of the earlier tramway strike, when over 70,000 tram workers walked out across the country over equal pay for female conductors. By this time, the role of the working class in the war effort could not be so easily ignored. It took state intervention (in the form of a direction issued by the Government's Committee of Production) to force Croydon Corporation to pay (albeit without precedence) female conductors the same rate for the job as men.

Clearly, one of the key lessons of the war, for working-class women in Croydon at least, was that the government was in many instances more effective in defending their interests than the official trade union movement, which resisted in many instances the recruitment of women members. The skilled engineers and compositors, whose position was under threat from dilution and female labour during the war, regained some of their influence when the soldiers returned from the front. After the war, the Aircraft Factory at Waddon was decommissioned by the Ministry of Munitions and 2,000 workers were discharged. A protest march, attended by the militant suffragette Sylvia Pankhurst, lobbied the Mayor and a deputation complained that the factory, which had cost £1,000,000 to build, and contained £800,000 worth of machinery, was to be used as a salvage store using discharged soldiers as a form of cheap labour contrary to the Wages Regulation Act.[82] A local shop stewards committee proposed that the factory be used for building new houses under the government house-building programme, but this was rejected by the Ministry of Munitions. The *Workers' Dreadnought* (before it became the official weekly newspaper of the CPGB in 1921, edited by Pankhurst) highlighted the weakness of

> the displaced workers, who now occupy a piteous position, their economic power broken. During the war, they greatly improved their position, because they were needed. Now, needed no longer, they appeal in vain to the Government, to Members of Parliament, and even to Executive Councils of Trade Unions.[83]

In contrast to Lambeth, Croydon experienced industrial expansion and population growth after 1918, but such changes did not provide a big enough social base which could guarantee any significant degree of support for the Labour Party. Although the party won Croydon South very narrowly in 1945, when it succeeded in attracting middle-class votes on a significant scale, it had to wait until the 1990s before it started to record any consistent success in local or parliamentary contests. By the end of the First World War, a fresh wave of workers, including many younger women, had come to work on the

---

82 *Pall Mall Gazette*, 13 January 1919.
83 *Worker's Dreadnought*, 25 January 1919.

trams and in the aircraft factories in Waddon. Like the largely rural area of Wembley, which became a manufacturing centre for military aircraft, supporting the nearby Aerodrome in Hendon, the war laid the foundations of post-war industrial development in the suburbs of London. After 1918, Croydon continued to attract both middle-class residents relocating from the centre of London as well as many members of the upwardly mobile and skilled working class escaping the slums and able to afford higher rents. But the suburbanites increasingly outnumbered the workers and the two new constituencies created in 1918 remained safe seats for the Conservatives. A Ratepayers Association (an alliance of local Conservatives and Liberals) politically controlled the corporation up to the 1970s.

Suburban areas like Croydon and Willesden experienced industrial expansion during the interwar period. Unemployed workers from the distressed areas, especially South Wales, joined younger female and adolescent workers from inner London to compete for semi-skilled jobs in light engineering and other small-scale manufacturing which developed on the sites no longer used for war production, such as the area around the Croydon Aerodrome, and the site of the 1924 Empire Exhibition in Wembley. Less expensive land prices than central London encouraged new industrial development in the suburbs, connected by good transport connections to the large market of consumers in the south-east. Population continued to expand rapidly as a result of migration and increased birth rate. Between 1919 and 1939, the number of polling districts in Croydon increased from 7 to 15 as new residential areas were formed around railway stations and tram stops. The Second World War injected new demand for labour into Croydon's industrial base. Manufacturing industries and especially light engineering expanded even further after 1945 reaching a peak in the 1960s. The *Croydon Times* noted how industry had come south during the war, putting enormous pressure on local housing:

> Some were residents here before the war; others have come to work from other parts of the country and now want to stay and make their homes here permanently. Figures from Croydon Trades Council illustrate the changes...Before the war 75% of the working population travelled to London for their employment. Today nearly 60% worked in Croydon. The town was becoming a centre of light engineering which would be one of the chief industries in post-war reconstruction.[84]

The number of well-paid jobs increased and the influence of the trade unions also grew in conditions of labour shortages. While many London boroughs experienced a decline in population, Croydon continued to grow at a faster rate than some other London suburbs. The office boom after 1956

84 *Croydon Times*, 8 and 29 September 1945.

114 *Thematic*

added further reasons for economic migrants to either live in Croydon or commute to work in its growing number of high-rise offices and its shopping centres. The number of parliamentary seats increased from two to three and then from three to four. The borough became politically polarised between an increasingly affluent and Conservative south and a more disadvantaged and marginal north, containing neighbourhoods of mixed social class, either identifying with Croydon or seeing themselves as Londoners. By the 1960s, retail and finance had replaced manufacturing as Croydon's primary industries, following the office boom engineered by the Corporation in the early 1950s. Like Lambeth a decade earlier, it also began to attract a growing number of black and ethnic minority citizens who started to relocate from inner London to socially upgrade and buy cheaper properties or rent flats, escaping from multi-occupied slums in the inner cities. As a result, the northern areas of the borough started to lose their more exclusive residential status which had underpinned the political domination of the Ratepayers Association.

De-industrialisation, gentrification and regeneration (1968–2020)

From the 1970s, London started to experience a process of social up-grading, referred to by sociologists as gentrification. In Lambeth, for example, this affected, in particular, Brixton, Clapham, Kennington and Vauxhall. Streatham also began to receive an influx of first- and second-generation black families moving southwards and further out to areas like North Croydon. In fact, by the1990s, the social changes identified by studies into the borough's inner-city problems published in 1974 had dramatically speeded up. During the 1970s, the percentage of those employed in manufacturing had declined further from 20% to 13.5%, while those employed in services had increased from 59% to 67%.[85] In 1966, employed men outnumbered women in manufacturing and transport, while employed women (mainly married) outnumbered men in services. There were about an equal and growing number of men and women working in national and local governments, with higher concentrations of white-collar workers in Vauxhall, close to County Hall and Westminster.[86]

A generation later, Lambeth began to attract an altogether different type of resident and the size of its working-class population contracted again, although it slightly increased to between 10% and 15% in the first decade of the twenty-first century as the number of unskilled and low-paid jobs in the service sector expanded to support London's growing population. London's new elites living in gentrified and segregated neighbourhoods needed a new

85 Census 1971 and 1981.
86 Census Parliamentary constituencies 1966.

Localities 115

service class to support its particular life styles. Many of these private sector jobs were created following the privatisation of public services after 1979. Thus, trade union membership in previously well-organised areas of local government, for example, started to decline in both blue- and white-collar areas. This was particularly marked in inner London, where trade union density reduced from 28% in 1995 to only 15% in 2018. Male density at 14% was significantly lower than that for women at 18%.[87] Although the figures for outer London were slightly higher (18% and 21%), the era of a labour market in the capital characterised by a culture of strong blue-collar trade union membership (predominantly male), with high levels of affiliation to the Labour Party through the political levy, had to a large extent disappeared by the 1990s. Trade union density for manual workers dropped from 65% in 1984 to 45% in 1990 and for non-manual workers from 37% to 31%.[88]

By the year 2000, whole neighbourhoods of inner London were being 'remade' by the combined forces of gentrification, immigration and related changes to housing and labour markets. Lambeth saw a remarkable expansion of the lower middle class as a proportion of its total population. This could be seen in changes to its socio-economic structure, its pattern of housing tenure, and in the age structure and level of educational attainment of its population. In the three parliamentary constituencies of Dulwich & West Norwood, Streatham and Vauxhall, the proportion of higher managerial residents increased from under 10% in 1991 to over 30% by 2011. There was a reduction in the number of intermediate and lower supervisory jobs, while the number of unskilled and semi-skilled jobs stabilised at just under 10%. This reflected a labour market composed of a group of highly paid professionals working in finance, computing and the creative industries, a significant proportion of whom were members of a trade union, especially in the public sector, and a mass of unskilled workers concentrated in the private sector, many on short-term contracts providing services to the more financially secure middle class, with only a very few belonging to a trade union. In some respects, the economic and social conditions of 'the gilded age' of late Victorian and Edwardian London had returned in the form of a widening gap between rich and poor, the presence of sweated service industries and an unskilled workforce untouched by trade unionism.

In London a hundred years later, the situation was in fact only marginally better, but with some important differences. Jewish immigration has now been replaced by the arrival of waves of new migrants from the New Commonwealth, Europe, the Middle East and Africa. The new public sector workers were far more likely than private sector employees to be trade union members. Union density rates for Londoners working in the public sector are 56% – four times higher than the rate for private sector employees

---

87 Labour Force Survey, ONS.

88 Martin, *Union Retreat and the Regions*, pp. 57–8.

116 *Thematic*

(14%). While the density rates are the highest in public administration, education and health sectors (49%), they are the lowest in the sectors dominated by private employers, such as wholesale and retail distribution (8%) and the finance and business sector (11%). Thus, there is little relationship between membership of a trade union and voting for the Labour Party in contemporary London, very different to the period after 1918 and before the onset of privatisation in the 1980s.[89]

In terms of housing tenure, the proportion of council housing reduced substantially under the impact of 'Right to Buy' and the availability of cheap mortgages before the financial crash in 2008. This was most dramatic in Vauxhall (from 50% to 23%), while the level of private rented accommodation increased in all three constituencies to something approaching 30%. Council housing had been replaced by a growth in the private rented sector. Lambeth is no longer a borough where council tenants form a majority of the population in its working-class districts. In the past, this guaranteed a degree of loyalty to the Labour Party, as it did, for example, when the house-building and slum clearance programmes of the LCC forged an identity between tenants and the party in the interwar period and after 1945. (It was for these reasons that Conservative-controlled Westminster, led by Shirley Porter, sought to reduce the number of council tenants through enforced relocation, for which it was found to have acted illegally.) But in other areas, Right to Buy reduced the number of council tenancies as a proportion of all tenures. In Dulwich & West Norwood, the number of residents who owned their homes outright fell from 50% in 1991 to only 15% in 2011. In Streatham, it fell from 45% to 15% and in Vauxhall from 24% to 9%. Property-driven gentrification prevented the majority of the resident population (rather than incomers) from purchasing a home for the first time, reducing the level of owner-occupation from a high point of 70% in the year 2000. This has created a level of insecurity for the growing number of tenants who now constitute 'generation rent.'[90]

A sociological survey into three areas of London (Brixton, Battersea and Isle of Dogs), carried out at the turn of this century, identified important differences in the way gentrification impacted on each area. Brixton, it concluded, was different to Battersea, for example, in the way that it was attractive to many incomers for its 'diversity and multi-culturalism':

> although this is more 'ideal' than lived. In reality, most respondents (to the survey), valued the fact that where they lived was relatively quiet and cut off from central Brixton. They took pride in saying that they lived in Brixton; it said something both to and about them. Those who had

---

89 Labour Force Surveys (ONS).
90 Census Parliamentary constituencies 1991–2011; Savage, *Social Class in the Twenty First Century.*

been there a long time wore their residence with pride. They regretted both what they saw as its passing and the emergence of a new Brixton that traded on its past but that now was in retreat before the twin forces of property driven property speculation and a commercially marketed night-time economy that appealed to white audiences attracted to its bad past.[91]

The age structure of Lambeth now conforms to the rest of inner and increasingly outer London. The previous over-representation of the elderly has been replaced by an over-representation of young adult age groups (aged 20–44), less likely to live in traditional family households and who make up most of the 'incomers.'[92] The over 65s have dropped to 7.6% of the population (the lowest level in London), while the 20–64 age group has grown to over 70%.[93] Furthermore, these young adults are now far better educated than their parents. The proportion of those with higher degrees increased from about 23% to over 50% in the 30 years since 1991.[94] They make up the largest number of those who state that they have no religion (37% in 2011), or who might be nominally Christian (just over 50%) but who do not practise or believe in God. However, there has been a change in the religious affiliations of Lambeth's population during the last 40 years, largely as a result of the growth of the black church-going community and the influx of asylum seekers and refugees, many of them Muslims attending what are thriving Islamic centres in Streatham and Norwood (see Chapter 7 on the politics of personal identity).

Many other areas of the capital were undergoing similar changes, especially in the suburbs. Croydon, for example, was well on the way to becoming a large, but slightly less prosperous multi-racial and cosmopolitan outer London suburb which in some ways imitated the inner cities of a previous generation. It still managed to retain a degree of civic identity as a separate town on the borders of London, an objective pursued by the corporation over many years as demonstrated by its failed attempts to achieve City Status. It now seeks to forge a new identity for itself, avoiding the mistakes of unregulated urban development, which destroyed the centre of Croydon in the 1950s and gave it a reputation for civic vandalism. By 2001, the population of Croydon had reached a record 330,700. It had become as ethnically diverse and cosmopolitan as many parts of inner London. After its last application for City Status was turned down in the year 2000, it joined the Edge Cities Network, which sought to promote a specific urban identity for major self-contained areas on the edge of capital or large provincial cities. 'Edge City' was a term coined by Joel Garreau, in which he argued that the

---

91 Butler and Robson, *London Calling*, pp. 94–5.
92 Buck, *Working Capital*, p. 145.
93 ONS, *Age Structure of London Boroughs*, 2011.
94 Census 1991–2011.

118   *Thematic*

edge city had become a new form of urban growth worldwide. He defined such areas as having

> more than five million or more square feet of leasable office space, 600,000 square feet or more of leasable retail space, more jobs than bedrooms, is perceived by the population as one place and was nothing like a "city" as recently as 30 years ago. Then it was just bedrooms, if not cow pastures.[95]

Certainly, Croydon met these criteria, unlike Brent, for example, which remains a more integrated part of Greater London, as it was not originally an independent town on the borders of London before 1900. Influenced by this concept, Croydon Council embarked on a regeneration programme in 1999 called *Croydon Vision 2020* designed by the Architect Will Alsop.

Working Capital & London Voices. London Lives (2000–2020)

Looking at Greater London more broadly than that provided by the examples of Croydon and Lambeth, a major survey (*Working Capital*) published in 2002 (in memory of the work of the sociologist Michael Young and the historian Roy Porter) identified six kinds of neighbourhood which made up the rapidly changing social and economic fabric of the capital by the turn of the twenty-first century.[96] Its findings provided a complex picture of the remarkable way that London's different areas have been socially and politically transformed. A further detailed survey was carried out by Sir Peter Hall (*London Voices. London Lives*) published in 2007, using and building on this earlier research.[97] The first study drew attention to the cultural distinctiveness of London's neighbourhoods and made some very relevant comments about class and race:

> London is probably the place where traditional class identities are weakest, and in which new identities, which may be most divergent from mainstream values, arise most rapidly. This in part reflects its character, which it shares with other big cities, as a tolerant environment. But that does not make it less class-divided, and some cultural forms play precisely the roles of exclusion and distinction that the (theorist) Bourdieu posited... (when he pointed) to the way in which culture is used as a resource in the formation of class, by establishing distinctions and boundaries with other classes...Global cities such as London play a key role in these processes. (However), ...ethnicity clearly provides a source of

95 Garreau, *Edge City*, p. 7.
96 Buck, *Working Capital*.
97 Hall, *London Voices. London Lives*.

Localities 119

cultural identity separate from class. There is therefore a question of how far processes related to ethnic identity, manifested for example in residential segregation, openness or closure of social networks, employment discrimination, school segregation, in a multi-ethnic city such as London, serve to consolidate social divisions which are of greater significance than those associated with class. This is generally perceived to be the case in US cities. It is much less clear in London.[98]

This tentative conclusion is borne out by the findings of *Working Capital* and in the follow-up report by Sir Peter Hall in 2007. In their descriptions of the many different kinds of areas which made up the capital, both reports painted a rapidly changing picture of the way London has been transformed by gentrification and migration. While class remains a key aspect of social and economic relationships, *Working Capital* concluded that London was not now

> and never was a city sharply divided into rich and poor neighbourhoods...Nor is it changing in a single unilateral or inevitable direction: London's neighbourhoods are not bifurcating into the upwardly mobile and the downward descending, and as a result is not – yet at any rate – in danger of becoming a dual city on the American or Brazilian model.[99]

The categories of neighbourhoods identified in these two research reports provide a useful way to explore what social and political trends were happening at a local level by the turn of the century. The changing social geography of the capital was producing a clear and quite distinctive political result. Support for the Labour Party was increasing in those areas undergoing gentrification and containing high concentrations of black and ethnic minority citizens. In those fewer areas not experiencing such changes, located mainly in some of the outer suburbs, political allegiances conformed to a different pattern found in non-metropolitan areas. The first kind of area the reports identified were those like Battersea, described as *'the New Melting Pots.'* They were once predominantly working-class districts 'where deindustrialisation and gentrification had brought huge changes. Artisan terraces have been bought by the young middle-class,' while many working-class residents had been decanted from their housing estates to make way for the newcomers, creating feelings of resentment.[100] Battersea had been a prime example of what Eric Hobsbawn described as the 'Red Belt' of solidly working-class constituencies that ringed inner London after 1918. The Communist Shapurji Saklatvala was elected for the working-class seat of

---

98 Buck, *Working Capital*, pp. 379–80; Bourdieu, *Distinction.*
99 Buck, *Working Capital*, p. 316–7.
100 Buck, *Working Capital*, p. 293; Hall, *London Voices*, pp. 15–55.

120   *Thematic*

Battersea North in 1922, in preference to the Liberals, who still attracted artisan votes after 1918, as they did, for example, in Lambeth North and Bethnal Green, but not more generally across London. From 1935 to 1983 when the constituency was abolished, it remained a safe working-class Labour seat. The more mixed area of Battersea South was highly marginal from the 1920s. Labour captured it in 1945 and retained it until the election of Alf Dubs in 1983. He lost it to the Conservatives in 1987 and like many London constituencies, party activists despaired that the 'London Effect' would consign them to permanent opposition.[101] But after 1997, Labour's record in this highly gentrified part of south London steadily improved. In parliamentary elections, it achieved 50% of the vote in 1997, dropping to 37% in 2015, but increasing to 45% in 2017 and 2019. The Borough of Wandsworth was a flag ship council for the Conservatives during the 1980s, promoting the privatisation of public services. Labour lost control of what had been a mainly working-class borough in 1978 (always being compared unfavourably with neighbouring hard-left Lambeth). The party has remained out of office since then reaching a low point in 2006 with only nine councillors. But despite rapid gentrification and an influx of middle-class professional residents (especially in areas around Battersea Park and opposite fashionable Chelsea on the north side of the river), Labour's record has steadily improved. In 2018, they were only seven seats short of a majority on the council.

The second kind of area identified were those like Bermondsey, described as '***Proletarian Islands Under Pressure.***' Up until the 1960s, it contained a long-standing and largely settled working-class population (another component part of the 'Red Belt'), living in close-knit homogeneous communities with strong family and neighbourhood networks, very similar to those areas investigated in *Family and Kinship in East London*. But after the 1960s, it experienced multi-dimensional change: the loss of traditional jobs in docks and factories; the arrival of newcomers to the public housing estates; the gentrification of working-class streets and the loss of a tight sense of community. Researchers described the area as 'amongst the unhappiest neighbourhoods in contemporary London.'[102] In parliamentary elections, Labour's share of the vote never dropped below 75% from 1945 to 1970. It fell to under 70% during the 1970s, and dropped spectacularly to under 30% in the notorious by-election in 1981 when the gay activist Peter Tatchell was defeated by a resurgent Liberal Party. However, it has now recovered after 2010 and Labour has retaken the seat, with over 50% of the vote in 2015, 2017 and 2019. The borough of Southwark was a Labour working-class stronghold during the interwar period and remained so up until 1964 winning nearly all the seats on the council, many of which the Conservatives did not bother to

---

101 O'Farrell, *Things can Only Get Better.*
102 Buck, *Working Capital*, p. 297; Hall, *London Voices*, pp. 57–82.

Localities 121

contest. It remained in control in 1968, one of the few councils not to fall to the Conservatives in that disastrous year for Labour, and quickly reasserted its dominance up until the early 1980s. The 1981 by-election provided the Liberals with a toehold in the borough and they have been in effect the main opposition to the Labour Party since then, with the Conservatives collapsing thereafter. During the last 20 years, Labour has increased the number of its seats on the council from 33 in 1998 to 49 in 2018 and is now in firm control, with the Liberal Democrats reduced to a minority of only 14 seats.

The third kind of area identified were those more socially mixed boroughs like Newham in the East End. The researchers described them as having *'potential,'* using the language employed by estate agents to call areas that were considered to be going 'up in the world.' They had seen an influx of white and ethnic minority households

> who, because of their stage in the life cycle or longer-term level of earnings, are towards the bottom of the home-owner market...It is a world apart from the classic, high-earning professional colonization of more desirable areas such as Battersea...It still bears the heavy imprint of its working-class history

but the sense of loss is much less than that found in Bermondsey.[103] Recent research into the East End has shown that 'the established minority groups have been clawing their way out of the social exclusion to which they were consigned when they, or their parents or grandparents, migrated to the UK two or three generations back,' motivated in part by a strong sense of aspiration for their children, making education a key political issue. Many of these families moved out to the suburbs to increase their chances of improvement, driven by the 'twin processes of gentrification and suburbanisation.'[104] The London Borough of Newham (the old areas of East and West Ham) were again constituencies which formed part of the 'Red Belt' before 1945, covering large parts of the old East End. West Ham had witnessed the election of the first independent Labour MP (Keir Hardie) in 1894 and the first Labour-controlled council soon after.[105] After 1918, the Labour vote in the various constituencies, which represented this dense and highly populated and solidly working-class part of East London (Plaistow, Silvertown, Stratford, Upton; then Newham North and South; now East Ham and West Ham), never fell below 60% and often rose to over 80%. In 2018, 2014 and 2010, the party won all 60 seats on the council (albeit on low turnouts). The swing to Labour in 2018 was 7.5%. The only time it lost to no overall control was in 1968, but normal service was resumed in 1971.

---

103 Buck, *Working Capital*, pp. 300–2; Hall, *London Voices*, pp. 83–126.
104 Butler and Hamnett, *Ethnicity, Class and Aspiration*, p. 240.
105 Marriott, *East of the Tower*.

122   *Thematic*

A fourth kind of area were those described as the *'**Challenged Suburb**.'*
Eltham in south-east London was like many interwar suburbs. In the recent
past, it was predominantly white upper working and middle class. Its mixed
social classes were less inclined to either vote Labour or Conservative. By
the turn of this century, it was 'being settled by groups who are following the
traditional path out of the inner city, seeking more space, a better suburban
environment and better schools for their children.' It is in such areas that
the existing community has faced less traumatic changes elsewhere in its life
and is less in competition with the newcomers for a wide range of resources.
Despite a reputation for racism following the Stephen Lawrence murder, 'it's
experience of transition is less fraught than in other similar suburban areas,'
undergoing more stressful pressures, such as housing decay or crime.[106] The
record of the British National Party and UKIP is poor. The constituency of
Eltham is a marginal Labour seat, where the share of its vote has not dropped
below 42% since 1997. In the election to the Royal Borough of Greenwich in
2014, which includes Eltham, Labour took 43 seats, while the Conservatives
only managed 8 – now par for the course in large swaths of suburban Greater
London where Labour is improving its position after 2015.

A different type of suburb, like Gants Hill, near Ilford in East London, was
described as an *'**Arcadian Suburb Under Pressure**,'* where 'at least in legend and
in fiction, nothing much happens.' For much of the twentieth century, these
areas – 'semi-detached London and its predecessor, the *"Diary of a Nobody"*
rows of late Victorian and Edwardian villas – were inhabited by the white
English middle-class, in its various stations and degrees, living comfortable
lives. They remain rather homogeneous in class terms though less white than
before.' The original Jewish and other white inhabitants of Gants Hill,

> many of whose families moved there from the East End in the 1920s and
> 1930s, were later succeeded by a wave of arrivals from the Indian sub-
> continent, now in their second or third generation, whose families also
> started in the East End slums.[107]

Gants Hill forms part of the London Borough of Redbridge, which Labour
gained for the first time in 2014, winning 35 seats. There are two constituencies
covering north and south Ilford. The Labour vote in Ilford South, the safer of
the two seats, increased from 58% in 1997 to 65% in 2019. Ilford North, which
contains Gants Hill, was a Conservative seat which went Labour in 1997 with
47%. Labour polled 58% in 2017 dropping to 50% in 2019. This drop may have
been the result of the increase in anti-Semitic attacks in the local area and
the controversy over anti-Semitism in the party after 2015 (see Chapter 7).[108]

---

106 Buck, *Working Capital*, pp. 303–6; Hall, *London Voices*, pp. 161–200.
107 Buck, *Working Capital*, pp. 306–7.
108 *Ilford Recorder*, 25 February 2015. See Chapter 7 for a discussion of anti-Semitism.

Localities 123

The sixth and last kind of area was described by the researchers as the '*Dynamic Edge Suburb*,' such as Dartford in Kent on the Thames Estuary. This archetype is best represented by large scale development outside London, though some similarities might be found in the Docklands developments. It is characterised by very rapid physical change: new housing, new roads and new shopping centres. These are not edge cities proper on the American model, like Croydon. Like many other multi-ethnic suburban growth hot spots, Croydon's two northern constituencies are now very safe Labour seats. The council has been Labour-controlled since losing to the Conservatives in 2006. In 2018, the party won 41 seats to the Conservatives 29, one of its best results in a century. This was not the experience in Dartford however, where 'change engulfs smaller settlements and some feel a sense of loss. Disruption, noise, congestion and pollution arise where none has previously existed, and there are crowded roads and schools.'[109] The Kent Thameside economy also includes a substantial manufacturing element, one of the highest proportions in the London region.[110] This makes it similar to many northern working-class seats and unlike many other metropolitan suburbs. Croydon, for instance, has lost much of its manufacturing capacity and has a much larger ethnic population and a greater sense of civic identity.

In political terms therefore, the parliamentary seat of Dartford (given its mix of urban mainly white working-class areas, and suburban and rural middle-class areas) has returned either Labour or Conservative MPs on an alternating basis since 1918. Labour won a spectacular by-election in 1920 on a swing of over 20%. It went Labour again in 1923, 1945 and 1950, but swung strongly to the Conservatives in 1983 and 1987. It swung back to Labour in 1997 on a swing of over 12% when, as we have seen, a large number of London suburbs unexpectedly 'turned red.' Labour held on to it just in 2005, but lost again in 2010. The Conservatives had a majority of over 19,000 in 2019. The borough council remains controlled by the Conservatives with 53% of the vote, holding 29 out of 42 seats, with Labour on only 10. Dartford is perhaps an area, which the researchers considered contained a higher proportion of long-established and elderly residents, who 'can only see what has happened to their locality as a loss,' rather than a higher proportion of newcomers and the young 'that welcome change the most.'[111] It is the former social group who voted to leave the EEC in 2016 and which supported the Conservative Party in 2019. In those other suburban parts of London which had lost nearly all of its manufacturing industries, and which had attracted a younger and more multi-racial population over time, such

---

109 Buck, *Working Capital*, p. 310; Hall, *London Voices*, pp. 235–8.
110 Hall, *London Voices*, p. 239.
111 Buck, *Working Capital*, p. 316.

124 *Thematic*

as Croydon, these social groups voted to remain in the EEC and they voted Labour by increasing margins after 2015.

Conclusion

In terms of the link between geography and politics, one recent study suggests that the electorate in the UK since 1950 has been more influenced by spatial than social polarisation, accounting for the 'class dealignment' of British politics, with suburbanisation in particular, 'shifting the geography of Conservative support.'[112] For others, the suburbs of contemporary London have come to imitate the inner cities of previous decades. The late nineteenth-century strongholds of 'Villa Toryism,' as exemplified by Hackney and Islington, for example, had become by the 1980s 'bedsitter' areas dominated by the political left.[113] The suburbs are now the sites of increasing poverty and ethnic and religious diversities.[114] After the riots in 2011, urban commentators started to refer to suburban Croydon and Ealing as the 'New Inner City.'[115] While boroughs like Hackney and Lambeth have given rise to political cultures influenced by gentrification, the suburbs are now sites of new electoral formations, posing challenges for the left in seeking political alignments which cut across traditional concepts of class and community.[116] Such questions raise the extent to which social class as a determinant of voting behaviour has now been replaced by political values based on new community identities (see Chapter 5 on voting and class). For the period after 1945, new political cultures were forged by the growth of affluence and the effects of class dealignment. A significant proportion of the population of London moved away from inner-city neighbourhoods to the suburbs or to new towns and experienced economic advancement and home ownership for the first time, creating different political cultures at a local level. After the year 2000, the search for community continued in an era characterised by rapid economic changes and where traditional boundaries of place of work or place of residence in metropolitan areas have been extended, made more fragile and where a sense of place (or belonging) has been weakened.[117]

The patterns of residential development in London over the course of the twentieth century present a social geography which is probably unique, if compared to other cities of the UK. In 2007, the urban planner Peter Hall

---

112 Walks, 'City-Suburban Electoral Polarisation in GB,' 500–17; Clapson, *Suburban Century*, pp. 169–90.
113 Baston, 'Rising Damp in the Suburbs.'
114 Dorling, 'Dying Quietly: English Suburbs and the Stiff Upper Lip'; Gilbert, Dwyer and Ahmed, 'Ethnic and Religious Diversity in the Politics of Suburban London.'
115 Huq, *On the Edge*, p. 12.
116 Cruddas, 'The Left's New Urbanism.'
117 Lawrence, *Me, Me, Me*; Dench, Gavron and Young, *The New East End*; Hall, *London Voices, London Lives*.

wrote in *London Voices, London Lives* that London was unique not only because it spreads out at relatively low densities, but that 'it has also achieved a new uniqueness, in being the sole major British city that is again growing.' Hall also emphasised that London 'forms one of the world's greatest magnets to migrants from other parts of the world; one of the very few global cities. These are making it a multi-ethnic, multicultural city that remains unique in Britain, and only comparable with other global cities like New York and Los Angles.'[118] Wilmott and Young characterised the old working-class communities of the East End of London as one based on strong kinship and neighbourhood ties. These bonds depended on close proximity and long residence and were forged by adversity, such as the fear of interwar unemployment and poverty.[119] These areas voted Labour as a means of expressing their class identity ('them and us') during the period described in this book as a municipal social democracy. The experience of the blitz (and the war more generally) also enhanced the status of London's working class (especially in the East End). This made possible the post-war settlement and welfare state, based on feelings of national solidarity and cross-class unity, and a type of moral economy ensuring an equitable distribution of state resources, such as housing and welfare.[120] However, this settlement was already beginning to break down when Wilmott & Young's research was published in 1957. The riots in Notting Hill Gate in 1958 exposed the racial tensions and social changes created by de-industrialisation and immigration after 1948.

The research carried out by Peter Hall 50 years later found that the new working class was struggling to make ends meet, with families needing two incomes to survive, living in polarised neighbourhoods, finding it difficult to get around on public transport and experiencing a severe housing crisis. 'We were in no doubt,' he concluded, 'that simple old-fashioned white racism survives...most strongly in traditional very homogeneous working-class estates in east and south-east London. The people here,' he continued,

> were among the most defensive of all the groups we interviewed. They have suffered from huge economic changes that have destroyed traditional male jobs in docks and factories, bringing structural unemployment and real difficulties for the children (especially boys) in responding to the needs of London's new advanced-service economy. Many such communities are geographically isolated, with a strong shared sense of solidarity: we found them far more like northern English factory towns than parts of a metropolis.[121]

118 Hall, *London Voices, London Lives*, p. 1.
119 Wilmott and Young, *Family and Kinship in East London*.
120 Field, *Blood, Sweat and Toil*.
121 Hall, 'London Voices 1957–2007,' 61.

126   *Thematic*

Such areas may have given rise to a greater tendency for these marginalised groups to vote other than Labour. By 2016, they were more likely to vote for Brexit or to not vote at all.[122] However, this response was not to be found in more multi-racial areas in both inner and outer London, such as Croydon and Lambeth, which showed perhaps a different type of working-class culture and resilience. Research into the Bangladeshi community in the East End, for example, demonstrated the strength of family and community ties in keeping ordinary people in control of their lives, part of a trend which the researchers described as 'Reclaiming Social Democracy.'[123] The well-attended black Pentecostal churches and Islamic centres also promote strong feelings of family and friendship (see Chapter 7 on the influence of religion). This is similar to the kinship ties identified by Willmott and Young in the 1950s (part of a labourist outlook), reflecting perhaps an equally non-party-political or cynical outlook. *London Voices, London Lives* confirmed the cliché that London is still politically apathetic. 'We get a strong sense that many people regarded local politics as a kind of racket monopolised by a small clique, and that the only kind of people who got into politics did so for bad reasons.'[124] The 2015 British Election Survey found that just a third of BAME respondents 'believed their MP would help if they wrote to them about an issue.'[125] This may account for the low membership of black people in political parties (estimated in 2009 as just under 6%).[126] For David Lammy, the black MP for Tottenham, the reason for such cynicism and why there are so few members of the BME population in the Labour Party,

> is due primarily to structural barriers, predominantly to education and employment. If you are black in this country, you are more likely to be racially profiled by the police, unlikely to be admitted to a Russell Group university, and on course for precarious employment waiting for you once school is over. (Combatting racism) is about reducing barriers to capital, to markets, to education.[127]

Yet, the black population of London vote Labour by large and increasing majorities, for reasons not dissimilar perhaps to the way the white working class did in previous generations (see Chapter 7 for further details on the influence of race).

---

122 Evans and Tilley, *The New Politics of Class*; Dorling and Tomlinson, *Rule Britannia*.
123 Dench, Gavron and Young, *The New East End*, p. 232.
124 Hall, 'London Voices,' p. 61.
125 McKeee, 'Signed, Sealed and Delivered ... Testing Politicians' Responsiveness to Voters.'
126 Whiteley, 'Where Have All the Members Gone?' This Percentage Probably Increased after 2015.'
127 Written evidence from David Lammy MP.

5 Voting and social class

Introduction

Class can be a descriptive term reflecting historic changes in the way that individuals are seen by themselves or others within changing social structures, or it can be regarded as 'an agent of change or progression (in the Marxist or Fabian sense).'[1] This chapter adopts the former definition. It will start with a short description of how the tables of election results for Greater London, listed at the end of this chapter to illustrate the links between voting and social class over time, have been compiled. This will be followed by an equally short discussion of the theoretical treatment of class by historians and sociologists. The remaining and more detailed part of the chapter will then go on to explore the relationship between social class and voting in four chronological periods, using Lambeth and Croydon as case studies and the charts of general election results to highlight the continuing importance of class in influencing voting behaviour. The first part ('Class Suppressed 1900–1918') looks at the period before the enactment of the Representation of the People's Act 1918, which widened the franchise in London to a probably greater extent than in other non-metropolitan areas of the country.[2] The second part ('Labourism 1918–1968') explores the growth of class politics after 1918, which was based on a particular type of social outlook defined by labour historians as 'labourism,' and which provided the social base of the municipal social democracy established by the Labour Party in the period 1929–1968.[3] The third part ('Dealignment 1968–1997') discusses the period characterised by Eric Hobsbawn as 'the Forward March of Labour Halted.'[4] The fourth and final part ('Working-Class Remade 1997–2020') examines the way the precariat in modern London now votes Labour as the historic party of the working class.

---

1 Navickas, 'What Happened to Class?,' 202; Cannadine, *The Rise and Fall of Class in Britain*; Lawrence, 'The British Sense of Class,' 307–18.
2 See Table 7 in Appendix.
3 See Chapter 2.
4 See Chapter 3.

128   *Thematic*

By way of introduction, it needs to be stressed that variations in geographical patterns of voting are not just the result of the social geography of particular localities, such as social class or the formation of local housing or labour markets, but reflect the influence of national politics as well. The history of popular politics in the capital cannot be considered in isolation from national political crises, such as, for example, the impact of war (Boer War, world wars, Iraq war), and the financial crises of 1929–1931, 1976 and 2008. The role of London as a capital city and the centre of Empire also cannot be ignored. Patriotic support for the Empire and the monarchy were features of London's political culture from as far back as the eighteenth century (see Chapter 1).[5] The political historian Ross McKibbin has recently pointed out, in response to some of his critics, that the development of party politics in England for the period 1914–1951 needs to take into account the national political crises of 1931 and the defeat of appeasement in May 1940.[6] The sociologist Michael Savage, in response to reviews of his account of the growth of the Labour Party in Preston, also acknowledged that national events influence local patterns of voting, a development which he argued started to increase during the interwar period with the spread of a national popular press and radio.[7] While the Labour vote in London reached a peak in 1929, it declined thereafter as a result of the damage which the Wall Street crash did to Labour Party unity in 1931, leading to the defection of Ramsay MacDonald to form a national Coalition with the Conservatives. The party did not really recover until the domestic impact of the Second World War transformed its political fortunes, although it continued to make steady progress in local elections after it took control of the LCC in 1934.

However, this does not deny the important influence of localities (see Chapter 4). In terms of social class more specifically, most historians of Labour have argued quite correctly, in the case of London at least during the first half of the century, 'that it would be foolish to deny the importance of local social factors such as economic class and tenure in affecting voting patterns.'[8] For the period after the Second World War however, the picture becomes more complex. Traditional class loyalties, identified by historians as 'labourism,' which derived its strength from homogeneous and white working-class neighbourhoods and particular types of gender relationships (the 'Red Belts' described by Eric Hobsbawn), no longer exercised the same degree of influence as they had done during the period of municipal social democracy (1918–1968). By the 1980s, historians acknowledged that 'the Forward March of Labour' had indeed been halted, although they disagreed about whether it was fatal or only an interruption. In the modern era, a new type of class

---

5 Cragoe and Taylor, *London Politics*; Bloom, *Violent London.*
6 McKibbin, *Parties and People*, p. 177.
7 Savage, 'Understanding Political Alignments. Do Localities Matter?'
8 Goss, *Local Labour and Local Government*, p. 143.

Voting and social class 129

consciousness, or indeed a new working class, has emerged which may help to account for the way Londoners voted after 1997.[9] It may also explain why about a third of the electorate (mostly working class) abstain from politics altogether, linked more than likely to levels of economic and social deprivation and a lack of confidence that party politics might represent their interests or make a difference to their lives.[10] This might hark back to earlier explanations of political abstention in London, when the working class in London was characterised as politically apathetic (see Chapter 1), although it should be noted that the franchise was particularly narrow in London before 1914, with the exclusion of many middle-class lodgers and students as well as those male heads of working-class households that could not demonstrate continuity of residence as a result of regular changes of accommodation.

In modern-day London, Labour is no longer an exclusively working-class party, where the middle class now forms a much larger proportion of the total electorate than it did in the past. The capital can no longer be described as a proletarian city in the way that it was before 1914 and during the interwar period. Historically, the party had always attracted a degree of cross-class support, especially from the large 'Black Coated Proletariat' supporting the capital's extensive and growing administrative and public functions following the establishment of the welfare state. The latest opinion polls show that over 50% of social class ABC1 vote Labour in London. The party also attracts the support of nearly 60% of the black and ethnic minority vote. However, it is losing the support of the white working class, which has been shrinking in the capital as a result of the severe loss of manufacturing jobs noticeably in the docks and related industries. Other social factors are also relevant, such as age, housing tenure and level of educational attainment. Age, for example, is now a major determinant of voting intentions, with over 60% of 18- to 49-year olds voting Labour, while the gender balance is about equal.[11] A revival in religious sentiment may now also play a part with the growth of the black Pentecostal churches and Islamic centres after the 1980s (see Chapter 7 for the influence of religion).

Electoral sociologists have employed a variety of different systems of classification for categorising constituencies in terms of their social class and other factors. This chapter will trace these changes over time in order to illustrate the way the socio-economic character of London has been transformed since 1900. For the period 1900–1970, a classification has been used based primarily on social class.[12] After 1970, a classification has been used

---

9 Ainsley, *The New Working Class.*
10 Evans and Tilley, *The New Politics of Class.*
11 YouGov/Queen Mary University London Survey Results (12–15 February 2018).
12 Pelling, *Social Geography of British Elections*; Turner, *British Politics and the Great War,* pp. 472–3 and Appendix A; Llewellyn-Smith, *New Survey of London Life and Labour,* Vol. 3, pp. 343–412 & Vol. 7, pp. 379–462.

130 *Thematic*

based on class, but supplemented by data on ethnicity, housing tenure, level of educational attainment and age.[13] After 1987, the classification adopted by the Office of Population and Census Studies has been used reflecting the growing importance of housing tenure.[14] After 1992, a classification has been used that divides London constituencies into six contrasting areas reflecting the growing importance of race as well as class, deprivation and status.[15] For the particular area examples used in this book, it has also been necessary in some instances to go below the level of constituencies to look at ward level results.[16] The various charts of general election results (starting selectively with December 1910 and finishing with 2017) have been compiled using these different systems of constituency classifications together with the published election results for Greater London. Each chart also gives the percentage turnout; the percentage share obtained by each party, broken down into inner and outer London; and the number of seats contested by each party.[17]

In terms of the theoretical treatment of class, the classic statement of the relationship between social class and voting was made by Butler and Stokes in 1969 when they argued that 'the emergence of Labour as a strong and explicitly class-based party was both cause and consequence of the decline of the religious alignment.' They concluded that the 'transition was accompanied by a fundamental change in the basis of party allegiance, especially the rise of class alignment which has dominated politics for fifty years.'[18] During the last 20 years, historians have sought to adapt this traditional model of electoral sociology to ask more relevant questions about class, community and voting, including the influence of gender, race, popular Conservatism and a type of politics more based on neighbourhood identities than class.[19] Before that, Edward Thompson had charted the way the

---

13 Wilmott and Young, 'Social Class and Geography,' 190–214 and Appendix A; *The Lambeth Inner Area Study*; Rowley, 'The Greater London Council Elections of 1964 and 1967,' 124; Census reports for the Greater London Area, parliamentary constituency tables 1966 to date.

14 Webber, *Parliamentary Constituencies*.

15 Johnston, Rossiter and Pattie, *Three Classifications of Great Britain's New Parliamentary Constituencies*.

16 See, for example, McHugh, *Labour in the City*, pp. 138–46. He distinguishes between business areas; suburban residential areas; socially mixed areas; working-class areas and slum districts.

17 Craig, *British Parliamentary Elections 1885–1918*; Craig, *British Parliamentary Elections 1918–1949*; Craig, *British Parliamentary Elections 1950–1973*; London Data Store, www.data.london.gov.uk/elections. See also Tables 5.12 and 5.13 in the Appendix for a summary of general election results in London compared to the UK for the period 1900–2017. It should be noted that the way in which statisticians define constituencies in terms of social class and other factors does not always coincide with more anecdotal evidence or impressions.

18 Butler and Stokes, *Political Change in Britain*, p. 172.

19 Lawrence and Taylor, 'Electoral Sociology and the Historians,' p. 18; Pugh, 'The Rise of Labour and the Political Culture of Conservatism.'

Voting and social class   131

working class had emerged as a new and clearly self-conscious social formation by the time of Chartism in the 1820s and 1830s.[20] Eric Hobsbawn pointed out in the 1980s that this class, which did not have the vote, was very different 'from the so-called traditional working-class about which cultural observers, sometimes of proletarian parentage like Richard Hoggart, began to write bitter-sweet elegies in the 1950s.' This book is concerned primarily with what Hobsbawn described as the emergence of 'the Andy Capp' working class – a

> proletariat which came to be recognisable not only by its headgear,… but by the physical environment in which they lived, by a style of life and leisure, by a certain class-consciousness increasingly expressed in a secular tendency to join unions and to identify with a class party of Labour.[21]

This definition is perhaps the most relevant in trying to understand the development of the Labour Party in London from about 1918 to the late 1960s, when a mass electorate for the first time started to exercise its right to vote. Distinct working-class communities, or 'red belts,' held together by loyalty to family, neighbours and work colleagues, voted Labour as a sign of their social class.[22] Historians have referred to this political expression of class loyalty as 'Labourism,' or a type of 'reformism' peculiar to the UK, where the trade unions were well-established as respectable and law abiding organisations before the formation of a socialist political party which sought, but did not always succeed in representing their interests.[23] Ralph Miliband was the first to critique 'Labourism' or 'Parliamentary Socialism,' subsequently elaborated in more detail by later commentators and historians.[24] Hobsbawn called this type of class consciousness more simply the working class of 'cup-finals, fish-and-chip-shops, palais-de-danse' and Labour with a 'capital L.' He questioned the extent to which it contracted and changed through what electoral sociologists refer to as the period of 'dealignment,' 'embourgeoisement' or 'affluence' after the Second World War. He argued that such theories were wrong to predict the dissolution of the working class, preferring instead to describe the decline in the number of people voting Labour after 1970 as the 'Forward March of Labour

---

20 Thompson, *The Making of the English Working Class.*
21 Hobsbawn, 'The Making of the Working-Class 1870–1914,' 194.
22 Hobsbawn uses the term 'red belts' to describe labour areas in large metropolitan cities like Berlin, Vienna ('Red Vienna') and London, during the interwar period. See his 'Labour in the Great City.'
23 Marriott, *The Culture of Labourism.*
24 Miliband, *Parliamentary Socialism*; Saville, 'The ideology of Labourism'; Macintryre, *A Proletarian Science*, pp. 47–65; Thompson, *The Long Death of British Labourism*; Elliott, *Labourism and the English Genius.*

132   *Thematic*

Halted.'[25] For Hobsbawn, the post-war secular boom, full employment and mass consumption transformed the lives of working-class people, undermining the strong sense of collectivity forged by poverty and the feeling of 'them and us,' during the first half of the twentieth century. But after 1970, 'prosperity and privatisation broke up what poverty and collectivity in the public place had welded together. The frontier between what was 'manual' and what was 'non-manual' work became 'fuzzy,' diffusing and dissolving 'the formerly clear outlines of "the proletariat."'[26] The meaning of working class had changed but it had not disappeared as hoped for by those politicians (both Labour and Conservative) who have argued since the 1950s, or even earlier that we are living in a classless society.

Theories of class 'dealignment' and the influence of 'affluence' have now been challenged and modified by historians and sociologists who argue that 'electoral sociology' is too reductionist and based on a simplistic assumption that voter interests and identities are predetermined and self-evident.[27] A new orthodoxy has now replaced the old in arguing 'that political values derive from local communities, where they are formed both by local workplace and neighbourhood experiences and by the political, social, economic, religious and recreational networks which underpin them.'[28] Most recently, historians and sociologists have reasserted the importance of social class, maintaining that it has not been destroyed by affluence and the rise of 'individualism' after 1970, but has in fact 'gone underground in twenty-first century Britain,' modified by a decline in deference and more fluid personal identities to mean a more general sense of 'ordinariness' or 'anti-elitism' – a new version, as it were of 'Them and Us.' But in contrast to the era of social democracy, when feelings of class were more self-conscious and more clearly defined, individuals in contemporary London do not necessarily seek with any degree of enthusiasm to define their position in the social hierarchy, particularly if people believe that society no longer holds out the promise of upward social mobility.[29] Interestingly, when polled in 2016, nearly 60% of people considered themselves to be working class even though the size of the manual working class has shrunk.[30]

However, gross inequality and the reduction in social mobility have now revived feelings of collective identity, especially amongst the young. This may help to account, amongst other factors, for why contemporary Londoners vote Labour in a capital city characterised by extreme disparities

---

25 Jacques and Mulhern, *The Forward March of Labour Halted*.
26 Hobsbawn, *Age of Extremes*, pp. 307–10.
27 Savage, 'Understanding Political Alignments in Contemporary Britain: Do Localities Matter?'; Majima and Savage, 'Contesting Affluence,' 445–55.
28 Stevens, 'The Electoral Sociology of Modern Britain Reconsidered.'
29 Sutcliffe-Braithwaite, *Class, Politics and the Decline of Deference*; Savage, *Social Class in the Twenty-First Century*.
30 Evans and Mellon, 'Identity, Awareness and Political Attitudes.'

Voting and social class   133

between rich and poor and where the evidence suggests that social mobility has flattened out if not gone into reverse. Parental background rather than meritocracy now exerts a stronger influence on the academic progress of recent generations of school children.[31] In their most recent book on class and politics in the UK, Evans and Tilley define class in terms of both the changing nature of occupations (secure and insecure), but with a new emphasis on education. They conclude that education shapes values and political preferences differently to occupational class, perhaps reinforcing existing class divisions.[32] Those from higher income groups are still over four times more likely to graduate than those from low income groups. London and other big cities now contain much higher proportions of graduates, who are more inclined to vote than the smaller and less visible working class, which has, according to Evans and Tilley, been left without political representation as both main parties seek to consolidate their support from within a growing middle-class electorate. One recent study of the political orientation of the white working class in the UK and the USA (both declining as a proportion of the total class structure, more so in metropolitan areas) assigns 'working-class status to people who did not complete university degrees.'[33] Such a definition reflects a new approach to understanding the social concept of class, where income and occupation are still relatively important, but where culture and possibly religion now contribute to a better understanding of contemporary class relationships.[34]

Class suppressed (1900–1918)

Before 1914, there were only four Labour MPs elected in London (Bow & Bromley, Deptford, West Ham South and Woolwich) out of 57 constituencies in the area covered by the LCC (not including the two City of London seats), and the 14 constituencies in outer London (Essex, Kent, Middlesex and Surrey).[35] By the time of the second general election in December 1910 (see Table 5.6), London was dominated by a resurgent and popular form of Conservatism and a Liberal Party which was finding it difficult to respond, especially in local elections to the LCC and the new borough councils. In parliamentary elections, fought on different and smaller electoral registers, the Liberals managed to maintain a certain degree of strength. The Labour Party had yet to pose a serious political threat to the strength of working-class Liberalism and Conservatism in London. They were a class party, but

---

31 Blanden and Machin, *Recent Changes in Intergenerational Mobility*; Henehan, 'Pick Up the Pace: The Slowdown in Educational Attainment Growth.'
32 Evans and Tilley, *The New Politics of Class.*
33 Gest, *The White Working Class*, p. 8.
34 Bennett et al., *Culture, Class and Distinction*; Bourdieu, *Distinction.*
35 Hertfordshire is sometimes included in definitions of outer London for this period but has not been included because it was not coterminous with the County of London.

134 *Thematic*

without significant support from the working class itself, apart from a minority of skilled male workers organised in trade unions, or what historians have called 'the Labour Aristocracy.'

Before 1914, Lambeth, for example, contained four parliamentary constituencies – Brixton, Kennington, Norwood and Lambeth North, in comparison to Croydon, which only had one, demonstrating the enormous disparity in population between inner and outer London, partly remedied by the redrawing of boundaries in 1918. They were segregated by class and housing. Both Brixton and Norwood were categorised by the historian Henry Pelling as middle class, given the number of domestic servants recorded in the census for each area. 'There was not much doubt about Norwood, which was the furthest south and the one most distinctly middle-class and suburban in character.'[36] Brixton, however, was much more mixed, with areas like Brixton Hill having pretensions towards 'villadom,' where the electorate was composed of a good proportion of 'City men.' Pelling found evidence of some limited non-conformity, but not sufficient to influence voting intentions, unlike in some of the outer suburbs, such as Croydon, where it played a more important role in forging a local political culture more favourable to organised labour or advanced Liberalism. Brixton did contain a number of congregational churches which attracted young men from the lower middle classes, such as policemen (like Herbert Morrison's father), railway officials and commercial travellers, as well as some of the 'more successful' entertainers of the day, like Charles Chaplin.[37] Some of these young men tended to hold more left-leaning views on Liberalism and socialism.[38] But the majority of those with the vote consistently voted Conservative in parliamentary elections, apart from in the Liberal landslide in 1906, and like middle-class Norwood, continued to do so after 1918 and up until the late 1950s.

Kennington however was categorised by Pelling as a mixed constituency which 'contained a good many railway men and potters' but they were outnumbered by a considerable middle-class population, living in areas close to Clapham.[39] Like Brixton, it went Liberal in 1906 and in both 1910 elections. In contrast, Lambeth North contained 'numerous blots of extreme poverty.' Pelling suggested that

> the complexion of the constituency was increasingly Conservative...a phenomenon to be explained largely by the growth of shop and industrial property at the expense of working-class accommodation, but possibly also by the appeal of Tariff reform to the workers in the local

36 Pelling, *Social Geography of British Elections*, pp. 34 & 55.
37 Donoghue and Jones, *Morrison*, pp. 3–5; David Robinson, *Chaplin*, p. 5.
38 Argent, *The Angels' Voice*.
39 Pelling, *Social Geography*, p. 39.

Voting and social class 135

industries, especially the 4,000 employees of the pottery works owned by the Conservative Sir Henry Daulton.[40]

The introduction of tariffs to protect industry and agriculture, including giving preference to the Empire, was a policy which very badly split the Conservative and Unionist Party at this time. In contrast, the Liberal Party and their Lib-Lab allies in London were staunch defenders of free trade (almost as a matter of faith) to keep the cost of imported food as low as possible for the working class. Support for the Empire however was a policy that permeated the politics of Victorian and Edwardian London and influenced all political parties, unable to ignore the hold which patriotic support for imperialism had across all classes.[41]

Class may have been a more influential factor in local elections, which were fought on a larger register containing many plural votes and women linked with their husband's enfranchisement. In the first election to the new Metropolitan Borough of Lambeth in 1900, the Conservatives (known as the Municipal Reform Party) won 35 of the 60 seats, picking up wards mainly in Brixton and Norwood, but also in the north of the borough, with the remainder going to the Progressives. Independent socialist candidates (SDF or ILP) stood in Bishop's and Princes wards in Lambeth North polling only 4% and 19%, respectively.[42] In the School Board elections a few weeks later, the Socialist Harry Quelch, a leading member of the SDF, obtained 4,159 votes in the Lambeth East Division, a quite respectable vote but he was still defeated by three Progressives and one Conservative.[43] The Lambeth and District Trades and Labour Council complained in 1904 that it had been a 'black year' for 'the labour interest independent of either Progressive or Moderate.'[44] This poor record continued up until the eve of the First World War with the Conservatives gaining the upper hand in local elections, as they did across London at the expense of the Liberals. In November 1906, just a few months after the Liberal landslide in the general election of that year, the Conservatives reduced the Progressives to only four seats on the Council although the first Labour Councillor (Charles Iremonger, a member of the Iron Founders Society and the ILP) was elected in Vauxhall ward.[45]

In 1909, the Conservatives won 52 seats, the Progressives only 6 and Labour 2 (Charles Iremonger and William Bishop). This was the first election when women were no longer disqualified from standing (Qualification of Women Act 1907) and two female Progressive councillors were elected in

40 Ibid., p. 50.
41 Windscheffel, 'In Darkest Lambeth,' 191.
42 *Times,* 3 November 1900; Woollard and Willis, *Twentieth Century Local Election Results.* Vol. 3, p. 32.
43 *Times,* 1 December 1900. The School Boards were abolished in 1902 and elementary education became the responsibility of the LCC.
44 MRC – MSS524/4/1/3 – Annual Report 1904.
45 *Times*, 3 November 1906.

136 *Thematic*

Lambeth – Dr Annie McCall and Miss Pearson. The Progressives fought the election on a radical programme, including the taxation of land values as a means of relieving the rate burden, slum clearance and reform of the Poor Law, while the Municipal Reformers fought on a programme of austerity, opposed to what they saw as the Progressive-Socialist attempts 'to capture the borough councils and to use them as a means of establishing Socialism.'[46] Land taxation featured again in the local elections in November 1912, at the height of Lloyd George's Land Campaign, when the Conservative consolidated their hold on London and the Progressives were nearly wiped out at a time of widespread industrial unrest in the docks and in transport, and militant action by the suffragettes.[47]

The Progressives did not fare any better in elections to the LCC, finally losing overall control in 1907 after nearly 20 years in power. Up to then, they had captured all four LCC divisions in Lambeth (corresponding to the parliamentary constituencies) in 1901 with over 55% of the vote. In 1910 and 1913, the Municipal Reformers captured Brixton and Norwood, but with the Progressives holding on to Kennington and Lambeth North on both occasions, even though Labour polled 14% and 32%, respectively, in these two northern divisions, facing accusations of splitting the Progressive vote. *The Times* had warned in 1913 that the 22 socialists standing in London as a whole 'of whom 10 are Labour, 7 are Progressives and 6 are Independent Socialists' could be 'sufficiently strong enough to dominate the situation.' Needless to say, a few days later it was relieved to report a Municipal Reform victory, including the election of two aristocrats in Kennington, Lord Peel (grandson of the Sir Robert Peel), a former Municipal Reform leader and Sir John Benn (grandfather of Tony Benn), a former Progressive leader, while the Labour candidate, John Dale, a prominent scientist and founder of the National Union of Police and Prison Officers (NUPPO), could only manage 8% of the vote.[48] But in so doing, the *Times* drew attention to the fact that 'of the 803,698 names on the register (in London), many are registrants of the same individuals two or three times over, but the actual number cannot be ascertained.'[49] Plural voting in local elections was not finally abolished until 1945 and it helped guarantee middle-class domination of local elections up to 1913 and to a more limited extent thereafter.[50]

In parliamentary elections, where the size of the electorate was smaller, the working-class seat of North Lambeth was held by the Liberal Party in 1892 when the famous explorer Henry Morton Stanley, standing as a Liberal Unionist, was defeated by just 130 votes. His imperial credentials formed a

---

46 *Times*, 12 & 30 October & 3 November 1909.
47 *Times*, 2 November 1912.
48 John Gilbert Dale (1869–6 March 1926) was a scientist who founded the National Union of Police and Prison Officers (NUPPO).
49 *Times*, 28 February & 8 March 1913.
50 Keith-Lucas, *The English Local Government Franchise*, p. 235.

Voting and social class   137

vital part of his election appeal and again in 1895 when he won the seat by a slim majority. He argued that

> the indigenous trades in North Lambeth – india-rubber, pottery and varnish – would benefit immeasurably from imperial expansion and exploitation...and when asked his opinion on the eight-hour day, he reportedly retorted that if he had worked 8 hours a day he would never have been ahead of the Germans in Africa. He would never have added 200,000 square miles of territory to this country.[51]

When the famous explorer announced his retirement in 1898, the Liberal and Radical Association in North Lambeth adopted Colonel Charles Ford, who had been an imperial volunteer in South Africa, in preference to Frank Smith, a Christian Socialist and close friend of Kier Hardie, who had already been elected as a Progressive to the LCC for Lambeth North in 1892.[52] Ford campaigned on the issue of 'housing of the workers' as well as highlighting his own imperialist credentials, boasting on his election leaflet that 'his flesh and blood helped to keep the flag up in Pretoria.' He was in favour of temperance reform and the disestablishment of the Church of England. While Stanley studied 'Darkest Africa,' he had studied 'Darkest London.'[53] As a Progressive on the LCC, Colonel Ford was supported by the local Gas Workers Union, the Amalgamated Society of Railway Servants and the United Builders Labourers Union. But despite his advocacy for workmen's train fares and the principle of manhood suffrage, he lost to the Conservatives in the Khaki Election of 1900, when the small mainly working-class electorate (but not disenfranchised slum dwellers) voted Conservative at the height of patriot fervour for the Boer War, especially after the relief of Mafeking, which prompted wild celebrations in the streets of London.

The voters of North Lambeth, like their counterparts in similar wards in other metropolitan cities such as Liverpool and Manchester, tended to vote Conservative influenced by the politics of imperialism rather than the values espoused by the organised Labour movement. The local evidence from these areas suggests that before 1914 the Labour Party drew its electoral strength from wards that were predominantly made up of more 'respectable' workers organised into trade unions and cooperative societies, and able to afford better housing. The relationship between housing conditions and voting is not clear cut, and local studies of voting patterns for this period take into account other factors such as age and religion.[54] The borough of

---

51 *Daily News*, 25 June 1892.
52 *South London Press*, 12 November 1898.
53 *Daily Chronicle*, 9 November 1898. See the papers of Charles Ford, Lambeth Archives (IV 206).
54 Davies, *Liverpool Labour*, pp. 197–232; McHugh, *Labour in the City*, pp. 137–46. For a smaller industrial town like Preston, see Savage, *The Dynamics of Working-Class Politics*.

138   *Thematic*

Lambeth contained electoral wards which might be best categorised as either suburban/residential (Norwood and parts of Brixton), socially mixed (Brixton and parts of Kennington) or as slum areas (North Lambeth and parts of Kennington). It did not contain wards which were either mainly business areas (which in the case of London were concentrated in the City or parts of the West End), or could be described as made up predominantly of the respectable working class, although such wards did exist in other areas of the capital like Battersea, Woolwich and Poplar, where organised Labour was stronger. As a result of this social segregation, the Conservative Party before 1914 won the majority of the Lambeth constituencies, with the Liberals only recording a success in Brixton and Lambeth North in the landslide election of 1906. Up to 1906, the Conservatives faced no opposition in Brixton and Norwood, where their Progressive opponents did not consider it worthwhile to contest the seats.

In the two bitterly fought general elections in 1910, during the constitutional crisis on Lloyd George's 'People's Budget,' the Conservatives easily held Norwood and regained Brixton, a marginal seat by this date. In the two northern seats, the Liberals held on to Kennington, with a majority of only 381 votes in January, and easily held off the challenge of the maverick socialist Victor Grayson in December, who lost his deposit polling only 400 votes before disappearing into obscurity.[55] In Lambeth North Harry Gosling, the General Secretary of the Amalgamated Society of Watermen, Lightermen and Bargemen (forerunner of the T&GWU) narrowly lost to the Conservatives, a defeat which demonstrated the continuing difficulty which organised labour in London had in countering the strength of popular Conservatism in working-class seats. Social class in London did not guarantee support for independent labour in boroughs like Lambeth, where the size of the electorate and the influence of Empire counted against it. Before 1914, the electorate (whether middle or working class) for all types of elections voted Conservative or Progressive. Independent Labour or socialist candidates fared very badly. Candidates sponsored by trade unions in Lambeth remained part of an alliance of radical Liberals and Fabians which made up the Progressive Party on the LCC and the new metropolitan borough councils established in 1900.

'Labourism' (1918–1968)

As we have seen, the First World War transformed the fortunes of the Labour Party in London. In terms of social class, the war undermined the legitimacy and role of charitable organisations in supporting the deserving

---

55 Victor Grayson had been sensationally elected as an independent socialist in a by-election in 1907 for Colne Valley, but lost this seat in January 1910, and then mysteriously disappeared in 1920.

Voting and social class 139

poor and enhanced a more assertive and confident type of working-class consciousness. The extension of the parliamentary franchise to all men aged over 21 and women aged over 30, made to some extent irresistible by the war itself, gave the working class the vote on a scale not thought possible before 1914, introducing class voting and mass democracy for the first time. Fearful of the outcome, Lloyd George called a general election as soon as the war ended in November 1918 to be held on Saturday, 14 December, the first to include on a single day all eligible voters. In the event, this was a highly effective move. On a low turnout before the army had been fully demobilised, the Coalition (without the Labour Party's involvement) was returned by a massive majority. As a result, the outcome of the general election in London was no different to that of December 1910 (see Table 5.7), with only four seats won, some without opposition from Progressive candidates giving Labour a free-run. This tactic still held out the possibility of a Progressive alliance with the Liberals, a strategy advocated by the parliamentary leadership before 1914, but not by a significant majority of the rank and file of the party.

In later years, Herbert Morrison argued that the 1918 general election result was a fluke which under-estimated the true class strength of Labour in London immediately after the war, hidden by the low turnout of new voters and demobilised soldiers. 'Less than 25% of the armed forces voted and less than 60% of the whole electorate.'[56] But in the circumstances of post-war hysteria, when Labour was identified with the Revolution in Russia and as pro-German in the popular press, the Conservatives retained middle-class Brixton and Norwood in Lambeth on behalf of the Lloyd George Coalition, capturing over 60% of the vote. But in the more socially mixed constituency of Kennington, a Coalition Liberal defeated an independent Conservative with only 42% of the vote after the Labour candidate William Glennie, sponsored by the Amalgamated Society of Engineers (AEU), secured a respectable 25% poll. This was a foretaste of future elections to come.

In 1922 after the collapse of the post-war Coalition government, Kennington was again contested by Labour. The candidate was the suffragist Mrs Ayrton Gould but she was defeated by the Liberal Frank Briant polling only 17% of the vote. To add insult to injury, Sir John Benn, the Progressive leader on the LCC before 1914, defeated Harry Gosling in a by-election to the LCC for Lambeth North in the same year. At a local level, the Progressives had formed an understanding with Labour in Kennington, unusual in the London context, causing consternation within Labour ranks. Gosling had been selected as the official Labour Party candidate and the party had ruled out any electoral arrangement with the Liberals after the war.[57] Labour finally took the parliamentary seat in 1923 when another middle-class candidate, Thomas Williams (a physician who had served as a Lieutenant-Colonel in

56 Coates and Topham, *The Making of the Labour Movement*, p. 689.
57 Weinbren, 'Building Communities, Constructing Identities,' 42 and fn. 5.

140   *Thematic*

the Indian Medical Service during the war), won a three-way contest with 40% of the vote, another sign of future election results to come. By this date, the political fortunes of working-class Liberalism, relatively strong before the war, had begun its slow decline to be finally replaced by a class-based Labour Party during the 1930s.

Such three-way contests helped Labour get established in London by splitting the anti-socialist vote. When the Liberals contested far more seats in the 1929 general election, for example, Labour did particularly well, able to form a minority government for the second time in a decade. This was Labour's best result during the interwar period, dominant in areas defined as predominantly working-class.[58] Labour also broke through in mixed-class areas like Fulham, Hammersmith and Islington, and even in some areas defined as middle-class such as Acton and Willesden. They reduced the Liberals to just two seats in Bethnal Green, where the ever-popular Percy Harris continued to attract working-class support (see Table 5.8).[59] However, in middle-class suburbs like Croydon, which contained only a small and geographically segregated working class, concentrated in only one or two wards, Labour could make little headway in an area undergoing rapid suburbanisation, and where class interests were represented by a powerful Ratepayers Association at a local level and by the Conservative Party in parliamentary elections. In the case of Croydon, the link between social class and voting was very pronounced. The suburban middle classes guaranteed Conservative domination, while Labour could only count on a small and diminishing proportion of the working-class electorate. But its limited performance also came to rely on a growing proportion of middle-class voters, attracted to the policies and values of the party in the absence of Liberal Party candidates in parliamentary elections. In fact, Croydon provides an example of a Labour Party which was far more middle-class in social composition in comparison to some of the inner London parties. This was a feature of suburban London during the interwar period.[60] In local elections, the Ratepayers Association was successful in defending the property interests of its growing suburban population of owner-occupiers.

The extension of the franchise in 1918 swelled the number of voters in Croydon to 88,784 (an increase of nearly 150%) for parliamentary elections,

---

58 *The New Survey of London Life and Labour* (1932–1934) classified the social composition of the London boroughs as follows: *Working Class*: (more than 80% poverty + unskilled + skilled) – Bethnal Green, Shoreditch, Stepney, Bermondsey, Poplar, Deptford, Greenwich, Woolwich, Barking, East Ham, Leyton, Tottenham, Walthamstow, West Ham, Finsbury, North Lambeth, Southwark, Fulham, Hammersmith, Islington, St Pancras, Battersea, Camberwell; *Mixed Class*: (more than 25% but less than 35% middle class) – Hackney, Lewisham, Stoke Newington, South Lambeth, Wandsworth; *Middle Class:* (only in the Western Area and more than 35% middle class) – Holborn, Westminster, Chelsea, Hampstead, Kensington, Paddington, St Marylebone, Hornsey.

59 Harris, *Forty Years In and Out of Parliament.*

60 Tanner, 'Labour and Its Membership.'

Voting and social class 141

Table 5.1 Croydon electorate 1915 and 1918 compared

1915			1918							
Consti-tuencies	Lodgers	Total	Consti-tuencies	Parliamentary			Local government			Service vote
				Men	Women	Total	Men	Women	Total	
CROYDON	1,593	31,009	Croydon North	25,263	18,406	43,669	17,011	18,260	35,271	9,937
			Croydon South	26,217	18,898	45,115	16,872	18,885	35,757	10,190
Totals		31,009		51,480	37,304	88,784	33,883	37,145	71,028	20,127

Sources: Compiled from Census Return Relating to Parliamentary Constituencies (February 1915) Cd. 120; Parliamentary and Local Government Electors (18 November 1918) Cd. 138.

and 71,028 for local elections. After 1918, Croydon's electorate was increasingly made up of a 'a variegation of City workers, with commuters to the fore, many at the managerial level but with clerks and typists lower down the social scale, alongside medium and small local businessmen.'[61]

The local government electoral register for 1918 included unmarried women and widows on the same terms as men, as well as women married to male voters and plural business voters. Many lodgers were denied the vote through stricter residency requirements than for the parliamentary register. Local elections therefore were more influenced by social class than for parliamentary contests, with a clear bias towards the middle classes, including business interests who had more than one vote.[62] During the debate on the Representation of the People Bill in 1917, the London Labour Party campaigned to enfranchise the 'Lodger Vote,' arguing that without it 'the power of "property" would be intensified in municipal elections.'[63] Local elections in Croydon resumed in December 1918. On a low turnout, Labour won a seat in South Norwood and North wards but lost in West ward, despite it being recognised 'as strong for Labour.'[64] By this date, the Ratepayers Association had grown into 'a formidable political machine,' known locally as 'The Association.'[65] New wards were created in 1921 as the population of commuters expanded. They became safe areas for ratepayers' interests. 'The Association' ended up controlling 50 out of 56 seats on the council. Labour gained ten seats in 1923 but was reduced back to five in 1926 against the national trend of steady improvement elsewhere. Labour collapsed badly

61 Davies and Morley, *County Borough Elections in England and Wales*, Vol. 3, p. 147.
62 See Table 5.4 in the Appendix for a comparison between 1915 and 1918 for Greater London.
63 *London Labour Party Circular*, July 1917.
64 *Croydon Advertiser*, 8 November 1919.
65 Davies and Morley, *County Borough Elections*, p. 147.

142 *Thematic*

in 1931, with its poll falling to only 25%. It recovered thereafter to reach a peak of 46% in 1937. But throughout the interwar years, it could not make any serious headway against the almost total domination of the Ratepayers Association, which represented an anti-Labour Coalition of Conservatives and Liberals.[66] The local Liberals clearly identified themselves as an anti-socialist force. 'The Liberal Party has no sympathy with the socialist cause,' wrote the editor of *Common Sense*, the magazine of the Croydon Liberal Party, 'but it does sympathise with the causes of socialism.'[67] This was very different to the pre-war situation where Labour demonstrated a much higher level of support.[68]

In terms of social geography, all the new wards created in the north of the borough in 1921, where the population of commuters was mostly concentrated, were middle-class and mainly strongholds of the Ratepayers Association. 'Labour's main area of potential support was in a small number of wards mostly near to the town centre.'[69] Unfortunately for the party, the absence of any large-scale factories and concentrated trade union organisation meant that it only had a base in two wards, insufficient to pose a real challenge. Lack of trade union candidates and finance for local elections was also a problem.[70] However, the growth of light engineering and other industrial developments towards the west of the town centre during the 1930s, along the Purley Way in Thornton Heath and Waddon, increased the size of the working-class electorate, as did the addition of the new ward of New Addington on the south-east outskirts of the borough in 1928, which after the war developed as an area of public housing. While such developments created new potential for Labour after 1945, it was not sufficient to challenge the continuing dominance of the Ratepayers Association. In parliamentary elections after 1918, Labour fared little better. By the end of the 1930s, the two Croydon constituencies formed part of the great swathe of suburban areas in London that voted Conservative, as can be seen in the result of the 1935 general election (see Table 5.9). By this date, Labour had replaced the Liberal Party as the main opposition to the Conservatives, winning seats in most areas defined as working class, as well as a handful of seats in the inner northern districts of the capital which were becoming increasingly socially mixed, such as Hackney and Islington. The Liberals had been reduced to only two constituencies: North Southwark and Bethnal Green South West.

The Second World War transformed the fortunes of the Party, the result of a combination of state intervention, working-class support for the war and the growth in the influence of the trade unions (see Chapter 2). The swing to Labour in London was much higher than elsewhere, making it one

66 Ibid., p. 151; Steel, *'True Blue'? The Political Representation of Croydon 1918–1931*, p. 2.
67 *Common Sense. Croydon Liberal Association*, January 1926, p. 6.
68 Tichelar, 'Labour Politics in Croydon.'
69 Davies and Morley, *County Borough Elections*, p. 150.
70 Ibid., p. 156.

Voting and social class 143

of the strongest regions in the country. It did particularly well in the middle-class suburbs (see Table 5.10), fulfilling the ambition of Herbert Morrison in winning over not just the 'black coated proletariat,' but a large swathe of middle-class opinion as well. Labour won Croydon South with a majority of 3,500, on a swing of nearly 25%. It very narrowly lost Croydon North by only 607 votes, with a popular local candidate Marion Billson, a local solicitor. (If an uncounted box of service votes had been taken into account, it may well have won.) Croydon North returned to being a relatively safe Conservative seat in a by-election in 1948, when a candidate imposed by Head Office, the upper-class diplomat Harold Nicolson, lost by nearly 12,000 votes. The constituency of Croydon South was abolished in 1950, replaced by two new seats (East and West), given the growth in the size of the electorate. Croydon East became a relatively safe seat for the Conservatives, while Croydon West was marginal, until the boundaries were re-drawn again in 1955.

After the Second World War, and despite a growth in its working-class population of skilled and semi-skilled engineers, Croydon remained a predominantly lower and middle-class suburb, with only pockets of support for Labour in areas characterised by local authority housing and small-scale industry, mainly light engineering. The sociologist Terrence Morris undertook a detailed survey of the borough in the early 1950s as part of a study on delinquency and social class. One of his reasons for choosing Croydon was the notorious criminal case of the 'Craig and Bentley affair.' In 1952, two teenagers were arrested for the murder of a police officer during the petty burglary of a sweet shop. The older of the two (Bentley) was sentenced to death for shouting to the younger boy (Craig) 'Let him have it Chris.' What interested the sociologist was that the boys came from

> decent middle-class homes where their parents would have been mortally ashamed of any trouble with the police…Craig was not the son of an unskilled labourer but of a bank clerk; his home was not a slum or a council housing estate but was in a highly respectable district from which other white collar workers went up to the city every day.[71]

While his sociological conclusions are now outdated, his detailed survey provides an excellent snap shot of Croydon in the early 1950s, broken down by ward and categorised by social class, housing tenure, land use, condition of property, political composition and rateable value (see Table 5.2). It demonstrates quite clearly the social differences within the borough and the reason for the Labour Party's difficulty in this suburb of London, before its centre became the site of an office building boom after 1956. The wards with large council estates (Addington, Broad Green and Waddon) are identified as Labour, and those undergoing a deterioration in the condition of its

---

71 Morris, *The Criminal Area*, p. 108.

Table 5.2 Social and economic characteristics of Croydon in the 1950s

Ward	Class	Land use	Period of development	Condition of property	Political composition	Persons per acre
Upper Norwood	M & LM	Residential	1889–1914	Well maintained	Ratepayer	18.3
Norbury *	M & LM	Residential	1910–1940	Well maintained	Ratepayer	28.5
West Thornton	M & LM	Residential & some industry	1910–1930	Well maintained	Ratepayer	35.5
Bensham Manor	M & LM	Residential	1900–1920	Well maintained	Ratepayer	46.9
Thornton Heath	LM & W	Residential & small industrial units	1890–1920	Deteriorating since 1940	Marginal	42.2
Bensham Manor	M & LM	Residential	1900–1920	Well-maintained	Ratepayer	46.9
Thornton Heath	LM & W	Residential & small industrial units	1890–1920	Deteriorating since 1940	Marginal	42.2
South Norwood	M, LM & W	Residential & small industrial units	1880–1914	Generally, well maintained but some deterioration	Ratepayer	28.9
Woodside	LM & W	Residential with large industrial unit	1870–1914	Deterioration since 1940	Labour	34.1
East	UM & M	Residential	1920–1940	Well maintained	Ratepayer	15.2
Addiscombe	LM & W	Residential & small industrial units	1880–1914	Some deterioration since 1940	Marginal	45.4
Addington *	UM & W	Residential	1930 +	Well maintained	Labour	4.9
Shirley	UM & M	Residential	1930–1950	Well maintained	Ratepayer	8.1
Whitehorse Manor	W	Residential & small industrial units	1870–1900	Badly bombed –deteriorating	Labour	41.1
Broad Green *	W	Residential with large industrial units	1870–1930	Deteriorating	Labour	42.6
Central	W & LM	Commercial with some residential	Roman times +	Commercial, well maintained residential deteriorating	Marginal	28.5
Waddon *	LM & W	Residential with largest industrial units	1920–1930	Well maintained	Labour	22.0
South	LM & W	Residential & small industrial units	1870–1914	Well maintained	Ratepayer	12.1

Key Class – UM = Upper Middle; M = Middle; LM = Lower Middle; W = Working Class.
Source: Adapted from Morris, *The Criminal Area*, p. 117.
* *Ward with large council estate*

Table 5.3 Differences in voting between areas where immigration was an important factor (1959 & 1964)

Constituencies	1959 % majority	1964 % majority
London Battersea South	Con. 6.0	Lab. 6.2
Brixton	Lab. 6.2	Lab. 16.2
Clapham	Con. 4.4	Lab. 1.4
Deptford	Lab. 23.9	Lab. 33.3
Holborn & St Pancras South	Con. 2.0	Lab. 9.4
Islington East	Lab. 15.1	Lab. 24.0
Kensington North	Lab. 2.6	Lab. 8.1

Source: Adapted from A W Singham, 'Immigration and the election' in D. Butler & A King, *The British General Election of 1964*, p. 361.

properties (Thornton Heath and Central) as marginal. The survey confirms the links made by other studies of voting and social class in London at this time between support for labour, housing tenure and 'labourism.'

By the time of the 1964 general election, the question of race in inner London had assumed a growing political significance, as it had done in other areas of high immigration such as Birmingham, Bradford and Manchester. The British General Election Study of 1964 provided for the first time a separate chapter on 'Immigration and the Election.' This showed the following different trends in voting between 1959 and 1964 in those constituencies where immigration was important, either because of its influence on the white vote or the size of the immigrant vote itself (see Table 5.3).

However, class remained an important determinant of voting Labour in London as demonstrated by the result of the 1966 general election. Inner London continued to be a stronghold of the party as it had been in 1945 (see Table 5.11 compared to Table 5.10). The BME community was predominantly working-class, especially the Afro-Caribbean population, less so some fractions of the Asian population, who were moving up the social scale.

Dealignment (1968–1997)

For most historians and sociologists, it is now a truism to argue that the link between class and voting began to decline after the Second World War in the UK, perhaps more so in London than elsewhere. Furthermore, inner-city boroughs like Lambeth saw a steady reduction in turnout for all types of elections, indicating a degree of apathy or disillusionment with party politics in an era of two-party domination where voters could not always distinguish between the programmes of their respective parties.[72] For local elections in Brixton, turnout dropped from 40% in 1949 to only 27% by 1961.

72 Turner, *Labour's Doorstep Politics in London*; Sharpe, *A Metropolis Votes.*

146   *Thematic*

The turnout for Vauxhall was lower still, averaging only 20% after 1955. Turnout was always higher in Norwood than in the more working-class districts of the borough and the local Conservatives complained that low polls favoured Labour in these areas. Labour never lost control of the council in Lambeth from 1937 to 1968, winning by large majorities in what had become by the 1960s a safe inner-London borough, with the overall population becoming more working-class and multi-ethnic. However, the first signs of a break in the pattern of two-party domination were in 1968 when the Conservatives swept to power in London at the height of the unpopularity of Wilson's second Labour Government in 1968 ('the pound in your pocket has not been devalued'), and just a few days after Enoch Powell's notorious 'River of Blood' speech. In all, Labour lost 431 seats in London polling only 28%.[73] The Conservatives took control of Lambeth gaining 43 seats (all from Labour) with the Liberals only polling 2.6%. The future prime minister, John Major, was elected at the age of 21 for the Ferndale Ward in Brixton becoming the chair of the housing committee. He pursued a 'one-nation' Conservative agenda in seeking to improve the borough's appalling housing conditions.[74] However, the position was reversed in 1971 when Labour won 871 seats in London on a poll of 52%. Labour regained control of Lambeth winning 56 seats to the Conservative's 14 and the Liberals declined to under 2% of the vote. The period of two-party domination reasserted itself to the dismay in London of those politicians who dreamed of a return to Progressive politics. They had to wait until the early 1980s before the formation of the SDP injected new life into the project.

In the meantime, a new generation of younger and more radical Labour councillors were elected after 1971 setting the scene for a conflict between the old guard who controlled the party at a regional level, and whose power-base was mainly in the blue-collar trade unions and the Royal Arsenal Cooperative Society. This close relationship between the cooperative, industrial and political wings of the Labour movement had been carefully fostered by Herbert Morrison during the interwar period. Morrison created a highly effective electoral machine under tight central control, attracting accusations of 'Tammany Hall' politics. Although he was in the forefront of rooting out corruption in local government, the machine he had created as the capital's most powerful 'City-Boss' had started to become too rigid and sclerotic by the 1960s.[75] But this machine politics began to breakdown after 1970 as Herbert Morrison's generation started to age and as the local party structures started to decay in the face of population change and de-industrialisation, with a corresponding decline in the influence of the blue-collar trade unions. The new generation of more radical Labour councillors

73 See Tables 5.15 and 5.16 in the Appendix for detailed results.
74 Major, *The Autobiography*.
75 *Times*, 24 September 1973.

Voting and social class   147

was perhaps best illustrated in Lambeth when the newly elected Tony Banks (Angel Ward) took down a picture of the Queen in the Town Hall and put it under a sofa. 'It might seem very flippant,' he told the press, 'but these gestures are, I hope, going to be symptomatic of the more positive things Lambeth Council is going to do.'[76] In 1971, Tony Banks was re-elected along with Ken Livingstone (Knights Hill Ward), who was then joined by Ted Knight and the barrister and civil rights activist Rudy Narayan in 1974.[77]

The example of Lambeth, and other inner-city boroughs like Hackney, supports the view that the period after 1970 was one of class dealignment. Other socio-economic factors need to be taken into account in discussing the way voting behaviour changed. After 1970, parliamentary constituencies start to be classified using criteria still based on class (working, mixed and middle), but taking into account 'status' and the way metropolitan areas saw the growth of 'poorer urban centres and peripheral council estates on their outskirts.'[78] The result of the February 1974 general election show London still divided by class in terms of voting, and with Labour making inroads into the outer ring of mixed and working-class suburbs (see Table 5.12). By this date, the Greater London Council had been established and the distinction between inner and outer London removed for recording election results. By 1979, this pattern of class voting continued but with Labour losing any gains it had made in the outer ring of mixed and middle-class suburbs, high-status metropolitan boroughs like Paddington and outer ring middle-class suburbs like Ealing North. Metropolitan low status constituencies like Acton, Fulham and Streatham still contained historic areas of middle-class support for the Conservatives (see Table 5.12); but by 1997, these had also largely disappeared, swamped by population change.

Working-class remade (1997–2020)

By the time of the 1997 general election, constituencies in London were defined in terms of inner and outer London immigrant concentrations, mixed inner-city seats and seats categorised as middle Britain, middle-class or high status.[79] If we take Lambeth as an example, Dulwich and West Norwood and Streatham changed from 'Metropolitan – Low Status' to 'Mixed Inner-City Area' reflecting the social upgrading associated with gentrification; and Vauxhall changed from 'Metropolitan – Low Status' to 'Inner London Immigrant Concentration,' reflecting the boundary changes which absorbed Brixton and Stockwell into Vauxhall. As we have seen in Chapter 1, these changes reflected a process of gentrification, which started

---

76 *Times*, 14 July 1971.
77 www. London Data Store Election Results.
78 Wilmott and Young, 'Social Class and Geography,' 190–214.
79 Johnston, Rossiter and Pattie, *Three Classifications of Great Britain's New Parliamentary Constituencies.*

148　*Thematic*

slowly and then accelerated after 1990, with significant increases in higher status occupational groups, immigrant concentrations, younger age groups with higher levels of educational attainment. The result of the 1997 general election using these new constituency classifications shows support for the Labour Party across all social classes ('When the Suburbs Turned Red') as was the case in 1945 (see Table 5.13).

For the period after 1997, the data for socio-economic groups in Lambeth show a dramatic increase in managerial occupations in the period 2001–2011 – in Dulwich and West Norwood from 14% to 32%, in Streatham from 14% to 30% and in Vauxhall from 14% to 33%, while the figures for the London region as a whole were 12%–26%. The figures for intermediate groups remained stable between 23% and 28%, while semi- and unskilled groups showed slight increases from about 8% to 9%.[80] There was a big rise in the number of residents with higher level qualifications.[81] The figures for ethnicity show the black population in the three constituencies stabilising at around 27% by 2011, indicating the outward movement of black citizens to the suburbs, such as Croydon, while there was a small increase in the Asian population. The proportion of residents defining as white continued to decline (approaching under 50%) while those defining as mixed race grew demonstrating a significant process of integration. The figures for housing tenure perhaps show the most dramatic changes reflecting the squeeze on the housing market arising from the impact of 'Right to Buy' after 1980 and following the financial crises of the 1990s and the crash of 2008. The proportion of those owning their houses outright dropped from about 16% to 14% in Dulwich and West Norwood and Streatham, and those with a mortgage from 29% to 25%. In Vauxhall, the figures show a small increase for outright ownership (from 8% to 9%), indicating the boom in luxury accommodation on the waterfront, while those with a mortgage dropped from 18% to 17% reflecting the contraction in the mortgage market.

The biggest and probably most significant change was in local authority housing. In Vauxhall, it dropped as a proportion of total households from 36% to 23%, in Dulwich and West Norwood from 24% to 18% and in Streatham from 22% to 15%. Council housing was replaced in the main by private rented accommodation. Lambeth by this period could no longer be characterised as an area with a high concentration of council tenants who traditionally voted Labour, as had been the case during the period of two-party domination. By 2011, Labour-voting council tenants had been replaced by 'Generation rent,' with higher levels of insecurity and eviction, compounded by diminishing real incomes for the precariat. The housing crisis had become the most pressing contemporary political issue in London, although housing had always occupied this position on this political agenda

---

80　Census 2001 & 2011.
81　From about 41% in 48% in all three constituencies while the average for London was 37%.

Voting and social class 149

in the capital, followed by education and transport. The reputation of the Labour Party before 1979 rested on its record of slum clearance and house building, epitomised by the slogan 'Down with the slums and up with the houses,' by far the most prominent poster circulated by the party in local elections during the 1930s and 1940s. But the squeeze on local authority spending and the effects of the Housing Finance Act of 1972 started to seriously undermine this reputation.

Despite these changes, the people of Lambeth continued to vote Labour and by larger majorities after 1997. By 2017, the three parliamentary constituencies had become safe Labour seats. From 1974 to 1987, Labour held Lambeth Central, Norwood and Vauxhall on votes ranging from 42% to 52%, while the Labour vote in Streatham increased from 34% to 39%.[82] From 1992 to 2017, Labour's hold on Norwood, Streatham and Vauxhall consolidated.[83] In Dulwich and West Norwood, its vote fluctuated from 61% in 1997 to 70% in 2017, dipping to 45% in 2005 and 2010. In Streatham, it ranged from 63% to 68% in the same period, dipping to 43% in 2010. In Vauxhall, Labour's hold weakened slightly, ranging from 64% in 1997 to only 57% in 2017, perhaps reflecting the more rapid reduction in council housing taking place in the gentrified areas close to the Thames.[84] The borough council had by this time returned to being a Labour stronghold, with the Liberal Democrats and the Green Party now recording respectable votes, while the Conservatives have been relegated to a poor fourth position. In the local elections in 2010, Labour polled 43% increasing to 54% in 2018. In the Greater London Authority elections, Labour polled 53% in 2012. In the referendum on EEC membership Lambeth voted 78.6% to remain, although turnout was only 67.3%. Nobody could mistake that Lambeth in 2017 was a Labour-voting borough by a significant margin.

The Times journalist Matthew Parris highlighted the influence of gentrification in his report on the Vauxhall by-election in 1989. He described the way white professional households were spreading out from traditional strongholds, such as around Clapham Common, of which 16% consisted of single non-pensioners living in private rented accommodation.[85] From the 1980s, cultural, ethnic and geographic differences started to play a more important role than social class in influencing political choice in Lambeth. By 2018, the Conservatives in Lambeth had been reduced to only 1 councillor, Labour had recovered to 57 from a low point of only 28 seats in 2002 after the defeat of the hard-left and the Liberal Democrats had been wiped out, for reasons to do primarily with their part in the Coalition government of 2010–2015.[86] The Green Party started to make inroads winning a seat

82 Craig, *Britain Votes 4 1983–1987*; Lambeth Central was abolished in 1983.
83 In 1997, Norwood became the new constituency of Dulwich and West Norwood.
84 London Data Base/Elections.
85 *Times*, 26 May 1989 – 'Divided they Stand in Vauxhall.'
86 London Data Store election results.

150   *Thematic*

in 2014 and increasing this to 5 in 2018. Local party membership figures in Lambeth are not publicly available, although the national figures show some clear trends, which were more than likely repeated at a local level. The UK membership had reached over 400,000 in 1997 at the height of the popularity of New Labour, but had declined quite quickly to only 177,000 by 2007, probably reflecting disillusion with Blair after the decision to go to war in Iraq. It had only partly recovered to 187,000 in 2012. But after the election of Corbyn as a Labour leader in 2015, the figures increased dramatically to 564,000 in 2017.[87]

In Croydon, a similar process of general social upgrading was taking place. For example, the proportion of higher managerial occupations in Croydon Central increased from 10% to nearly 22% between 2001 and 2011, while the number of intermediate and lower supervisory groups increased from 22% to 30%. Working-class occupations (semi-routine and routine) remained stable at about 18%. The number of people with higher educational qualifications (level 4 and above) increased from 22% to 30%. The private rented sector grew from 12% to 20% of all tenures at the expense of those who were owner-occupiers with a mortgage, which dropped from 40% to 32%, while all social housing (local authority and housing associations) remained stable at around 22%. The same changes were taking place in Croydon North, which was becoming more ethnically diverse, while Croydon South remained an area predominantly occupied by owner-occupiers, and was much less ethnically diverse, but with a higher proportion of Asians rather than Afro-Caribbeans.[88] These trends can be seen in the general election result for the Greater London Area in 2017. The Conservatives were confined to middle-class suburban seats and high-status inner London seats like Chelsea and Fulham and Cities of London and Westminster (see Table 5.14).

London is now a city with an almost equal balance of people who self-define as either working or middle class, with a higher proportion of people saying they 'don't know' in comparison to other areas of the country. This is in contrast to the results of a national survey which found that despite the long-term decline in the size of the working class, the proportion of the public who identify themselves as working class has remained stable over time at about 60%.[89] Ambivalence is more pronounced among younger age groups in London, reflecting perhaps the more socially fluid environment of a capital city. In a YouGov survey carried out in 2017, the self-identity figures for London were 41% working class, 41% middle class, 2% upper class with 16% don't knows. Inner London is more middle class than outer London (48%–38%) and outer London is more working class (45%–33%).[90] In terms

---

87 Audickas, *Membership of UK Political Parties.*
88 Census, 2001 & 2011.
89 Evans and Mellon, 'Identity, Awareness and Political Attitudes.'
90 YouGov Survey Results, 'How Would You Describe Your Own Social Class?' (September 2017).

Voting and social class 151

of headline voting intentions as measured just before the 2019 general election, Labour is ten points ahead of the Conservatives (39% –29%), a fairly consistent figure after 2015. The gender balance of those voting Labour is about equal (37% male to 41% female), a very different situation from earlier in the century, when a much larger proportion of women voted Conservative. In terms of age, 62% of 18- to 24-year olds voted Labour, while only 18% of the over 65 did so. In terms of social class, 37% of ABC1s voted Labour, while 41% of C2DE did so. In terms of race, Labour attracted 53% of the BME electorate, with the Conservatives only obtaining 22%.[91] These figures confirm London as a city which is increasingly middle class, young and multi-ethnic. It is the least working-class region of the country at 41%, while the North is 58%, the Midlands 57%, Wales 55% and Scotland 49%. Its ten-point lead in voting intentions is also in marked contrast to its so-called traditional heartlands in the North, Midlands and Wales (whereas in Scotland it has been wiped out by the SNP and in Northern Ireland it does not exist as a separate party).

The turnover of population, the changing age structure, the growth of a much enlarged lower middle class of intermediate and supervisory occupations and the significant upgrading of educational levels during the last 20 years have had a major impact on voting intentions in London. It is generally accepted that London remains an integrated city unlike some big cities in the USA or South America where racial segregation is more polarised.[92] However, the gap between rich and poor has needless to say widened creating a high degree of polarisation between rich and poor.[93] The working-class population of many London constituencies stabilised or increased slightly after 2000, no doubt satisfying a labour market which increasingly services (literally in some cases providing servants) to London's highly paid executive class living in gentrified neighbourhoods. These two social groups (intermediate and working-class) make up the capitals increasingly insecure precariat. They are a markedly different type of working class to that which voted Labour during the 'Golden Age' of municipal social democracy. They do not live in relatively stable predominantly white working-class districts in inner-city boroughs joined together by a common tradition of work, family and street life, specific gender relationships and defensive of their neighbourhoods against incomers. They do not express their position in the social hierarchy in terms of a distinct 'Labourist' type of class consciousness ('them and us'). It is certainly the case that their aspirations have been severely restricted by the acceleration of inequality following the financial crash of 2008. Some of the traditional white working class have been dispersed to the outer suburbs and new towns, or they have escaped altogether

91 YouGov/QMUL Survey Results – Headline Voting Intentions (November 2019).
92 Hall, *London Voices, London Lives*; Buck, *Working Capital. Life and Labour in Contemporary London*.
93 Dorling, *Peak Inequality*.

152   *Thematic*

('white flight') to other areas of the country. Those left behind (who are more economically disadvantaged) have been forced out to cheaper areas in the suburbs, like Croydon, unable to afford inner-city rents or obtain mortgages, or they make up small and declining pockets of poverty in inner-city areas, living side by side in gentrified neighbourhoods, now the subject of documentary film makers.[94]

The speed of these changes had important implications for local politics and strategies. At a national level, they gave rise to a debate about the best strategy for Labour to win elections in such areas in the future. While social class was still regarded as relevant, other factors such as geography now inform a different understanding of the social basis of support for the party. Jon Cruddas, the Labour MP for the outer London suburban constituency of Dagenham and Rainham, which like Croydon has experienced significant ethnic diversification, argued that it was necessary to understand the changing meaning of suburbia in terms of a new political culture, if Labour was to win support in this new social environment. 'Suburbia,' he suggested, infers a certain lifestyle and the idea of the suburbs is often used to identify a community or class of people who inhabit a specific territory. He maintained that 'a geographical realignment, influenced by cultural or lifestyles should redefine the "base" of the left in terms of class and community.'[95] This debate is of particular relevance for London. It has drawn attention to a sharpening divide between working-class areas outside of London and metropolitan cities like London with their younger, better educated, multi-ethnic and more mixed-class populations.

But this should not be exaggerated. There remains a significant working-class population in the Greater London area. They either do note vote (a third of the electorate in London that abstains from politics altogether) or a majority of those that do vote support the Labour Party. This constituency is made up of a mix of social classes and ethnic groups stretching across the whole spectrum of the way individuals define their position in the social hierarchy. From being a largely proletarian city during the interwar and post-war period (up to the 1960s), London has been transformed into a post-industrial region of remarkable economic vitality but marred by growing inequality. As a result, social mobility has flattened out. Disadvantaged students from the multi-racial areas of inner London 'are more likely to attend higher educational institutions than other students (nearly 60% do so), but are less likely than non-disadvantaged students to attend Russell Group universities.'[96] While education therefore provides a potential route out of poverty for many of London's children, their working-class parents are either not registered to vote or over a third that are registered abstain from

---

94 See the film *The Street* (2019), directed by Zed Nelson, based in Hackney over a period of four years.

95 Cruddas, 'The Lefts New Urbanism.' See also Huq, *On the Edge*.

96 Tinson, *London's Poverty Profile*.

Voting and social class   153

Table 5.4 Labour vote (%) by social class (general elections 1945–1966)

Date general election	Upper middle class (%)	Middle class (%)	Working class (%)	Very poor (%)
1945	14	24	57	57
1950	9	17	53	64
1951	6	22	52	67
1955	9	21	57	54
1959	6	16	54	68
1964	9	22	53	59
1966	8	24	61	72

Source: Gallup Poll (1976), 206; Adapted from Fielding, *The Labour Party*, pp. 87–8.

Table 5.5 Labour vote (%) by social class (general elections 1964–1997)

Date general election (%)	Higher service (%)	Lower service (%)	Routine non-manual (%)	Petty bourgeoise (%)	Foreman & technicians (%)	Skilled working class (%)	Unskilled working class (%)
1964	18	20	26	15	48	70	66
1966	19	29	41	20	61	73	70
1970	22	32	40	20	56	63	61
1974	17	26	29	18	39	59	61
1974	17	30	32	13	52	62	65
1979	24	19	32	13	45	58	53
1983	8	16	20	12	28	47	49
1987	11	19	26	16	37	48	48
1992	16	21	30	17	45	50	60
1997	34	42	49	40	62	67	69

Source: Evans, Heath and Payne, 'Class: Labour as a catch-all Party?' in Evans & Norris (eds.), *Critical Elections* (1999); Adapted from Fielding, *The Labour Party*, pp. 87–8.

politics altogether, a figure which is higher in London than other smaller towns and rural areas.[97]

Throughout long periods of the twentieth century, the strategy of the leadership of the Labour Party was to continue 'to appeal to voters from all classes, a need that became ever stronger as post-war social change caused the manual working-class to decline.'[98] This strategy was pursued with some effectiveness by Herbert Morrison in the way he built the London Labour Party during the interwar period.[99] Certainly, the party succeeded in London in appealing to both middle- and working-class voters, as perhaps uniquely demonstrated in the general election of 1945 and again in 1997. But even after 1945, the national figures (see Tables 5.4 and 5.5) show a

97 Evans and Tilley, *The New Politics of Class*.
98 Fielding, *The Labour Party*, p. 85.
99 Donoghue and Jones, *Morrison*.

154   *Thematic*

clear and continuing relationship between the labour vote and the working class; however, much of the definition of what it means to be working class has changed in the modern era (taking into account fluid categories such as occupations, geography, status, education and race).

If class is measured in terms of deprivation (economic disadvantage), then there is also a clear link between levels of such disadvantage and voting Labour, which suggests that class continues to be a relevant consideration across the country, not just in London. In fact, poverty levels in London are higher than in the rest of the country. The most recent survey published in 2017 shows that

> the cost of housing is the main factor explaining London's higher poverty rate. The majority of people living in poverty (58%) are living in a working family. The number has risen to 1.3 million over the last decade, an increase of around 50%. More people in poverty live in the private rented sector than any other housing tenure, nearly 1 million. The number of children living in poverty in this sector has tripled over the last decade. Wealth inequality is more pronounced than income inequality in London. The top 10% of households received nearly 30% of income but owned just over 50% of total wealth. The bottom 50% of Londoners received nearly 25% of income but owned only 5% of wealth.[100]

Recent analysis by the University of Sheffield also shows that the most deprived areas voted Labour in the 2017 general election, even after taking into account higher levels of abstentions.[101] Although the size of the middle class has grown in the capital as a result of gentrification and immigration, there are those sociologists who argue that the post-industrial working class in London has not disappeared; rather, it is made up of several fractions which reduce its visibility.

> These fractions include a new migrant 'reserve army of labour' doing many of the city's socially invisible, often 'dirty jobs'; alongside white and established black and Asian groups who intermit over time between routine employment (manual and non-manual) and various forms of non-employment; plus an older largely white although increasingly multi-ethnic retired population. What tends to unite this disparate, unevenly organised post-industrial working-class, is considerable exposure to poverty, either of the in-work or out-of-work varieties, alongside various forms of deprivation including lamentable housing conditions.[102]

---

100 Tinson, *London's Poverty Profile*; Dorling, *Peak Inequality*.
101 www.statsmapsnpix.com (Alasdair Race, University of Sheffield).
102 Watt, 'The Only Class in Town?' 209.

Conclusion

Social class (however defined) therefore continues to play a role in determining voting intentions, although support for the two main parties is now more evenly spread between the middle and working classes. For some political sociologists, studying the period after the Second World War, it is 'an important cleavage at both elite and mass level...and the two-party system has largely remained intact,' dependent to a large extent on the electoral first-past-the post system.[103] Whether the introduction of proportional representation would destroy the class basis of support for the Labour Party remains a hypothetical question. However, national opinion poll evidence shows that working-class disengagement is a significant problem for the Labour Party, either as a result of abstentions or a decline in the support of skilled manual workers (from 50% in 1997 to 30% in 2010), and semi-skilled and unskilled workers (from 60% to 40% in the same period). Turnout was also much lower amongst working-class voters, at 63%, while it was 70% for higher social groups. The party 'recovered just enough by the 2017 election to allow many Labour "heartland" seats to be spared' with Labour increasing its support amongst managerial and professional workers.[104] But as suggested by one recent analysis, 'the party merely deepened its coalition in the regions,' such as London, 'where it had already been strong; it is not expanding to reach white working class voters or other constituencies,' questioning whether Labour had 'an appetite for reconnecting with its lost base.'[105]

The centre of London now contains very high concentrations of higher social groups (ABC1s) where property prices are beyond the reach of many, in areas like Kensington and Chelsea, and those boroughs close to the City, such as parts of Islington, and in bohemian quarters like Hampstead and Hackney.[106] Although Labour's share of the vote dropped in the 2019 general election in London, it held up remarkably well in comparison to other areas of the country where Labour lost support heavily from amongst skilled and unskilled manual workers, especially from the white working class. From the 1980s, the decline in this latter constituency was more dramatic in London than elsewhere. But in the capital, it was replaced by the growth of a new type of working class, younger, better educated and more multi-ethnic. However, outside of the big cities, the size of white working class was also diminishing but probably to a lesser extent. It was still 'great in number,' but in line with trends in both the UK and the USA, it had become according to one analysis 'an anachronism that was derided as lazy, bigoted and simple. Many continued to vote for centre-left parties, but remained relatively side-lined and frustrated for decades,' disengaged

---

103 Curtice, 'Political Sociology, 1945–92,' 41–2.
104 Berry, 'Class, Place and Values: Labour's Lost Tribe,' 56–68.
105 Gest, *The White Working Class*, p. 115.
106 Savage, *Social Class in the 21st Century*, pp. 319–21.

156   *Thematic*

from party politics (especially a Labour Party which was perceived as not representing its interests), 'until the recent populist wave harvested their anger and generated a string of shocking electoral triumphs' (Trump and Brexit).[107] In London, Labour was more cushioned from the dissertation of the white working class by the support of a higher concentration of middle- and lower-middle-class groups. This helps to account for Labour's greater success in the capital and in big cities 'where feelings of relative deprivation played a significant part.' Did many 'left-behind voters ('some well-educated, some less so') join or vote for the Labour Party for the first time when a candidate (Jeremy Corbyn) with a clearly radical profile' was elected as a leader?[108]

For many rank and file members of the party however, especially socialists, the one-nation strategy pursued by the leadership for most of the twentieth century was controversial in that it implied a weakening of socialist principles in order to win the support of the working class. This dilemma had been present since the formation of the Labour Party in Parliament in 1906. It also reflects the current sense of crisis within the Party – a tension 'between *socialism* as a radical movement of idealists pioneering new ways of living and *Labour politics* as a vote maximising strategy for securing political power necessary to implement practical social reforms.'[109] This will be explored in more detail in the next chapter looking at party organisation and membership and the influence of socialism over the course of the twentieth century.

107 Gest, *The White Working Class*, p. viii.
108 Whiteley, 'Oh Jeremy Corbyn!' 80–98.
109 Lawrence, 'Movement Politics, the Electoral Machine and the "masses."

Appendix – Tables of general election results for Greater London area 1910–2017

Table 5.6 1910 (December) general election result for Greater London

Inner London (57 seats)			Outer London (14 seats)		
Working class (23)	Mixed class (15)	Middle class (19)	Working class (3)	Mixed class (7)	Middle class (4)
South London	*South London*	*South London*	*North London*	*North*	*North*
Battersea & Clapham	Deptford	Battersea,	*Middlesex*	*London*	*London*
Bermondsey	Fulham	Clapham	Tottenham	*Middlesex*	*Middlesex*
Camberwell, North	Greenwich	Camberwell		Brentford	Ealing
Camberwell, Peckham	Lambeth-	Dulwich	*East London –*	Enfield	Hornsey
Lambeth, North	Kennington	Chelsea	*Essex*	Harrow	Uxbridge
Newington, Walworth	Woolwich	Finsbury,	Walthamstow		
Newington, West		Holborn	West Ham,	*South*	*South*
Southwark – Bermondsey	*Inner North*	Hackney, North	South	*London –*	*London –*
Southwark, Rotherhithe	Hackney, Central	Hampstead		*Surrey*	*Surrey*
Southwark, West	Hackney, South	Kensington,		Croydon	Wimbledon
	Hammersmith	South			
East End	Islington, East	Lambeth, Brixton		*East*	
Bethnal Green, NE	Islington, North	Lambeth		*London –*	
Bethnal-Green SW	Islington, South	Norwood		*Kent*	
Shoreditch- Haggerston	Kensington-	Lewisham		Dartford	
Shoreditch-Hoxton	North	Wandsworth			
Southwark,	St-Pancras,			*East*	
Southwark,	North	*Business & Class*		*London –*	
Tower-Hamlets-Bow &	St-Pancras-South	*Residential*		*Essex*	
Bromley	St-Pancras, West	Marylebone, East		Romford	
Tower-Hamlets- Limehouse		Marylebone,		West Ham,	
Tower-Hamlets- Mile End		West		North	
Tower-Hamlets- Poplar		Paddington,			
Tower-Hamlets- St George's		North			
Tower-Hamlets-Stepney		Paddington,			
Tower-Hamlets-Whitechapel		South			
		St George's			
Inner North		Hanover-			
Finsbury, Central		Square			
Finsbury, East		Strand			
Islington, West		Westminster			
St Pancras East					
Shoreditch- Hagerstown					
Shoreditch-Hoxton					

Colour code – White = Liberal; Light grey = Conservative; Dark grey = Labour.
Turnout Inner London 85% (88% UK); Outer London 84%; Percentage vote share – Inner London: -Con & Unionist 53% (47% UK), Lab 1.5 % (7% UK), Lib & Progressive 45% (43% UK), Outer London: Con & Unionist 53% (47% UK; Lab 5% (7% UK); Lib & Progressive 42% (43%); Number of candidates: Con & Unionist 71 (out of 71); Labour 2 (of 71); Lib & Progressive 68 (of 71).
Source: Craig, *British Parliamentary Elections 1885–1918; 1918–1949; 1950–1973*; London Data Store – www.data.london.gov.uk/elections.

158   Thematic

Table 5.7 1918 general election result for Greater London

Inner London (59 seats)			Outer London (37 seats)		
Working Class	*Mixed Class*	*Middle Class*	*Working Class*	*Mixed Class*	*Middle Class*
South London	*South London*	*South London*	*North London –*	*North London*	*North London –*
Battersea, North	Battersea South	Camberwell,	*Middlesex*	*Middlesex*	*Middlesex*
Bermondsey,	Deptford	Dulwich	Tottenham	Edmonton	Acton
Rotherhithe	Greenwich	Hackney	North	Brentford &	Ealing
Bermondsey, West	Islington East	North	Tottenham	Chiswick	Hornsey
Camberwell	Islington North	Lambeth	South	Enfield	Richmond
North	St Pancras North	Brixton		Finchley	Spelthorne
Camberwell NW	St Pancras SW	Lambeth	*North London –*	Harrow	Twickenham
Camberwell,		Norwood	*Essex*	Hendon	Willesden
Peckham	*Business & Class Residential*	Lewisham	East Ham		East
Lambeth,		East	North	*East London –*	Willesden
Kennington	Paddington	Lewisham	East Ham	*Essex*	West
Lambeth, North	North	West	South	Ilford	Uxbridge
Southwark,		Balham &	Leyton East	Maldon	Wood Green
Central	*Inner North*	Tooting	Leyton West	Romford	
Southwark, North	Fulham East	Wandsworth –	Walthamstow		*South London –*
Southwark, SE	Fulham West	Central	East	*East London – Kent*	*Surrey*
Woolwich East	Hammersmith	Clapham	Walthamstow	Dartford	Wimbledon
Woolwich West	North	Putney	West		
	Hammersmith	Streatham	West Ham	*South London –*	*South London –*
Inner North	South		Plaistow	*Surrey*	*Kent*
Islington, South	Islington East	*Business & Class Residential*	West Ham	Croydon	Bromley
Islington, West	Islington North	Chelsea	Silvertown	-North	
St Pancras SE	St Pancras North	Hampstead	West Ham –	Croydon-	
	St Pancras SW	Holborn	Stratford	South	
East End		Kensington	West Ham	Mitcham	
Bethnal Green,		South	Upton		
NE		Paddington			
Bethnal Green		South			
SW		St Marylebone			
Finsbury,		Westminster			
Hackney, Central		Abbey			
Hackney, South *		Westminster			
Poplar, Bow &		St Georges			
Bromley					
Poplar, South					
Shoreditch					
Stepney,					
Limehouse					
Stepney, Mile End					
Stepney,					
Whitechapel &					
St Georges					
Stoke Newington					

* Hackney South was held by the independent – Horatio Bottomley.
Colour code -White = Liberal (non-coupon); Light grey = Conservative and Liberal Coalition; Dark Grey = Labour.
Turnout Inner London 45% (57% UK); Outer London 48%; Percentage vote share – Inner London: -Coalition 57% (47% UK), Lab 13% (21% UK), Lib 13% (13% UK), Outer London: Coalition 57% (47% UK; Lab 20% (21% UK); Lib 14% (13%); Number of candidates: Coalition 97 (out of 97); Labour 54 (of 97); Lib 47 (of 71).
Source: Craig, *British Parliamentary Elections 1885–1918; 1918 – 1949; 1950- 1973*; London Data Store – www. data.london.gov.uk/elections.

Voting and social class   159

Table 5.8 1929 general election result for Greater London

Inner London (59 seats)			Outer London (42 seats)		
Working Class	*Mixed Class*	*Middle Class*	*Working Class*	*Mixed Class*	*Middle Class*

South London
Battersea, North
Bermondsey,
  Rotherhithe
Bermondsey, West
Camberwell
  North
Camberwell NW
Camberwell,
  Peckham
Lambeth,
  Kennington
Lambeth, North
Southwark,
  Central
Southwark, North
Southwark, SE
Woolwich East
Woolwich West
	South London
	Battersea
	  South
	Deptford
	Greenwich
	
	Business &
	Class
	Residential
	Paddington
	  North
	
	Inner North
	Fulham East
	Fulham West
	Hackney
	  North
		South London
		Camberwell,
		  Dulwich
		Hackney North
		Lambeth
		  Brixton
		Lambeth
		  Norwood
		Lewisham East
		Lewisham West
		Balham &
		  Tooting
		Wandsworth –
		  Central
		Clapham
		Putney
		Streatham
			North
			London –
			Essex
			East Ham
			  North
			East Ham
			  South
			Leyton East
			Leyton West
			Walthamstow
			  East
			Walthamstow
			  West
			West Ham
			  Plaistow
			West Ham
			  Silvertown
			West Ham
			  Stratford
			West Ham
			  Upton
				North
				London
				Middlesex
				Edmonton
				Brentford &
				  Chiswick
				Enfield
				Finchley
				Harrow
				Hendon
				
				East
				London –
				Essex
				Ilford
				Maldon
				Romford
					North
					London –
					Middlesex
					Acton
					Ealing
					Hornsey
					Spelthorne
					Twickenham
					Willesden
					  East
					Willesden
					  West
					Uxbridge
					Wood Green
					
					South
					London –
					Surrey
					Richmond
					Wimbledon

Inner North
Islington, South
Islington, West
St Pancras SE
	Hammersmith
	  North
	Hammersmith
	  South
	Islington East
	Islington
		Business & Class
		Residential
		Chelsea
		Hampstead
			West Ham
			Upton
				East
				London –
				Kent
				Dartford
					South
					London –
					Kent
					Bromley

East End
Bethnal Green,
  NE
Bethnal Green
  SW
Finsbury,
Hackney, Central
Hackney, South
Poplar, Bow &
  Bromley
Poplar, South
Shoreditch
Stepney,
  Limehouse
Stepney, Mile End
Stepney,
  Whitechapel &
  St Georges
Stoke Newington
	North
	Islington
	  South
	Islington West
	St Pancras
	  North
	St Pancras SE
	St Pancras SW
		Holborn
		Kensington
		  North
		Kensington
		  South
		Paddington
		  North
		Paddington
		  South
		St Marylebone
		Westminster
		  Abbey
		Westminster St
		  Georges
		
		East End
		Hackney North
			North
			London –
			Middlesex
			Tottenham
			  North
			Tottenham
			  South
				South
				London –
				Surrey
				Croydon
				  -North
				Croydon-
				  South
				Mitcham	

Colour code – White = Liberal; Light Grey = Conservative; Dark Grey= Labour.
Turnout Inner London 67% (76% UK); Outer London 72%; Percentage vote share – Inner London: -Con 38% (38% UK), Lab 44% (37% UK), Lib 18% (23% UK); Outer London: Con 40% (38% UK; Lab 39% (37% UK); Lib 21% (23% UK); Number of candidates: Con 97 (out of 97); Labour 94 (of 97); Lib 85 (of 97).
Source: Craig, *British Parliamentary Elections 1885–1918; 1918–1949; 1950–1973*; London Data Store – www. data.london.gov.uk/elections.

160 Thematic

Table 5.9 1935 general election result for Greater London

Inner London (60 seats)			Outer London (49 seats)		
Working Class	*Mixed Class*	*Middle Class*	*Working Class*	*Mixed Class*	*Middle Class*
South London	*South London*	*South London*	*North*	*North*	*North*
Battersea. North	Battersea South	Camberwell,	London –	London	London –
Bermondsey.	Deptford	Dulwich	Essex	Middlesex	Middlesex
Rotherhithe	Greenwich	Hackney North	East Ham	Edmonton	Acton
Bermondsey.		Lambeth	North	Brentford &	Ealing
West	*Business &*	Brixton	East Ham	Chiswick	Hornsey
Camberwell	*Class*	Lambeth	South	Enfield	Richmond
North	*Residential*	Norwood	Leyton East	Finchley	Spelthorne
Camberwell NW	Paddington	Lewisham East	Leyton West	Harrow	Twickenham
Camberwell,	North	Lewisham West	Walthamstow	Hendon	Willesden
Peckham		Balham &	East		East
Lambeth,	*Inner North*	Tooting	Walthamstow	*East*	Willesden
Kennington	Fulham East	Wandsworth –	West	*London –*	West
Lambeth, North	Fulham West	Central	West Ham	*Essex*	Uxbridge
Southwark,	Hackney North	Clapham	Plaistow	Ilford	Wood Green
Central	Hammersmith	Putney	West Ham	Maldon	
Southwark,	North	Streatham	Silvertown	Romford	*South*
North	Hammersmith		West Ham		*London –*
Southwark, SE	South	*Business &*	Stratford	*East*	*Surrey*
Woolwich East	Islington East	*Class*	West Ham	*London –*	Richmond
Woolwich West	Islington North	*Residential*	Upton	*Kent*	Wimbledon
	Islington South	Chelsea		Dartford	
East End	Islington West	Hampstead	*North*		*South*
Bethnal Green.	St Pancras	Holborn	*London –*	*South*	*London –*
NE	North	Kensington	*Middlesex*	*London –*	*Kent*
Bethnal Green	St Pancras SE	North	Tottenham	*Surrey*	Bromley
SW	St Pancras SW	Kensington	North	Croydon	
Finsbury,		South	Tottenham	-North	
Hackney, Central		Paddington	South	Croydon-	
Hackney, South		North		South	
Poplar, Bow &		Paddington		Mitcham	
Bromley		South			
Poplar, South		St Marylebone			
Shoreditch		Westminster			
Stepney,		Abbey			
Limehouse		Westminster St			
Stepney, Mile		Georges			
End					
Stepney,		*East End*			
Whitechapel &		Hackney North			
St Georges					
Stoke Newington					

Colour code – White = Liberal; Light Grey = Conservative; Dark Grey = Labour.
Turnout Inner London 61% (72% UK); Outer London 67%; Percentage vote share – Inner London: -Con 51% (53% UK), Lab 45% (38% UK), Lib 3% (7% UK); Outer London: Con 55% (53% UK; Lab 43% (38% UK); Lib 2% (7% UK); Number of candidates: Con 97 (out of 97); Labour 96 (of 97); Lib 23 (of 97).
Source: Craig, *British Parliamentary Elections 1885–1918; 1918–1949; 1950–1973*; London Data Store – www.data.london.gov.uk/elections.

Voting and social class 161

Table 5.10 1945 general election result for Greater London

Inner London (60 seats)			Outer London (49 seats)		
Working Class	*Mixed Class*	*Middle Class*	*Working Class*	*Mixed Class*	*Middle Class*
South London	South London	South London	North	North London	North
Battersea, North	Battersea	Camberwell,	London –	Middlesex	London –
Bermondsey,	South	Dulwich	Essex	Edmonton	Middlesex
Rotherhithe	Deptford	Lambeth	East Ham	Brentford &	Acton
Bermondsey,	Greenwich	Brixton	North	Chiswick	Ealing East
West		Lambeth	East Ham	Enfield	Ealing West
Camberwell	*Business &*	Norwood	South	Finchley	Hornsey
North	*Class*	Lewisham East	Leyton East	Harrow East	Richmond
Camberwell,	*Residential*	Lewisham	Leyton West	Harrow West	Southall
Peckham	Paddington	West	West Ham	Hendon North	Spelthorne
Camberwell NW	North	Balham &	-Plaistow	Hendon South	Twickenham
Lambeth,		Tooting	West Ham	Wembley	Willesden
Kennington	*Inner North*	Wandsworth –	-Silvertown	North	East
Lambeth, North	Fulham East	Central	West Ham-	Wembley	Willesden
Southwark,	Fulham West	Clapham	Stratford	South	West
Central	Hackney	Putney	West Ham		Uxbridge
Southwark,	North	Streatham	Upton	*East*	Wood Green
North	Hammersmith			*London – Essex*	
Southwark, SE	North (ind.	*Business &*	*North*	Barking	*South*
Woolwich East	Labour)	*Class*	*London –*	Ilford South	*London –*
Woolwich West	Hammersmith	*Residential*	*Middlesex*	Ilford North	*Surrey*
	South	Chelsea	Tottenham	Maldon	Sutton &
Inner North	Islington East	Hampstead	North	Romford	Cheam
Islington, South	Islington	Holborn	Tottenham	Walthamstow	Wimbledon
Islington, West	North	Kensington	South	East	
St Pancras SE	St Pancras	North		Walthamstow	*South*
	North	Kensington		West	*London –*
East End	St Pancras SE	South		Woodford	*Kent*
Bethnal Green,	St Pancras SW	Paddington			Bromley
NE		North		*East*	
Bethnal Green,		Paddington		*London – Kent*	
SW		South		Dagenham	
Finsbury,		St Marylebone		Dartford	
Hackney, Central		Westminster			
Hackney, South		Abbey		*South*	
Poplar, Bow &		Westminster St		*London –*	
Bromley		Georges		*Surrey*	
Poplar, South				Bexley	
Shoreditch		*East End*		Croydon	
Stepney,		Hackney North		-North	
Limehouse				Croydon-	
Stepney,				South	
Mile End				Mitcham	
(Communist)					
Stepney,					
Whitechapel &					
St Georges					
Stoke Newington					

Colour code – White = Liberal; Light Grey = Conservative; Dark Grey = Labour.
Turnout Inner London 68% (73% UK); Outer London 72%; Percentage vote share – Inner London: -Con 33% (39% UK), Lab 59% (48% UK), Lib 4% (9% UK); Outer London: Con 35% (39% UK; Lab 54% (48% UK); Lib 9% (7% UK); Number of candidates: Con 109 (out of 109); Labour 108 (of 109); Lib 49 (of 109).
Source: Craig, *British Parliamentary Elections 1885–1918; 1918–1949; 1950–1973*; London Data Store – www. data.london.gov.uk/elections.

162 *Thematic*

Table 5.11 1966 general election result for Greater London

Inner London (49 seats)			Outer London (49 seats)		
Working Class (16)	Mixed Class (11)	Middle Class (22)	Working Class (10)	Mixed Class (24)	Middle Class (15)
South London	South London	South London	North London – Essex	North London Middlesex	North London – Middlesex
Battersea, North	Battersea South	Camberwell, Dulwich	East Ham North	Edmonton	Acton
Bermondsey	Deptford	Lambeth Brixton	East Ham South	Brentford & Chiswick	Ealing North
Camberwell, Peckham	Greenwich	Lambeth – Norwood	Leyton	Enfield East	Ealing South
Lambeth, Kennington		Lambeth Vauxhall	West Ham -Plaistow	Enfield West	Hornsey
Lambeth, North	*Business & Class Residential*	Lewisham North	West Ham -South	Feltham	Richmond
Southwark	Paddington North	Lewisham West	West Ham-North	Finchley	Southall
Woolwich East		Lewisham South		Harrow East	Spelthorne
Woolwich West	*Inner North*	Balham & Tooting	*North London – Middlesex*	Harrow West	Twickenham
	Barons Court	Wandsworth Central	Tottenham	Hendon North	Willesden East
Inner North	Fulham	Clapham	Hayes & Harlington	Hendon South	Willesden West
Islington, South-West	Hackney North	Putney		Heston & Isleworth	Uxbridge
St Pancras SE	Hammersmith North	Streatham		Wembley North	Wood Green
	Islington East			Wembley South	
East End	Islington North	*Business & Class Residential*		*East London – Essex*	*South London – Surrey*
Bethnal Green	St Pancras North	Chelsea		Barking	Sutton & Cheam
Hackney, Central		Hampstead		Ilford South	Wimbledon
Stoke Newington and Hackney North		Holborn & St Pancras		Ilford North	
Shoreditch & Finsbury		Kensington North		Maldon	*South London – Kent*
Poplar		Kensington South		Romford	Bromley
Stepney		Paddington North		Walthamstow East	
		Paddington South		Walthamstow West	
		St Marylebone		Wanstead & Woodford	
		Cities of London and Westminster			
				East London – Kent	
				Dagenham	
				Erith & Crayford	
				South London – Surrey	
				Bexley	
				Croydon N West	
				Croydon South	
				Croydon - North E	
				Mitcham	

Colour code – White = Liberal; Light Grey = Conservative; Dark Grey = Labour.
Turnout Inner London 65% (76% UK); Outer London 74%; percentage vote – Inner London: -Con 35% (42% UK),
Lab 58% (48% UK), Lib 7% (9% UK); Outer London: Con 40% (42% UK; Lab 47% (48% UK); Lib 11% (9% UK);
Number of candidates: Con 91 (out of 91); Labour 91 (of 91); Lib 58 (of 91).
Source: Craig, *British Parliamentary Elections 1885–1918; 1918–1949; 1950–1973*; London Data Store – www.
data.london.gov.uk/elections.

Voting and social class 163

Table 5.12 1974 (February) general election result for Greater London

Greater London (92)

Working-Class	*Mixed-Class*	*Middle-Class*
Metropolitan Centre – low status	*Outer Ring – mixed-class suburbs*	*Metropolitan Centre – high status*
Acton	Croydon Central	Chelsea
Battersea North	Croydon North East	City of London &
Battersea South	Croydon North West	Westminster South
Bermondsey	Edmonton	Hampstead
Bethnal Green & Bow	Enfield North	Kensington
Brent East	Erith & Crayford	Paddington
Brent South	Feltham & Heston	St Marylebone
Deptford	Finchley	
Dulwich	Greenwich	*Outer Ring – Middle-Class*
Fulham	Hayes & Harlington	*Suburbs*
Hackney Central	Hendon South	Beckenham
Hackney North & Stoke	Hornchurch	Bexleyheath
Newington	Ilford South	Brentford & Isleworth
Hackney South &	Lewisham East	Brent North
Shoreditch	Lewisham West	Carshalton
Hammersmith North	Mitcham & Morden	Chingford
Holborn & St Pancras	Putney	Chipping Barnet
South	Romford	Chislehurst
Hornsey	Uxbridge	Croydon South
Islington Central	Walthamstow	Ealing North
Islington South & Finsbury	Woolwich West	Harrow Central
Lambeth Central		Harrow East
Leyton		Harrow West'
Newham North East		Hendon North
Newham North West		Ilford North
Norwood		Kingston Upon Thames
Peckham		Orpington
Southall		Ravensbourne
St Pancras North		Richmond Upon Thames
Stepney & Poplar		Ruislip & Northwood
Streatham		Sidcup
Tooting		Southgate
Tottenham		Surbiton
Vauxhall		Sutton and Cheam
Wood Green		Twickenham
		Upminster
Outer Ring – growth areas,		Wanstead & Woodford
poorer urban centres and		Wimbledon
peripheral council estates		
Barking		
Dagenham		
Woolwich East		

Colour code – White = Liberal; Light Grey = Conservative; Dark Grey = Labour.
Turnout 75% (79% UK); percentage votes Con 38% (38% UK), Lab 40% (37% UK), Lib 21% (19% UK); Number of candidates: Con 92 (out of 92); Labour 92 (of 92); Lib 89 (of 92).
Source: London Data Store – www.data.london.gov.uk/elections.

164 *Thematic*

Table 5.13 1979 general election result for Greater London

Greater London (92)

Working-Class	Mixed-Class	Middle-Class
Metropolitan Centre – low status	*Outer Ring – mixed-class suburbs*	*Metropolitan Centre – high status*
Acton	Croydon Central	Chelsea
Battersea North	Croydon North East	City of London &
Battersea South	Croydon North West	Westminster South
Bermondsey	Edmonton	Hampstead
Bethnal Green & Bow	Enfield North	Kensington
Brent East	Greenwich	Paddington
Brent South	Erith & Crayford	St Marylebone
Deptford	Finchley	
Dulwich	Feltham & Heston	*Outer Ring – Middle-*
Fulham	Hayes & Harlington	*Class Suburbs*
Hackney Central	Hendon South	Beckenham
Hackney North & Stoke	Hornchurch	Bexleyheath
Newington	Ilford South	Brent North
Hackney South &	Lewisham East	Brentford & Isleworth
Shoreditch	Lewisham West	Carshalton
Hammersmith North	Mitcham & Morden	Chingford
Holborn & St Pancras South	Putney	Chipping Barnet
Islington Central	Romford	Chislehurst
Islington North	Uxbridge	Croydon South
Islington South & Finsbury	Walthamstow	Ealing North
Lambeth Central	Woolwich West	Harrow Central
Lewisham Deptford		Harrow East
Leyton		Harrow West'
Newham North East		Hendon North
Newham North West		Ilford North
Newham South		Kingston Upon Thames
Norwood		Orpington
Peckham		Ravensbourne
St Pancras North		Richmond Upon Thames
Southall		Ruislip & Northwood
Stepney & Poplar		Sidcup
Streatham		Southgate
Tooting		Surbiton
Tottenham		Sutton and Cheam
Vauxhall		Twickenham
Wood Green		Upminster
		Wanstead & Woodford
Outer Ring – growth areas, poorer urban centres and peripheral council estates		Wimbledon
Barking		
Dagenham		
Woolwich East.		

Colour code – White = Liberal; Light Grey = Conservative; Dark Grey = Labour.
Turnout 72% (76% UK); Percentage votes: Con 46% (44% UK), Lab 40% (37% UK), Lib 12% (14% UK); Number of candidates: Con 92 (out of 92); Labour 92 (of 92); Lib 92 (of 92).
Source: London Data Store – www.data.london.gov.uk/elections.

Voting and social class 165

Table 5.14 1997 general election result for Greater London

Greater London (74)

Inner City and Outer London Immigrant	Mixed Inner City	Middle Britain, Middle Class & High Status
Cluster 10 Inner London – Immigrant concentration	*Cluster 3 Mixed Inner-City areas*	*Cluster 5 Middle Britain*
Bethnal Green & Bow	Battersea	Barking
Camberwell & Peckham	Cities of London & Westminster	Carshalton & Wallington
Greenwich & Woolwich	Dulwich & West Norwood	Croydon Central
Hackney North & Stoke Newington	Ealing Acton & Shepherd's Bush	Dagenham
Hackney South & Shoreditch	Hammersmith & Fulham	Dartford
Holborn & St Pancras	Hampstead & Highgate	Eltham
Ilford North	Hornsey & Wood Green	Enfield North
Islington North	Streatham	Lewisham East
Islington South & Finsbury	Tooting	Lewisham West
Poplar & Canning Town		Spelthorne
Regent's Park & Kensington North		
North Southwark & Bermondsey		*Cluster 6 Middle-Class Suburban*
Vauxhall		Beckenham
		Bexleyheath & Crayford
Cluster 14 North London – Immigrant --deprived areas		Bromley & Chislehurst
Brent East		Chingford & Woodford Green
Brent South		Chipping Barnet
Deptford		Croydon South
East Ham		Finchley & Golders Green
Tottenham		Hornchurch
West Ham		Kingston & Surbiton
		Old Bexley & Sidcup
Cluster 15 – Outer London – Immigrant Concentrations		Orpington
Brent North		Putney
Brentford & Isleworth		Richmond Park
Croydon North		Romford
Ealing North		Ruislip & Northwood
Ealing Southall		Sutton and Cheam
Edmonton		Twickenham
Erith & Thamesmead		Upminster
Feltham & Heston		Wimbledon
Harrow East		
Harrow West'		*Cluster 20 – High Status Inner London*
Hayes & Harlington		Kensington & Chelsea
Hendon		
Ilford South		
Leyton & Wanstead		
Mitcham & Morden		
Walthamstow.		

Colour code – White = Liberal; Light Grey = Conservative; Dark Grey = Labour.
Turnout 68% (71% UK); Percentage share – Con 31% (31% UK), Lab 50% (43% UK), Lib 15% (17% UK); Number of candidates: Con 74 (out of 87); Labour 74 (of 74); Lib 74 (of 74).
Source: London Data Store – www.data.london.gov.uk/elections.

166 *Thematic*

Table 5.15 2017 general election result for Greater London

Greater London (74)

Inner City and Outer London Immigrant	Mixed Inner City	Middle Britain, Middle Class & High Status
Cluster 10 Inner London – Immigrant concentration	*Cluster 3 Mixed Inner-City areas*	*Cluster 5 Middle Britain*
Bermondsey & Old Southwark	Battersea	Barking
Bethnal Green & Bow	Cities of	Carshalton & Wallington
Camberwell & Peckham	London &	Croydon Central
Greenwich & Woolwich	Westminster	Dagenham & Rainham
Hackney North & Stoke Newington	Dulwich & West	Dartford
Hackney South & Shoreditch	Norwood	Eltham
Holborn & St Pancras	Ealing Acton &	Enfield North
Ilford North	Shepherd's	Enfield Southgate
Islington North	Bush	Lewisham East
Islington South & Finsbury	Hammersmith	Lewisham West & Penge
Poplar & Canning Town	Hampstead &	
Regent's Park & Kensington North	Kilburn	*Cluster 6 Middle-Class*
North Southwark & Bermondsey	Hornsey & Wood	*Suburban*
Vauxhall	Green	Beckenham
	Kensington	Bexleyheath & Crayford
Cluster 14 North London –	Mitcham &	Brentford & Isleworth
Immigrant – deprived areas	Morden	Bromley & Chislehurst
Brent East	Regent's Park &	Chingford & Woodford
Brent South	Kensington	Green
Deptford	North	Chipping Barnet
East Ham	Streatham	Croydon South
Tottenham	Tooting	Finchley & Golders
West Ham	Westminster	Green
	North	Hornchurch & Upminster
Cluster 15 – Outer London –		Kingston & Surbiton
Immigrant Concentrations		Old Bexley & Sidcup
Brent Central		Orpington
Brent North		Putney
Croydon North		Richmond Park
Ealing Acton & Shepherd's Bush		Romford
Ealing Central & Acton		Ruislip, Northwood &
Ealing North		Pinner
Ealing Southall		Sutton and Cheam
Edmonton		Twickenham
Erith & Thamesmead		Upminster
Feltham & Heston		Uxbridge & South Ruislip
Harrow East		Wimbledon
Harrow West'		
Hayes & Harlington		*Cluster 20 – High Status*
Hendon		*Inner London*
Ilford South		Chelsea & Fulham
Leyton & Wanstead		
Mitcham & Morden		
Walthamstow		

Colour code – White = Liberal; Light Grey = Conservative; Dark Grey = Labour.
Turnout 70% (69% UK); percentage share – Con 33% (42% UK), Lab 55% (40% UK), Lib 9% (7% UK); Number of candidates: Con 73 (out of 73); Labour 73 (of 73); Lib 73 (of 73).
Source: London Data Store – www.data.london.gov.uk/elections.

6 Party organisation, membership and the influence of socialism

Introduction

This chapter describes the growth and development of local Labour Party activity in some selected areas of London, using Croydon and Lambeth again as case studies to illustrate wider developments. It will look at the way organisation and membership, including the influence of socialist groups, changed over time. It is divided into four sections. Section I discusses the period before 1918 ('Socialists, Progressives and Labour 1900–1918'). Section II discusses the period characterised in this book as a municipal social democracy ('Growth and decline of a mass party 1918–1968'). Section III explores 'The rise and fall of the New Left 1968–1997.' Section IV discusses the revival in the fortunes of socialism within the party after 2015 ('Momentum – the Old Left Reborn 1997–2020').

The chapter will help to identify those issues which motivated individuals to either join or vote for the Labour Party at particular points in time (not related to questions of wider social structure), whether it be national events, socialism or other beliefs and values. This will correct some of the more critical and sometimes static historical interpretations of the party, and add to the growing collection of local studies on the history of the labour movement, such as recently published works on Liverpool, Manchester and Oxford.[1] In doing so, the chapter adopts the approach advocated by 'the new political history' (see below) and 'history from below,' championed by Edward Thompson.[2] There are a large number of local studies on the history of the labour movement, but these have tended to focus on Labour's strength in its traditional northern heartlands, rather than on those areas where it was relatively weak during the first half of the twentieth century, such as the big cities and the suburbs.[3] For London, there are only a small

---

1 Davies, *Liverpool Labour*; McHugh, *Labour in the City (Manchester)*; Bowie, *Reform and Revolt in the City of Dreaming Spires (Oxford)*.

2 Thompson, *The Making of the English Working Class*.

3 Reynolds and Laybourn, *Labour Heartlands*; Lancaster and Mason, *Life and Labour in Coventry*; Savage, *The Dynamics of Working-Class Politics (Preston)*. There are a

168   *Thematic*

number of books dealing with the labour movement in the twentieth century as well as a recently awarded doctorate on the history of the party in West London, a neglected area of the capital as historians have been drawn to the East End with its more identifiable working-class communities and concentrations of immigrant populations, such as the Jews.[4] The historical works dealing with London have concentrated on the earlier part of the twentieth century and there is almost nothing specific on the period after 1945, apart from a number of publications covering the New Left and the crisis in local government during the 1980s.[5]

As we have seen in Chapter 1, the party's championing of local government and state intervention to defend working-class interests, especially the provision of municipal housing and rate equalisation across the capital, in a region of weak trade unionism, raised its profile during and after the First World War. As we have seen in Chapter 2, the First World War laid the foundations of its electoral success as a party of the working class after the extension of the franchise in 1918. The ability of the party to secure alliances between middle- and working-class voters, and within the working class itself between different religious and racial interests, such as Catholics and Jews, helps explain in part its success during the interwar period (see Chapter 7). Individual socialists and socialist groups and parties played a significant part in all these developments. As affiliated socialist societies, the Independent Labour Party (ILP) and to a lesser extent the Social Democratic Federation (SDF) supported independent labour representation before 1914, albeit without much success in London. Along with local trade union branches, the ILP was crucial in providing candidates (less so money) to fight elections in London before and after 1918. It disaffiliated in 1932, ideologically caught between the CPGB and the Labour Party, but many members remained in the party as individuals or they joined the Communist Party of Great Britain (CPGB), formed in the wake of the Russian Revolution by members of the SDF and others, such as the suffragist Sylvia Pankhurst.[6] The CPGB made numerous failed attempts to affiliate to

---

considerable number of unpublished theses listed in the journal *Labour History Review*, three of which have been relevant – Hugh Atkinson, 'The Rise and Fall of the London New Urban Left in London Labour Politics 1976–1987' (PhD South Bank University, 1995); Michael Passmore, 'The responses of Labour-controlled London local authorities to major changes in housing policy, 1971–1983' (PhD University of London, 2015); Heidi Topman, 'A Study of the Rise and decline of selected Labour Halls in the Greater London Area, 1918–1979' (PhD University of Kingston, 2006).

4 Bush, *Behind the Lines* (East End First World War); Goss, *Local Labour and Local Government* (Southwark); Marriott, *The Culture of Labourism* (East End); Humphries, 'The origins and development of the Labour Movement in West London, 1918–1970' (University of Reading, PhD, 2019). There are a number of very useful articles on London in *Labour Heritage, a Labour history society for the London area* (www.labour-heritage.com).

5 Lansley, Goss and Wolmar, *Councils in Conflict*; Body and Fudge, *Local Socialism?*

6 Dowse, *Left in the Centre*.

Party organisation 169

the party nationally, but it was relatively weak in London during the 1920s, even during the General Strike, only becoming stronger in the build-up to the Second World War when many people joined to oppose the rise of fascism. Over a dozen constituency parties and local trades councils were expelled from the party and the TUC in the capital after 1927 for their co-operation with the CPGB, a much higher figure than in other parts of the country.[7] London has remained an important centre of socialist activity since that time. Socialism has been and continues to be a feature of its metropolitan and radical political tradition.[8]

Socialism continued to exert influence thereafter through affiliated internal pressure groups, like the Socialist League, set up in 1932, which sought to influence the party on issues like unemployment, the Spanish Civil War, including the very popular demand for a 'People's Front' against the rise of fascism in the late 1930s.[9] This led to further expulsions, including the high-profile MP for North Lambeth, George Struass, and Stafford Cripps, the MP for Bristol East, although they re-joined the party later. After the war, the CPGB was relatively strong in the coal fields, as it always had been, and achieved some limited influence in, for example, the munition factories in the outer suburbs of London (e.g. Napiers in Acton), and it stood candidates in local and parliamentary elections. But its influence diminished during the early 1950s in the context of the post-war boom. It suffered a dramatic drop in membership after the invasion of Hungry in 1956.[10] After the war, the main left-wing group within the party was that which coalesced around Aneurin Bevan, Richard Crossman and Michael Foot opposed to the modernisers in the Party represented by Hugh Gaitskell and Tony Crosland, who wanted to water down the party's commitment to nationalisation.[11] The Trotskyists were of only minor influence. Following the formation of the Fourth International 1938, members of various Trotskyist groups joined local constituency parties after the war, like Ted Knight in Norwood. They campaigned on issues like nuclear disarmament and racial discrimination, amongst other issues, but while Labour Party membership reached a high point of over 1 million in 1951, they remained only a very small minority. Many individuals were expelled, particularly in London, with some re-joining during the 1970s with the revival of the New Left.

---

7 Clinton, *Trade Union Rank and File*, pp. 138–66.

8 Cragoe and Taylor, *London Politics*.

9 The attempt to create a 'Popular Front' in Britain against fascism in the late 1930s took the form of a failed political alliance against the National Government's appeasement of Nazi Germany. It was made up of left-wing elements in the Labour Party, the Liberal Party, the ILP, the CPGB and some rebellious members of the Conservative Party, such as Winston Churchill. However, it was opposed by the Labour Party, which objected to the involvement of the CPGB. See Joyce, 'The Liberal Party and the Popular Front.'; Pimlott, 'The Socialist League: Intellectuals and the Labour Left in the 1930s.'

10 Morgan, Cohen and Flinn, *Communists and British Society 1920–1991*.

11 Jenkins, *Bevanism*.

170   *Thematic*

Socialist influence increased after 1970. The success of the New Left in local government, especially the GLC (less so in national politics), was based on its ability to bring together a 'rainbow alliance' of different political interests and voluntary organisations, not always successfully, reflecting the changing demographic and social make-up of London.[12] 'For feminism and the black movement, the existence of the GLC and its grants strategy had a number of important effects,' especially in building opposition to Thatcherism in the 1980s beyond the traditional confines of class voting.[13] In London, such alliances embraced both national and international interests (anti-capitalist as well as anti-imperialist, such as support for Palestine and anti-apartheid), as well as groups defined by their personal identity (see Chapter 7 on the influence of gender, race and religion). However, the defeats of the left in London during the early 1980s (ratecapping, abolition of the GLC, to name but two) were in part the result of the way this alliance fragmented socially and politically, and in part a fightback by the traditional social democratic wing of the party.[14] New alliances across social classes and racial groups were made with the advent of New Labour in the 1990s. However, many socialists left the party over the direction of New Labour following the Iraq War, but re-joined following the election of Jeremy Corbyn as a leader in 2015. A new left-wing pressure group Momentum was formed after Corbyn's election, reviving the fortunes of the old New Left. Many older ex-members came back, together with a very large intake of new younger members. It was particularly strong in London, always seen by the party leadership as a troublesome bastion of a variety of different socialist groups, such as the CPGB during the 1920s and 1930s and the Trotskyists after 1950.

There have been a range of different historical interpretations of the party as an organisation since the 1950s. The first serious historian of the Labour Party was Henry Pelling, who focused primarily on the organisational growth and development of the institutions of the labour movement, such as the party and the trade unions, including the Communist Party. Although his interests stretched to social geography and the importance of class, he was not a Marxist. His empirical and evidenced-based approach is unfairly regarded by some as worthy but dull.[15] Later historians like Ross McKibbin sought to interpret the party in the broader context of social class, out of which grew an understanding of the British working class as uniquely 'labourist,' unlike its continental partners, such as the German Social Democratic Party. He argued that the rise of the Labour Party to replace the Liberals as the main opposition to the Conservative Party by the 1930s was

---

12 A 'Rainbow Alliance' is a group of people from many different types of backgrounds working together politically.
13 Campbell, 'Politics, Pyramids and People.'
14 Campbell & Jacques, 'Goodbye to the GLC.'
15 Reid, 'Class and Politics in the Work of Henry Pelling.'

Party organisation 171

the result of 'an acutely developed working class consciousness' that was able to identify with Labour as a class party once universal manhood suffrage, and limited female enfranchisement, had been achieved in 1918. However, he said that it was a class consciousness of a defensive and non-political nature, 'which obstructed the spread of socialism and excluded Labour from many areas of working-class life. Though the party remained ideologically vague, it was unable to become the sort of catch-all "people's party" which some of its leaders desired.'[16] There was 'No Marxism in Britain' because the working class was above all constitutional, respectable and deferential towards royalty and state institutions, more enthusiastic about sport than politics.[17] Left-wing historians, writing from a highly critical Marxist perspective after 1956, like Ralph Miliband, Perry Anderson and Tom Nairn argued that the Labour Party could not break out from the hopelessly reformist ideology of 'Labourism' or 'Parliamentary Socialism.' There is now an extensive academic and popular literature which has explored the nature of 'Labourism,' in order to account as the authors see it, for the party's various failures and weaknesses.[18] One historian of the party likened this 'to blaming the working class for the failings of the Labour leadership.'[19]

Later historians have attempted to confront and challenge what they see as these monolithic, negative and static interpretations of the party's development. A new approach to political history has emerged which is critical of an electoral sociology which sees the link between class and voting too broadly, ignoring local details, such as politics, religion and other factors influencing political choice, such as identities with neighbourhoods (see Chapter 4 on localities). This argues 'that political values derive from local communities, where they are formed both by local workplace and neighbourhood experiences and by the political, social, economic, religious and recreational networks which underpin them.'[20] One of the leading proponents of this 'new political history' was Duncan Tanner. He rejected the view that the extension of the franchise in 1918 was responsible for the rise of the Labour Party, arguing that restrictions on registration before 1918 did not deny working-class men the vote, but disadvantaged all single and young men, although he did stress the importance of labour movement activism in maximising the labour vote after the war, especially amongst new female voters. It was not class consciousness, he argued, that benefited Labour after the war, but the failure of Liberalism during the war, when it split with Lloyd George who then joined with the Conservatives in a right-wing post-war coalition. The Liberals became over-identified as an anti-socialist party. In the gap created, Labour inherited the mantle of radical Liberalism

16 Callaghan, 'Ross McKibbin: Class Cultures, the Trade Unions and the Labour Party.'
17 Ghosh, 'The Guv'nor: The Place of Ross McKibbin in the Writing of British History.'
18 Ibid.; Allender, *What's Wrong with Labour.*
19 Thorpe, *A History of the Labour Party*, p. 4.
20 Stevens, 'The Electoral Sociology of Modern Britain Reconsidered.'

172   *Thematic*

(in London the Progressives) and was not therefore a socialist party in a clearly defined sense, but one which united a coalition of interests around the need for state intervention.[21] The 'New Political History' is the latest reiteration of a variety of different theoretical approaches that have been used to interpret the history of the Labour Party. It rejects the view that the party is 'peculiarly 'British' or warranting a specific approach ('Labour History') (but) situates Labour in a broader re-thinking of political history'.[22] More recent and local studies of Labour have also emphasised 'history from below,' an approach taken forward by historians such as Matthew Worley and Dan Weinbren.[23]

Socialists, Progressives and Labour (1900–1918)

Before 1918 and the adoption of individual party membership, the Labour movement was made up of a variety of different trades and labour councils, representing local trade union branches, many of them formed with the help of socialist groups after the 'New Unionism' of the unskilled had swept through London and the docks in the late 1880s and early 1890s. The federal structure of the movement also included branches of the Marxist SDF set up by Henry Hyndman in 1881 and the socialist ILP set up by Keir Hardie in 1893. The SDF was stronger in the capital, and more working class than the ILP, whose influence was greater in smaller northern towns, like Halifax where labour was better organised around the activities of the chapels and the trade unions.[24] The Fabian Society did not really see itself as part of the labour movement in London, preferring to work through the Progressives which controlled the LCC before 1907, although they did affiliate to the Labour Representation Committee in 1900, which became the Labour Party in Parliament in 1906. These various organisations contested elections to the LCC, the new borough councils created in 1900, boards of guardians (which administered the Poor Law) and the school boards (until education was taken over by the LCC in 1902). But they did so on only an intermittent basis, sometimes in alliance with other Liberal and Radical political bodies, including religious and temperance interests. The moves towards independent Labour representation in London had great difficulty in breaking away from the influence of the Progressives (see Chapter 1). The SDF disaffiliated from the LRC after only a year, distrustful of the relationship between the trade unions and the Liberal Party, seen as too close to the employers.

To take Lambeth as an example, in 1898, the SDF branch in North Lambeth nominated Harry Quelch, one of its leaders as a candidate to the

---

21 Tanner, *Political Change and the Labour Party 1900–1918*.
22 Callaghan, *Interpreting the Labour Party*, p. 35.
23 Weinbren, *Generating Socialism*; Worley, *Labour Inside the Gate*; Worley, *Labour's Grass Roots*.
24 Howell, *British Workers and the Independent Labour Party, 1888–1906*.

Party organisation 173

Lambeth East School Board. He polled a respectable vote but still failed to be elected.[25] A year later, Charles Iremonger, from the Kennington branch of the ILP and a member of the Friendly Society of Iron Founders (which was one of the first unions to affiliate to the LRC in 1900), stood unsuccessfully as a Progressive in the election to the Prince's Ward of the Lambeth Vestry.[26] He had been previously elected to the Vestry in 1894 and campaigned for the recognition of trade union rights, more investment in road repairs in the northern wards and for improved working conditions for the female dust sorters in the crowded and insanitary wharfs on the south-side of the Thames.[27] Up to about 1905, the Lambeth Trades Council remained part of a Progressive Alliance linked to but increasingly suspicious of the Liberal Party. Such councils played a key role in cementing relationships between the working-class movement and the Liberal Party, over international issues like opposition to the Boer War.[28] In 1903, a *North Lambeth Labour and Progressive Association* (NLLPA) was formed and they ran a slate of trade union candidates in the second election to the new borough council, polling 20%, but losing out to the Progressives as a result of the intervention of a number of independent candidates. In the 1903 council elections, the Municipal Reform Party won 34 seats and the Progressives 26.[29] In the same year, the North Lambeth Liberal and Radical Association (NLLRA) supported the adoption of Dadabhai Naoroji, a Parsi intellectual and veteran leader of the Indian Congress Movement, as the parliamentary candidate for North Lambeth.[30] He had been elected as the first Indian MP for the working-class seat of Finsbury Central in 1892, defeating the sitting Conservative by only 5 votes. He was later known as the 'Grand Old Man of India,' for his advocacy of Indian nationalism.[31] Along with his fellow Parsi, the barrister Sir Mancherjee Bhownaggree, who had been elected as the Unionist MP for Bethnal Green North East in 1895 (ousting the veteran radical George Howell, who complained that he had been 'kicked out by a black man, a stranger from India), these candidates represented the strong connections that existed between the empire and the politics of both main parties in London at this time, including trade union interests defending free trade but calling for immigration controls.[32]

By 1905, a number of trade unions affiliated to the Lambeth Trades and Labour Council had severed their links with the Liberal Party, although

---

25 *Justice*, 8 February 1898.
26 *South London Press*, 7 May 1898.
27 Ibid., 4 March 1899 and 17 February 1900.
28 Clinton, *The Trade Union Rank and File*, p. 34.
29 *South London Press*, 10 October 1903; Woolard and Willis, *Twentieth Century Local Election Results*, p. 38.
30 *South London Press*, 9 May 1903.
31 Craig, *British Parliamentary Elections. Guardian*, 26 July 2013 – 'Britain's first Asian MP.'
32 Windscheffel, 'In Darkest Lambeth', 193–4.

174   *Thematic*

many individual trade unionists remained loyal to the Progressives. A year before, the local press had reported that William Lock, its treasurer and a member of the Gas Workers Union had been adopted as a Labour candidate for the LCC, describing him as 'a thorough-going Progressive – in a socialist sense.'[33] But after the election, this confusion was only partly resolved when the trades council (which was affiliated to the NLLRA) withdrew its support of Naoroji, following, it alleged, his 'reactionary conduct' during the campaign.[34] In 1905, the ILP nominated Charles Iremonger for a by-election in Vauxhall to the borough council, a local contest which the trades council considered had a chance of winning, unlike parliamentary or LCC contests for which it did not have the resources to fight. The radical newspaper, the *London Daily News*, owned by the temperance reformer and Quaker George Cadbury, encouraged all Progressives to vote for Iremonger, as did the vicar and members of St Anne's Church, South Lambeth Road, following a sermon by Stewart Headlam on the 'Church as an instrument of social reform.'[35]

Ethical socialism in London brought the churches and left-wing politics into a close relationship on a range of Progressive issues, such as temperance reform (see Chapter 7 for the influence of religion).[36] The socialist parson 'was increasingly in evidence in London' during the Edwardian period (and to some extent after 1918).[37] George Lansbury, for example, who re-joined the Church of England in 1901, had three parsons on his platform when he stood as a parliamentary candidate for Bow in January 1910.[38] Iremonger was no different in this respect and had close links with the church. He won the by-election in 1905, described by the *Labour Leader*, as the 'first Labour representative to gain a seat on the Borough Council.'[39] The *South London Press* reported that he had refused the help of the official Liberal Party, 'maintaining an independent Labour attitude.' This attitude continued after 1905 resulting in a vitriolic exchange of letters from those anti-socialist trade unionists who remained politically attached to the Liberal Party, accusing the trades council of being controlled by class-war elements in the SDF.[40]

From the early 1880s, there were over 120 different branches of the Marxist SDF in London, mainly concentrated in the old industrial quarters in the centre but also well represented in some of the suburbs such as Croydon and Walthamstow, where industry was growing and relocating.[41] In Hackney, for

33 *South London Press*, 5 March 1904.
34 Ibid., 13 May 1905.
35 *London Daily News*, 23 September 1905; *Labour Leader*, 22 September 1905. Stewart Headlam was a Progressive councillor in Bethnal Green.
36 Cox, *The English Churches in a Secular Society.*
37 McLeod, *Class and Religion in the late Victorian City*, pp. 118–20.
38 *East London Observer*, 15 January 1910.
39 *Labour Leader*, 4 November 1905.
40 *South London Press*, 9 April 1904.
41 Thompson, *Socialists, Liberals and Labour*, Appendices C & D.

Party organisation 175

example, there had been five different branches of the SDF, the first one covering Hackney and Shoreditch. A branch was set up in 1903 which attracted some Jewish workers and it successfully stood one independent socialist candidate for the borough council.[42] But in suburban areas of London, their influence was declining in the face of a resurgent form of ethical socialism. This was the case in Croydon, where a branch of the SDF had been formed as early as 1884.[43] This was followed by a branch of the breakaway Socialist League in 1886, the national membership of which included William Morris, but it lapsed two years later. In October 1890, the Fabian Society organised a demonstration in support of the Eight Hour Day addressed by George Bernard Shaw.[44] Socialists provided the political platforms that gave birth to the demand for independent labour representation. As a result, a Croydon Trades and Labour Council was formed in 1890, following a mass meeting in support of the Great Dock Strike in 1889, organised by the Croydon Working Men's Liberal and Radical Club. It was attended by over 500 and described in the local press 'as remarkably revolutionary and socialistic.'[45] High levels of continuing unemployment in the building trades led to further demonstrations and strikes during the course of 1890 and 1891.[46]

The Croydon Advertiser complained in an editorial that extremists were seeking to sow division within Progressive ranks by 'pledging the Croydon Liberal Association to a strict labour policy.'[47] But at a meeting of the Croydon Federation of Trades and Labour Unions in 1891, a union member made it clear that 'as a trade unionist of 26 years he was happy to say his union had never done anything against the law, and their principal object was to keep wages up to which he thought no gentleman present could object.'[48] In 1893, Henry Muggeridge, a socialist convert from the Penge Liberal Party, was instrumental in setting up the Croydon Socialist Society, widening its appeal to a larger group of non-aligned socialists and Progressives, including many from the Labour churches. It called for the abolition of private property, an eight-hour working day and trade union rates of pay for council workers.[49] The secularists (or materialists) within the SDF fell out with the Brotherhood Church, and with its member Henry Muggeridge, over religion and the influence of the church in politics.[50]

Branches of the ILP did not become fully established in Croydon until after 1903.[51] This coincided with a more concerted move towards independent

---

42 Rothstein, *The Hackney and Kingsland Branch of the SDF.*
43 *Justice,* 10 May, 1 & 8 November 1884.
44 *Croydon Times,* 11 October 1890.
45 *Croydon Chronicle,* 7 & 14 September 1889.
46 Ibid., 17 January and 13 June 1891.
47 *Croydon Advertiser,* 21 May 1892.
48 *Croydon Times,* 25 March 1891.
49 Creighton, *Radical Croydon 1860–1939,* p. 10.
50 *Justice,* 25 August, 1 September & 10 November 1894.
51 Ibid., 3 September 1892.

176 *Thematic*

labour representation after 1900, more so than in other more working-class areas of inner London where the Progressives had more established links with the trade unions. In 1902, a Croydon Labour Electoral Council (CLEC) was formed and it affiliated to the national LRC in 1903.[52] Its initial programme was concerned primarily with education, which was one of the most controversial political questions in Croydon at the time over the implications of the 1902 Education Act. In 1903, the Croydon and District Trades and Labour Council nominated a local stonemason, Sidney Stranks, arguing that he was the best Progressive candidate following the withdrawal of two potential Liberal candidates. It stressed its Progressives credentials by arguing that 'the Labour Party in Croydon is not a socialist organisation, but composed of different circles of thought who have found for the time being a common ground to work from to advance Labour representation.'[53] This level of local support may have been one of the reasons why Croydon had been initially included in the list of single-member constituencies where the Liberal Party was prepared to stand down as part of the pact between the Liberal Chief Whip Herbert Gladstone and Labour's Ramsay MacDonald.[54] In the event, the local Liberals were not willing to do so, leading to a three-cornered fight in the 1906 general election. This created great bitterness and tensions within the local Progressive alliance over the split vote, which allowed the Conservative Liberal Unionist to win with the support of less than 45% of the electorate.

The local Labour movement in Croydon was badly damaged by this split. It did not fully recover thereafter, overtaken by the suburbanisation which undermined its social base within the manual working class. After 1906, socialists (SDF and ILP) broke away from supporting the Trades and Labour Council as did a number of trade unionists. However, at the same time, the tradition of ethical socialism continued to flourish if not expand through new branches of the ILP which met the needs of more unattached socialists and especially women who were campaigning for the vote. Up to that time, the SDF and the building trade unions had dominated the local labour movement, but thereafter the ethical socialism of the ILP and the labour churches recruited more members from Croydon's increasingly fluid population of residents and commuters with its metropolitan connections. In 1907, a Socialist Sunday School was established and a Labour Church in South Norwood had an audience of 400 to hear Henry Muggeridge, now a prominent member of the Fabian Society, expound on the doctrine of 'Socialism, Pure and Scientific.'[55] Social tensions between working-class

---

52 Report of the Third Annual Conference of the Labour Representation Committee (February 1903).
53 Stranks, 'Liberalism and Labour', *Croydon & District Trades and Labour Council* (December 1904).
54 Bealey and Pelling, *Labour and Politics*.
55 *Justice*, 5 October & 23 November 1907.

Party organisation 177

trade unionists ('the fustians') and lower-middle-class socialists ('the black coated proletariat') became more marked after the split in the Progressive alliance arising from the 1906 general election. In some of the better class districts of London where trade union organisation was relatively weak or weakening, the ILP

> was taking the place of the SDF as the socialist element in the Labour Party. In others it was developing into the middle-class socialist party which had been the ambition of some of the Fabian rebels. In contrast to the scarcity of trade union leaders, it was easy to find school masters and clergy, rich City men, stockbrokers and company secretaries in the ILP ranks.[56]

Despite initial talks in Croydon about socialist unity between the ILP and the SDF, by the time the SDF had been renamed the British Socialist Party (forerunner of the CPGB) in 1911, the West Croydon branch had ceased to exist and the Woodside branch was also in a 'languishing condition.'[57] By 1911, the history of the SDF in Croydon had come to an end. Its existence had ebbed and flowed since the early formation of a Croydon branch in 1885, before finally expiring in 1911. A West Croydon branch had existed between 1904 and 1909.[58] It would take the impact of the First World War to create the circumstances for the formation of a branch of the CPGB, which received some support from the workers in the Aircraft Factory at Waddon and from ex-members of the ILP radicalised by the Russian Revolution.

The situation in Lambeth was little different. By 1910, the trades council had been reconstituted as the Lambeth and District Labour Representation Committee (LDLRC) and affiliated to the National Labour Party.[59] This created problems for individuals like Frank Smith, a close friend of Keir Hardie, who had been elected as a Progressive, albeit a Labour socialist one, as the LCC member for North Lambeth in 1907 and 1910. Hardie, had to intervene in April 1910 on behalf of the NEC of the Labour Party over the unhappiness of the LDLRC with his nomination, reporting that Smith had only been 'provisionally' selected as the candidate for North Lambeth. The nomination went ahead in any case.[60] The Brixton branch of the ILP equally complained about Will Crooks, the Labour MP for Woolwich, for speaking at a Progressive candidate's hustings in 1913, but again the national party

---

56 Thompson, *Socialists, Liberals and Labour*, p. 231.
57 *Justice*, 22 March 1913.
58 Young, 'Social Democratic Federation Membership in London.'
59 Labour Party Archives (LPA): NEC 13 April 1910; Labour Party Annual Report 1916 – Lambeth LRC was regarded as a local Labour Party and not a trades council, which operated under different rules.
60 Ibid., NEC 13 & 21 April and 30 June 1910. Smith was defeated by 13 votes in the 1913 LCC election for North Lambeth.

178   *Thematic*

took no action, tacitly acknowledging the strength of Progressive politics in London.[61] The problem for the LDLRC was summed up when just before the general election of December 1910, its secretary wrote to *The Times* to say why it could not support the Lib-Lab candidature of Henry Gosling for North Lambeth. This was despite the fact that Gosling was one of the heroic trade union leaders of the Great Dock Strike of 1889, Lambeth born and bred, Progressive LCC member for St George's in the East since 1898, and General Secretary of the Watermen, Lightermen and Bargemen, sitting on the Parliamentary Committee of the Trades Union Congress. 'He has not been considered as a candidate,' the secretary wrote

> by any representative Labour Party in North Lambeth, and is not there-fore, in any sense whatever a candidate of the Labour Party. He is in reality, the candidate of the North Lambeth Liberal and Radical Asso-ciation, and his own union. At the conference of delegates called by the political council of the North Lambeth Liberal and Radical Club, to which every trade union in North Lambeth was invited, the delegates decided by 17 votes to one that they could not endorse the candidature of Mr. Gosling.[62]

In practice therefore, Labour in London had great difficulty before 1914 in forging a clear identity as an independent political force. It remained a loose alliance of trade unionists and ethical socialists, such as the Fabians and the ILP as well as some Progressives on the radical wing of the Liberal Party. Liberal reforms, such as old age pensions, land reform and national insur-ance, blurred the distinction between Labour and the Progressives. Lloyd George had argued in 1906, and was proved correct, that the only chance of carrying Croydon for the Progressive Party 'was by supporting the Liberal candidate.'[63] Given the changing social composition of the borough during the Edwardian period, similar to many other suburban areas, and the re-stricted franchise, it is unlikely that Labour in Croydon would have made any more progress than the limited presence it had achieved on the council and the board of guardians by 1914. It was certainly not in a position to field candidates during the two general elections in 1910, when the constituency had become marginal. Talk of a Progressive League in Croydon attracted derisory comments in the local press.[64] But a Progressive tradition contin-ued throughout the war and into the interwar period when the Labour Party in Croydon recruited an increasing number of ex-Liberals angry about their party's anti-socialist and pro-war stand.

61 LPA: NEC, 6 March 1913.
62 *The Times*, 30 November 1910.
63 *Times*, 6 January 1906.
64 *Croydon Advertiser*, 18 & 22 October 1910.

Party organisation 179

The war split the labour movement between pro- and anti-war factions. In Croydon, for example, many of the leading party members supported the war, although not all were super patriots like Will Crooks MP or the trade unionist Ben Tillett. The two eldest sons of Henry Muggeridge joined up, as did Percival Cosedge, Labour councillor for South Norwood, who before 1914 had supported Keir Hardie's call for an international General Strike to prevent war. He was killed at Mons in December. According to Muggeridge's other more famous literary son Malcolm, the outbreak of war elicited a pragmatic response from his father, who had been a committed pacifist before the war, but supported the conflict 'in the hope that, once won, it would be possible to take steps to prevent anything of the kind oc-curring again.'[65] Croydon became a centre of anti-war sentiment and or-ganisations. The number of conscientious objectors in total numbered over 200.[66] The Quakers played a pivotal role as did the Croydon and Thornton Heath branches of the ILP. By 1915, Croydon had an active branch of the Non-Conscription Fellowship (NCF), and branches of the Union of Dem-ocratic Control (UDC) and the Fellowship of Reconciliation (FOR). The UDC attracted the growing support of 'not only radicals – left-wing or social reform Liberals – who objected to their party's backing of wartime policies but also of Labour...and facilitated the transition of a significant number of Liberals to the Labour Party.'[67] Opposition to conscription and the war more generally was expressed through a local newsletter called *The Epistle*, edited by Harry Curtis Jones, a Co-op salesman, conscientious ob-jector and ILP member. Three months later, it reported the formation of a local branch of the National Council against Conscription which quickly became the Croydon branch of the National Council of Civil Liberties. A 'Peace Conference' was held in November 1916 calling for early negotiations to secure a just and lasting peace.[68]

Thus, the war only partly resolved the confusion between Progressivism and independent Labour which had diluted the party's identity in London before 1914. But in other respects, as we have seen in Chapter 1, the war (together with the extension of the franchise in 1918) laid the foundations for Labour to replace the Liberals as the main opposition to the Conserv-atives. In Croydon, for example, the Ratepayers Association had by this date developed into an effective anti-socialist political body, representing Conservative and Liberal opinions. As a result, many Progressives drifted towards Labour, giving the party a particular middle-class ethos in some of the suburbs of the capital. This marginalised some of the more working-class trade unionists who had been members of the SDF before 1914 and who had supported the candidacy of the working-class stonemason Sidney

---

65 Muggeridge, *Chronicles of Waster Time*, pp. 68–9.
66 Pearce, 'The Anti-war Movement in Croydon 1914–1918,' (unpublished manuscript).
67 Swartz, *The Union of Democratic Control*, p. 1.
68 Pearce, 'The Anti-war Movement in Croydon.'

180   *Thematic*

Stranks in the 1906 general election. He stands out as probably the only truly working-class Labour candidate for election in Croydon.

Growth and decline of a mass party (1918–1968)

After the adoption of Labour's new constitution in 1918, which created individual membership for the first time and adopted a clearly socialist objective (clause four), constituency or divisional parties were established fairly rapidly in London.[69] In Lambeth, only Kennington was able to field a parliamentary candidate, polling a respectable 28% of the vote, utilising the electoral machinery of the old trades council and the active members of the local ILP branch. There were two new affiliations to the National Labour Party during 1918 – Lambeth Central and Brixton.[70] Brixton CLP applied unsuccessfully for a grant from the London Labour Party (LLP) in November 1919 to help fight the local elections, but the regional party was equally short of money. At the time, Herbert Morrison was pleading with affiliated trade unions and cooperative societies to contribute to a special election fund, complaining that the regional party had run the LCC elections in February on a budget of only £350 for the whole of London.[71] Out of 77 London Labour Parties in the early 1920s, only 27 had full-time agents. They were reliant on good trade union organisation to fight elections rather than large individual memberships. Woolwich and Bermondsey were perhaps the only two examples of parties with mass membership covering whole geographical areas within the London region, and in the case of Woolwich the membership of the Royal Arsenal Cooperative Society (RACS).[72]

It is not clear how many of these new parties had enrolled individual members in the immediate post-war period as accurate membership figures are not available until the late 1920s (see Table 6.1 on page 182). Trade union delegates would have constituted a large element of the membership together with members of socialist societies affiliated to the party (see Table 6.2 on page 184). Indeed, the leaders of the pre-war local labour parties in London may have been rather reluctant to change the structure of the party by introducing paid officials and individual membership.[73] The trades councils before the war had been the vehicles for organising the registration of voters, before this

---

69 Clause four was a commitment

> to secure for the workers by hand or by brain the full fruits of their industry and the most equitable distribution thereof that may be possible upon the basis of the common ownership of the means of production, distribution and exchange, and the best obtainable system of popular administration and control of each industry or service

> Labour Party Annual Report 1918

70 *Labour Party Annual Report* 1919.
71 LMA: LLP EC, 25 April and 19 November 1919.
72 Berger, *The British Labour Party and the German Social Democrats,* p. 93.
73 Ibid., p. 92.

Party organisation 181

responsibility was taken over by the borough council registration officers in 1918, and for ensuring turn-out during elections. The Liberals in particular had been reliant on them in many areas of London to get their working-class voters to the polls, in the absence of a strong London Federation or well-resourced constituency parties. This was certainly the case in Kennington and North Lambeth, which were both strongholds of Progressivism before and after the war, although increasingly threatened by the move towards independent Labour thereafter. The trades council in Southwark, for example, played a vital role in Labour politics during the 1920s, campaigning on local issues such as housing, health and relief for the unemployed, as well as promoting trade union rights.[74] The trade unions, and to a much lesser extent the affiliated socialist societies, provided most of the funds and the nominations to contest elections in the early 1920s before individual membership started to take-off towards the end of the decade.[75] The party's failure to become financially independent of the trade unions at a local level restricted the influence of both the national party and in the case of London, the regional party, to direct and control the growth of local parties. Certainly, Herbert Morrison would have liked to have exercised more control in imitation of his much-admired SPD (Social Democratic Party of Germany) in Germany, but he met resistance from local parties keen to protect their independence.[76]

By 1925, individual party membership in London started to pick up while the number of affiliations from trade union branches and socialist societies declined as a result of expulsions, disaffiliations and government legislation. Individual membership was higher in London, given the general weakness of the trade unions.[77] In London, the ILP had joined on a nominal membership of 2,700, while the Fabian Society did so on a figure of 800. Many socialists had probably become individual members of the party rather than through their affiliated societies, with some perhaps joining more than one organisation, either the ILP or the Fabians, or after 1933 the newly formed Socialist League. Membership levels were influenced by a number of factors. By far, the most important for trade unionists was the Trades Disputes and Trade Union Act 1927 enacted by the Baldwin government in revenge for the General Strike. The Act outlawed secondary action and mass picketing. Most importantly, it also mandated trade union members to 'contract-in' to any political levy which their union made on their behalf, resulting in a reduction in membership levels and a significant fall in income for the LLP. Moreover, it forbade civil service unions from having political objectives, a problem for London where there was a higher proportion of white-collar trade union members than in other areas of the country. Over 10,000 civil servants disaffiliated from the LLP in 1927 leading to a loss of £86 a year in affiliation fees.

74 Goss, *Local Labour and Local Government.*
75 McKibbin, *Evolution of the Labour Party.*
76 Berger, *The British Labour Party and the German Social Democrats,* p. 102.
77 Tanner, 'Labour and Its Membership.'

Table 6.1 Party membership figures and affiliations – London Labour Party 1894–1929

Year	Membership figures	Affiliations
1894	No reliable figures available before 1927 Strongest parties before 1914 were Bermondsey Poplar West Ham Woolwich	Battersea (1908–1912); Bermondsey Labour Representation Committee (LRC) 1912–1914; Bethnal Green LRC 1910–1913; Croydon LRC; Deptford LRC 1906 & 1911–1914; Ealing LRC 1906–1907 and 1912–1914; East Ham LRC 1908–1914; Erith LR Ass. 1908–1911; Fulham 1909; Greenwich LRC 1905–1906; Hackney LRC 1906; Hammersmith LRC 1907–1914; Islington 1911–1914; Lambeth LRC 1910–1913; Lewisham LR Ass. 1904–1906; Poplar LRC 1906–1913 and then Labour Party 1914; St Pancras LRC 1905–1906; Shoreditch 1908–1909 than Shoreditch LRC, then Shoreditch Trades and Labour Council from 1911; Stepney Labour League 1903; Tottenham 1910; West Ham LRC 1906; Willesden 1908–1914; Wood Green LRC 1906–1907; Woolwich LRC 1905–1906.
1914 (May) 1914 1915	The inaugural conference to set up the LLP was attended by 338 delegates from trade unions and 86 delegates from socialist societies (ILP, Fabian & BSP) & Women's Labour League, Cooperative societies, Women's Socialist Circles and Women's Cooperative Guild. Chairman – John Stokes (Glassblowers) Treasurer – Dr Alfred Salter (Local Labour) Secretary – Fred Knee then Herbert Morrison ILP – James Mylles BSP – E C Fairchild Fabian Society – Susan Lawrence Women's Organisations – Dr Marion Phillips 134,951 (aggregate membership of trade unions and socialist societies) 151,549	The following local parties were affiliated to the National Party – Bermondsey LP; Croydon LRC; Deptford Labour Ass; Ealing & Acton Labour Council; Hackney Trades Council & Lab Rep. Ass.; Hammersmith Labour Council; Islington LRC & Trades Council; Lambeth LRC; Poplar LP; St Pancras LRC; Willesden LP. The following trades councils were also affiliated – East Ham; Enfield; Ilford & District; London; Woolwich. Trade Union section of the Executive Committee of the LLP: Fred Bramley (Nat. Ass. Of Furnishing Trades) Miss E Cook R M Gentry Will Godfrey (National Union of Vehicle Workers). George Isaacs (NATSOPA) Joseph Fineberg (BSP) Mary McArthur (Women's Trade Union League and suffragist)

Year	Affiliations	Notes	Members
1916	New national affiliations – Local Parties – Woolwich LR Ass. Trades Councils – Hampstead; Southwark, Walthamstow, West Ham.		189,854
1917	New affiliations: Local Parties – Bermondsey TC & LP; London; Westminster. Trades Councils – Battersea; Bromley; Ealing, Acton & Chiswick, Richmond, Tottenham; Watford; Wimbledon.	London Labour Party affiliates to the National Party. London Trades Council does not raise any objections but fears being eclipsed.	215,098.
1918	New affiliations of local parties and trades councils: Acton LP; Balham & Tooting; Battersea Trades & Labour Council (Central); Bethnal Green TC & LP; Bow & Bromley Local LP; Brixton LP: Camberwell LP: Camberwell North (Divisional LP); Camberwell Peckham Local LP; Croydon (Central) LP; Croydon (North) LP; Croydon (South) LP; Ealing LP; Edmonton LP; Finchley Divisional LP: Fulham (Central) LP; Fulham (East) LP; Fulham (West) LP; Greenwich KLP: Hackney (Central) LP; Hackney (South) Divisional LP; Hammersmith (Central) LP; Hampstead LP; Hendon LP; Hornsey LP; Ilford LP; Islington (East) Local LP; Kensington (North) LP; Kensington (South) LP; Lambeth (Central) LP; Marylebone LP & TC; Mile End LP; Mitcham LP; Norwood (Lambeth) LP; Poplar TC & Central LP; Putney & Southfields LP; St Pancras LP & TC (new title; St Pancras North LP; St Pancras SE LP; Southwark Central LP; Southwark (Northern) LP; Southwark (SE) LP; Stepney (Central) LP; Tottenham (South) LP; Twickenham Divisional LP; Wandsworth (Central) LP; Wandsworth (Central Division) LP; Willesden LP; Willesden (West) LP; Willesden (East) LP; Whitechapel & St Georges LP; Wimbledon LP; Wood Green & District TC & LP; Woolwich LP.		228,603
1919			290,958
1920			364,426
1921			385,969
1922			355,129
1923			353,886
1924			370,304
1925	In 1924 59 borough and divisional parties and a London University branch were affiliated to the LLP on notional figures. Deptford (1,100), Greenwich (1,440) and Woolwich (over 3,000) were the only parties with over 1,000 members.		374,238
1926			371,260
1929	By 1929 there were 60 borough and divisional parties and a London University branch still affiliated to the LLP on notional figures. Bermondsey, Rotherhithe (1,000); Bermondsey West (1,800); Deptford (1,600), Greenwich (2,250); Lambeth North (1,440); Lewisham East (2,000); Bow & Bromley (1,200); Poplar South (1,612); Woolwich East (2,188) and Woolwich West (2,117) had over 1,000 members.		

Sources: Compiled from Thompson, *Socialists, Liberals and Labour*, pp. 313–21; Labour Party Annual Reports for 1916–1919; London Labour Party Annual Reports 1924–1925 and 1928–1929.

184 *Thematic*

Table 6.2 Organisations affiliated to the London Labour Party in 1933

Local parties *(fees above £5 indicating high* *membership – in bold)*		*Trade unions* *(number of branches).* *Large affiliation fees – in bold.*	
Battersea Borough LP	Lambeth North LP	Asylum Workers	Musicians Union
Battersea North	Lambeth Norwood LP	Amal. Soc. of Bakers & Confectioners	**Nat. Ass. of Plasterers (£20)**
Battersea South (£5)	Lewisham TC & LP	Amal. Soc. of Boot & Shoe Makers (2)	National League of the Blind (2)
Bermondsey & Rotherhithe TC & LP	**Lewisham East LP (£20)**	Amal. Soc. of Electrotypers & Stereotypers	Nat. Soc. of Brassworkers
Bermondsey Rotherhithe LP	**Lewisham West LP (£6)**	Amal. Soc. of Farriers	Nat. Soc of Painters
Bermondsey West LP (£12)	Paddington Borough LP	Amal. Soc. of Woodworkers (5)	**Nat. Soc. of Printers (3) (£82)**
Bethnal Green TC & LP	Poplar TC & LP	Bakers Union, London Jewish.	Nat. Union of Cigar Makers
Bethnal Green NE LP	**Poplar Bow & Bromley LP (£5)**	Boilermakers, Iron & Shipbuilders	Nat. Union of Clerks (5)
Bethnal Green SW LP	**Poplar South LP (£16)**	Clothing Employees Union	**Nat. Union of Public Employees – London District (£27)**
Camberwell TC & LP	St Marylebone TC & LP	Constructional Engineering Union	**Nat. Union of Railwaymen (31) (£75)**
Camberwell Dulwich LP	St Pancras Borough LP	**Distributive & Allied Workers (Woolwich £13 + 4)**	Nat. Union of Shop Assistants (2)
Camberwell North LP (£6)	**St Pancras North LP (£7)**	Engineering Union (4)	Nat. Union of Vehicle Builders
Camberwell NW LP	St Pancras SE LP	Electrical Trades Union (9)	Nat. Union of Water Works Employees
Camberwell Peckham LP (£7)	St Pancras SW LP	Fire Brigades Union	Patternmarkers Ass.
Chelsea LP	**Shoreditch TC & LP (£5)**	Furnishing Trades Ass (4)	Plumbers & Domestic Engineers
Deptford LP (£20)	Southwark TC & LP	**General & Municipal Workers Union – London District (£100)**	Railway Clerks Ass.
Finsbury LP	Southwark Central LP	Gold, Silver & Allied Trades	Soc. of House & Ship Painters
Fulham TC & LP	Southwark North LP	Heating & Domestic Engineers (3)	Tailors & Garment Workers Union (2)
Fulham West LP (£6)	Southwark SE LP	Iron & Steel Trades Ass	
Fulham East LP (£5)	Stepney TC & LP	**London Society of Compositors (£67)**	
Greenwich LP (£22)	**Stepney Limehouse LP (£6)**		
Hackney TC & LP	**Stepney Mile End LP (£6)**		
Hackney Central LP	Stepney Whitechapel LP		
Hackney North LP	Stoke Newington LP		
Hackney South LP (£8)	Wandsworth LP & TC		
Hammersmith Borough LP	Wandsworth Balham & Tooting LP		
Hammersmith North LP			

(Continued)

Local parties (*fees above £5 indicating high membership – in bold*)		*Trade unions* (*number of branches*). Large affiliation fees – in bold.	
Hammersmith South LP	Wandsworth Central LP	**Machine Managers Trades Soc. (£17)**	**Transport & General**
Hampstead LP	Wandsworth	Mental Hospital &	**Workers Union**
Holborn LP	Clapham LP	Institutional	**(London Area)**
Islington Borough LP	Wandsworth Putney &	Workers Union (3)	**(£262)**
Islington East LP	Southfields LP		United French
Islington North LP	Wandsworth		Polishers
Islington South LP	Streatham LP		Union of
Islington West LP	Westminster LP		Operative
Kensington North LP (£5)	University of London LP		Plumbers
Lambeth TC & LP	Woolwich LP		
Lambeth Brixton LP	**Woolwich East LP (£14)**		
Lambeth Kennington LP	**Woolwich West LP (£14**		

Socialist Societies	*Cooperative Societies*
Fabian Society (£5) – membership 800	**Royal Arsenal Cooperative Society (RACS)**
Independent Labour Party (ILP) – London Divisional Council; Bermondsey; Clapham; Dulwich; London Central – membership about 2,700	**(Guild Council and 50 local guilds including the London Political Committee) (£452)** London Cooperative Guild (Clapton Branch)

Source: Compiled from LLP Papers (Executive Committee, February 1933). The annual affiliation fees to the LLP were – Borough LP in divided boroughs £1; Divisional LPs, including LPs in undivided boroughs 2d per individual member with a minimum of £1. Trade union branches could affiliate on a minimum of £1. The affiliation fee for the RACS was by negotiation.

A similar number disaffiliated from the Union of Post Office Workers, one of the larger blue-collar trade unions making sizeable financial contributions.[78] A year later, the London Trades Council (LTC) disaffiliated as a result of the Trades Dispute Act. The LLP always had an uneasy relationship with its older industrial wing of the movement, established as far back as 1860. The LTC provided a more ideologically comfortable home for a range of socialist opinion, such as the ILP, SDF and syndicalists before and during the First World War (acting as a break on the formation of the LLP before 1914), and for communists after the formation of the CPGB in 1920. Its left-wing stance on issues like unemployment was in stark contrast to

78 LLP EC June 1927.

186 *Thematic*

the parliamentary reformism represented by the Labour Party. Its influence had declined as the political wing of the movement grew after 1918. It became one of the channels for the CPGB to infiltrate the trade unions and the borough labour parties during the 1920s, souring relationships even further with the Labour Party and the TUC as they took ever stronger measures to expel suspected members of the CPGB from trades councils and constituency parties.[79] Herbert Morrison had encouraged merger talks between the LTC and the LLP but the two executives could not agree, suspicious of each other's motives.[80] The expulsion of 15 constituency and borough parties in London by the end of the 1920s for refusal to exclude communists from membership, and the disaffiliation of the LTC itself in 1928 due to the anti-trade union legislation, had a significant impact on membership levels. The reorganisation of new parties and trades councils also took up a great deal of time and staff resources in contacting previous trusted members and affiliated organisations.

While the number of members affiliated through their trade unions or socialist societies reduced, the party sought to recruit new members, especially women which probably made up about half of total members, by running regular membership drives, well organised by the regional party (see Chapter 7 for female membership). Membership figures at the time were based on negotiation rather than actual numbers, determined by cost rather than on real membership levels. The Labour movement in London did not fulfil the dream of Herbert Morrison to create a mass membership party in imitation of his much-admired German SPD. At certain times, local parties struggled to recruit members during 1925, for example, 'as they have been devoting themselves mainly to raising funds for the miners.'[81] The small number of election agents appointed to constituency parties at this time (21 full-time and 1 part-time by 1924 as well as two full-time London organisers) considered the capital to be a challenging district characterised above all by the alleged political apathy of the capital. At a meeting of agents held at Alexandra Palace in 1922, they reported, or rather complained that

> London with all its wonderful life of gaiety for the idle rich and tragedy for the wage earner ...London the workshop of the Labour Party agent, where in the hard conditions of toil for apathetic humanity, there is no equal in any other part of the country.[82]

Morrison worked extraordinarily hard to overcome such apathy and create a London-wide political machine. Although successful, he did not win many friends, attracting criticism for employing Tammany Hall-type tactics and

79 Clinton, *Trade Union Rank and File*, pp. 138–66.
80 Ibid., pp. 148–9.
81 LMA: LLP The Work of the London Labour Party 1925–26, p. 7.
82 Ibid., *Labour Organiser*, August 1923, p. 19.

Party organisation 187

behaving like an all-powerful 'city boss.'[83] He bombarded every organisation with requests to affiliate and donate money for election purposes. He succeeded in getting most borough parties (based mainly on previous trades council structures) and the new divisional or constituency parties, to affiliate to the LLP by the end of the 1920s. Privately, he hoped that the trades councils would wither and die on the vine as his objectives were above all political rather than industrial.[84] One of the problems for the Labour Party in London was the necessity, as Morrison saw it, of maintaining a central as well as a local organisation. Not all constituency parties and affiliated trade unions agreed, as it involved paying two sets of affiliation fees, one to their national organisations and one to the region. Morrison's attempt to abolish the borough parties and make the regional party the borough party for the whole of London met stiff opposition and failed.[85] During the 1920s, he had more success, at least in the short term in setting up a range of cultural and sporting organisations within the party coordinated at a regional level, in order to encourage 'communities of solidarity.'[86] Morrison wanted to attract new members that were not just trade union or socialist activists, but included a wider range of working- and middle-class voters, kept informed by local collectors and newsletters. For example, in 1924, he set up a Dramatic Federation, utilising existing organisations, such as the Clarion Dramatic Clubs, the Woodcraft Folk and the Cooperative guilds. Seventeen constituency parties had drama societies by the end of 1925. A Choral Union was established in the following year and a Sports Association in 1928, with its own football league and individual cricket, tennis, darts, billiards and swimming clubs. However, when faced with the growth of a powerful commercial leisure industry and national sporting organisations, as well as the cinema, such party initiatives could not compete and were not sustainable in the long term.

Morrison was more successful in building a highly effective relationship with the Transport & General Workers Union (T&GWU) and its General Secretary Ernest Bevin (although they thoroughly disliked each other), which secured the financial and organisational future of the party. Bevin generously supported the party at a regional and local level (affiliating over 24,000 members at two pence per person), exercising a powerful influence in helping to expel communists. Along with the London Society of Compositors (LSC) and the National Union of Railwaymen (NUR), such

---

83 Tammany Hall was the HQ of the executive committee of the Democratic Party in New York City historically exercising political control through lists of carefully selected candidates and a blend of charity and patronage. It became a byword of political corruption. Herbert Morrison was at pains to root out corruption in local government and rejected accusations of city-boss tactics. See Donoghue and Jones, *Morrison*, pp. 196–7.
84 *Labour Organiser* (October–November 1924), pp. 14–15.
85 LMA: LLP The Work of the London Labour Party 1929–30, pp. 7–8.
86 Berger, 'The British Labour Party and the German Social Democrats.'

188 *Thematic*

support put the LLP on a firm financial and organisational foundation, providing Morrison with an important power base for his breakthrough into national politics.[87] In a private document which fell into the hands of Herbert Morrison in 1927 describing their infiltration tactics, the CPGB referred to the LSC as the 'handmaid of the London Labour Party,' for the way it funded the regional power base of its ambitious secretary.[88] Morrison was also successful in recruiting the RACS, a major source of funding and loyalty. But despite repeated requests and some underhand tactics, he could not persuade the London Cooperative Society (LCS) to affiliate to either the LLP or the party nationally. It was suspected of communist influence and it jealously guarded its sizeable political funds (£17,000) for its own Co-operative Party, a considerable sum which Morrison could not get his hands on.[89]

In London, the role of the ILP was crucial in capturing the 13 London boroughs in the local elections of November 1919, with five members becoming mayors, including George Lansbury in Poplar and Clem Attlee in Stepney. The ILP in particular

> began most readily to merge itself in the wider Labour movement. It was in London that the development of really independent Labour Parties went ahead at great speed; in this development local ILPers played a big part, while themselves tending to move away from their own Party.[90]

It is likely that the newly formed local Labour parties recruited many ILP members and probably quite a few Liberal Party converts as well.[91] But the ILP had never been a centralised socialist party like the CPGB and to a lesser extent the SDF. It had difficulty in imposing much discipline on its mixed and strongly independent membership, estimated in 1918 to be anywhere between 80,000 and 35,000 nationally, having attracted many new members during the war over its opposition to conscription. This included many Liberals moving to the left and disillusioned by the right-wing policies of the Lloyd George coalition after 1918.[92]

In contrast, the CPGB operated much more centrally (democratic centralism) and was created from a merger between the British Socialist Party (formerly the SDF) and other smaller Marxist groups following the decision of the Third International to set up parties across the world following the Russian Revolution of November 1918. It attracted the affiliation of some ILP branches and members, influenced by the need to adopt a more revolutionary

---

87 Donoughue and Jones, *Morrison*, p. 65.
88 LMA: LLP Executive Committee Papers February 1927.
89 Donoughue and Hones, *Morrison*, pp. 211–2.
90 Marwick, 'The ILP 1918–1932,' p. 49 & pp. 57–8.
91 Cline, *Recruits to Labour*.
92 Dowse, *Left in the Centre*, p. 70.

Party organisation 189

stand in contrast to the reformism represented by the Labour Party's clause four.[93] 'Caught in the cross-fire, it steered a consistently left course, but it constantly lost members to both the Labour Party and, in the later 1920s, to the CPGB.'[94] It is safe to say that some members almost certainly joined the Labour Party, allowing their membership of the ILP to lapse, while others joined the CPGB. The ILP maintained a relatively stable membership during the 1920s, doing quite well in London ('home of bourgeois extremism' according to one historian), but collapsing after 1929 and finally disaffiliating from the Labour Party in 1932, never to really recover.[95] The membership of the CPGB fluctuated between 5,000 in 1922, 12,000 in 1926, dropping to 2,500 in 1930 and then recovering to a peak of 45,000 by the Second World War. It was strongest in London and Scotland, the only areas to elect communist MPs, including Shapurji Saklatava, another Parsi Indian nationalist, who was adopted by the Battersea Labour Party and Trades Council in June 1921 and was elected as a Labour MP for Battersea North in 1922 and then as a communist MP in 1924.[96] In the capital, the proportion of CPGB members ranged from 31% in 1922, dropping to only 14% in 1926 at the time of the General Strike, but reaching 40% by 1939 following the adoption of the Popular (or People's) Front policy endorsed by the Seventh Congress of the Comintern in 1935.

Unlike the ILP in the capital, London always had a 'critical mass of communist members to sustain a network of social and cultural institutions as well as a central party apparatus.' The CPGB also had a good presence in some of the newly industrialising areas of North West London which attracted party members migrating to new jobs from the depressed areas of South Wales and the North East. There were also more 'middle-class' branches, like London West Central.[97] 'London's pre-eminence was not unpredictable,' according to the historian of the Party:

> The city had been one of the main areas of strength for the SDF and the BSP. Its sheer size in terms of population meant it was likely, in any case, to produce a significant proportion of members of any political party. Before the 1930s it was probably the one significant district of the party which did not depend largely on miners for its membership; and it was able to expand when the party's industrial efforts became better organised from 1926 onwards. Only during the rapid expansion of 1932 and its aftermath did London lose its pre-eminence within the party;

93 See footnote 61.
94 Ibid., p. 75.
95 Marwick, 'The ILP 1918–1932,' p. vi.
96 Squires, *Saklatava*, 13–193.
97 Morgan, *Communists and British Society 1920–1991*, p. 7, 47, 90, 156.

190 *Thematic*

thereafter, it first regained and then exceeded its former share of the party's membership. By1939 two in every five lived in London.[98]

The principal strongholds in the capital were the East End, especially in Bethnal Green and Stepney (known as 'Little Moscow'), where there was an expanding base of support from the Jewish community, and south of the Thames around Battersea and Clapham, active in the transport trade unions, especially the railways. These branches and groups carried on with the work of the SDF 'and at least in the early part of the 1920s they enjoyed comparatively harmonious relations with the local Labour parties.'[99]

The communists had an effective presence on the LTC and this was one of the reasons for its deteriorating relationship with the regional party (LLP) after 1918. The CPGB was also heavily involved in organising the London Busmen's Rank and File Movement during the 1930s (the transport industry was one of the few areas where trade unionism was strong and well organised), when they voted against the recommendation of their union leaders in a series of strikes which severely embarrassed Herbert Morrison as Minister of Transport.[100] The CPGB was more effective in infiltrating local trades councils than constituency labour parties. It set up what they described in internal documents as 'Left-Wing Groups,' or by undertaking 'Fraction Work' in factories.[101] However, the LLP was in the forefront of moves by the national party and the TUC to publicly disassociate the labour movement from such influence, seeing it as essentially malign and undemocratic. According to his biographers, Herbert Morrison pursued 'communists with such implacable intensity that by 1928 he was renowned as "our chief witchfinder," stating in an American radio interview that he was proud that in Great Britain I was the man who did the most fighting to prevent the communists from capturing the British Labour Party.'[102]

After the national party had rejected communist affiliation in 1921 by a large majority, the CPGB changed tactics and communists started to join the Labour Party as individual members. Not everybody agreed with Morrison's hard-line approach. George Lansbury, for example, thought that there should be no barrier against them at all. But in 1924, the TUC imposed model rules on the trades councils in order to separate 'political' from 'industrial' functions, thereby preventing them from cooperating with the CPGB. This included communist-front organisations like the Minority Movement organising the unemployed. Most of the communist infiltration of trades councils took place in London and the south of England. But in May 1927, the communists were ousted from the executive of the LTC and

98 Thorpe, 'The Membership of the Communist Party of Great Britain,' 781 & 790–1.
99 McIntryre, *A Proletarian Science,* p. 30.
100 Clegg, *Labour Relations in London Transport.*
101 Harmer, 'The Failure of the Communists.'
102 Donoghue and Jones, *Morrison,* p. 98.

from the London District Committee of the General and Municipal Workers Union.[103] However, the CPGB was not dislodged from the London District of the Electrical Trades Union until after 1945.[104] A large number of trades councils were either reorganised or de-recognised by the TUC, 'culminating, most famously, in the battle for the control of the London Trades Council in 1950–53, a battle that the TUC won despite stiff resistance.'[105]

But communist influence was also present in the formation of a new left-wing pressure group, the Socialist League established in 1932 by a number of guild socialists, ex-communists and ex-ILP members who disagreed with the decision to disaffiliate from the Labour Party. The League was more successful in gaining affiliation to the party as a left-wing pressure group, advocating, amongst other things, the nationalisation of the Bank of England. It attracted the support of a number of mainstream London MPs, including Clement Attlee and Alfred Salter. But by the time it launched a 'Unity Campaign' in 1937, these high-profile members had resigned, concerned about its relationship with the CPGB, leaving Stafford Cripps and George Strauss, the Labour MP for North Lambeth, to propose a united front (Popular Front) of all left-wing groups, including the CPGB, to oppose fascism. This was too much for the Labour Party which regarded the campaign as yet another example of communist infiltration. The League was dissolved in May 1937, but George Strauss and Stafford Cripps continued to push for unity (publicised through the left-wing journal *Tribune*, which they funded) leading to their expulsion from the Party. The unity campaign demonstrated the strength of left-wing opinion in London over the rise of fascism. Many socialists wanted more urgent action than the Labour Party was prepared to take.[106] Such opposition to communism persisted into the war, despite support for Stalin after Russia became allies in the fight against the Nazis.

When Labour joined the Churchill Coalition in 1940, it agreed an electoral pact with the Conservatives not to fight each other during by-elections. Despite attempts to keep constituency organisation intact, individual national membership fell from just over 400,000 in 1939 to 225,000 by 1941. The decline was particularly marked in London as a result of evacuation and bombing, as population decanted out of the capital altogether or to the suburbs, some never to return.[107] Membership fell from 63,888 in 1939 to 22,200 by 1941, and the number of full-time agents dropped from 31 to only 7. Some suburban and more middle-class constituencies retained their membership, able to maintain a network of volunteers capable of collecting

103 Clegg, Fox and Thompson, *A History of British Trade Unions since 1889*, Vol. 2, p. 420.
104 Lloyd, *Light and Liberty*, pp. 126–404.
105 Stevens, 'Containing Radicalism.'
106 Pimlott, 'The Socialist League.'
107 Donoghue and Jones, *Morrison*, p. 322.

192   *Thematic*

weekly or monthly subscriptions.[108] Following the Nazi-Soviet Pact in September 1939, the CPGB was directed by Moscow to oppose the war against Germany, setting up another front organisation, the 'People's Convention' demanding a 'People's Peace.' As a result, the CPGB alienated many Labour Party members and its membership fell, until the German invasion of Russia in June 1941 reversed its fortunes when it joined the allies. After 1941, the CPGB waged 'an intensive campaign to affiliate to the party,' but it met with little local success. Norwood Labour Party, for example, voted against further attempts by the CPGB to affiliate to the party in May 1943, arguing that it would 'imperil the unity and power of the labour movement.'[109]

During the war, public opinion within London shifted leftwards, perhaps more so than in other areas of the country. The record of the Commonwealth Party, founded in 1942 by an alliance of two left-wing groups, is a possible measure of this move to the left. It stood for a type of Christian socialism and common ownership of land and had over 300 branches and a membership it claimed of over 12,000 by 1944, many in the armed forces. It fought a series of remarkable by-elections winning safe Conservative seats mainly in suburban areas.[110] The swing to Labour in London in 1945 was much higher than in other areas of the country and it did particularly well in the middle-class suburbs. In Kennington and North Lambeth, for example, Labour increased their share of the vote by 10% in both seats. In Brixton, Marcus Lipton overturned a Conservative majority of 6,500 by the same amount. But the biggest swing was in middle-class Norwood, when Ronald Chamberlain, regarded as 'a maverick MP,' overturned a Conservative majority of 12,500, reducing its share of the vote from 67% to 42% and winning the seat for the first time. In a similar neighbouring constituency, 'Herbert Morrison's victory in East Lewisham, which had returned a Tory throughout the interwar years, was taken to signify the defection of much of the lower middle-class to Labour's cause.'[111]

Membership of the Labour Party increased steadily after the war. By 1951, Labour had reached 5,849,002 (mostly trade union affiliates) with individual membership peaking at 1,014,524 in 1952 (a proportion of 6 trade unionists to 1 individual member), while Conservative Party membership rose to over 2 million in the same period. The published membership figures for London showed a similar increase, but the proportion of individual members to trade union affiliates was much higher at 3 to 1 in London, or about 200,000 trade union members to about 70,000 individual members in 1950, not including the largely passive members affiliated through the RACS, calculated at over 50,000.[112] In contrast, the LCS, operating north of the Thames,

---

108 Thorpe, *The Parties at War*, pp. 110 & 126.
109 *South London Press*, 14 May 1943.
110 Fielding, *'England Arise'*, p. 55; Morgan, *Labour in Power*, p. 23.
111 Fielding, *'England Arise'*, p. 63.
112 LMA: Roughly calculated from the Work of the London Labour Party 1947–1956.

had a peak membership of about one million members in the early 1950s, often providing much needed election funds for constituency parties where trade union support was lacking.[113] The high ratio of individual members to trade unionists in London was a measure of the relative weakness of the trade unions in London compared to the more unionised areas in Labour's industrial heartlands.

But by 1959, national individual membership of the Labour Party had dropped to 847,526 on a minimum affiliated rate of 800 members per CLP.[114] It has been suggested that political activism in the form of allegiance to a multi-issue mass party, like the early Labour Party, forged by open-air mass meetings and demonstrations, such as May Day, had been undermined by more home-based leisure patterns. Political views were influenced more by television and newspapers and single issues, like nuclear disarmament, involvement in which tended to either replace or indeed compliment membership of a political party.[115] In inner London, the membership figures had dropped from 70,000 to about 40,000 by 1956, and if Middlesex is taken into account, there were about 150,000 individual members in total by 1955 for the Greater London Region as a whole, reflecting the larger party memberships in some of the suburban constituencies. Areas like Woolwich West and Lewisham South had a tradition of high membership, but in other areas of south London, the decline continued through the 1950s. Bermondsey, Peckham, Dulwich and Southwark, for example, had over 12,000 members in 1952, but by the late 1960s, they could not muster more than 2,000 members between them.[116] The fall after this date is then very rapid. The figures for Brixton before it was absorbed into the new constituency of Lambeth Central in 1970 show a startling reduction from 1,212 in 1965 to only 342 in 1969, the year following the disastrous borough council elections of 1968. The membership of the newly formed party in 1970 amounted to only 292. The outgoing officers described 1970 as 'a very hard year for the Brixton Labour Party.'[117]

The Report on Party Organisation (Wilson Report), commissioned by the National Executive Committee after the election defeat of 1955, painted a depressing picture. It described the party as 'rusty and deteriorating with age.' Compared with Conservative Party organisation, recently reformed under Lord Woolton, it concluded that the party was 'still at the penny farthing stage in a jet-propelled era.'[118] A similar reflection of the state

---

113 Wilson, Webster, and Vorberg-Rugh, *Building Co-operation*.

114 Seyd, *Labour's Grass Roots*, pp. 13–26.

115 Parry, Moyer and Day, *Political Participation in Britain,* Donnelly, *Sixties Britain, Culture, Society and Politics*.

116 Syd, *Labour's Grass Roots*, p. 15.

117 Lambeth Archives: Records of the Lambeth Central Labour Party (IV 156/1/13) – Annual Report for 1970.

118 Black, '" Still at the Penny-Farthing Stage in a Jet-Propelled Era".

194 *Thematic*

of 'local democracy' in Lambeth, for example, was provided by Cynthia Cockburn in her critique of the 'Local State.' She reported that Lambeth Central had between 600 and 1,000 members ('They did not know exactly how many'), of which about 10% were estimated to be active. Things had obviously picked up since 1970, probably reflecting an influx of new younger more left-wing members.[119] Cockburn thought Streatham was somewhat different. It returned only four Labour councillors at the 1974 elections, but it provided the leadership of the Labour Group controlling the council. It attracted a slightly younger and more professional or business-style intake, but membership was no more than about 450, with only 10% active. They were considered by some members of Norwood Labour Party to be 'right-wing.'

However, Norwood Labour Party stood out for its left-wing tradition. In 1945, it selected a hard-left parliamentary candidate, Ronald Chamberlain, who was closely identified with the journal *Socialist Outlook*, which started to be published in 1948 by a group of left-wingers, fellow travellers and some Labour MPs. This was influenced, in turn, by a Trotskyist Group called *Socialist Fellowship*, linked to the Revolutionary Communist Party (RCP), although it was beginning to fragment as was the case of Trotskyist groups in general.[120] According to Cockburn, Norwood CLP had over 1,000 members, typically in their thirties, mainly teachers, such as Ken Livingstone and his partner Christine, some active in supporting squatting groups, including the famous squat in Villa Road in Brixton. The northern parties criticised Norwood for being 'militant, passing extreme resolutions and acting "en-bloc." People get pissed off with it.'[121] These changes are the first signs of the growth of the New Left in London after a period of defeats over nuclear disarmament and nationalisation.

Rise and fall of the New Left (1968–1997)

Before Norwood CLP sent Ken Livingstone and Ted Knight to Lambeth Council in 1974, the party had been purged on two occasions during the 1950s for Trotskyist entryism. Along with Islington East, Norwood was one of two London constituencies regarded as suspect by the national party. The first investigation was in 1954 when three members were suspended, David Finch, a former member of the RCP who joined the Labour Party in 1947, Thomas Mercer, who had been expelled from Glasgow Labour Party for selling a Trotskyist journal, and Ted Knight, its 21-year-old secretary.[122]

---

119 Cockburn, *The Local State*, p. 88.
120 Jenkins, *Bevanism,* pp. 90–112; Wood, 'Socialist Outlook and Socialist Fellowship.'
121 Cockburn, *The Local State*, p. 91.
122 *Norwood News*, 3 December 1954; Wood, 'Socialist Outlook', p. 12.

The second purge took place in 1959 when Brian Behan, brother of Irish novelist and playwright Brendan Behan, was expelled, together with his wife and five others belonging to the *Socialist Labour League*, including Vivien Mendelsohn, who had moved unsuccessfully, the famous Norwood resolution at the 1957 Annual Conference calling for unilateral nuclear disarmament.[123] The subsequent appeal against the expulsions failed, prompting its press officer, Alderman W R Knight, 'to blame the party for not crushing the revolutionary group before it spread to other members.'[124]

By the 1960s, the Labour Left in its various forms was relatively weak. This followed a series of bruising and debilitating policy conflicts over public ownership, clause four[125] and nuclear disarmament. It had lost many of these disputes within the party in favour of those who wanted to consolidate the gains made in 1945, keep nuclear weapons and maintain a good relationship with America during the Cold War. However, clause four was retained after a bitter fight with the leadership. In 1961, Ralph Miliband's powerful critique of the Party 'as one of modest social reform in a capitalist system' seemed to many an accurate description of a moribund and ineffective political force, rendered impotent by the 'age of affluence,' a term which came to be used by Labour revisionists to characterise the entire period of the Conservative government's so-called 'thirteen wasted years.'[126] The threat of nuclear war and support for CND, along with opposition to the Vietnam War, were probably the main issues which radicalised young people at this time.[127] The values which had inspired an earlier generation of socialists, ethical rather than Marxist, such as peace and disarmament, housing, welfare reform, defence of local communities, and trade union rights, were to many Labour activists and socialists being compromised by a party machine characterised by apathy, sclerotic organisation and declining membership. Yet from a position of considerable weakness the Labour Left re-emerged as such a powerful force that by the beginning of the 1980s it had become *the* Labour Party in the sense that this faction predominated within much of the Party.[128] This turnabout in the fortunes of the left was particularly marked in London and in local government. But its duration was relatively brief before the right wing made a comeback after 1981, compounded by the actions of Mrs Thatcher in abolishing the GLC in 1986.

123 *Norwood News* 12 June 1959; Foot, *Bevan*, Chapter 8.
124 *Norwood News*, 4 September 1959.
125 See footnote 67.
126 Miliband, *Parliamentary Socialism*; Middleton, 'Affluence' and the Left in Britain, c.1958–1974.'
127 Lent, *British Social Movements since 1945*.
128 Seyd, *The Rise and Fall of the Labour Left*, p. 17.

196 *Thematic*

Ken Livingstone rather typically but unfairly characterised local government in the 1960s as being nothing 'much more than white old men coming along to general management committees and talking about rubbish collection.'[129] Municipal politics and the defence of working-class communities had been a major factor in the growth and success of the LLP before the Second World War, particularly in terms of slum clearance, house building and welfare. But this tradition had to a significant extent died by the late 1960s, dramatically bought home by the disastrous local election results of 1968 and the re-emergence of fascism in the form of the National Front. Livingstone played a central part in restoring the fortunes of the left, riding a wave of popular opposition to the way local government came under attack after the IMF crisis of 1976, an assault carried on by Margaret Thatcher after her election as Prime Minister in 1979. Hilary Wainwright, an activist in the women's movement and a key member of the GLC's Popular Planning Unit, described it in terms of an 'explosion of party and popular democracy in local government in the late 1970s, and throughout the eighties...a spark lit by the new-style GLC and Sheffield Council...and which spread to the London borough councils and further afield.'[130]

Lambeth Council was one of those most dramatically affected by this explosion of left-wing popular democracy. The borough contained two constituencies, Norwood and Streatham, both regarded by the party leadership as controlled by Trotskyists during the 1950s (not including Brixton). Ted Knight, the future council leader, had been identified as 'a convinced and committed Healyite.' Gerry Healey was a member of the RCP and Streatham Labour Party until he was expelled along with other Trotskyists in 1954. They tried to form unofficial 'suspended' parties but without much success.[131] It was thought that Ken Livingstone might have been a fellow traveller, but according to one of his biographers, he opposed Ted Knight when he stood for the chairmanship of Norwood Party in 1972, although by the end of that year, they were starting to work together. Ted Knight had been readmitted to the party in 1970 and together with Livingstone, they organised a purge to deselect all the Labour councillors representing Norwood who had not voted to defy the Housing Finance Act of 1972, which enforced rent increases and led to a rebellion by Labour councillors in Clay Cross, Derbyshire who were surcharged by the District Auditor. This revolt was similar to the way Poplar councillors and Poor Law guardians in 1920 were imprisoned for refusing to levy the precepts for the LCC in order to maintain unemployment relief.[132]

---

129 Boddy and Fudge, *Local Socialism*, p. 263.
130 Wainwright, *Labour – A Tale of Two Parties*, p. 94.
131 Shaw, *Discipline and Discord*, pp. 131–7.
132 Carvel, *Citizen Ken*, p. 43; Passmore, 'The Response of Labour-controlled Local Authorities to Major Changes in Housing Policy, 1971–1983,' (PhD London, 2015), p. 66. The Housing Finance Act forced local authorities to move towards charging commercial

Party organisation 197

As in many other inner London councils, in the local elections in May 1974, 'Norwood returned a solid block of left-wingers who joined with a scattering of other leftists from other parts of the borough to form a disciplined group on the council, in conflict with the majority Labour administration.' In May 1978, Ted Knight succeeded in displacing David Stimpson as leader, but he was dependent on the support of a group of 'soft-left' councillors determined to prevent the return of the former right-wing leadership.[133] In the meantime, Ken Livingstone focused on his role as the GLC member for Norwood, elected in 1973. The 1982 elections produced a hung council in Lambeth (32 Labour and 32 Conservatives and Liberal/SDP Alliance members), but after six months, Ted Knight resumed his leadership making clear his intention of fighting central government cuts at the party's annual conference in 1980. This set the scene for a major conflict between the council and the Conservative government when he persuaded other Labour-controlled councils across London (and in Liverpool and initially Sheffield) to refuse to set a rate in 1985 in protest against central government reductions to its rate support grant. However, support for the strategy slowly dissipated, leaving only Lambeth and Liverpool to continue the campaign. As a result, the Labour councillors in Lambeth were surcharged by the District Auditor and disqualified from office in 1986, along with councillors from Liverpool, unlike GLC and other Labour councillors who had voted against the strategy as the deadline loomed.[134] The left in London was seriously split, and the GLC was one of the authorities who in the end did not follow Ted Knight's lead. Ken Livingstone was the leader of the GLC by this date, heavily criticised for his alleged betrayal, but was embroiled in an altogether different but related conflict with the Conservative government leading to the eventual abolition of the GLC in 1986 – a historic defeat for the Labour Party in London.

A number of developments combined to mark the beginning of the decline of the New Left from the mid-1980s. Nationally, this decline started with the narrow defeat of Tony Benn for the Deputy Leader of the Labour Party in 1981 and the subsequent waning of the Campaign for Labour Party Democracy (CLPD); a major split leading to the formation of the Social Democratic Party (SDP) in March 1981 after a special party conference agreed to an electoral college for electing the leader; the defeat of Labour (led by Michael Foot) in the general election of 1983 and above all the defeat of the miners' strike in 1985. In London, the decline started with the Liberals and SDP winning a number of parliamentary by-elections. In 1981, the Liberal Simon Hughes took the safe Labour seat of Bermondsey, capturing nearly 60% of the vote, defeating the left-wing candidature of the

---

rents for council housing by ending subsidies. For Poplar, see Booth, *Guilty and Proud of it*; Branson, *Poplarism, 1919–1925*.

133 Lansley, *Councils in Conflict*, p. 15.

134 Lambeth Labour Group Minutes 1985–86 (Lambeth Archives: IV 273/1/6).

198 *Thematic*

gay activist Peter Tatchell. In 1983, the Liberals took Croydon North West on a swing of 25% with the Labour vote dropping by 15%. In 1987, the SDP took the safe Labour seat of Greenwich on a swing of 28% defeating Diedre Wood, a former GLC and ILEA councillor closely identified with Ken Livingstone. Although the Militant Tendency was not nearly as strong in London as it was in Liverpool, the start of Neil Kinnock's purge when he became a leader in 1983 represented a further weakening of the left. 'Division, fragmentation and realignment occurred within the Labour Left from the end of 1981 onwards. The wide community of interest which prevailed throughout the 1970s broke down and in its place considerable personal tensions and antagonisms manifested themselves on a wide range of issues.'[135] In Lambeth, these divisions showed themselves in the formation of a local branch of the SDP and the beginnings of a fightback by 'Labour's traditional right.'

One of the first signs of an organised right-wing campaign in Lambeth was a letter in *Labour Weekly* in August 1981 from three Labour councillors representing Stockwell ward, an area which had undergone some gentrification. Peter Mandelson, Patrick Mitchell and Paul Ormerod gave a warning in a letter to *the Times* that the party was in danger of putting itself out of office for a generation.[136] In the autumn of 1981, the Streatham Liberal Association started discussions with the SDP about fighting the next borough elections in an alliance. In Vauxhall, Roger Liddle was involved in negotiating an electoral agreement targeting Oval ward, and confirmed that all his members were ex-Labour, while his potential Liberal allies joked that 'there was no claret on offer.' The Association of Liberal Councillors was faced with a tactical dilemma, worried about their identity. However, the real fightback against the left was taking place within the Labour Party. In Lambeth, Dianne Hayter, who was a member of Norwood Labour Party and General Secretary of the Fabian Society (1976–1982), was collecting evidence and was particularly interested in the Council's budget strategy after 1986. Joan Twelves, elected leader in 1988, was trying to obstruct the collection of the notorious Poll Tax (which the Conservative had introduced to replace local rates) and repeat the defiance showed during the ratecapping campaign, not without some success, leading eventually to a major riot in London in March 1990, marking the beginning of the end of Mrs Thatcher's premiership. But in the meantime, Hayter had formed a 'Londoners for Labour' group in 1987 with other 'traditionalist right-wing London Party members.' They boasted that it would reclaim Labour in London from 'the loonies.'[137] She went on to become part of an effort by the 'traditional right' to regain control of the party through the 'Labour Solidarity Campaign,' an

135 Seyd, *The Rise and Fall of the Labour Left*, p. 170.
136 *Times*, 10 August 1981.
137 Heffernan and Marqusee, *Defeat from the Jaws of Victory*, p. 75.

internal pressure group of trade unionists and MPs which supported Neil Kinnock in trying to replace the electoral college for the leadership with 'One Member One Vote' (OMOV). Such a strategy was designed to reduce the influence of the left, an objective eventually achieved in 1993, leading to the election of John Smith and then Tony Blair.[138] The defeat of the left in Lambeth however took a bit longer.

After Linda Bellos was deprived of the leadership in 1988 (having taken over from Ted Knight in 1986 following his disqualification), a right-wing faction within the Labour Group took control of Lambeth Council, but it was quickly replaced with a new left-wing administration led by Joan Twelves in 1989. Although Labour retained control of the council in the local elections of 1990, winning the same number of seats they had done in 1986, the number of hard-left councillors fell and they could not always command a majority. In 1990, the District Auditor imposed yet further fines on the disqualified councillors for lost interest and legal fees, making it difficult for Ted Knight in particular to make any concerted comeback. The NEC of the Party also refused to allow his name to go forward for possible selection as a labour council candidate after the end of his period of disqualification from office.[139] Joan Twelves had been returned in Angel Ward together with about a dozen hard-left councillors. Undaunted, she gave notice of continuing to oppose the collection of the Poll Tax and provoked further controversy by calling for a ceasefire in the Gulf War. This proved too much for the Labour Party NEC which suspended 13 rebel councillors together with the secretary of the All Britain Anti-Poll Tax Federation.[140] In the 1994 local elections, Joan Twelves was narrowly defeated by a Liberal Democrat and the hard-left group of suspended councillors was reduced to nine. Four years later, the Liberal Democrats doubled their number of council seats, largely at the expense of the Conservatives, but in 2002 they won the same number of seats as the Labour Party.[141]

This marked the end of an era for the left in the Lambeth party as it did across London more generally. While the fortunes of the Liberal Democrats had revived, there was also a change of political mood within the Labour Party, best captured in John Fraser's election address for his re-adoption as Labour's Norwood's parliamentary candidate in 1990. It achieved a careful balance between pragmatism and socialist values. In it, he reported that

> I have tried to relate much of my contributions in debate on policies to what impinges on or promotes the interests of people in Lambeth.

---

138 Hayter, 'The Labour Party: Crisis and Prospects'; Hayter, *Fightback!*
139 Heffernan and Marqusee, *Defeat from the Jaws of Victory*, p. 7.
140 Ibid., pp. 282–91 for a left-wing account of this conflict; *Times*, 28 March 1991.
141 London Data Store – election results.

200   *Thematic*

> Housing, rates (and now the Poll Tax), inner city and race issues have been constant themes... I have consistently voted on and shared the local party's policy on abortion, homosexuality and like issues which are usually 'free-vote' matters...In putting Labour policies to voters I believe we should not promise what we cannot deliver. What we do promise and what we have a duty to deliver must be of high quality, efficient, reliable and consistent... As a socialist I remain committed to individual freedoms and equality of opportunity... I remain committed to unilateralism...British nuclear weapons are an impediment to peace not a sign of security.[142]

Such a statement represented a partial restoration of the policies and values which had informed, and was largely responsible for the success of the Labour Party in London during the interwar period and to a declining extent after 1945. The commitment to delivering on issues which were of pragmatic benefit to working people, living in local communities, such as housing and welfare, combined with a strong belief in peace and disarmament, is part of what may be defined as a tradition of both middle-class 'progressive' and working-class 'labourist' politics in the capital. These were not necessarily missing from the agenda of the hard left in London, but they were not necessarily its priorities. The beliefs and values espoused by John Fraser were those which more closely reflected the policies of the Labour Party in London for much of the twentieth century. John Fraser was a devout Catholic. They could also be further defined as ones which were not explicitly socialist. Rather, they represented a more general belief in fairness and equality, or 'them and us,' which had always been an important feature of 'labourist' ideology before 1968.

Momentum – the Old Left Reborn (1997–2020)

It took another generation for the left in London to stage a comeback after disillusionment with New Labour had run its course by the time of the 2015 general election. It revived in the form of a grass roots organisation called Momentum, which was particularly strong in London and other metropolitan areas. It was founded by Jon Lansman, a veteran from the CLPD in the 1970s and 1980s, which had backed Tony Benn for deputy leadership in 1981. It enrolled many left-wing activists, including many young recruits completely new to politics. In 2018, Jon Lansman said that four years before, 'the biggest cohort of Labour Party members was in their sixties. Now it is people in their twenties.' Local constituency parties 'that had been moribund for years reported surges in membership and supporters, with the majority

---

142 Lambeth Archives: Records of Norwood Labour Party (iv 256/7) Election Address for Parliamentary Selection July 1990.

Party organisation 201

of these in London and the south.'[143] Together with 17,000 volunteers and 130,000 supporters, Momentum succeeded in getting Jeremy Corbyn elected as the leader of the Labour Party in September 2015. Over 250,000 party members voted for Corbyn in the first and only round of voting. For one commentator, 'the parliamentary and non-parliamentary parts of the left had never worked together so effectively to pull off a victory that one could have predicted.'[144] The movement was inspired by *Syriza* in Greece, *Podemos* in Spain and Bernie Sanders in the USA, all opposed to the politics of austerity and espousing a wide range of socially liberal positions, from peace to sexual identity, combined with a tradition of direct action. Its early history was marked by a degree of sectarianism as various Trotskyist groups sought to influence its direction and create a new party outside of Labour. But after the second leadership election confirmed Corbyn as the leader in 2016, Lansman was successful in getting a new constitution adopted which made Momentum a Labour Party membership organisation, similar to previous socialist pressure groups affiliated to the party, like the ILP, SDF and Socialist League. The right of the party accused it of being a new type of Militant Tendency, but this misread its intentions as a more broadly based and wider social movement which had resisted the entryist tactics of the traditional hard left.[145]

Momentum was heavily involved in mobilising support for Labour in the general election campaign of 2017, targeting marginal seats and running highly effective social media campaigns. This significantly boosted its membership. By September 2017, the membership had reached 31,000 across 170 local groups, with 15 members of staff. By January 2018, it had grown to 35,000 and by July 2018 to 42,000, mostly based in England and largely concentrated in big-city areas. On polling day in 2017, it was estimated that 10,000 Momentum activists had knocked on 1.2 million doors in the UK.[146] It was also active in promoting socialists as candidates in local, mayoral and parliamentary elections. In London, it successfully backed Rokhsana Fiaz as the Mayor of Newham and Joseph Ejiofor as the leader of the London Borough of Haringey.[147] In the build-up to the 2020 local elections, a change of selection procedures by the LLP allowed Momentum to put forward a slate of candidates in order to push Sadiq Khan's election manifesto to the left. In Croydon, councillor Patsy Cumming ran against the journalist Rowenna Davis, who wrote a book on 'Blue Labour' (an attempt to rebrand the party in terms of a religious emphasis on family and community), and had previously stood as a parliamentary

---

143 Beckett and Seddon, *Jeremy Corbyn and the strange rebirth of Labour England*, pp. 241 & 229.
144 Kogan, *Protest and Power*, p. 247.
145 *Guardian,* 28 April 2016 (Review of Michael Crick, *Militant Tendency*, by Andy Beckett).
146 *New Statesman*, 4 December 2019.
147 *Guardian*, 25 February 2019.

202   *Thematic*

candidate.[148] In Lambeth, Momentum endorsed Maurice McLeod, a journalist and trustee at Race on the Agenda (ROTA), a BAME-led organisation promoting issues of health, education and criminal justice.[149] Many activists are members of other campaigning organisations, such as Stop the War Coalition, which organised one of the largest demonstrations in London in February 2003 against the Iraq War, although some of the views of Muslim affiliates and members have embroiled the organisation in the controversy over anti-Semitism. Jon Lansman, a prominent Jewish member of Momentum, played a role in trying to bring people together over the controversy (see Chapter 7 for a discussion of anti-Semitism).[150]

Momentum has made a big contribution to the growth of Labour Party membership since 2015. Leaving aside those members affiliated through their trade union (always low in London), the membership figures have fluctuated since the high point of 1952, when they reached just over a million. By 1995, it had dropped to about 300,000, particularly pronounced in London, where membership declined from 91,000 in 1952 to just under 56,000 in 1995 (London and Middlesex combined after local government reorganisation in 1965).[151] However, the advent of New Labour saw the national figures increase to about 400,000. But by 2008, they had dropped to just 166,000 as Tony Blair's popularity faded. Such figures tend to be unreliable as they have been based in the past on minimum affiliation rates of either 800 or 1,000 per constituency, but many parties either had less than this figure or affiliated on a reduced number. The case of Woolwich stands out in London, as it always had. In 1977, for example, both constituencies (East and West) had a combined membership of over 8,000, based to some extent on their relationship with the RACS, an important funder of the LLP since the 1920s.

National membership recovered to 193,000 by 2010. But by 2015, it had jumped to 388,000, and then soared to 544,000 by 2016, reaching 564,000 by the end of 2017. The figures for London are not available, but it is certainly the case that Momentum has helped revive the fortunes of Labour since it became an affiliated membership organisation (like the ILP and Fabian Society) in 2016.[152] Limehouse and Poplar had a membership of 2,400 published on their website. The number of socialists active in the party now stands at probably an all-time high, although Momentum does not state explicitly that it is a socialist party, rather that

---

148 Geary, *Blue Labour.*
149 www.labourlist.org.
150 Kogan, *Protest and Power*, p. 365; Beckett and Seddon, *Jeremy Corbyn and the strange rebirth of Labour England*, pp. 282–3.
151 The Work of the London Labour Party 1926/27 to 1938/39.
152 Tanner, *Labour's First Century*; Audickas, *Membership of UK Political Parties*; Bale, 'Grassroots: Britain's Party Members.'

Party organisation 203

it aims 'to transform the Labour Party, our communities and Britain in the interests of the many, not the few.' Before the disaffiliation of the ILP in 1932, the number of socialists in affiliated groups to the LLP was just under 2,500, dropping to only 753 in 1938. By this date, most socialists were individual members of the party rather than through an affiliated society, making it very difficult to identify the true number of members who regarded themselves as socialist. In terms of overall current membership, London only represents about 12% of total party membership, in comparison to 34% for the South of England, 29% for the north and 21% for the Midlands and Wales, but this may be an underestimate. Only 32% are members of a trade union and the majority regard themselves as left-wing and socially liberal.[153] The dichotomy between low levels of party membership and high levels of voting Labour in London (as is the case in the BME electorate) is an issue worthy of further research (see Chapter 7 on race).

Conclusion

In an age of mass democracy after 1918, individuals joined single-issue pressure groups as well as political parties, the leaders of which hoped, like Herbert Morrison, to enrol a mass membership.[154] But mass membership of multi-issue parties was never fully realised, unlike the SPD in Germany, apart perhaps from the decade after 1945 when individual membership levels for both main parties exceeded 1 million. In London, no different from other areas of the country, many individuals became party members if they thought that it would help achieve specific ends, such as communists or Trotskyists, peace activists or feminists, or even those just pursuing a career in politics, in the way, for example, the LCC provided a route to national politics for ambitious middle-class politicians during the interwar period.[155] However, the demands for peace and disarmament (CND), feminism (women's sections) or racial equality (black sections) are good examples where the party in London was joined by individuals for specific single-policy aims, given the particular strength of these demands, more pronounced in metropolitan areas with their higher concentrations of young people, single women and immigrant communities (see Chapter 7 for the politics of personal identity). All such reasons for joining the party were well represented in the capital, perhaps more so than in other areas of the country where the trade unions were in some cases stronger and where they might have exercised more control over selection of candidates or submission of radical policy resolutions

153 Ibid., pp. 15–19.
154 Thane, 'The Impact of Mass Democracy,' 54–86.
155 Clifton, 'Members and Officers of the LCC, 1998–1965.'

204 *Thematic*

to annual conference. This added an extra dimension to the character of local constituency parties in London.

The relative weight of these different interests was both a strength and a weakness. It created unity, for example, during the interwar period in building opposition to fascism and again during the 1970s and 1980s in helping to cement the rainbow alliance of interests which underpinned the growth of the New Left. But it also created disunity in the way that communists and Trotskyists were either expelled or tolerated, damaging the reputation of the party in the eyes of the wider electorate. It may be the case that the strength of Momentum in metropolitan areas, especially in London, has had the effect of exacerbating the geographical and social differences between London and Labour's so-called traditional heartlands in the north and Wales. The success of the Labour Party in London has been to an extent more dependent on it obtaining the support of citizens motivated by single issues or wider values. For the peace movement, research suggests that the higher levels of involvement from middle-class citizens were based on psychological or emotional factors, or age such as youth radicalisation.[156] This is perhaps a very different type of motivation from working-class support for the Labour Party, which during the course of the twentieth century was based more on non-ideological factors, such as 'labourism,' a defence of working-class interests expressed in terms of 'them and us.'

Momentum is an example of a relatively large-scale popular movement of predominantly young people, motivated by a variety of different issues, not necessarily socialism but other socially liberal values common to metropolitan areas, such as support for European integration.[157] Under the new rules introduced by Ed Miliband when he was a leader in 2014, many people joined the party (and Momentum) in order to vote for particular individuals rather than to support a clearly agreed socialist programme. Attempts by Trotskyists to take it over were successfully resisted. Ideological conflict over socialist objectives has been an ever-present feature of internal debates within the party since its formation in 1900. The most recent attempt to plot the history of socialists in the Labour Party concluded that

> Labour has never been a socialist party, even if – in the words of Tony Benn – it has always had socialists in it. How does their ideology compare to the wider politics of Labourism? Is it defined by a commitment to nationalisation or to pacifism? Perhaps it is simply more of a mood, an instinct rather than a consistent strategy. Certainly, historically, what has been considered 'left' is a moving target. What was deemed 'right' in the 1950s became left policy in the 1970s; and while Corbynism is far

---

156 Parkin, *Middle Class Radicalism.*
157 See Table 20 in the Appendix for details of Referendum result in London.

to the left of Tony Blair's New Labour, it is not economically radical as the Labour policy of the early 1970s. Understanding these shifts and the politics behind them is crucial to our understanding of the present.[158]

The next and final chapter explores the influence of gender, race and religion, and their sometimes-difficult relationship to the wider universalism of the left. This also distinguishes London from other non-metropolitan areas of the country.

---

158 Hannah, *A Party with Socialists in it,* pp. xii–xiv.

7 The politics of personal identity – gender, race and religion

Introduction

Gender, race and religion are aspects of Labour politics in London that cannot be ignored in discussing the relative strengths and weaknesses of the party in comparison to other non-metropolitan areas. They were sometimes a source of conflict, but at other times offered grounds for alliances uniting different interests. After 1970, following the enactment of equality legislation in the 1960s, introduced by a Labour government, issues of personal identity (based on gender, race and religion) became a prominent feature of the ideology of the left wing of the party. Such issues had influenced the party in London before this date, but not quite in the same way it did after the 1970s. Class interests had tended to subsume matters of gender, race and religion in the earlier period, while they provoked division and controversy in the later period, but also provided grounds for some cooperation.[1] The socialist bulletin, *London Labour Briefing*, ran a series of articles during the 1980s promoting 'the personal as the political.' The GLC under Ken Livingstone was in the forefront of promoting equal opportunities, grant-aiding a wide range of voluntary organisations to promote the interests of different single-issue groups. This was not always welcomed by those socialists, such as Eric Hobsbawn, who maintained that identity politics undermined 'the universalism of the left' and relegated questions of class solidarity to a secondary position.[2] However, other socialists, like the Marxist Stuart Hall, of a more cultural orientation, argued that the renewal of the left in the 1980s (to counter Thatcherism) could be best achieved by mobilising around something beyond class, such as personal identity.[3] The growth of the New Left owed a lot to this type of politics, more so in London than in other metropolitan areas like Sheffield, for example. An analysis of Sheffield City Council's policies on race and gender,

---

1 Fielding and Geddes, 'The British Labour Party and 'ethnic entryism.'
2 Hobsbawn, 'Identity Politics and the Left.'
3 Stuart Hall, *The Hard Road to Renewal.*

The politics of personal identity   207

for example, showed that the politics of class were prioritised over New Left identity politics.[4]

Public opinion often regarded the politics of personal identity as evidence of the party being out of touch with 'ordinary life.' The popular press ran, sometimes very unfairly, campaigns parodying the equal opportunity policies of the GLC as the 'looney left.' Identity politics also alienated many older and more traditional white working-class voters leading to higher levels of abstention from politics altogether or the switching of allegiance to other parties. The defeat of the gay activist Peter Tatchell in the by-election for Bermondsey in 1981, following a campaign marked by overt homophobia, is an example of such a response.[5] More generally, identity politics has been identified as one of the reasons for the decline of social democratic parties in the USA and Europe, undermining their support in traditional white working-class communities.[6] In London, it was partly responsible for widening the political gulf between the capital and Labour's working-class support in its northern heartlands and in Wales and in areas of Scotland outside of the metropolitan centres of Edinburgh and Glasgow. Cultural diversity (and social liberalism) is now a feature of the politics of big cities and their younger and more educated populations, but who are often characterised by the right-wing media as being preoccupied by questions of personal identity, such as sexual identity.[7] This growing social group or educational elite has been described by the economist Thomas Picketty, as the 'Brahmin left,' opposed to the free-market economic policies of the 'merchant right' and the right-wing populism of politicians like Nigel Farage, who rail against 'Generation Snowflake' and make patriotic calls for stronger immigration controls.[8] This constituency voted Labour in London in 2017 and 2019, unlike a significant proportion of more elderly working-class voters in non-metropolitan and less ethnically diverse areas. It was such areas that voted to leave the European Union in 2016 and which then went on to vote for the Conservative Party in 2019 in order to 'Get Brexit Done,' while their children in the big cities voted Labour in solidarity with European ideals of integration and social liberalism (as well as opposing austerity).

This chapter discusses some of the tensions and divisions relating to race, religion and gender within Labour politics in London during the twentieth century. It explores, for example, the relative strengths of nonconformity, more pronounced in the suburbs during the first half of the century, and the religious revival amongst the black community in the second half of the century, and their influence on voting intentions. Did such religious sentiments cut across or reinforce class interests? Did the demand for black sections in

---

4 Payling, 'Socialist Republic of South Yorkshire,' 602–27.
5 Tatchell, *The Battle for Bermondsey.*
6 Kaufman, *White Shift*; Fukuyama, *Identity.*
7 Milburn, *Generation Left*, pp. 7–12.
8 Picketty, *Capital and Ideology*; Mudde and Kaltwasser, *Populism.*

208   *Thematic*

the party during the 1980s represent a new type of politics based on personal identity that came into conflict with those socialists who prioritised the class struggle? The same question can be asked about those feminists who campaigned for all female shortlists in the selection of candidates for election. Why should identity politics take precedence over broader political questions? The chapter is divided into three sections. Section I discusses the role of women in the London Labour Party from the formation of the Women's Labour League (WLL) in 1906 up to the influence of second wave feminism in the 1980s and thereafter. Section II looks at the influence of race and focuses in particular on the demand for black sections in the 1980s, using Lambeth as a case study. Section III briefly looks at the influence of religion, such as nonconformity, Judaism and Catholicism in the first half of the century, and the resurgence of the black Pentecostal churches and Islam in the modern period. It will conclude by putting the recent controversy over anti-Semitism into historical perspective, an example where the interests of race, class and religion came into conflict spanning generations.

The role of women (1900–2020)

The influence of gender played a significant part in the development of local parties in London, particularly during the interwar period and after 1970 with the growth of popular individualism and second wave feminism. Although the term identity politics came into use in the period after 1970, to suggest a certain and now more contemporary definition of equality ('the personal is political'), it does not apply in the same way when discussing the period before 1970. At the birth of the labour movement, women faced cultural, legal and structural inequalities specific to that time. Women did not have the vote before 1914, neither did they have other legal rights defining their role as citizens. Their demand for equal treatment, and what they understood to be socialism, came into conflict with the interests of men in the party as fathers, husbands, politicians and trade unionists. A century of legislative change has achieved a degree of equality in certain spheres, but for many women there is still much to be achieved and their demands, either as feminists, socialists or party members, are now expressed in different ways.[9] Historians continue to find the concept of social class relevant in understanding questions of gender during the second half of the twentieth century (as they do to some extent race), influenced by changing cultural definitions of identities and lifestyles.[10]

While the families of women sometimes provided a good base of support to enter politics, London and other large metropolitan cities also offered a wide range of activities and employment for both single and married women.

---

9 Zweiniger-Bargielowska, *Women in Twentieth Century Britain.*
10 Howarth, *Classes and Cultures in England after 1951*; Devine, *Rethinking Class.*

The politics of personal identity 209

Such opportunities were not available in smaller towns and rural areas. This continues to distinguish London from many other areas of the country to this day. The presence of large numbers of universities and colleges, maternity and teaching hospitals, literary, publishing and journalistic outlets all provided opportunities for middle-class women seeking independence. Before 1914, the WLL, and organisations supporting women's suffrage, had many active branches in the capital, as did women's sections after 1918, which attracted large memberships, especially in the suburbs of London.[11] London also offered more political opportunities for women than other areas. During the 1930s, women played an important role in the London Labour Party, with higher than average numbers of women amongst elected councillors.[12] One of them Agnes Dawson persuaded Herbert Morrison in 1935 to remove the marriage bar for women teachers, doctors and nurses employed by the LCC, an important but isolated victory in the cause of women's rights. Herbert Morrison encouraged well-educated women to stand for election to the LCC and by the 1950s its education committee was dubbed 'the Shrieking Sisterhood.'[13] A generation later, the GLC women's unit in the 1980s, and similar ones in borough councils were a source of employment and promotion of women's issues. By 1986, the Women's Committee at the GLC had a budget of £90 million and a staff of 96.[14] As a result, gender equality was a prominent feature of local Labour party politics more so in the capital than elsewhere.

Thousands of working-class women joined the Labour Party and the Cooperative movement after winning the right to vote in parliamentary elections in 1918. A large number of middle-class women were also recruited and by 1939 women in total made up nearly half of the membership of the party. Many of these women were enrolled through special women's sections created in 1918. These took over the role of the WLL, set up in 1906 in order to give them a voice in the party as an affiliated organisation before the introduction of individual membership. For one historian, these new sections played a substantial role in building the party organisation and its growing vote in the interwar years. They brought more women into public life, chiefly at a local level, though only a handful of women were voted into parliament. They were notably more successful in London than elsewhere. In the local elections of 1934, of 729 Labour borough councillors elected in London, 150 were female: 15 of them on Bermondsey Council, 15 in Hackney, 16 in Southwark, 12 in Poplar, all poor boroughs. Compared with their ambitions, however, it was a minimal achievement.[15]

11 Tanner, 'Labour and Its Membership.'
12 Thane, 'The Women of the British Labour Party and Feminism.'
13 Martin, 'Engendering City Politics and Educational Thought.'
14 Bruely, *Women in Britain since 1900*, pp. 69 & 160–1.
15 Thane, 'The Women of the British Labour Party and Feminism,' 140; *Labour Woman*, December 1934.

210   *Thematic*

Between 1880 and 1914, the women's movement had grown in parallel with the socialist and labour movements, existing side by side and often in an uneasy relationship, in particular over the vexed question of women's enfranchisement. After the introduction of individual party membership in 1918, the relationship between the newly created women's sections and the leadership of the party was difficult.[16] Compromises had to be made on many policy issues, such as birth control or family allowances. In the end, most women's sections supported the male-dominated leadership because their primary loyalty was to a party which they saw as the vehicle for achieving social change. However, for one historian, this compromise had collapsed by 1933, by which time 'women had become a large but mostly silent minority in the National Labour Party (which) had lost its post-war reputation as the party that supported women's social and economic emancipation. British feminists, who had seen Labour as their best parliamentary hope in 1918, had come to see it as the enemy, not an ally. "Socialism and feminism were effectively divorced."'[17] However, not all historians accept that the sections became 'traitors to a feminist movement.'[18] Others have argued that 'during the 1930s the party was quietly moving forward, paying more attention to the stated concerns of Labour women members,' such as family policies, housing and maternity rights. Women members also offered loyalty and unity to a beleaguered party leadership.

> Although this hardly meant constructing an overtly feminist agenda, it could and did mean that some progress was made in some areas which had concerned labour feminists, alongside major advances in areas of social policy where women were vociferous advocates of change.[19]

It would take a second feminist wave in the 1970s for progress to be made on questions of equality and pay, but even then it was blocked by entrenched patriarchal attitudes.

The new party constitution in 1918 allowed women to join for the first time as individual members. Before this date, the WLL was the only way women could support the party. It became an affiliated organisation in 1908. A branch in Croydon, for example, was established in 1909, made up of female ILP members and others drawn from Progressive political circles and those demanding the vote.[20] In 1910, the Thornton Heath branch of the WLL, together with the Women's Cooperative Guild (WCG), urged the Croydon Education Authority to provide free school meals and dental

16 Francis, 'Labour and Gender,' 191–220.
17 Graves, 'An Experiment in Women-Centred Socialism,' 180–214.
18 Thane, op. cit., p. 141.
19 Tanner, 'Gender, Civic Culture and Politics in South Wales.'
20 *Croydon Citizen*, 13 February 1909.

The politics of personal identity   211

services for children with defective teeth.[21] In 1910 at a well-attended meeting of the Croydon branch of the Men's League for Women's Suffrage, a cross-party pressure group, the Mayor of Croydon, argued

> that it was indefensible that ladies who had a very great stake in the country, who paid large sums in weekly wages, were denied a vote, while the labouring man, who could neither read nor write…could vote.[22]

Support for women's suffrage also formed part of the local nonconformist political tradition, which was a significant feature of the labour movement in the suburbs. At the Penge branch of the Free Church League for Women's Suffrage, the local preacher argued that it was impossible to dismiss politics from religion, emphasising 'the spiritual side of the emancipation of women.'[23]

Before 1914, as we have seen, the WLL had an uneasy association with the Labour Party which was dominated by male trade unionists. There were very few female trade union members, women did not have the vote and the leadership was divided on the question of women's suffrage. Leading figures like Keir Hardie and George Lansbury campaigned for women to have the vote on the same terms as men, but most trade union leaders resisted change. Lansbury lost a by-election in Bow and Poplar in 1912 fighting as an independent on a platform of female suffrage. The WLL was initially concerned with recruiting and electioneering, but it also campaigned on issues regarded by the party at the time as relevant to women. For the party leaders, this meant matters of domesticity and the home, a view widely shared within the labour movement. In party propaganda, women were often referred to as 'chancellors of the exchequers of the homes.'[24] The WLL had fewer branches than the WCG, founded by socialist feminists in 1883, which had a membership of over 30,000 in 1910 in comparison to about 5,000 for the WLL. The WCG advocated minimum wages and maternity benefits for women workers, and like the WLL it called for peace during the Great War, a tradition which carried on into the 1930s.[25]

Their joint campaigning activities during the later stages of the First World War raised the general profile of the labour movement by addressing the needs of working-class women. Many of these women over 30 who gained the vote in 1918 did not forget the stand taken by the WLL, WCG and socialists like Sylvia Pankhurst in defending their interests. For it was during the war that members of the WLL sought and won representation on the numerous local committees which proliferated dealing with relief of

---

21 *Croydon Advertiser*, 4 June 1910.
22 *Croydon Advertiser*, November 1910.
23 *Norwood News*, 1 April 1911.
24 Francis, 'Labour and Gender,' 192.
25 Gaffin, *Caring and Sharing.*

212   *Thematic*

distress, munitions tribunals and war pensions. But despite the large-scale recruitment of women into war industries, particularly in munitions and transport in London, the WLL and its industrial partner the National Federation of Women Workers (NFWW) were not influential enough to defend the interests of female war workers, especially if it involved conflict with male trade unionists over such controversial questions as dilution of skills in craft trades. The NFWW agreed that women's industrial work would only last for the duration of the war and that they would leave when peace came and the men returned from the front. 'Thus, despite women's proven ability to work in industry, the sexual division of labour remained unchallenged, both in men's unquestioned priority in employment and the continuing assumption of gender as a criteria for determining suitability for a particular job.'[26] These female activists, many of them socialists but also converts from other parties, had more influence after the war in campaigning within the wider movement for better housing, medical treatment and relief from poverty, seen as uniquely female issues, rather than seeking equality with men in the workplace.[27] Above all, they stressed the harsh realities of working-class domestic life and the maternal constraints on 'good motherhood.' Their feminism appealed directly to working-class women. By asserting the value of their work in the home, it gave women houseworkers a sense of their own worth and value to the community and the confidence to fight to improve the unbelievable drudgery that was domestic labour in the early twentieth century.'[28]

In 1918, the Executive Committee of the London Party congratulated itself that the party had through the creation of women's sections retained the mass of women members from the WLL.[29] In the same year, full-time women organisers were appointed in each of the nine regions as part of the major reorganisation of the party's electoral machinery.[30] Just before the end of hostilities, a Women's Advisory Committee of the London Labour Party was established following a conference at the Kingsway Hall in October. The LCC member for Poplar, Susan Lawrence (an ex-Conservative who had joined the Labour Party in 1913), drew attention to 'the grave problems with regard to women's labour that will come with demobilisation,' while Dr Marion Phillips (who became the Labour Party's first Chief Woman's Officer in 1918) 'dwelt especially on the need for watchfulness with regard to food policy.'[31] The women's organiser for London was Annie Somers, a graduate, suffragist and member of the National Union of Clerks and Administrative Workers.

---

26 Rowan, 'Women in the Labour Party, 1906–1920,' 77.
27 *Labour Women*, January 1918.
28 Ibid., p. 82.
29 LMA: LLP Report of the Executive Committee for 1917–18.
30 Hannam, 'Women and Labour Politics,' 171–2.
31 *Labour Women*, July & November 1918.

The politics of personal identity   213

Nationally, the number of women's sections grew from 271 in 1919 to over 1,000 in 1923. The numbers continued to increase rapidly reaching a peak of just under 2,000 in 1930, after which numbers slowly declined.[32] The extension of the franchise had led to a massive surge in female membership. By 1922, 100,000 women had joined the party as individual members. The average female membership during the interwar period was over a quarter of a million, which accounted for at least half of Labour's individual membership at this time. 'These new women activists came from a variety of social backgrounds and occupations: housewives, manual workers, professionals, nurses and social service workers...In the interwar period the parliamentary party possessed more university-educated women than the Conservatives... Labour activism was a further stage in the long tradition of middle-class female philanthropy.'[33] The capital contained the headquarters of an extraordinary range of charitable and social welfare bodies addressing the needs of the deserving poor before the war, specialising in visiting and rescuing working-class households from poverty and the evils of drink. After 1918, the party tried to play down this tradition which was regarded by many working-class women as intrusive and patronising. In London, the party promoted a different approach in, for example, women's work in municipal housing, arguing that too many visitors are resented by tenants. It proposed that women's housing managers should be professionally qualified and recognised, marking the beginnings of a move towards state provision of public services, such as social work and health visitors.[34]

The London-wide Women's Advisory Committee met on a regular monthly basis in central London. Seasoned campaigners like Susan Lawrence and Marion Phillips initiated a number of high-profile campaigns on education and housing. These centralised campaigns probably diverted resources away from the more routine activities of local women's sections in the suburbs. At a constituency level, women's sections were encouraged to focus on social events, sewing clubs and fundraising rather than on controversial political issues. While improved organisation was vitally important in ensuring the growth of the party after 1918, the leadership discouraged the involvement of women in issues thought to be too controversial, such as abortion rights and birth control, taboo subjects in electoral terms at this time and likely to upset Catholic members of the party in metropolitan areas like London and Liverpool. The leadership regarded this demand as coming into conflict with the party's quest for respectability. In the same way, the campaign for family allowances, launched by women in the 1920s, met resistance from male trade union negotiators who worried that it would weaken their bargaining position with employers.[35] Female involvement in

32 Calculated from Labour Party Annual Conference Reports 1919–1930.
33 Francis, 'Labour and Gender,' 192.
34 *Labour Woman*, September 1938.
35 Graves, 'An Experiment in Women-Centred Socialism,' 198.

214   *Thematic*

support for the republicans in the Spanish Civil War and the Popular Front in the late 1930s also led to expulsions for cooperating with communists. The full-time women's organisers were paid employees of their regional parties and would have had to 'toe-the-party-line,' but although they were constrained in this respect, they did seek to promote women's participation in the party as political activists and trade union members.[36] Women's sections had no formal power within the party's decision-making procedures. In 1918, they were regarded by the leadership as a temporary expedient for 'closing down the WLL (about which many delegates were extremely angry).'[37] Demands for more influence over policy were met by setting up advisory bodies such as the annual Women's Conference and the Women's Advisory Committee.

> They were also given a reserved seat on the NEC of the party – later expanded to five – but this was to be elected by the conference as a whole, and therefore determined by the trade union block-vote rather than by the constituencies or the women's sections themselves.[38]

This device was designed to weaken the left in the party, particularly the ILP which had been in the forefront in the campaign for female suffrage.[39]

In many respects, the Conservative Party in London was quicker off the mark in setting up women's branches and in responding to the challenges of mass democracy. The Norwood Association in Lambeth, for example, set up a branch in March 1921, although it was equally confined to non-political and social concerns such as fundraising and canvassing. It elected a female 'chairman' to its executive council and nominated a female candidate for the LCC election. Its total individual membership increased to over 2,000 by 1923 and it was able to employ a clerk on 'a salary of 35 shillings a week.' After 1918, Norwood was a safe middle-class Conservative constituency with small pockets of poverty where Labour stood little chance of success. The Norwood Conservative Association was vehemently anti-socialist, pro-tariff reform/imperial preference and concerned more by the threat posed by 'the so-called Socialist-Labour Party' than by the local Liberal Party in parliamentary elections. It did feel socially threatened by the formation of London-wide choral and dramatic societies, carefully cultivated by the regional Labour Party to attract a mass membership, and it wanted their London Office to do likewise. As well as forming a women's branch, the Norwood Association also set up a Labour Advisory Committee to recruit trade union members, stating that it was important 'that there should be no distinction of class or occupation in Conservative organisations.' But given

36 Hannam, 'Women as Paid Organisers and Propogandists,' 69–88.
37 Wainwright, *Labour: A Tale of Two Parties*, p. 176.
38 Ibid., p. 178.
39 Rowan, 'Women in the Labour Party.'

The politics of personal identity   215

the size of its majorities in all elections, it did not feel it necessary to spend any money in canvassing in the poorer districts of the constituency.[40]

It has been estimated that the Conservative Party nationally was able to attract the votes of nearly half of the working-class electorate during the interwar period and it was certainly more successful than either the Labour or Liberal parties. In the general election of 1945, Labour's lead over the Conservatives stood at almost 20% among men, but it shrank to 2% among female voters.[41] However, after 1945, opinion poll evidence suggests that there was a small net move of women towards Labour. It has been argued that women supported austerity as long as the Labour government increased taxation on

> their husbands beer and tobacco and used the proceeds to subsidise food prices and fund the welfare state...It was the men, more than women, whose impatience with the politics of self-sacrifice put an end to Labour's secure majority in February 1950.[42]

Support for Labour in this instance could be seen as a vote for state intervention rather than for the ability of male trade unionism to protect working-class living standards. However, the political effect of rationing and austerity also undermined Labour support for women as both consumers and citizens, predicting the extent to which the Labour Party struggled to adapt to the era of affluence after 1950.[43]

Women members of the party exercised very little influence over party management or policy. This created unresolved tensions within local constituency parties. The experience of women members in Bexley CLP after 1945, for example, demonstrated that the party was firmly run by men, with women complaining that 'they did not have enough opportunities to take part in the running of the party.'[44] Although the party may have started to attract more female voters after 1945, it made only limited progress in selecting female candidates for all types of elections. The domestic impact of the Second World War had transformed the lives of many working- and middle-class women, but 'feminist issues continued to be sacrificed to other goals, and this hiatus was only ended by the re-emergence of an organised feminist movement after 1968.'[45] During the war, a 'Women for Westminster Movement' had been set up by the feminist Women's Publicity Planning Association to campaign for the adoption of more female candidates across

---

40 Lambeth Archives: Minutes and Annual Reports of the Norwood Conservative Association for 1920–1925 (IV/166/1/13).
41 Pugh, *Making of Modern British Politics*, p. 256.
42 Hinton, 'Women and the Labour Vote, 1945–50,' 59–66.
43 Black and Brooke, 'The Labour Party, Women and the Problem of Gender,' 419–52.
44 Todd, 'Labour Women,' 163.
45 Francis, 'Labour and Gender,' 200.

216   *Thematic*

all parties. However, the Labour Party regarded the movement as influenced by the communists and called on its two most prominent proponents, Edith Summerskill (MP for Fulham West) and the LCC councillor Freda Corbett, to withdraw support. At the Labour Women's Conference in 1942, a motion 'urging selection committees to look favorably on potential women candidates was defeated by 211 votes to 192 on the grounds that women did not want special treatment.'[46] In the 1945 general election, there were only seven female parliamentary candidates in inner London (out of 61 seats), of which only two were elected, Mrs Ganley in South Battersea and Dr Edith Summerskill in West Fulham.[47] The other five had been selected in safe Conservative seats and were not expected to win. In local elections, the number of women councillors in London had increased by 1954 to 255. But this was out of a total of 1,356 councillors and represented only 19%, indicating the extent to which women in the party remained marginalised and largely unrepresented during the 1950s.[48]

In the elections of 1951 and 1955, 'Labour's vote among women lagged twelve to thirteen percentage points behind that of the Conservatives and in only two elections between 1945 and 1970 did Labour enjoy leads among female voters.'[49] Labour finally obtained a majority of female voters for the first time in the general election of 1966, despite a decade of failing to give women a more equal role in the party or to promote legislative change to give women more equal rights. By this date, it was difficult to ignore the way the post-war labour market had been transformed by the presence of married women in the workforce and the extent to which gender was increasingly acknowledged as a source of structured social inequality, although some leading sociologists of the day did not agree with this conclusion.[50] Young unmarried women had formed nearly 30% of the entire occupied population in 1921 following the use of such labour during the First World War. This figure remained about the same in 1951 following the greater involvement of women during the Second World War and had grown to nearly 34% by 1960. But the important difference was that this increase came mainly from the ranks of older, married women. Many women were also undertaking different types of paid work, such as taking in lodgers, child minding and casual domestic work. 'In 1931, 10% of married women worked, but 22% did so by 1951. They now represented 43% of all female employees...and by 1958 this

46 Thorpe, *Parties at War*, p. 88.
47 *Labour Woman*, July–August 1945. Unsuccessful candidates were – Dr Elizabeth Jacob – St Marylebone; Miss I Marcouse – Holborn; Miss M D Shufeldt – Chelsea; and Mrs P Strauss (wife of George Strauss) – South Kensington.
48 *Labour Woman*, December 1954.
49 Black and Brooke, 'The Labour Party, Women and the Problem of Gender,' 420.
50 Hart, 'Gender and the Rise and Fall of Class Politics,' 20; Goldthorpe et al., *The Affluent Worker in the Class Structure*. Goldthorpe was criticised for submerging women's class position with that of their husbands (as male heads of households) rather than as actors in their own right.

The politics of personal identity 217

had risen to 52%.'[51] However, despite these changes, women continued to be 'more firmly trapped within patriarchal relations at work and at home,' but in the long run their new position in the labour market may have 'prompted women collectively both to attack inequalities at work and to challenge the sexual division of labour in the home.'[52]

By the 1960s, the Labour Party started to take equal rights for women more seriously and this may account for the increasing number of females who voted Labour.[53] In 1966, it acknowledged the need to adapt the party's organisation to fit in with the outlook of modern women. Two strikes in London for equal pay (Dagenham in 1968 and Trico in 1976) may have been responsible for this new perspective. In 1968, the party established a Study Group on Discrimination against Women which dealt with social security, taxation and conditions of work. Labour's policies towards women began to change. An Equal Pay Act was finally passed in 1970, followed by legislation on matrimonial property, employment protection and sex discrimination. 'A Labour Women's Action Committee was set up to investigate and improve the position of women within the labour movement. In 1980, a NEC Women's Committee was established... Party literature increasingly reflected a greater level of concern and realism about women's interests...a more defiant and less deferential generation of women entered the party after the late sixties...a cohort of party activists more firmly and confidentially associated with "second wave" feminism.'[54] While the formal structures for gender representation in the party remained in place (annual conference and representation on the NEC), the publication of *Labour Woman* was discontinued in 1971 and merged with the new *Labour Weekly*. This may have signified the view that women's issues no longer needed a separate journal. But in its final editorial, it noted that progress had been irregular, as it continues to be so to this day.

> It is not a smooth continuous process. Backward steps are sometimes taken – particularly when a Conservative Government is in power. Although equal pay is now a statutory obligation, equal access to employment, training and promotion is not. Nor can it be easily legislated for, because unequal access arises from deeply entrenched attitudes – attitudes instilled into men and women employers and employees, teachers and pupils, parents and children. This is the next target for attack by the National Joint Committee and the National Labour Women's Advisory Committee.[55]

51 Summerfield, *Women Workers in the Second World War*, p. 189.
52 Ibid., p. 191.
53 Bruley, *Women in Britain since 1900*, pp. 158–81.
54 Black and Brooke, 'The Labour Party, Women and the Problem of Gender,' 450–1.
55 *Labour Woman*, September 1971.

218   *Thematic*

After 1970, the growth of 'popular individualism' injected new energy into the demand for gender equality. The rise of the Women's Liberation Movement (WLM), known as 'Second Wave Feminism,' coincided with the passage of Equal Pay and Sexual Discrimination Acts and an increase in the number of working-class married women working outside the home. However, there remained a tension between the WLM, which was supported mainly by educated middle-class women, and the aspirations of the majority of females in work or at home who were trapped in domestic and patriarchal relationships. 'This was partly because the social and economic opportunities that would allow women to live an alternative existence' (as promoted by the desire for greater personal autonomy and self-determination which emerged during the 1970s) 'were limited at this point.'[56] Working-class women were never drawn to the WLM in large numbers and other groups, such as lesbians feminists and black feminists, challenged the claims of the WLM to speak for all women.[57] But feminist and socialist literature after 1970 began to emphasise the need to accept that 'the personal' had become 'the political,' and that socialism could not be divorced from 'the domestic.'

But 'Second Wave Feminism' lost momentum during the 1980s. It fragmented when questions of race, religion, ethnicity and sexual orientation introduced unresolved tensions into debates, for example, on abortion.[58] It would take another generation for 'equality of opportunity' to extend into areas which challenged male preserves in employment, in politics and in the home, but even then, entrenched attitudes persisted. 'Third' and 'Fourth Wave Feminism' continued to be a largely middle-class movement without deep roots in wider society. Although the entry of women into a wider range of public roles has broadened and a number of formal barriers have been removed, deeper structural and cultural barriers still operate to prevent women from fully engaging in public life. The Women's Officer of the London Labour Party complained in 1990 that only superficial gains were being made by quotas and the policy of one woman on every shortlist, and that London still had only six female MPs in London out of total of 22.[59] By 1995, the party reported that the policy of all women shortlists was being challenged in the courts.[60]

But by the turn of the century, the Labour Party was selecting more female candidates for election and not just in unwinnable seats, and the introduction of quotas as part of a programme of modernisation was helping to transform the masculine culture of the party.[61] A record number of female MPs were elected in 1997 (including 16 out of 57 in London), but were

---

56 Robinson, 'Telling Stories about Post-war Britain,' 268–304.
57 Hannam, *Feminism*, p. 82.
58 Ibid., p. 89.
59 Annual Report of the Greater London Labour Party 1990.
60 Ibid., 1995 and 1996.
61 Perrigo, 'Women and Change in the Labour Party 1979–1995.'

The politics of personal identity   219

still described in the media in condescending terms as 'Blair's Babes.' The journalist Matthew Parris commented somewhat archly: "'So many purple suits! So much hairspray!" It all reminded me of that picture of Hugh Hefner by his Playboy Bunnies, except of course that these women are not bunnies, they are, say it again, MPs.'[62] In London local government, white women had achieved broad numerical representation by 2018, while black men were the least represented.[63] In terms of voting, the 2017 general election found significantly fewer women voting Conservative than men in the UK, while the Labour Party was 8 percentage points ahead amongst women compared to men. Although pollsters think that this might have been a blip, the result is in stark contrast to earlier in the twentieth century when the trend was the opposite by a considerably larger margin. It was only during the period 1974–2015, following the enactment of gender-equality legislation, that the gap 'rarely reached statistical significance.'[64]

Black sections – the case of Lambeth (1970–1990)

Labour politics in London, like in other metropolitan centres, such as Glasgow, Liverpool and Manchester, has been strongly influenced at different times by religious and racial conflicts. Divisions between Catholics and Protestants are a well-known and important feature of politics (as well as football clubs) in Glasgow and Liverpool, and to a lesser extent in Manchester.[65] In London, waves of Irish immigration during the nineteenth century, of Jews from Eastern Europe and Russia before 1914, of Afro-Caribbean's and Asians from the New Commonwealth after 1945, and of asylum seekers and refugees from many parts of the world in the modern period created ethnic and religious conflicts that did not exist to the same extent as in other non-metropolitan areas of the country. The trade unions in London, for example, called for immigration controls in the early 1900s (supporting the Aliens Act 1905) arguing that cheap Jewish immigrant labour suppressed the wages of indigenous workers.[66] Londoners rioted against aliens (Germans, including Jews) during the First World War.[67] The Labour MP for North Kensington (George Roberts) called for restrictions on New Commonwealth immigration after the race riots in his constituency in 1958.[68] London Dockers and other blue-collar workers marched in support of Enoch Powell in 1968, following his notorious 'Rivers of Blood' speech. During

62 *Independent*, 9 May 1997.
63 Muroki and Cowley, 'Getting Better Slowly.'
64 Campbell, 'The Average Voter Is a Woman: Sex and Gender Differences.'
65 Davies, *Liverpool Labour*; Fielding, *Class and Ethnicity*; Gallaher, *Glasgow*; McHugh, *Labour in the City*.
66 Schneer, *London 1900*.
67 White, *Zepplin Nights*.
68 LP archives: GS/Race/49 ii.

220   *Thematic*

the 1990s, the Bangladeshi community in the East End was subject to racial hostility from the indigenous white working-class population over housing and welfare provision.[69] After the Iraq War in 2001, the large Arab population in London (estimated at over 106,000 according to the 2011 census, and which had been present in the capital since the 1920s) faced regular hostility and their young men accused of being terrorists.[70]

However, as well as conflicts between class and race, there are also examples of where alliances were forged across these divisions to counter a common threat. The labour movement at a local level in London has been in the forefront of combating racial and religious prejudice. For instance, in 1934, large crowds, supported by communists and Labour party members, prevented Oswald Moseley and the British Union of Fascists from attacking Jewish communities and taking over the streets in the East End (Cable Street).[71] In the 1950s, left-wing Labour MPs like Fenner Brockway and the first black Labour councillor elected to the LCC for Hackney, Dr David Pitt, initiated the Campaign against Racial Discrimination (CARD) seeking to introduce legislation outlawing racial hatred as well as campaigning for colonial independence.[72] During the 1980s, the Anti-Nazi League fought street battles against the National Front in areas like Brixton and Lewisham. In the modern era, the Stand Up to Racism movement has joined together with Labour-controlled local authorities, trades councils and inter-faith organisations in a number of London boroughs like Lambeth, for example, to make refugees and asylum seekers welcome and ensure that their legal rights are protected.[73]

Lambeth provides a good example of the role of race in London Labour politics, similar in many respects to areas like Brent, where race divided opinion over issues such as education ('the McGoldrick affair'), resulting in bitter internal party conflicts.[74] Indians from Punjab in Southall and Bengalis in Tower Hamlets, for example, provided a different type of black politics to that which the Afro-Caribbean community developed in areas such as Brixton.[75] After the Second World War, Lambeth started to become a mainly residential area with a less-skilled but increasingly unionised workforce employed in delivering a wide range of services in the expanding public sector across London, such as in local and national governments, in education and health, and in public services like the Post Office and London Transport. These were all areas experiencing significant increases in trade

---

69 Dench, Gavron and Young, *The New East End.*
70 Aly, *Becoming Arab in London.*
71 Rosenberg, *The Battle for the East End.*
72 Perry, *London is the Place for Me*, pp. 216–7.
73 Cockburn, *Looking to London.*
74 Moher, *Stepping on White Corns.*
75 Butler and Hamnett, *Ethnicity, Class and Aspiration*; Dench, Gavron and Young, *The New East End. Kinship, Race and Conflict*; Wills, *Lovers and Strangers.*

The politics of personal identity 221

union membership and density. By the 1950s, shortages in these expanding labour public sector markets were increasingly filled by citizens from the West Indies, some recruited directly to the NHS by the government in the Caribbean, but most of them taking jobs where there were severe post-war labour shortages and which employers found difficult to fill with British-born white people. At the same time, these newly arrived British citizens encountered high levels of racial discrimination in employment and housing.

Before 1945, the population of Lambeth had been predominantly white. But after 1948, Brixton was one of the chosen areas for migrants from the West Indies, building on the existing and relatively small Jamaican community which had lived there from before the war. The British Nationality Act of 1948 granted citizenship to all residents of the Commonwealth irrespective of race, colour or nationality although the government had not anticipated the flow of migrants increasing from the West Indies. Taking advantage of the prospect of self-improvement (and able to say 'London is the Place for Me'), by the early 1960s, there were already some 100,000 West Indians in Brixton and Notting Hill, in addition to Irish communities in Camden, Kilburn and Fulham and Greek Cypriots in Camden and Haringey.[76] Like previous concentrations of black people in Britain, such as the seafaring communities in interwar Cardiff and Liverpool, and in Midland cities like Nottingham, they experienced discrimination and violence. An early sociological study of West Indian workers in Brixton during the late 1950s, conducted by the anthropologist Sheila Patterson, identified hostility towards 'foreign' labour, both male and female, restricting job opportunities to unskilled work, although many migrants were skilled workers. A high level of discrimination was also endemic in the private housing market where migrants were excluded from many areas.[77] By 1971, the black population of London had increased to 170,000, constrained by the Commonwealth Immigration Act of 1962, but preceded by an upsurge before the Act came into force. The proportion of residents in inner London whose both parents were born in the New Commonwealth was officially estimated at only 8% in 1961, but this was clearly an under-estimate. Thirty years later when the census started to record ethnic origins for the first time, the black and ethnic minority population in Greater London had reached 20% and in inner London 25%. By 2001, this had increased to 28% and 34%, respectively.

By the year 2000, London had been transformed into a multi-ethnic city described as a 'true cosmopolis.' 'In the former heart of the British Empire, less than half a century after its demise, a city has emerged that would,' according to a leading academic on immigration, 'not exist without the contribution of immigrants and their offspring. They have become part of the geographical, social, economic, cultural, sporting, culinary and political

76 Perry, *London Is the Place for Me.*
77 Patterson, *Dark Strangers*; Perry, *op cit.,* p. 86.

222   *Thematic*

landscape of the one truly global city in the British Isles.'[78] This rapid growth was due primarily to different age structures rather than fresh waves of migration after 1980, and children joining their families from overseas at a later date. By 2011, the proportion of black and Asian residents in the three parliamentary constituencies in Lambeth exceeded 30%, with Afro-Caribbean's constituting 25% and Asians between 5 and 7%. By the turn of the century, the proportion of non-ethnic minority pupils in Lambeth secondary schools had fallen below 40%.[79] In addition, there were 7,500 residents of Arabic and other ethnicities, reflecting the growth in the number of asylum seekers and refugees making Lambeth their home.[80]

While the size of Lambeth's ethnic minority population was under 10% in the early 1970s, the government could no longer ignore the economic and social problems of the inner cities caused by the loss of manufacturing industry, poor housing and the increase of immigration, and not least the on-going level of racial violence. Black people were increasingly characterised as representing a 'coloured problem' giving rise to policies designed to improve 'race relations,' but also to restrict immigration. The riots in Notting Hill Gate in 1958 and the notorious housing scandals of the early 1960s ('Rachmanism') in London brought home the brittle nature of race relations in a country experiencing decolonisation. Stuart Hall, the Marxist academic who had moved in 1951 from a middle-class life in Jamaica to study at Oxford University (Rhodes Scholarship), wrote that it was impossible to ignore the 'palpable presence of racism' at this time:

> The 1950s were, after all, a watershed period as far as overt expression of racist attitudes in public places was concerned. The local hostility and resentment at the formation of the early ghetto areas and the competition for jobs and housing; the discrimination on the doorstep; racketeering landlords who presided over the multi-occupation archipelago; all were sharpening at this time, culminating in the violence of Notting Hill.[81]

In 1958 after moving from Oxford to London, he lodged with Jock and Millie Haston in Clapham, both activists in socialist and Labour Party circles. Before becoming an editor of the *New Left Review*, he took a job as a supply teacher in Stockwell Secondary Modern School, an experience which introduced him to the reality of class and race in the borough. The school, he wrote, was composed of the children of the white working class with

---

78 Panayi, 'Cosmopolis,' 75–6; Hamnett, *Unequal City*, p. 110; Storkey and Lewis, *Ethnicity in the 1991 Census,*

79 Department of Education and Science, *Minority Ethnic Pupils in Maintained Schools* (1999).

80 Census, 1991–2011; Cockburn, *Looking to London.* pp. 167–210.

81 Hall, *Familiar Stranger*, p. 257.

The politics of personal identity 223

about a quarter made up of black boys from around Brixton and the Oval... Many of the white fathers were in the newspaper trade and their sons were guaranteed work in 'the print,' like hereditary peers destined for the House of Lords. He witnessed some of these Teddy Boys travelling to Notting Hill Gate on the underground (knowing they rarely left their 'manor') to join the fascist Mosleyites in attacking black people on their way home to the ghettos of North Kensington.[82] After the riots in 1958, the National Union of Fascists (NUF) targeted Brixton, but came bottom of the poll in the 1962 local elections. In the general election of 1970 leaflets circulated in Clapham which were purported to have come from the Conservative candidate, read, 'If you desired a COLOURED for your neighbour vote LABOUR...If you are already burdened with one vote TORY.'[83]

Under pressure, the Labour government in the 1960s started to address the problems of the inner city.[84] It targeted such areas, including Lambeth, for extra investment through the inner area programme. The Lambeth Inner Area Study, published in 1974 by the Department of the Environment, concluded that the borough as a whole was undergoing a number of complex social changes, although it did not highlight the issue of racism directly. It identified some limited gentrification, the outward migration of the skilled working class to areas outside the borough (colloquially known as 'white flight') and the consequent polarisation, and the shorter-distance migration of the less skilled to areas within the borough south of Brixton, such as Streatham and Norwood. It thought that gentrification had been exaggerated in comparison to other areas of London with better transport links (the Victoria underground line had arrived in Brixton in 1971 but was yet to become one of the busiest stations on the network). It argued that gentrification had led to some social upgrading in certain pockets, with older houses being improved with the availability of government renovation grants seeking to address the problem of slum housing. There was evidence however that some residents had been harassed or persuaded out of their homes as a result of redevelopment. While it noted that the loss of skilled working men was more marked in Lambeth than elsewhere, this did not apply to white-collar jobs working in local or national government. The Inner Area Study predicted, an under-estimate as it turned out, that if the borough continued to lose 5% of the skilled working-class every ten years, as it did between 1961 and 1971, the 'proportion of such men would in twenty years be down to just over a quarter, and the population structure would be transformed.'[85]

82 Ibid., p. 258.
83 Bloom, *Violent London*, p. 428.
84 Stoker, 'Inner-city Policy in Britain,' 378–402.
85 Lambeth Inner Area Study, pp. 27–8.

224 *Thematic*

The study warned of what it saw as the danger of polarisation, a popular concept amongst sociologists at the time. If the proportion of middle-class professional groups increased as a result of gentrification and the proportion of less-skilled people remained fairly constant (as it seems to have done between 1961 and 1971), 'then Lambeth would indeed become increasingly "bi-polarised" in terms of social class.' It speculated that gentrification and large-scale redevelopment have made it difficult, or perhaps just unpleasant, for some residents to stay in areas that no longer generated feelings of strong community identity. It concluded that such residents:

> searching for a home, they have moved slightly further 'out', where declining privately-rented property could still be found. In consequence, their new areas have probably begun to take on some of the characteristics, and some of the problems, of the inner-areas themselves. To oversimplify, it may be, ironically, that the more the inner-city is improved by gentrification and council redevelopment, the further out it spreads.[86]

This conclusion downplayed the issue of racial discrimination. The Scarman Report, which was the official government enquiry into the so-called 'Brixton Disorders' of 1981, had described the neighbourhood as

> a lively and prosperous place in the late nineteenth and early twentieth centuries. The railway gave it excellent access to the centre of London: business and professional people (including members of the acting profession) lived there, some of them in large, dignified houses standing in their own grounds.

Before 1914, 'streets of small terraced houses, not unlike those which are currently fashionable in Chelsea and Islington, were built for the wage-earners who found excellent employment opportunities not only in Brixton itself but in the centre of the Metropolis. Economic decline, however, set in shortly after the First World War, and has continued to the present time'.[87] Such social problems, especially housing and unemployment, were according to Scarman the underlying causes of the Brixton riots. 'The disturbances,' he concluded, were the result of severe overcrowding and poverty, triggered by the institutional racism of the police in seeking to reduce crime by stop and search tactics (called 'Operation Swamp 81'). Above average levels of unemployment, as the economy entered a sharp downturn following the election of Mrs Thatcher in 1979, and the severe housing crisis combined, Scarman argued, to 'create a predisposition towards violent protest.'[88]

---

86 Ibid., p. 29.
87 *Scarman Report*, p. 18.
88 Ibid., p. 36.

The politics of personal identity   225

A good deal of damming evidence about multi-occupation had already been highlighted in the Milner Holland Report of 1965, an enquiry set up in the wake of the Profumo scandal and the associated outrage over rack-renting and the intimidation of tenants by the notorious Peter Rachman.[89] It showed that as a result of the abolition of rent controls in 1957, the London conurbation contained about 26,000 dwellings with four or more households (that is over 100,000 families or over a quarter of a million people living in multi-occupation), but the bulk of these were in certain districts where there were high levels of immigration. Islington came on top of the list with 8,500 dwellings containing three or more households. Kensington had 3,600, Paddington 3,500, Lambeth 3,400 and Hackney 3,300.[90] Scarman had described the housing situation in Lambeth as 'one of considerable stress.' There was a shortage of 20,000 dwellings and a housing waiting list of 18,000 households, with 12,000 living in overcrowded conditions.[91] After the second riot in the late summer of 1985, the Church of England published a damming report on the state of the inner cities called *Faith in the City*. It described the Urban Priority Areas, which included Lambeth, Hackney, Docklands and Islington in London, as in a state of 'social disintegration,' reflecting an intractable and structural inequality in the inner cities.[92]

The matter of black political representation was first raised in Lambeth in the mid-1970s, but it did not become a heated or divisive issue until the early 1980s. The demand for black sections (similar to long-established youth and women's sections in the party) was very much a feature of London politics. Such demands

> were strongest in London, but had little success in other parts of the country. In Bradford and Leicester, a pre-existing form of ethnic political action based on religion prevented their development. In Liverpool, the Militant dominated Labour Party was hostile to black representation which it saw as deflecting energies from the class struggle.[93]

In 1987, a black councillor in Brent and Lambeth Council's Principal Race Relation's Adviser wrote to the press complaining about the coverage of race issues in the media. 'As long as ago as January 1975,' he wrote, 'a group of black people met together and agreed that:

> There is a dire and long-standing need for black people in this country to be afforded an opportunity amongst themselves to express their point of view, their concern, opinion and general experience in relation

---

89 Wills, *Lovers and Strangers*. p. 247.
90 Milner Holland Report (1965).
91 *Scarman Report*, p. 20.
92 Archbishop of Canterbury, *Faith in the City*, p. 25.
93 Fielding and Geddes, 'The British Labour Party and 'ethnic entryism,' p. 67.

226   *Thematic*

to policies/programmes produced by a host community that condones racist discriminatory legislation and rather paternalistic programmes. The blacks have a clear perception of their contribution to this society but must be allowed to define their own problems, solutions and priorities.'[94]

Black citizens arriving from the Caribbean in the late 1940s, encountered as we have seen extreme anti-black racism, which went on to influence the political views of first, second and third generations of immigrants settling in Lambeth, many who were made to feel 'strangers' in their own land.[95] In the neighbouring borough of Southwark, for example, the council's housing programme, which favoured relatively 'respectable' families, concealed an ideology that rendered the black population invisible. As slum-clearance families started to be allocated most of the new housing after 1960, 'the wards that first turned against Labour were those dominated by the white working-class.'[96] In Southwark, where there had been different political cultures among the Labour groups in Bermondsey, Camberwell and the old Southwark Borough, members tended towards parochialism over policy and this was particularly evident with housing.[97] In the face of such hostility, ethnicity became a dominant factor in local politics during the 1980s in those areas of London where there were high concentrations of black people.

At a national level, the Labour Party was deeply compromised over immigration and race relations. During the fifties, the anti-colonialist activist and left-wing Labour MP Fenner Brockway had introduced a private member bill almost every year to outlaw racial discrimination and incitement. But none of these got past second reading. However, after Labour took power in 1964, the party pursued an official race policy that was contradictory. It accepted that the country had a moral duty to foster inclusion and keep the pernicious 'colour bar' at bay, but at the same time, it 'viewed Britain as an island nation under siege in need of protection from the invasion of Commonwealth "immigrants."'[98] The effect of the controversial election in Smethwick, in the 1964 general election, exercised an extremely negative influence on the new area of policy known as 'race relations.' The Conservative candidate Peter Griffiths defeated the shadow Labour Home Secretary Patrick Gordon Walker through the circulation of leaflets bearing the now

---

94 Lambeth Archives: Minutes of the Lambeth Labour Group 1980–1987 (IV/273/3) – Letter from Phil Sealy to *The Guardian* 9 April 1987.
95 Perry, *London is the Place for Me*, pp. 1–23; Hall, *Familiar Stranger*; Patterson, *Dark Strangers*; Wills, *Lovers and Strangers*.
96 Cater, 'Building the Divided City,' 155–85.
97 Passmore, 'The Response of Labour-controlled Local Authorities to Major Changes in Housing Policy, 1971–1983 (PhD London 2015), p. 35.
98 Perry, *London is the Place for Me*, p. 199.

The politics of personal identity 227

infamous slogan 'If you want a Nigger for a Neighbour, Vote for Labour.' It characterised his opponent as an anti-white working-class candidate who had lost touch with his constituents. It transformed Smethwick 'into a symbolic bastion of anti-black sentiment.'[99] Such an outcome imposed significant constraints on the cross-party CARD, causing it to disintegrate as an organisation 'less than two years after it had begun.' It had also been undermined by internal conflicts over 'Black Power,' and the influence of the civil rights movement in the USA.[100]

But at a local level the labour movement in Lambeth campaigned against race hatred. In 1953, the trades council, influenced by the Communist Party and Trotskyist groups, called on all trade unionists to boycott the George Pub in Railton Road (the future front line of the riots in 1981) for operating a colour bar. In December 1958, it helped set up a 'Campaign Against Racial Discrimination,' fearful that the Notting Hill riots would spread south of the river. It convened a conference of over a dozen trade union branches, the Movement for Colonial Freedom, the *West Indian Gazette*, the Association for the Advancement of Coloured People and the local WCG, at which David Pitt, the first black member of the LCC, spoke together with some of the expelled Trotskyist members of Norwood Labour Party. The conference condemned all racist attacks 'pledging to take steps to develop and strengthen the bonds of solidarity and unity between coloured and white workers' as well as calling for the end to immigration controls.[101] Racism in the borough was explicit at this time. For example, in banner headlines, the Medical Officer of Health reported in 1961 that 'public health is worsened (sic) by coloured immigrants.' Fourteen Lambeth Tory councillors caused outrage when they publicly demanded a ban on all immigration, provoking a bitter complaint from the Lambeth branch of the National Union of Teachers.[102] But such local opposition was far removed from the official Labour Party policy of supporting the restrictive Immigration Act of 1962 when out of power, but introducing race relations legislation when in power, which sought to make race hatred punishable by heavy fines and a maximum two years in prison.

The demand for black sections took off in the early 1980s as black activists in the party grew increasingly critical of the discrepancy between the party's reliance on black votes and its long-term failure to address racism in a serious way or to promote black candidates in elections, especially to parliament. The publication of the highly influential '*The Empire Strikes Back*' in 1982 by black academics from the Centre for Contemporary Cultural Studies, following the race riots of the previous year, was extremely critical of the response of the labour movement to the growing evidence of racial

99 Ibid., p. 188.
100 Ibid., pp. 242–3.
101 Modern Record Centre: Records of the Lambeth Trades Council.
102 *South London Press*, 8 September 1961.

228   *Thematic*

discrimination.[103] By the late 1970s, a number of black councillors had been elected across London and in 1979 a black councillor in Lewisham, Russell Profit, organised a 'Black People's Manifesto Conference,' to put pressure on the leadership to endorse more black parliamentary candidates. The *West Indian World* complained that while the Conservatives are at least making a pretence of trying to attract black votes, 'Labour doesn't even appear to be aware there's a black vote around.'[104] In 1981, Tony Benn caused controversy by calling on black organisations to affiliate to the Labour Party in the same way as did the Fabians and the trade unions. But he was condemned for 'Labour's abysmal record on immigration and race and the deep-seated racism of white working-class people.'[105] A Greater London Labour Party Black Section held its first meeting in December 1983 at which Russell Profit reported with some disappointment that it was not yet recognised by the leadership of the party. The annual conference in 1982 had remitted a resolution in favour of black sections, in exchange for a working party.[106] The first national black sections conference was held in Birmingham in 1984, 'attracting over 300 participants. This was, however, the moment when the left's influence within the Party had begun to decline.'[107] In the eyes of the party leadership, the demand for black representation was associated with the left wing. Their official position was that there would be 'problems of definition' and that autonomous black sections would be 'deeply patronising.' The deputy leader Roy Hattersley argued that positive discrimination was needed instead 'in order to support the aspirations of black and Asian British people.'[108] Resolutions in favour of black sections at the annual conference in 1984 were defeated by over 4.5 million votes and by a narrower but similar margin in 1985.

In Lambeth, the campaign for black sections was led by Sharon Atkin, a black Labour councillor for Town Hall ward and chair of the Black Sections National Committee of the Labour Party. This committee was regarded as illegal by the leadership. She had been selected as the parliamentary candidate for Nottingham East. In an interview for local radio, she answered accusations of promoting apartheid or 'some kind of separatism' by replying 'that black sections attracted black people into the party in the same way that women's sections and youth sections attracted more women and more youth into the party.' But she acknowledged that she was breaking the rules.[109] In 1987, Atkin was deselected from her candidature for Nottingham East on the

103 Gilroy et al., *The Empire Strikes Back*.
104 *Labour Weekly*, 12 October 1979; *West Indian World*, 26 April 1979.
105 *Times*, 17 November 1980; *Guardian*, 27 November 1980.
106 *New Life*, 23 December 1983.
107 Fielding and Geddes, 'The British Labour Party and 'ethnic entryism,' p. 67.
108 *Times*, 11 June 1983.
109 LBC phone in 28 March 1985 – transcript in the records of the Vauxhall Liberal Association 1981–88 (Lambeth Archives IV 326/1).

The politics of personal identity   229

grounds of being in breach of the constitution. She had called Neil Kinnock and the party racist at a public meeting in Birmingham. Her deselection was more likely the result of a purge of the hard left in Lambeth.[110]

Similar disputes broke out in the party over the selection of candidates in key by-elections. On the death of Marcus Lipton in 1978, the party selected John Tilley, a white councillor from Wandsworth, without any major controversy or internal opposition. He retained the seat for Labour, but with a reduced majority. He did, however, face opposition from a long-list of independent socialist candidates, including Brixton Socialist Unity, Workers Revolutionary Party, Socialist Workers Party and the Socialist Party of GB. The National Front beat the Liberals into fourth place.[111] However, ten years later in the by-election for Vauxhall, there was fierce opposition from within the party to the selection of a white candidate. In 1987, the academic Stuart Holland resigned as MP to take up a research post in Florence. The leadership imposed their own candidate, Kate Hoey, a physical education lecturer who was a Kinnock supporter. Meetings ended in chaos after the local party abandoned their selection meeting to demand the reinstatement of Martha Osamor, a left-wing black female councillor, who had been excluded from the short list by party HQ.[112] A new organisation in Lambeth, the People's Movement for Electoral Justice, selected Rudy Narayan, the black barrister and previous Labour councillor to fight the seat as an independent. He had left the party in 1983. A black Methodist minister was also put up as an independent. In the event, Labour regained the seat with a majority of just under 10,000.

By the 1990s, the demand for black sections had abated after the defeat of the hard left in London and the election of a small number of black MPs such as Paul Boateng in Brent and Dianne Abbot in Hackney. The Black Section's National Committee was wound up in 1993 and replaced by the Black Socialist Society, which could affiliate to the party, but it was an unhappy compromise in the circumstances.[113] Thereafter, the black population of London continued to vote Labour, in line with a trend that has not changed significantly since the late 1970s. In 1978, a National Opinion Poll survey on attitudes towards immigration indicated that the party attracted over 90% of both Afro-Caribbean and Asian voters from all social classes.[114] After the 2017 general election, the Runnymede Trust concluded

> that 1 in 5 of Labour's voters were from an ethnic minority background; for the Conservatives it was 1 in 20. This is the same as in the 2010

---

110 Hefferman, *Defeat from the Jaws of Victory*, pp. 75–7.
111 *Times*, 22 April 1978.
112 *Independent*, 18 May 1989.
113 Riddell, 'The Catholic Church and the Labour Party,' 166; Fielding, *Class and Ethnicity*; Shukra, *The Changing Pattern of Black Politics in Britain*.
114 *New Society*, 12 April 1979, p. 76.

230   *Thematic*

general election. In this remarkable period of political change, ethnic minority voting patterns have changed little. However, changes at the margins – increasing Conservative support among Hindus, and more Muslims voting for the Labour Party – suggests that demography need not be destiny.[115]

While the record for elections to parliament has improved (with over 50 MPs with black and ethnic minority backgrounds elected in 2017), performance in local elections remains poor. A reporter for the Runnymede Trust complained that in 2008 the proportion of ethnic minority councillors was only 3.7%. 'In Lambeth, ethnic minority councillors make up less than 20% of the elected members, despite the local population being 60% black.' The report argued that the demands of family and jobs may be one factor, given the higher proportion of BME people having young families and the much smaller proportion who are retired.[116] The estimated figures for party membership suggest that while BME people vote Labour, they do not join the party. An internet survey carried out in 2008 put the non-white membership at 5.7% (in contrast to 6.1% for the Conservatives.)[117] This may have been an over-estimate as later surveys put the non-white membership of the party at 4%.[118] This low figure is despite the growth of overall national membership to 552,000 by 2018, an increase of 198,000 since 2015.[119] However, this figure is almost certainly too low for BME membership of the Labour Party in those parts of London where there are very high concentrations of the BME population.

Sir Peter Hall put low rates of BME political participation in London down to apathy and cynicism.

> We were surprised by the intensity of that cynicism, which seemed to regard any attempt at consultation as a piece of manipulation or of spin. We got a strong sense that many people regarded local politics as a kind of racket monopolised by a small clique.[120]

A recent survey of BME candidates in local elections concluded that there was little agreement over why there were low levels of representation. London contained the majority of BME-elected councillors. But the survey found that about a third of respondents thought that lack of confidence was an issue; a third agreed that family pressures were to blame; while about a half explained the paucity of numbers on the confrontational style of local

---

115 Martin and Kkan, *Ethnic Minorities at the 2017 British General Election.*
116 Holloway, *Where Are All the BME Councillors?*
117 Whiteley, 'Where Have All the Members Gone?' 242–57.
118 Bale, Webb and Poletti, *Grass Roots*, p. 6.
119 Whiteley, 'Oh Jeremy Corbyn!'
120 Hall, 'London Voices 1957–2007,' 61.

The politics of personal identity   231

politics.[121] The record of the GLC in promoting a certain type of ethnic minority politics through its grant programme has also been criticised by black Londoners for marginalising black interests.

> In the absence of a consistent direction, the politics of the ethnic minorities throughout the last decade of the twentieth century were preoccupied with miscarriages of justice and police accountability...and in the event there was no serious black rival for the post of mayor.[122]

However, the election of Sadiq Khan in 2016 as Labour mayor may be the start of a new political chapter which properly reflects the multi-ethnic character of London. Progress is slow however. A recent survey of ethnicity and gender in local government found that London's Asian population is now represented proportionately, although black Londoners as a whole remain under-represented.[123] However, the evidence clearly indicates that

> Labour are seen as the best party to defend minority interests, and that minorities tend not to abandon white Labour candidates to vote for a non-white candidate from another party, even if that candidate is from the voters own ethnic group.[124]

After the Windrush scandal, and Labour's historic record of enacting race-equality legislation (apart from the party's support for racist immigration controls in the 1960s), it is likely that this trend will continue, especially in London.[125] While the controversy over black sections in the 1980s, 'written-off as the 'looney-left,' 'the message of equality and diversity had been accepted, rhetorically at least, by front-bench politicians of both main parties...culminating in the 2010 Equality Act,' which was one of the last acts of the Labour government of Gordon Brown.[126] However, after the Iraq War, New Labour was criticised for not fully embracing 'a democratic and multicultural future,' unable 'to mourn its imperial ghosts,' according to some of its critics.[127] But Labour's manifesto in 2017 (*For the Many, Not the Few*) coincided with the emergence of popular anti-racist movements, such

---

121 Thrasher, 'BAME Candidates in Local Elections in Britain,' 286–304.
122 Phillips, *London Crossings*, p. 178.
123 Muroki and Cowley, 'Getter Better, Slowly.'
124 Fisher, 'Racism at the Ballot Box: Ethnic Minority Candidates.'
125 The Windrush scandal is a 2018 political controversy concerning people who were wrongly detained, denied legal rights, threatened with deportation and, in at least 83 cases, wrongly deported from the UK by the Home Office. Many of those affected had been born British subjects and had arrived in the UK before 1973, particularly from Caribbean countries as members of the 'Windrush generation.'
126 Bunce, 'Race Today cannot fail': Black Radicalism in the Long 1980s,' 17.
127 Back et al., 'New Labour's White Heart: Politics, Multiculturalism and the Return of Assimilation.'

232　*Thematic*

as Black Lives Matter and the formation of refugee support networks. This encouraged other commentators to argue that 'we may be entering a new period of sustained collective action against racist discrimination, as well as class inequalities.'[128] Thus, Corbyn's long-standing support for anti-racism may well have contributed to the party's electoral success in multi-ethnic metropolitan areas.

Religious decline and then a religious revival (1900–2020)

Religious differences have also been present in London, more so than in the provinces or rural areas, as a result of significant concentrations of Jewish, Catholic, Hindu and Muslim populations, as well as Black Christians. Religion is a different type of personal identity to race and gender, which are more immutable, but can be equally controversial as demonstrated by current controversies over anti-Semitism. As well as conflict however, there are also examples of inter-faith cooperation, which was a feature of Jewish and Irish working-class politics in East London before 1914.[129] During the interwar period, the Catholic Church was influential in certain inner London constituency parties, supporting Herbert Morrison in his moves against the influence of communist infiltration. In 1918, the working-class constituency of Whitechapel & St Georges, which contained a large Irish and Jewish population, nearly elected Dr Robert Ambrose as its Labour MP, the previously Irish nationalist MP for West Mayo. There were large Irish settlements in Islington and Kilburn. Irish party members or voters took particular policy positions on the education of their children, on Irish independence (before and after 1922) or on women's rights, such as abortion or divorce, influencing party choice.[130] Recent controversies over anti-Semitism, to take another example, can only be properly understood in the context of the pattern of Jewish immigration and its dispersal to the suburbs over the course of the twentieth century. The views of Jewish party members, some pro-Zionist in the earlier period and others anti-Zionist in the later period, on Palestine or the State of Israel, came into conflict with a particular type of socialist politics that emerged in London during the 1970s and 1980s, which advocated the rights of oppressed peoples, such as the Palestinians. The issue badly split the party, especially in London under Jeremy Corbyn's leadership after 2015 and may have affected the Labour vote in those London suburbs where there is a high concentration of Jewish voters, such as Hendon, Ilford North and Finchley & Golders Green.[131] These are now areas populated

---

128　Virdee and McGeever, 'Racism, Crisis Brexit.'
129　Renshaw, *Socialism and the Diasporic 'other.'*
130　Hutchinson, 'Diaspora Dilemmas and Shifting Allegiances,' 107–25; Riddell, 'The Catholic Church and the Labour Party,' 165–93.
131　Kogan, *Protest and Power*, pp. 331–74.

The politics of personal identity   233

by the largely middle-class descendants from the original Jewish ghetto in Whitechapel.

Since the middle of the nineteenth century, London has long been associated with the modern trend towards secularisation, although it is far too simplistic to argue that 'the conversion of the working-classes to "socialism" or to Labour in the 1920s led them to reject organised religion.'[132] There is an important difference between recorded church attendance and the wider beliefs and values of society as a whole. The 1851 religious census recorded very low church attendances in working-class districts, but not in the middle-class suburbs. There was some anti-clericalism as part of the radical Chartist tradition prevalent in the working men's clubs, although not as much as in continental Europe. In terms of voting patterns, it has been suggested that before 1900 the relatively small electorate 'divided religiously because most of the voters were moulded by religious institutions,' and that the party system was based around either the Church of England ('the Conservative Party at prayer') or nonconformist churches (Liberal or Labour).[133] The Church of England has always been perceived as middle-class and out of touch as it is today, unable especially to relate to the needs of its working-class parishioners. It was the development of state-supported non-sectarian elementary education towards the end of the nineteenth century (especially in elections to locally elected school boards no longer controlled by different religious denominations) which broke this pattern. It may have been one of the factors that allowed a more class-based system of voting to develop, especially after the extension of the franchise in 1918, although its influence continued in the suburbs of London after the First World War.[134] Religion still influences party choice in Britain today through parental transmission of party affiliations, suggesting that secularisation may have been over-estimated as a motivation in voting behaviour.[135]

Conscience and politics came together to create a powerful movement for political reform before 1900. This can be clearly seen in Liberal Party support for temperance, educational reform and opposition to imperialist wars, such as the Boer War. Such religious impulses also formed the bedrock of the ethical socialism of the early labour movement. Croydon, for example, saw the short-lived birth of both a Ruskin Labour Church and a Brotherhood Church, inspired by an evolutionary form of socialism. The peak of the political involvement of these 'Free Churches' 'came in the era of the "Nonconformist conscience" around the opening of the Twentieth Century, when educational reform, temperance, social purity and anti-gambling

---

132 Field, 'Faith in the Metropolis,' 68–84; Fielding, *Class and Ethnicity.*
133 Thompson, *Socialists, Liberals and Labour*, pp. 17–38.
134 Wald, *Crosses on the Ballot*, pp. 250–54; Koss, *Nonconformity in Modern British Politics*;
      Tichelar, *A History of the Labour Movement in Croydon* (unpublished manuscript).
135 Tilley, 'We Don't Do God.'

234   *Thematic*

were among the key issues.'[136] After 1900, the close association between the Liberal Party and nonconformism culminated in the Liberal landslide in the 1906 general election. The survey of religious life in London carried out for the *Daily News* by the author Richard Mudie-Smith in 1904 concluded that the nonconformists show 'the best returns' in church attendance in the huge and ugly dormitories which are being built around London.[137] He had campaigned against the worse effects of sweated industry in London, bemoaning 'the aversion of the great mass of workpeople from Christianity. 'The Labour world,' he noted, with its separate organisations, is almost wholly cut off from the religious world and its organisations...The church-going employer and the stay-away trade unionist are alike suspicious of each other. So wide has the gulf become that workpeople have themselves started Labour churches.[138]

The Labour Church movement had been founded by John Trevor, a Unitarian minister who resigned to establish the first Labour Church in Manchester in 1891.[139] One of its converts was the Reverend E M Geldhart, a Unitarian Pastor of the local Free Christian Church in Croydon. He was converted to socialism, becoming the secretary of the local branch of the SDF in 1884. As a result, he lost the confidence of some of his congregation, his health deteriorated and it was believed that he took his own life on the night ferry from Newhaven to Dieppe in 1885.[140]

The twentieth century saw an absolute decline in church attendance in London. By the 1970s, a local survey estimated that only 15% of married men attended church at least 12 times a year.[141] Historians have debated the extent and timing of the decline of religious belief during the twentieth century.[142] Recent scholarship, for example, suggests that the Church of England responded positively and built new churches in middle-class suburban London after 1918.[143] Others have argued that secularisation did not really start to take effect until the 1960s, when liberalising attitudes to sex and authority emerged strongly amongst a younger generation.[144] After the First World War, housing reform and unemployment were two of the major challenges faced by the Christian churches in seeking to proselytise in the big cities and the distressed areas. Some 4 million new dwellings were built during the interwar period and by 1937 12 million people lived on new estates,

136 Husselbee and Ballard, *Free Churches and Society,* p. 64.
137 Mudie-Smith, *The Religious Life of London*, pp. 342–3.
138 Op. cit., p. 343.
139 Bevir, 'The Labour Church Movement 1891–1902,' 217–45.
140 *Justice,* 25 April 1885.
141 Morris, *The Nonconformist Experience in Croydon*, p. 14.
142 Morris, 'Secularisation and Religious Experience.'
143 Walford and Morris, *The growth of 'New London' in suburban Middlesex.*
144 Brown, *The Death of Christian Britain.*

The politics of personal identity 235

often devoid of community facilities or in areas of ad hoc and unregulated development in new residential areas. William Lax, a Methodist preacher from one of the poorest inner London boroughs (Poplar), lamented 'that too often a large estate is built upon and the houses occupied before we have a church ready for the new residents.'[145] Community centres and settlements sought to fill the gap and connect with an increasingly urban and secular society. But where the Free Churches set up chapels in suburban areas, they often met resentment and resistance from existing congregations to incomers from inner London, who by moving to the suburbs had lost a sense of community and experienced isolation and disorientation until they started to integrate.

While the influence of nonconformism declined after the First World War, Jewish migrants in London had established a vibrant and separate religious community (a ghetto) in the East End. The overwhelming majority of Jewish immigrants chose to remain within a square mile of Stepney, south of Cable Street. 'Toynbee Hall investigators put the total East London Jewish population at around 100,000,' in 1914. 'Whitechapel boasted no less than four daily Yiddish newspapers'; there were 35 synagogues and 'at least 16 state schools observed Jewish holidays.'[146] Many Russian Jews returned to their homeland after the 1917 revolution, 'including many traditionalists who had never wished to integrate,' plus those at risk of deportation as aliens, but those that stayed, sought wider horizons, 'trickling steadily up the "north-west passage" out of Whitechapel into the English-speaking, English living suburbs and beyond.'[147] Later research has shown that, for the most part, Jews in London neither desired residential segregation nor actively sought

> to be separated or isolated from others in the general population... They maintain an overall communal cohesiveness although spread out throughout Greater London...They may be typical of middle-class ethnic minorities which are freed from many of the financial – and perhaps even social – constraints that worked against immigrant and working-class ethnic minority groups in the past.[148]

Before the process of integration gathered pace after 1918, the largely working-class Jewish population in East London developed their own trade unions and socialist organisations, strongly influenced by the political culture they brought with them as immigrants from Eastern Europe

145 Husselbee and Ballard, *Free Churches and Society,* p. 126; Lax, *Lax of Poplar* (1927).
146 Bush, 'East London Jews and the First World War,' 140.
147 Ibid., 159.
148 Waterman and Kosmin, 'Residential Patterns and Processes,' 79–95.

236   *Thematic*

and Russia.[149] In 1906, the Jewish Social Democratic Labour Party ('Poale Zion') was formed in Russia by Marxist Zionist and Jewish Workers. In the UK, it urged Jewish voters to vote Labour in 1918 and the party affiliated to Labour in 1920. During the interwar period, many working-class Jews were active in anti-fascist movements, with a minority joining the CPGB and many recruited to the Labour Party.[150] The Jewish population as a whole tended to support the Labour Party 'not so much on ideological or socio-economic grounds, as through a process of elimination.'[151] The discrimination showed by the LCC, controlled by the Municipal Reform Party up to 1934, towards aliens on questions such as access to education, encouraged a move towards support for Labour. But after 1945, support for the party declined as the Jewish population (estimated at about 150,000 during the interwar period) dispersed to the suburbs and as the size of the Jewish working class contracted in line with general trends. By the 1970s and 1980s, Jewish suburbs like Hendon, Ilford and Golders Green & Finchley were safe Conservative seats.[152]

Similar patterns of dispersal can be found amongst Roman Catholics. Like for Jewish immigrants, 'the secular culture of the wider East End proletariat did not extinguish religious or cultural identity.'[153] In 1918, there were over two-and-a-half million Catholics in Britain, the vast majority were from the poor working class, many of them Irish. They were concentrated in Lancashire (Liverpool and Manchester), London, Leeds, Tyneside and Birmingham. The majority 'held on to their religion as a means of identity in a society where they were seldom accepted as equal citizens by their Protestant neighbours.'[154] 'Throughout the inter-war period, the Irish were one of the most consistently pro-Labour elements within the working-class.'[155] They exercised an important influence on the party, most notably on issues such as birth control, divorce and education. Moreover, class conflict and socialism were anathema to the Catholic hierarchy and Labour's constitutional and moderate approach during the interwar period, when it expelled a number of local parties and trades councils for communist infiltration, may have strengthened Catholic support for the party.[156]

At the same time, the influence of the nonconformist churches (as institutions) was not as important to the party in the way they had been before 1914,

149 Hofmeester, *Jewish Workers and the Labour Movement*, pp. 105–206; Renshaw, *Socialism and Diasporic 'Other.'*
150 Alderman, *London Jewery and London Politics*; see also Emanuel Litvinoff, *Journey Through a Small Planet.*
151 Alderman, *London Jewery*, p. 95.
152 Ibid., p. 140.
153 Renshaw, *Socialism and Diasporic 'Other.'*
154 Riddell, 'The Catholic Church and the Labour Party,' 166–7.
155 Fielding, *Class and Ethnicity*, p. 105.
156 Riddell, 'The Catholic Church and the Labour Party,' 193.

The politics of personal identity 237

such as the role of the Labour churches. But a large number of individual nonconformists were still active and influential, becoming the main carriers 'on the nonconformist conscience' on issues such as drink and gambling. They made 'a distinctive and important contribution to the development and ideals of the party.'[157] In Croydon, for example, a Brotherhood Church survived into the 1920s. It was part of a Progressive political tradition that proved attractive to many ex-Liberals who gravitated towards the Labour Party when their party formed anti-socialist alliances with local ratepayers' associations or did not put up candidates on a consistent basis in local and national elections. However, during the Second World War, a significant number of the capital's places of worship were destroyed or damaged during the blitz along with the communities which they served.[158] A Mass Observation survey conducted in London after the war concluded that 'the decline in religious faith is but one symptom of an all-round decline in faith in the future, accelerated by war, accentuated by the inevitable anxieties of peace.'[159]

State intervention after 1945 further undermined the influence of the Church of England and the nonconformist churches, which in many cases struggled to adapt following the creation of the welfare state. The staple of charitable activities, the domestic visitor, all but disappeared, replaced by local social services. As one Unitarian enquiry put in 1969, "Where the church led the Welfare State followed and went further, catering for the social needs not merely of the poor but of almost all classes." Lax of Poplar had established dental and other medical clinics before 1945, but only chiropody and psychotherapy services survived the blitz and the creation of the NHS.[160] Reports like *Faith in the City*, published in 1985 after the riots in Brixton, highlighted a continuing crisis for many of the established churches. A revived concern for the disadvantaged was also in part a response to the free-market ideology of Thatcherism. It started a process of revival amongst faith groups responding to inner-city deprivation, racial discrimination and unemployment.

However, a religious revival towards the end of the twentieth century, based primarily on the growth of the black and ethnic population in London after 1960, revitalised the nonconformist tradition. Before this date, London's Christian churches had largely served a white population. But by 1991, 20% of the population of Greater London was non-white. When black citizens migrated to London during the 1960s, they had come from a mostly Anglican English-speaking Caribbean, and they 'felt rejected by English Anglicanism. As a result, they developed a black Christian church

157 Catterall, 'Morality and Politics,' 667–85.
158 *Faith in the City*, pp. 27–46.
159 Mass Observation, *Puzzled People*, p. 158.
160 Husselbee and Ballard, *Free Churches and Society,* p. 127.

238   *Thematic*

community that was to become, in the last quarter of the twentieth century, one of the few thriving sectors of British Christianity.'[161] The London Church Census (2005–2012) found that two new London churches opened every week in the seven-year period and two-thirds of those were Pentecostal black majority churches and a third catered for a particular language or ethnic group (such as Polish Lutheran or Ghanaian Seventh-Day Adventist). This growth was driven by London's ethnic diversity and was strongest in the parts of London that already had significant African and/or Caribbean populations. Southwark, Lambeth and Newham saw at least a 25% growth of new churches. Church attendance in these boroughs also grew over the same period, with Lambeth seeing a 50% increase. The census found that nearly half of churchgoers in inner London (48%) are black, compared with 13% of the capital's population. That means nearly one in five (19%) black Londoners goes to church each week. Two-thirds attend Pentecostal churches, though the black community is represented in every denomination.[162] For non-Christians it was calculated in 1996 that, whereas Greater London hosted 7 per cent of all Christian places of worship in the United Kingdom, it was home to 16 per cent of Sikh gurdwaras and 12 per cent of Muslim mosques.[163] Recent research has demonstrated that the most dynamic churches in suburban London include the black Pentecostal churches, the evangelical wing of the Anglican Church and a wider set of churches associated with the 'new expressions movement.' They have made a significant impact on local politics through their ability to raise money, and in the context of cuts to local government funding, to build new places of worship, such as Islamic centres.[164]

Inter-faith cooperation is now a feature of local politics in London where there are large concentrations of refugees, 'where people and communities of Jewish, Muslim and Christian faiths are able to work together constructively to welcome refugees...a partnership of local community and local state.'[165] The Church Forum in Croydon, for example, run projects in the community, with initiatives labelled under the Croydon Churches banner, showing that they represent the wider, united Church rather than promoting individual churches. This includes the Croydon Churches Floating Shelter, which sees 70 churches work together to provide a bed and hot meal for homeless people. Other projects include Christians Against Poverty, debt advice centres, food banks, street and school pastors.[166]

---

161 Brown, *Religion and Society in Twentieth Century Britain*, p. 255.

162 www.lcm.org.uk.

163 Brierley, *UK Christian Handbook: Religious Trends*.

164 Gilbert, 'Ethnic and Religious Diversity in the Politics of Suburban London,' 78; Dwyer, 'Faith and Suburbia.' 403–19.

165 Cockburn, *Looking to London*, pp. 194–210.

166 www. Church Forum Croydon.

The politics of personal identity 239

Whether this inter-faith cooperation is a return to the religious pattern of voting prevalent in London a century earlier (in terms of an alliance between Labour and the churches) is perhaps too early to say, but it does provide the basis for the formation of political alliances around common left-wing values, such as human rights, equal treatment and combating poverty. A recent survey into the involvement of young people in politics from different migrant groups in London shows that Muslim South Asians in particular are better integrated and more politically active as citizens, than Christian Black British Jamaicans, although both share the same concerns and problems associated with migrant communities.[167] More recent research into London's religious geography concluded that the capital is the most religious region in Britain with many Christians opposed to welfare benefit cuts and supportive of tax increases, seen as a top priority for ensuring a healthy society. The report found that 62% of Londoners identify as religious (compared to 53% in GB, excluding London), a profile driven largely by immigration and diaspora communities; and that London is the most intensively religious place in Britain with 30% of Christian Londoners attending services and praying regularly, compared to only 13% in Britain. It also found that the capital is not as socially liberal as many commentators like to believe. 'Londoners are more conservative than the rest of Britain on moral questions such as sex before marriage, same-sex relationships, and assisted suicide; and that 76% of Christian Londoners think that political correctness has gone too far.'[168]

Anti-Semitism (1917–2020)

Such potential religious cooperation however was sorely tested in the controversy over anti-Semitism which engulfed the Labour Party after 2015, although the issue had been present since the birth of the labour movement. Leading socialists, such as Henry Hyndman, founder of the SDF, and Robert Blatchford, author of *Merrie England* and editor of the *Clarion* Newspaper, railed against the influence of Jewish bankers.[169] It also arose in the 1970s, when the New Left started to campaign for Palestinian rights in the name of anti-imperialism. For example, in 1981, Ted Knight founded the *Labour Herald* (funded by the Palestine Liberation Organisation), which helped change Labour Party policy on Palestine. Before this, the Labour Party had been predominantly pro-Zionist. The leadership supported the Balfour Declaration of 1917 although its support for the state of Israel in 1948 was

167 DeHanas, *London Youth, Religion and Politics.*
168 Bickley and Kladin, *Religious London: Faith in a Global City*; *Guardian*, 24 June 2020.
169 Renshaw, *Socialism and the Diasporic 'other.'*

240 *Thematic*

more muted by concerns over the extent of Jewish migration following the holocaust and the violent circumstances surrounding the creation of Israel itself when British soldiers were attacked by Jewish insurgents. But a commitment to the creation of a Jewish homeland in Palestine had become firmly entrenched as party policy by 1945. By the time of the Arab-Israeli war in 1948, 'the party's past debates on Palestine bequeathed it an outlook sympathetic to (Israel) and uncomprehending of the tragedy that it entailed for the Palestinians.'[170]

However, after the rise of the New Left from the 1970s, and the dispersal of the Jewish population in London to the middle-class suburbs, Labour Zionism 'imploded' as anti-racism and human rights issues became more prominent in the political outlook of the left. Socialists started to reject the 'blood and soil' nationalism of Zionist ideology and oppose Israel's expansion into the occupied territories.[171] Support for the Palestinians became part of an anti-imperialist campaign, in much the same way as the black struggle did against the apartheid state of South Africa. The Six Day War in June 1967 marked a turning point, after which the politics of anti-racism came into conflict with the leadership of the Jewish community in London over the status of Israel and its continued existence.[172] There had been examples of cooperation between Catholics and Jews in Stepney during the early 1920s.[173] But the tensions created by the conflict over Palestine had by the 1980s, and in particular the election of Ken Livingstone as the GLC leader in 1981, destroyed the previously close relationship between 'London Jewery and the Labour Party.'[174] Black antipathy to Jews combined with left-wing anti-Zionism to create a toxic political atmosphere. This is best illustrated by the geographical divide in Brent during the 1970s, 'whereby the Jews had congregated at the northern end of the borough, leaving the southern extremity to the Blacks – (reflecting) a deepening political chasm.'[175] The left-wing newsletter, *London Labour Briefing*, ran a series of articles during the early 1980s supporting the Palestinians, one which condemned Israel's invasion of Lebanon as a 'holocaust' and another arguing that 'support for feminism is incompatible with support for Zionism.'[176] The Brent East CLP called on Israel to come to terms with the Palestinians 'just as the whites in Zimbabwe had to acknowledge black majority rule.'[177]

The question of Israel became an issue which exposed racial and religious tensions but it also reflected a growing division between left and right in the

---

170 Keleman, 'Zionism and the British Labour Party.'
171 Keleman, *The British Left and Zionism*, p. 220.
172 Alderman, *London Jewery and London Politics*, pp. 111–41.
173 Ibid., 84.
174 Ibid., 137.
175 Ibid., 127.
176 *London Labour Briefing*, August 1983 and April 1983.
177 *Brent Socialist*, Issue 7 (Summer 1980).

The politics of personal identity   241

party. These tensions played out in new ways after the defeat of the New Left by the 1990s and the advent of New Labour. Contemporary studies of the revival of the left within the party under the leadership of Jeremy Corbyn have described the way the controversy became a dispute between left and right more generally, more than just a difference of opinion over foreign policy.

> Several prominent Jews had supported Margaret Thatcher as MP in Finchley. In the 1990s this support switched to Tony Blair and Gordon Brown who were both strong advocates of Israel. For the left this demonstrated a consistent pattern of supporting the wrong people. Being a Blarite was as bad as being a Tory, particularly after Iraq in 2003. From 2015, the accusations of anti-Semitism were countered by descriptions of being a Blairite plot.[178]

In London, the controversy proved particularly damaging in the 2017 general election. The four London constituencies with the largest Jewish populations (the so-called Bagel belt of Finchley, Golders Green, Hendon and Chipping Barbet) 'resisted Labour's sweep of the capital.'[179] The controversy resurfaced in 2018, when the Jewish Board of Deputies called for a demonstration against anti-Semitism and in support of a Labour MP Luciania Berger who was trying to raise the issue of an anti-Semitic mural which Jeremy Corbyn had allegedly supported in 2012.[180] The controversy could not be resolved by the leadership and it remained an on-going and highly divisive issue into the 2019 general election, exacerbated by the way the social media created a highly toxic environment.[181] The party's failure to capture the London Borough of Barnet in 2018 (where 15% of the electorate was Jewish) has been attributed to the mishandling of the controversy by the Labour leadership.[182] Luciania Berger resigned from the party in 2019 to stand for the Liberal Democrats in the Jewish constituency of Finchley and Golders Green. She reduced the Labour vote by about a half, but did not poll enough to defeat the Conservative in what was previously a marginal seat. The day after the election, the *Guardian* reported that in London, anti-Semitism and what people perceived as the absence of an apology 'appeared to be a key issue.'[183] It remains to be seen if the election of Keir Starmer as a leader in 2020, to replace Jeremy Corbyn after Labour's defeat in the 2019 general election, will make a difference, although his first action on being elected was to apologise to the Jewish community for the hurt caused by the

---

178 Kogan, *Protest and Power*, p. 337; see also Beckett and Seddon, *Jeremy Corbyn*, pp. 257–87.
179 Beckett and Seddon, *Jeremy Corbyn*; p. 291; *Times of Israel*, 9 June 2017.
180 Kogan, *Protest and Power*, pp. 348–69.
181 Beckett and Seddon, *Jeremy Corbyn*, pp. 279–87.
182 Gilbert, 'Ethnic and Religious Diversity in the Politics of Suburban London,' 77.
183 *Guardian*, 13 December 2019.

242   *Thematic*

undoubted presence of anti-Semitism in some sections of the party, but its full extent is yet to be fully established.

Conclusion

Gender, race and religion have had the potential in London to create conflict and division as well as unity. These divisions became more pronounced after 1970 with the birth of the politics of personal identity, although they had always been a feature of political life before this date, especially in London, given its role as an imperial city, attracting continuous waves of migrants. This can be seen, for example, in the way the white working class did not always welcome, and in some cases rioted against aliens and immigrants before and during the First World War, calling for stronger immigration controls. The politics of racial identity seriously divided the party over the demand for black sections, but this did not prevent the BME population from voting Labour for reasons other than race, where new class identities, based on culture, education and age, seem to be a more relevant in determining voting intentions. The growth of the Muslim community in London added a new level of racial and religious conflicts into the controversy over anti-Semitism, when radical Islamic interests denied the holocaust, seriously embarrassing its mainstream leaders. Divisions over gender were present after the formation of the WLL in 1906 but they became more prominent during the 1970s with the growth of individualism and second wave feminism, accentuated by the way the politics of personal identity sometimes outweighed questions of class or mainstream family values.

These divisions interacted with questions of social class to forge a new type of contemporary politics, which now distinguish metropolitan areas, with their more cross-class and multi-ethnic populations, from other smaller towns and rural areas, which produce a different political outlook. In terms of ideology, the younger, better educated and more middle-class voters in London are best characterised as socially liberal, while the traditional white working class (now in decline in the capital but still very much present in non-metropolitan areas) are characterised as socially authoritarian on issues like immigration, family life and crime.[184] Other types of issues might also come into conflict with the politics of personal identity. Attitudes to immigration, for example, might reflect a particular outlook on national identity, such as the need to defend the country's borders from uncontrolled immigration. However, a socially liberal perspective, which is more tolerant of immigration, might undermine working-class support for the Labour Party because it is perceived as unpatriotic. This division of opinion supports the idea that contemporary politics is not so much a matter of 'right' or 'left' (reflecting different views about wealth distribution), but is now determined by culture

---

184 Evans and Tilley, *The New Politics of Class*, pp. 59–88.

The politics of personal identity 243

and identity, or what a recent study described as a divide between cosmopolitans and patriots.[185] But this difference can be exaggerated. It is not clear that social liberalism alienates traditional working-class opinion. In terms of contemporary views on gay rights, for example, an important political battle-ground during the 1980s between Thatcher and the New Left, Labour support is not 'wedded *en masse* to the ideals of social conservatism.' This view is borne out by polling for the British Social Attitudes Survey in 2012, 'which found that only 29% of respondents viewed same-sex relationships as always or mostly wrong, reflecting a rapid decline in opposition to the LGBT community from the mid-1990s onwards.'[186]

In London, gender, race and religion have also had the potential to create alliances as people from different backgrounds came together to achieve particular economic, social and political objectives. The relationship between class, religion, gender and race is perhaps too complex to arrive at firm conclusions about their political implications without more in-depth research. The Jewish, Catholic and other members of the white working class in interwar London were united in supporting a Labour Party which represented their class interests above their religious beliefs. As Catholics and Jews became less segregated, many developed a stronger sense of national rather than religious identity, sometimes expressed in patriotic terms. The same goes for attempts by the Muslim communities in London to integrate and participate in modern-day politics. However, the politics of the New Left in the 1980s championed personal identity (specifically gender and race) over class and national identity, espousing internationalism and anti-imperialism, seen as potentially unpatriotic by its critics. Feminism, for example, may have brought together a new alliance of interests seen as the best means of revitalising the Labour Party against Thatcherism in the 1980s, but it also alienated many white working-class voters who could no longer identify with Labour as a party which did not support certain mainstream family values, such as opposition to gay rights.[187] However, contemporary feminist beliefs do not necessarily contradict the more general desire within society to see greater gender equality, now achieved in many but not all spheres of life.

Contemporary campaigns in London based on inter-faith and political cooperation to defend the interests of asylum seekers, the poor and dispossessed, such as food banks, reflect a new set of political values that now inform support for the Labour Party. Such campaigns are not necessarily based on social liberalism or political correctness. A recent study into London youth, religion and politics shows that despite different levels of integration between Muslim South Asians and Christian Black British Jamaicans,

185 Wheatley, *The Changing Shape of Politics.*
186 Bloomfield, 'Labour's Liberalism: Gay Rights and Video Nasties,' 18.
187 Campbell, 'Politics, Pyramids and People.'

244 *Thematic*

it is possible to create understanding between people from different faiths and ethnicities on matters of social justice and culture.[188] The pro-remain and black Labour MP for Tottenham David Lammy has recently advocated such socially liberal values. 'Together,' he argued,

> we can build a society that provides opportunity for all classes, ethnicities, genders, sexualities and identity groups... Together, we can replace tribes with inclusive and dynamic communities of which we can be proud. Together, we can find spaces and places to belong.[189]

This may reflect a cosmopolitan perspective, but it does not necessarily reflect the dominant political culture of non-metropolitan areas. Labour may as a result lose support in these areas if it is seen as just a party of the big cities like London. However, the black church-going community in London does not identify as socially liberal, yet it continues to vote Labour in large numbers opposed to austerity and in support of improved welfare.

188 DeHanas, *London Youth, Religion and Politics.*
189 Lammy, *Tribes*, p. 306.

Conclusion

The conclusion is in three parts – a summary and historical review covering the period from 1900; a discussion of the changing definition of social class in London and a discussion of the future prospects of the Labour Party in London and nationally in the light of historical experience.

Summary and historical review

Before 1914, the move towards independent Labour representation in London was constrained within a Progressive Alliance made up of Liberals, Radicals, Fabians and trade unionists. This alliance controlled the LCC from 1889 to 1907. The Liberal Party, despite its landslide victory in 1906, was struggling in the face of a resurgent form of popular conservatism and losing heavily in pre-war local elections, less so in parliamentary contests. Labour was unable to develop an independent identity of its own, restricted to being a regional pressure group representing some but not all male trade unionists in only certain neighbourhoods of the capital. Labour representatives had an ambivalent attitude towards socialism, some were members of a socialist party (ILP, SDF, Fabian Society), but many were not, identifying as Progressives rather than socialists. However, the First World War transformed the fortunes of the Labour Party in London, despite the bitter divisions which existed between pro- and anti-war factions. The war did more damage to the Liberal Party resulting in splits and weak constituency organisation. The Labour Party also benefited from promoting state intervention as a viable policy, supporting a working-class struggling with wartime inflation and other problems. In London, the war helped reduce endemic poverty and unemployment; laid the foundations of suburban industrial development after 1918 and fostered a belief in the role of the state to bring about improvements after it intervened to protect groups of workers, such as, for example, bus conductresses on the trams and others many of whom were not in a trade union. Moreover, it reduced the influence of the large number of charities in London which supported the so-called deserving poor, creating a more assertive and enhanced sense of working-class-consciousness. It also gave legitimacy to many of the welfare reforms

246   *Conclusion*

introduced by the pre-war Liberal Party, such as old age pensions and national insurance. Consequently, the reputation of the Labour Party was enhanced by its participation in the wartime coalition and its role in the management of labour relations, food and rent control. This helped transform it from a regional into a national party, able to compete during the 1920s with a revitalised and popular form of Conservativism under Stanley Baldwin, which had also adapted well in a new age of mass democracy, unlike the Liberals. Finally, and most importantly, the introduction of universal manhood suffrage and limited female enfranchisement in 1918 was made inevitable by wartime circumstances. The size of the electorate in London tripled if not quadrupled in many districts, enfranchising for the first time London's sizeable proletariat.

Although only winning the same number of parliamentary seats it had done in 1910, from a position of no borough representation at all, Labour captured 13 councils in the local elections of November 1919, transforming its electoral prospects and laying the foundations of a future municipal social democracy. It did spectacularly well in predominantly working-class areas, especially in the East End where pre-war electoral registration was very low, but not so well in middle-class suburban areas like Croydon and Willesden. It began to break through in socially mixed areas like Lambeth and Lewisham in the 1930s, when 'the black coated proletariat' voted Labour in larger numbers. In 1934, Labour captured the LCC, an achievement which enhanced its reputation as a national party, a position it then held for over 30 years. Together with the borough councils, the Labour-controlled LCC transformed the life chances of the capital's working-class population through programmes of slum clearance, municipal housing and other social improvements, such as maternity and health care provision, all local services paid for by rate equalisation across the capital. The adoption of a new constitution in 1918 allowing for individual membership for the first time, and creating constituency party organisations, saw a significant increase in party membership, especially women who made up about just under 50% of activists by the 1930s. The party also attracted middle-class recruits from the Liberal Party, who found a new political home with Labour over issues like peace and disarmament and many of whom were opposed to the anti-socialist pacts their party had formed with the Conservatives in national elections and with ratepayer associations locally. Growth in membership was particularly high in middle-class suburban areas as well as in working-class areas like Poplar and Woolwich, although many constituency parties in London did not recruit large numbers until the late 1920s, if at all. Herbert Morrison did not succeed in creating a mass-membership party, like his much-admired German counterpart (SPD).

Support for industrial militancy was patchy in London culminating in the disappointment and failure of the General Strike in 1926. Thereafter, the party turned away from industrial militancy, especially during the interwar depression when trade union membership declined very rapidly.

Rearmament in the late 1930s revived the fortunes of the trade unions in the light engineering and other factories of the suburbs in areas like Croydon and Wembley. After 1926, Labour focused on becoming a party of local government. It was again through the benefits obtained by local state intervention, in terms of slum clearance and welfare benefits, paid for by rate equalisation, that the reputation of the party was built, locally at first and then in parliamentary elections by 1945, following a war which again enhanced but also consolidated its reputation as a national party.[1] The LCC built nearly 80,000 flats and houses during the interwar period, mainly outside the LCC boundaries in large estates at Beacontree (Dagenham) and St Helier (Morden). The domestic impact of the Second World War strengthened a move towards state intervention and patriotic support for a party which had proved itself in coalition government. Like the first, it also raised the status of the working class as a result of its contribution to the war effort, laying (unlike the first) the more permanent foundations of the post-war welfare state and the commitment to full employment. Trade union membership flourished after 1945 and party membership reached a peak in London during the early 1950s. The high point of Labour's municipal social democracy was reached by the 1960s, although by this date, the loss of manufacturing jobs, very pronounced in London, post-war affluence and class dealignment had begun to undermine the proletarian base of Labour Party support in the 'Red Belt' of inner London constituencies and the industrial suburbs.

From the mid-1950s, the party experienced a severe contraction in membership and organisation, culminating in the major electoral disaster of the 1968 local elections. By this date, it had lost its reputation for municipal housing and the provision of locally run services, such as health, welfare, transport and utilities, when they were nationalised and run by Whitehall. It struggled to respond to the demographic and social changes that started to transform many inner-city areas, such as deindustrialisation, immigration, inner-city decay, poverty and race riots. Its share of the vote began to shrink in line with trends across the country, but more so in London as a result of the severe contraction in manufacturing industries. The old guard associated with the blue collar-unions and the cooperative movement, which controlled the party machine at regional and borough levels (and which represented the interests of a declining white working class in many boroughs), began to be replaced by a new generation of more left-wing, middle-class and younger members radicalised by the Vietnam War and feminism. This younger cohort of members gave birth to the New Left. Its greatest success was taking control of the GLC in 1981, and a number of borough councils

---

1 See Edgerton, *The Rise and Fall of the British Nation*, pp. 195–221, for a useful discussion of the way Labour had become by 1950 a party which stood more for the nation than for class or socialism.

248   *Conclusion*

from the late 1970s, inaugurating an era of a new type of socialism, epitomised by the policies of equal opportunities, workers control and identity politics. It was internationalist, and vehemently opposed above all to the 'New Right' policies of Mrs Thatcher. However, by the late 1980s, the left had suffered a series of dramatic defeats in London and nation-wide, starting with the failure of Tony Benn to be elected to the Deputy leadership in 1981, followed by the collapse of the anti-rate capping campaign in 1985, the abolition of the GLC & ILEA in 1986 and 1990, respectively, a series of by-election defeats (Bermondsey, Croydon North West and Greenwich), the disaster of 1983 general election and the defeat of the Miners' Strike. For many in London, the demise of the party seemed to be fatal, a disease named by activists as 'the London Effect.' The social base of the party in London no longer provided a sound foundation for opposing Thatcherism in the way that 'labourism' had created the circumstances for a social democratic settlement taking root during the interwar period and consolidated after 1945.

Right-wing elements (representing as they saw it the old interests of social democracy) staged a fightback, leading eventually to the election of Tony Blair, via Neil Kinnock and John Smith. There was a revival in membership during the late 1990s, mainly if not exclusively middle class, but not on a par with peak membership achieved in 1951. The appeal of New Labour, and the demographic and social changes brought about by gentrification and immigration, especially the growth of a new middle class and a precariat experiencing the detrimental effects of austerity after the financial crash of 2008, revived the party's fortunes. The swing to Labour in London in 1997 ('When the Suburbs Turned (unexpectedly) Red') was higher than in other regions, a repeat of the landslide of 1945. However, membership declined quickly during the early 2000s, due in part to New Labour's decision to go to war in Iraq and its unquestioned support for globalisation and various neo-liberal policies. Labour's share of the vote also reduced but not seriously enough to dent the advantage the party had over the Conservatives in London. This advantage only increased after the election of Jeremy Corbyn in 2015, but at the expense of a loss of support in non-metropolitan areas outside of London. There was a dramatic rise in membership, especially concentrated in London. Many ex-members re-joined, including a number of socialists from fringe organisations, but also by a much larger number of a new type of younger and non-sectarian members. They were more centre-left, reflecting the rapidly changing social base of the capital, made up a younger, multi-racial, socially liberal and lower-middle-class constituency, the size of which was unique in the UK. This 'new working-class,' as it has been called, had been adversely affected by years of austerity after 2010 and the financial crash of 2008, and it was more inclined to vote Labour as the historic party of the traditional working class. By 2011, London contained some of the highest levels of poverty in the country, and the gap between the very rich and very poor widened. By this date, the traditional and mainly

Conclusion 249

white working class had been dispersed to the outer suburbs and beyond, or they remained as a not so new 'under-class,' largely hidden from view and politically unrepresented, in certain inner-city mainly East End neighbourhoods, but also in other small pockets of deprivation across the capital. To the outsider, London may have appeared a super-prosperous and unaffordable place to live, populated by an elite of highly paid executives, but it contained a large precariat struggling to cope with very high levels of relative deprivation and for black people racial discrimination.

Labour's electoral record in London has highlighted several different factors that played a key role in influencing the way electors voted. Before 1914, the people of London either voted Conservative or Liberal, with Labour not breaking out of a Progressive Alliance with the radical wing of the Liberal Party, given the limitations of the franchise. During the 1920s following the extension of the vote, the massively enlarged electorate in London, made up of many first voters, had the choice of voting for either of the main three parties, with Labour competing with the Liberals to become the official opposition to the Conservatives, a target it reached after 1929, perhaps a few years later than the rest of the country. From the 1930s, the electors either voted for the Conservatives or Labour, in a period characterised as the beginning of two-party domination. Support for Labour was based primarily on social class (defined as labourism), with significantly more men voting Labour than women, reflecting in part its base in the trade unions. From the 1960s, this two-party domination began to break down, with the Liberals and then the Social Democrats experiencing a revival as well as the British National Party winning occasionally in working-class areas like Barking and Dagenham. The Green Party also started to make inroads into Labour's Progressive base of support and now attracts higher levels of support even than the Conservative Party in many inner-city areas. Electoral sociologists and historians have viewed this period as one of class dealignment, driven by economic and social changes, such as deindustrialisation, growing affluence, higher levels of education and more regional voting. Some suggested an increasing north/south divide, although this was always in danger of some exaggeration, hiding the extent of polarised poverty in the capital.

There are a complex range of reasons that are relevant in accounting for these changes in voting behaviour. The nature and extent of enfranchisement and the degree of turnout in elections is one such factor. The Municipal Reform Party in London always argued that low turnout benefited Labour. The effectiveness of party organisation is another. For Labour, the level of trade union finance, involvement and organisation in local constituency parties was of crucial importance in London during the interwar period but is now not so important with the decline in trade union membership and density in London, which are the lowest in the country. Another reason is changing political attitudes to the state at times when industrial militancy could not defend working-class living standards. This can be seen in the way local government served class interests after 1918, in elections, for example,

250   *Conclusion*

to the boards of guardians, until they were abolished in 1930 when welfare relief was made a responsibility of Whitehall. The concept of 'Labourism' is also relevant in trying to understand the way Londoner's voted Labour, certainly for the first half of the twentieth century. Allegiances to family networks and neighbourhood loyalties, rather than any specific commitment to religion or socialism, are equally important, as is the influence of socialism in particular periods. The ILP before it disaffiliated in 1932, made a vital contribution in terms of candidates during the early 1920s, while local trade union branches provided most of the money. In the 1930s, London became a stronghold (outside of the mining districts) of the CPGB over its opposition to fascism. There was evidence of some very limited Trotskyist entry tactics in certain London constituencies during the 1950s. The growth of the New Left in the 1970s and 1980s revitalised constituency organisation, but its strategy of confronting Thatcherism in the 1980s, without the benefit of wide community support previously provided by 'labourism,' perhaps damaged its reputation. Thereafter, the changing nature of London's social structure during and after the 1990s laid the foundation for a new class base of support for a Labour Party no longer identified with labourism, but reflecting a different set of values, driven above all by race, and followed by age, class and education.

Finally, policy issues advocated by the Labour Party when they were able to achieve power either locally or nationally, such as welfare, housing, education and equality, need to be acknowledged as reasons for voting Labour to help counter the sometimes-static approach of some electoral sociologists in explaining voting behaviour. For example, a large proportion of the BAME electorate currently vote Labour for its record of opposing racism and discrimination, not necessarily during the period before 1970, when the position of the party was seriously compromised over its support for racist immigration controls, but certainly following the enactment of equality legislation after 1970. However, black people remain suspicious of institutional racism within organisations, including political parties, creating barriers to real equality, and this is likely to be one of the main reasons why the Labour Party has so few BME members. The middle-class ethos of the Labour Party, where less than 2% of MPs are working-class, also does not help.[2] Municipal housing was probably the most important policy issue during the interwar period which cemented support for Labour in working-class neighbourhoods benefiting from slum clearance and large-scale public house building with controlled rents. Adequate welfare payments by boards of guardians were also a reason why Labour attracted support after paupers (recipients of welfare payments or the so-called 'slum vote') were no longer disqualified from voting in 1918.

---

2 Heath, 'A Growing Class Divide: MPs and Voters.'

Conclusion 251

Housing and redevelopment are now the most pressing contemporary political issues in the capital, particularly the desperate need for more affordable housing and opposition to large-scale redevelopment schemes. The precariat struggle to afford unregulated private rents has been totally priced out of mortgages, and is no longer eligible for the much reduced availability of social housing, forcing many residents into higher density occupation, especially non-white households.[3] Education is also a vitally important policy issue, given the aspirations of London's BME communities to improve the life chances of their children, whose social mobility has been thwarted most recently by growing inequality. The LCC's education policies were also very influential in garnering support for Labour after 1934, particularly its world-class adult and nursey education provision, badly damaged by the abolition of the ILEA in 1990. In terms of national politics, financial crises, such as the Wall Street Crash and the banking collapse of 2008, as well as public reaction to going to war, also played a part in voting behaviour. Opposition to the war in Iraq in 2003 and its aftermath, and support for the peace movement during the interwar period were quite different responses when compared with the patriotic and wild enthusiasm on the streets of London that followed the relief of Mafeking during the Boer War in 1901, a reflection of Britain's loss of an overseas empire.

The changing definition of social class

But is it accurate to say that there is now a 'new working-class' in London as suggested by some commentators hopeful of revitalising support for the Labour Party, not so much in London where it is relatively strong, but in other non-metropolitan areas where the party is struggling to retain its working-class support?[4] Is this new social formation capable of being defined as a 'class' in traditional sociological terms, given the way it is divided by race, legal status (as in the case of asylum seekers), age, education and the degree to which it is exploited within a highly hostile labour market, where trade union organisation is often fragile, limited or non-existent? Or are there other social and political processes which are creating alliances across this fragmented class structure which provide some answers for why a significant proportion of London's electorate vote Labour (but always noting the high level of abstentions by those economically disadvantaged voters who have no confidence in party politics addressing their needs)? London remains more polarised between rich and poor than other regions. 'The growth of poverty between 1980 and 2010, as measured by the share of households that are poor, has been 80%.'[5] Opposition to austerity can

---

3 Johnstone et al., 'House Price Increases and Higher Density Housing Occupation.'
4 Ainsley, *The New Working Class.*
5 Dorling, *Peak Inequality*, p. 184.

252 *Conclusion*

be seen as a particular feature of its left-wing politics after the financial crash of 2008 and part of a growing class-based response to inequality, as epitomised by Labour's manifesto in 2017 ('*For the Many. Not the Few*').

Furthermore, recent evidence from a number of social surveys suggests that ethnicity, the presence of strong family and religious networks within the BAME population, especially amongst Asians in the East End, youth culture combined with educational aspirations, have all provided examples of the creation of a new type of politics, more favourable to the Labour Party than to the Conservative Party, which now to a significant extent represents the interests of older, white and wealthier property owners across the country in non-metropolitan areas, including a growing number of working-class voters. It is perhaps in the area of trade union organisation amongst the precariat, such as contract cleaners and catering workers, and related campaigns for the 'living wage' in London, which show that such movements can reach out beyond specific shop-floor issues to connect with wider community interests. Such connections may represent a new form of working-class identity. The Unite Union, for example (previously the T&GWU), has been in the forefront of organising contract cleaners in Canary Wharf and in the City of London involving a wide variety of individuals and organisations representing a multiplicity of interests, including political parties, voluntary organisations and the media. This has been described as an attempt to break out of an old style of left-wing politics which has not been sensitive enough to the ethnic, religious and gender needs of super-exploited contract workers.

> In contrast, community organisations like the East London Communities Organisation (TELCO) Living Wage Campaign, have highlighted the scope for finding common ground around issues such as job quality, housing, welfare, immigrant rights and street safety, all of which potentially embrace a much wider group of actors at a much larger geographical scale. Workers' issues have been recast as community-wide concerns and class interests have been read through the lens of community, immigration, 'race' and religion.[6]

While some researchers are finding that deeper racial divisions are emerging between foreign-born workers in London's service sector (described as a new hierarchy of inequality),[7] others are more hopeful in identifying other forms of resistance to precarious labour markets, such as shown, for example, by casual cleaning and teaching staff employed by London University. Since the creation of the Living Wage Foundation in 2011, to campaign for a Living Wage throughout the UK, it has won over £1 billion of additional

---

6 Wills, 'Making Class Politics Possible.'
7 McDowell, 'Precarious Work and Economic Migration.'

Conclusion 253

wages in London and lifted over 200,000 people out of working poverty. The campaign for a London Living Wage and the growth of alternative forms of trade unionism are considered to be important new forms of organisation, some of which are linked politically to 'the Right to the City' movement.[8]

'The Right to the City' offers another avenue of potential resistance to the way the capital is being redeveloped as part of large-scale speculative urban renewal schemes, like the Aylesbury estate in Southwark, which was once one of the largest municipal council estates in Europe, but is now undergoing gentrification, displacing previous working-class tenants who can no longer afford to live in central London. There are examples of fightbacks against the redevelopment plans of developers and local authorities, such as Cressingham Gardens in Lambeth.[9] The East London Community Land Trust, for example, one of Britain's first urban CLTs, has secured common land in Tower Hamlets in the interests of tenants and against the interests of private developers. But successes are small in comparison to the scale of redevelopment taking place across the capital. Such initiatives are not powerful enough by themselves to address the severity of the housing crisis in London, neither are they approaches supported by mainstream politics.[10] The current Labour Mayor of London is struggling to meet his target of building more affordable housing in the face of rising land prices; planning delays; slow or delayed starts to building works in order to keep the price of accommodation inflated; very large reductions in central government housing subsidies and not least opposition from some Labour councils like Haringey, which are opposed to redevelopment schemes with private developers. The very low levels of affordable housing and the enormous profits arising from planning gain are just two of the reasons why an increasing number of Labour councillors in London are now opposed to such redevelopment schemes.[11]

In terms of new class formations, the political nature of working-class life in London after the year 2000 has been influenced by other factors, such as developments in urban youth culture, although it is not clear what the exact political impact has been on voting behaviour. Ethnographic studies have shown, for example, that religious and non-religious youth from different ethnic backgrounds share a high level of political awareness combined with a low level of identification with British culture and citizenship. This translates into active participation in politics and a strong desire for integration.[12] Age is thus an important influence on social cohesion in different

---

8 Woodcock, 'Precarious Workers in London.'
9 Minton, *Big Capital,* p. 130.
10 Loretta Lees, 'The Urban Injustices of New Labour's "New Urban renewal."'
11 Minton, *Big Capital.*
12 DeHanas, *London Youth, Religion and Politics*; Kim, 'We're Just Like Everyone Else!' pp. 125–40.

254   *Conclusion*

neighbourhoods. Ethnic diversity in London has been found to be positively related to feelings of social cohesion

> once the level of economic deprivation is accounted for...On the other hand, ethnic segregation within neighbourhoods is associated with lower levels of perceived social cohesion. Both effects are strongly moderated by the age of individual residents. Diversity has a positive effect on social cohesion for young people but this effect dissipates in older age groups.[13]

The younger age groups in London, including second-, third- and fourth-generation migrants, who are more socially liberal than their parents as a result of higher educational achievement, have it seems a more positive attitude to the benefits of integration and the possibilities of political participation. If we add the importance of family and community ties amongst the ethnic communities in the 'New East End' ('in keeping ordinary people in control of their lives'), we are perhaps seeing a rebirth of the type of strong community cohesion identified by Willmott in the white working class in the 1950s.[14]

How far this translates into support for more left-wing politics, similar to a previous adherence to 'labourism' in such communities, is open to some speculation, although the electoral evidence suggests a strong connection. Some have argued that growing opposition to austerity represented 'a class struggle within the Labour Party' against the neo-liberal policies of New Labour, mirroring a shift to the left in the wider electorate. This may be the case in London where inequality is more pronounced and where the party responded to public pressure to come out more strongly against austerity, especially after the massive influx of new and younger members after 2015 ('generation rent'). The election of Jeremy Corbyn as a leader can be seen as one of the consequences of such growing opposition, which accelerated after the financial crash of 2008, culminating in, for example, the People's Assembly Against Austerity in London in 2015, attended by over 250,000 people and addressed by Jeremy Corbyn as part of his leadership campaign.[15] However, political opposition to austerity may be lower in those non-metropolitan working-class areas of the country, in the north of England, for example, where inequality is less marked as a consequence of higher levels of property wealth and where labour markets offer relatively more protection to workers through stronger trade union organisation that exists in the capital.

13 Sturgis et al., 'Ethnic Diversity, Segregation and Social Cohesion of Neighbourhoods in London.'
14 Dench, Gavron and Young, *The New East End.*
15 Panitch and Leys, *Searching for Socialism*, pp. 183–200.

Conclusion   255

The history of the Labour Party shows that geographical differences were present in the early formation of the Labour Party during the first half of the twentieth century. As we have seen in Chapter 1, the origins of the party began as a regional force or left-wing pressure group with a stronger power base in the more homogeneous working-class communities in the smaller industrial towns of the north and in the coalfields. It developed a generation later in the bigger cities, partly as a result of the industrial impact of total war, especially rearmament. As we have seen in Chapters 4–7, the relative importance of different types of localities and workplaces, trade union organisation, class formations, socialism, gender differences, race and religion all played a role in the growth of Labour as a national party and the cross-class alliances it was able to forge to win elections in London. By 1950, it had become an effective national party representing the nation (more patriotic than socialist), competing with the Conservatives who had also adapted with more success than the Liberal Party to the age of mass democracy after 1918. Labour remained a national political force during the period of 'golden age of social democracy' up to the late 1970s, prior to the advent of 'popular individualism' and neo-liberalism set in train by Thatcherism.

But during the last quarter of the twentieth century, these local factors have also helped to differentiate (if not to drive apart) areas like London from other non-metropolitan parts of the country, as can be seen in differences over economic policy (opposition to austerity) and 'the politics of personal identity' (gender, race and religion). London had experienced a remarkable economic and social transformation by the year 2000 – from 'a municipal social democracy' into a 'City of Rampant Capitalism.' It has produced a new type of working class quite distinct from that which exists in non-metropolitan areas, more ethnic, younger, better educated and with less property wealth, and crucially less able to withstand the effects of austerity. This class (or precariat) votes Labour in a cross-class alliance with key segments of middle class in London. This largely accounts for the success of Labour in the capital. The middle class of London, the values of which have been characterised as socially liberal on questions of political identity, has been described by the economist Thomas Picketty as the 'Brahmin Left,' opposed to the 'Merchant Right,' which supports the policies of the free market and votes Conservative. This, he argued, changed the structure of political conflict.[16] These types of alliances have been crucial at different times in guaranteeing Labour's national electoral triumphs, as was the case in the general elections of 1945 and 1997. However, the gap between London and the rest of the country has now widened to an extent that astonishes contemporaries. Paradoxically, this gap is in large part responsible for undermining Labour as a national party. Will Labour revert to being a

---

16 Picketty, 'Brahmin Left' vs 'Merchant Right.'

256   Conclusion

regional party or pressure group unable to forge effective electoral alliances across regions and classes as was the case before 1914? Or will it be able to create new alliances which will ensure its future as a national party able to represent the nation in the way it had done in the past?

Future prospects for the Labour Party in London

This book started with a discussion on the way politicians at the turn of the twentieth century regarded the influence of the suburbs on London politics (see Chapter 1). The Municipal Reform Party thought that suburbanisation would guarantee political success when it believed most of the population would be living in these areas in the near and distant future. The Progressives attributed their loss of the LCC in 1907 to the malign influence of the suburbs as sites of uniformity and blandness, essentially supporting a Conservative outlook (an overly cynical view of suburban life which persisted for long periods of the twentieth century).[17] Certainly, the suburbs of London during the interwar period were dominated politically by the Conservative Party or related ratepayers' associations, as in Croydon, for example. However, the suburbs of London during the last quarter of the twentieth century did not continue to develop along these lines; in fact, almost the opposite has occurred.[18] They have become sites of ethnic and religious diversity, as well as poverty and deprivation, and many of their residents now vote Labour. The most recent analysis of suburban politics in London stated that

> Religious and ethnic diversity in suburbia poses significant challenges for political parties. In particular, Labour's difficulties in appealing to different constituencies, often expressed geographically in terms of the differences between inner London and the white working-class areas of post-industrial Britain, are also present in the micro-politics of adjacent areas of London. New forms of religion, and especially the development of large new worship spaces, increasingly common in outer London, also have significant consequences for the local politics of suburbia.[19]

Labour broke the Conservative grip on the London suburbs in the 1945 general election with a much higher swing than the rest of the country. While Thatcherism strongly appealed to the suburbs in the 1980s (Thatcher was the MP for Finchley), Labour broke the Conservative grip again in 1997 ('When the Suburbs Turned Red'), also on a bigger swing than elsewhere. This book has attempted to answer the question 'Why London is Labour'? In 2019, *The Political Quarterly* devoted a whole issue to a discussion of

17 Balderstone, 'Semi-detached Britain?'; Silverstone, *Visions of Suburbia.*
18 Cross, 'The Suburban Weekend,' 108–31.
19 Gilbert, 'Ethnic and Religious Diversity in the Politics of Suburban London,' 72–9; Dwyer, 'Faith and Suburbia,' 403–19; Naylor and Ryan, 'The Mosque in the Suburbs.'

Conclusion 257

the changing political nature of suburbia. Its various contributions sought to identify the causes of Labour's success in ending Conservative political domination of the suburbs. They highlighted two clear historical trends: first, the outward movement of population to interwar suburbia (with many incomers bringing their politics with them); and second, Labour's increasing appeal to middle-class electors.[20]

In the case of London, this book has, however, added two more equally if not more important trends. The first and by far the most significant is the support of the BME electorate. In November 2019 just before the general election, 53% of BME voters in London intended to vote Labour, while only 22% indicated support for the Conservatives.[21] For the postponed Mayoral election, scheduled for May 2020, the lead of Sadiq Khan, the sitting Labour Mayor, was 25 points over all the competition (attracting 49% of first round votes and 67% of second round votes). In terms of voting intentions, Sadiq Khan obtained the support of 61% of BME voters, while the Conservatives could only muster 15%.[22] The second trend is the degree of poverty and inequality in the capital. For some, it might be argued that an important factor behind support for left-wing politics in London is not so much the liberal values espoused by the middle classes, but the continuing and increasing levels of inequality and poverty, and the way the slowdown in educational attainment growth has blocked upward social mobility. Many of London's suburbs, like South Acton and Southall, for example, are some of the most deprived areas of the country. Thus, taking all these factors together (outward movement of population; the growth of the middle class; the voting record of the BME electorate; poverty and inequality; and the decline in social mobility), Labour in London has benefited far more from these trends than any other political party. For one commentator, it has 'outperformed the party's national achievement' in the suburbs since 1955. The party's exceptional results here in the 2017 election (confirmed again in 2019) 'are therefore, a new peak on a long-term trend rather than a breakthrough.'[23] In fact, as this book demonstrates, this trend started as early as the 1945 general election.

Thus, London has remained a Labour city for most of the twentieth century. It looks like it will continue to do so for the foreseeable future, given population projections, especially the growth of the BME population, and the extent to which it remains an ethnically integrated and relatively tolerant city. In a context where nationally the Conservative Party does relatively better with Indian voters, for example, in London, Boris Johnson fared badly in those wards with high concentrations of Asians, performing

---

20 Bastion, 'Rising Damp in the Suburbs, 64–71; Huq, 'Postcards from the Edge? 6–9; Huq, *On the Edge.*
21 YouGov poll 4 November 2019.
22 YouGov poll 11 March 2020; Heath, 'Why Ethnic Minorities Vote Labour: Group Norms.'
23 Bastion, 'Rising Damp in the Suburbs,' 64–71.

258 *Conclusion*

even worse than Zac Goldsmith amongst BME voters in 2016.[24] The polling intentions for Mayor of London in early 2020 were 58% for Labour in inner London and 44% in outer London, with 50% coming from social grades ABC1 and 47% coming from C2DE, an even spread of cross-class support.[25] Labour in the capital is dependent on the votes of a cross-class constituency, where age and level of education attainment (graduate status) are the key drivers of voting intentions. It still attracts a sizeable proportion of C2DE votes, but this is likely to decline in the future, given population projections. These trends pose a serious challenge to the Labour Party as its support in non-metropolitan areas also continues to decline, with the Conservatives picking up higher proportions of low-income working-class votes. In terms of strategy, which constituency should Labour aim for in the future, a discussion which now dominates internal-party debate or can it put together an alliance which can unite both sets of interest?

The demographic data indicates that between 2016 and 2041, the population of London is projected to increase by 1.98 million (22%) to 10.8 million. London remains an integrated city, far more than some similar conurbations in other parts of the world. The White British population is projected to increase by 6% to 3.76 million. The BAME population is projected to increase by 32% to 4.94 million. The White British group will remain as the biggest individual ethnic group, by a significant margin, over the 2016 to 2041 period. The next largest groups will be Black African (increasing by 31% to 828 thousand in 2041), Indian (increasing by 32% to 811 thousand in 2041) and Other Asian (increasing by 42% to 671 thousand in 2041). The most stable groups (i.e. smallest relative change), apart from White British, are projected to be the White Irish (increasing by only 6% to 196 thousand in 2041), and Black Caribbean (increasing by only 6% to 370 thousand in 2041).[26] However, some of this population growth is not necessarily made up of new or extra people, 'but people living longer.'[27] Therefore, it remains to be seen that as the population of London starts to age, whether this will be to the advantage or disadvantage of the Labour Party in the future. Pollsters have pointed out that

> as later generations of ethnic minority voters, who have faced less racial prejudice than their parents, access middle-class jobs and do not associate the centre-right as strongly with racism and xenophobia, may be more willing to give such parties a hearing...the left cannot take ethnic minority loyalty for granted.[28]

24 Omar Khan, 'One Nation Boris?'
25 YouGov poll 11 March 2020.
26 GLS Intelligence 2016-based ethnic group projections (November 2017). Dorling, *Peak Inequality*; Dorling and Thomas, *People and Places*.
27 Dorling, *Peak Inequality*, p. 160.
28 Martin, 'A Demographic Time Bomb: The Right and Ethnic Diversity.'

Conclusion 259

Finally, will the party's new leader, Keir Starmer, be able to forge successful electoral alliances across the country, particularly in terms of geography, race and class, that will hold Labour together as a viable national party and not just a regional or sectional pressure group as it was before 1914? The rise of nationalism in Scotland, and to a lesser extent in Wales has undermined Labour as a national party seeking to represent the whole of the UK.[29] Britain's electoral system (first-past-the-post) requires such broadly based alliances for national rather than regional parties to form governments. Or will the fact that Starmer represents a London constituency prevent the party from being able to revive its fortunes in the north of England, let alone Scotland? While leading positions in the previous shadow cabinet were taken by London-based MPs, such as Jeremy Corbyn, Dianne Abbott, John McDonnell and Emily Thornbury, Starmer has sought to change the balance of geographical representation by appointing figures such as Angela Rayner (Ashton under Lyne) and Lisa Nandy (Wigan). But will Labour be able to challenge the ability of the Conservatives to appeal not only to its traditional (property-owning) middle-class base, but important segments of the working class in different parts of the country, in the way previous Conservative leaders have succeeded in doing so? For example, the Liberal Unionist Joseph Chamberlain (championed by Theresa May in 2017) promoted policies for the working class (e.g. slum clearance and 'gas and water socialism') during the 1880s. The Conservative leader Stanley Baldwin appealed to newly enfranchised working-class women in the 1930s?

The historical origins of the party were found in the homogeneous and predominantly working-class communities of the coal fields and the smaller heavy-industrial towns of the north of England, Scotland and Wales, characterised during the interwar period as the distressed areas. The big cities, like London (where trade unionism was weaker), took a bit longer to develop a strong Labour tradition, although this was weaker in those suburban areas, but not those suburbs undergoing new waves of industrialisation after 1918. This 'big-city' Labour tradition was based on the strength of neighbourhood identities expressed in terms of municipal politics, rather than through local labour movements organised around chapels and trade union branches which exercised a more cohesive but now declining influence in smaller towns and urban districts. The enormous loss of manufacturing jobs after 1960 significantly undermined the social basis of Labour Party support in London during the 1970s and 1980s, when popular Conservatism (Mrs Thatcher) appealed to the individualism of the white working class, leading many commentators to predict the death of the Labour Party, especially in London.

---

29 See Barnett, *The Lure of Greatness*, for a useful discussion of the impact of nationalism on constitutional reform.

260   *Conclusion*

However, the spectacular growth of new service industries, especially finance, banking, ICT and the creative industries, following the deregulation of the City of London in 1985, accompanied by gentrification and the considerable expansion in the size of the BME population, had by the turn of the twentieth century, created the foundations of a new political alliance in the capital which votes Labour. This alliance is made up of a combination of interests – class, race, age and education. London (or 'World City') is now unique in terms of the size of its population (which will continue to grow rapidly during the next few decades) and the integration of its extraordinary multi-ethnic communities, although not necessarily including fresh waves of asylum seekers or refugees. The working-class elements of this new alliance or precariat have replaced the old 'Labourist' white working class of the traditional inner cities, who have either died out or escaped to the outer suburbs. It is a class that is culturally rich but economically poor. The era of austerity introduced by the Conservatives in 2010 after the financial crash of 2008 has effectively blocked its social aspirations to a greater extent than perhaps other areas of the country. Opposition to austerity is one of the primary motivations for its support of the Labour Party in London. It is a very different type of working class that exists in non-metropolitan areas – white, older, less educated, culturally poor but with greater property wealth. The challenge for Labour as a historic national party is to develop a programme which appeals to both types of working class across England, Scotland and Wales. The forces of nationalism and populism may make this very difficult to achieve in practice (worthy of further discussion and research but outside the scope of this book).[30]

The history of the party in London (and nationally) suggests that it will only succeed in forming such alliances by appealing to a broad spectrum of interests which together will allow the party to become electable. Herbert Morrison achieved a unifying electoral programme in London during the interwar period by securing the party's working-class base in the East End and certain industrial suburbs, as well as the 'black coated proletariat' in the mixed class suburbs of inner and outer London. Working-class Jews and Catholics put their class interests (expressed as 'labourism') before their religion. He tried to distance the party from the CPGB and the trade unions, both seen as sectional interests (and in the case of the CPGB anti-democratic), a strategy which made him unpopular with socialists within the party, but in the longer term ensured electability. Ken Livingstone forged a rainbow alliance of different interests (socialism, gender and race but deprioritising class) during the 1980s, although this fragmented after the defeat of the left and the abolition of the GLC in 1986. Tony Blair achieved a landslide for New Labour in 1997 through a cross-class alliance (he denied the importance of class), but this also fragmented after the Iraq war. Jeremy Corbyn

---

30 Barnett, *The Lure of Greatness.*

Conclusion 261

revitalised the socialist base of the party by adopting anti-austerity policies, very popular in London, but his profile as a London-centric politician, mercilessly attacked by the populist press, was not broad enough to hold on to working-class voters in the north of England, who were less socially liberal on questions of personal identity or international issues, such as European integration. The Labour Party has always needed to make alliances with other social classes and interests in the different regions of the country to win power. The history of Labour in London proves the point.

Appendix
Demographic and election statistics

Contents

1 Background
2 Population and ethnicity 1891–2041
   Table A1: Population for inner, outer and greater London 1901–2041
   Table A2: Changes in ethnicity in London 1991–2011
   Table A3: Current ethnicity in London compared to England & Wales
   Table A4: Population of London's Sub-regions (2006–2016) compared to England
   Table A5: Current demographics of London (race, religion, languages)
3 Size of electorate and turn out, 1889–1964
   Table A6. Inner London 1889–1964 electorate, turnout and number of seats
   Table A7: Inner London: Percentage of parliamentary electorate to population in 1901 and 1911
   Table A8: Growth of the suburban electorates before 1914
   Table A9: Comparison of the electorate between 1915 and 1918
   Table A10: Inner London: Size of parliamentary electorate (male and female) 1918–1945
   Table A11: Greater London electorate and turnout 1964–2018
4 Parliamentary elections
   Table A12: Labour results in parliamentary elections in London compared to the UK 1900–1970
   Table A13: Labour results in parliamentary elections in London compared to the UK 1974–2019
5 Regional elections – LCC, GLC, London Assembly 1889–2016
   Table A14: Results London County Council (LCC) 1889–1961
   Table A15: GLC Election results 1964–1981
   Table A16: Percentage share of vote London Assembly elections 2000–2020
   Table A17: Percentage share of the vote London Mayoral elections 2000–2020

264   *Appendix*

6   Metropolitan Borough council election results (1900–2018)
    Table A18: Metropolitan Borough elections 1919–1937
    Table A19: Share of votes and seats in the London Boroughs 1900–1962
    Table A20: Percentage share of vote London Borough elections 1964–2018
7   Referendum result
    Table A21: Referendum on Europe 2016 – results for Greater London

1   Background

> The first problem with London is to define it. London has never taken kindly to attempts at delimitation, whether by people who wanted to govern it, or by those who just wanted to fix it statistically; every time this was done, London outgrew its administration or its figures.[1]

The area of Greater London is defined in the London Government Act 1963. It stretches from Enfield in the north to Coulsdon in the south, and from Uxbridge in the west to Hornchurch in the east. The London County Council (LCC), which was created in 1889 after many years of pressure to reform the archaic and vestry dominated system of local government, 'was artificially created out of parts of the counties of Middlesex, Surrey and Kent.'[2]

However, by 1888, London had already outgrown the boundaries of the LCC. The new authority did not include all the built-up area, particularly Tottenham and West Ham. Many of the future LCC housing projects, including the Becontree Estate, were outside its boundaries.[3] The boundaries of the LCC were very similar to those of what is now known as 'inner London.'[4]

The London Government Act of 1899 set up 28 metropolitan boroughs. But the proposal to amalgamate the City of London with the LCC was not implemented. The City Corporation has remained unchanged since the Norman Conquest, successfully preserving its ancient rights and privileges. This system of two-tier government (the LCC and metropolitan boroughs but excluding the City of London) lasted until 1965.

The LCC and the 28 metropolitan boroughs were

> analogous to county and municipal boroughs elsewhere, but with a unique division of powers between them, in which the LCC came increasingly to be the dominate partner... Beyond the boundary was the

---

1 Hall, *London 2001*, p. 1.
2 Ruck and Rhodes, *The Government of Greater London*, p. 19.
3 Saint, *Politics and the People of London*.
4 Travers and Jones, *The New Government of London*, p. 50.

normal local government pattern of county boroughs, municipal boroughs, urban and rural districts.[5]

The reform of local government in London became an on-going source of controversy and conflict between local interests and central government.

After half a century of further population increases and turnover, the London Government Act 1963 created an area known as Greater London, replacing the administrative counties of Middlesex and London, including the City of London, where the LCC had limited powers, and absorbing parts of Essex, Hertfordshire, Kent and Surrey. The Act came into force on 1 April 1965, creating a two-tier system of local government, with the Greater London Council (GLC) sharing power with the City of London Corporation and the 32 London borough councils.

The GLC was abolished in 1986 by the Local Government Act 1985. Its functions were devolved to the City Corporation and the London boroughs, with some functions transferred to central government and joint boards.[6]

In 1999, the Greater London Authority was established made up of the London Assembly and the directly elected mayor of London.[7]

Its boundaries remained unchanged from the Greater London Area set up in 1965.

2 Population 1891–2041

Table A1 Population for inner, outer and greater London 1901–2041

Year	Inner London	Outer London	Greater London
1891	4,442,340	1,143,516	5,565,856
1901	4,670,177	1,556,317	6,226,494
1911	4,997,741	2,160,134	7,157,875
1921	4,936,803	2,616,723	7,553,526
1931	4,887,932	3,211,010	8,098,942
1941	4,224,135	3,763,801	7,987,936
1951	3,680,821	4,483,595	8,164,416
1961	3,336,557	4,444,785	7,781,342
1971	3,030,490	4,418,694	7,449,184
1981	2,425,534	4,182,979	6,608,513
1991	2,625,245	4,262,035	6,887,280
2001	2,765,975	4,406,061	7,172,036
2011	3,231,900	4,942,100	8,173,900
2041.est.			10, 430,000

Source: Compiled from Census; GLA Intelligence, 2018-based trend projection results.

5 Ruck and Rhodes, *The Government of Greater London*, p. 20.
6 Rhodes, *The Government of London: the struggle for reform.*
7 Greater London Authority Act 1999.

266   *Appendix*

Table A2 Changes in ethnicity in London 1991–2011

Ethnic group	1991		2001		2011		Change 2001–2011
	Number	%	Number	%	Number	%	
White	5,333,580	79.80	5,103,203	71.15	4,887,435	59.79	Down 4.23
Asian or Asian British	690,031	10.33	946,894	13.20	1,511,546	18.49	Up 59.63
Black or Black British	535,216	8.01	782,849	10.92	1,088,640	13.32	Up 39.06
Mixed			226,111	3.15	405,279	4.96	Up 79.24
Other	120,872	1.81	113,034	1.58	281,041	3.44	Up 148.63
Total	6,679,699	100.00	7,172,091	100.00	8,173,941	100.00	Up 13.97

Source: Compiled from Census 1991–2011.

Table A3 Current ethnicity in London compared to England & Wales (%)

Place	White	Asian	Black	Mixed	Other
East Midlands	89.3	6.5	1.8	1.9	0.6
East of England	90.8	4.8	2.0	1.9	0.5
Eng. & Wales	86.0	7.5	3.3	2.2	1.0
London	**59.8**	**18.5**	**13.3**	**5.0**	**3.4**
North East	95.3	2.9	0.5	0.9	0.4
North West	90.2	6.2	1.4	1.6	0.6
South East	90.7	5.2	1.6	1.9	0.6
South West	95.4	2.0	0.9	1.4	0.3
Wales	95.6	2.3	0.6	1.0	0.5
West Midlands	82.7	10.8	3.3	2.4	0.9
Yorkshire & Humber	88.8	7.3	1.5	1.6	0.8

Source: www.trustforlondon.org.uk.

Table A4 Population of London's sub-regions (2006–2016) compared to England

	Total population (millions)	Population increase 2006–2016	People per square km	% BME	% not UK-born
Inner South & East	2.4	24%	11,200	46%	39%
Inner West	1.2	8%	10,700	34%	45%
Outer East & north East	1.9	16%	4,400	38%	32%
Outer South	1.3	10%	3,600	28%	28%
Outer West & North West	2.1	15%	4,500	44%	44%
London	8.8	16%	5,590	38%	38%
Rest of England	46.5	7%	360	11%	11%

Source: www.trustforlondon.org.uk.

Appendix 267

Table A5 Current demographics of London (race; religion and languages)

After the UK Census of 2011, it had revealed that about 37% of the London's populace is based on immigrants that came from various parts of the world. Due to such large number of foreigners, it is proclaimed that London is the second largest city, incorporating such figures of emigrants after New York City. By gender, females make up of 52% of the London's population while the remaining 48% comes into the male's hand. The standard age of London's inhabitants is about 40 and half years.

London is a multi-racial city. 59.8% out of the total population are White, among which 44.9% are White-British, 2.2% of Irish White and 12.2% of White from various parts of globe.

Asians are filling 20.9% of the London populace. Asian statistics include 6.6% of Indians, 2.7% of Pakistan and 2.7% of Bangladesh. 1.5% of the population is covered by Chinese, with 1.3% of Arabs dwelling the Mainland and the rest came from various area of Asia.

15.6% of Black and mixed-black ancestries cover up the London's population. Among those, 13.3% belong to absolute Black ancestries and only 2.3% of them are from mixed-Black ancestries. 7.0% of Black Africans constitute in the London populace, with 4.2% of Black Caribbean and 2.1% of Black belonging to other tribes, make up the list and 5% of population is based on half-breeds.

In London, 300+ languages are spoken, among which English is spoken by 77.9% of population as their first language. Some of the population is unable to speak English language. Thus, they preferred to speak their national languages. Thus, 1.9% of them speak polish, 1.5% converse in Bengali, 1.3% make communications via Gujarati, etc.

The people of London have varied religions. The ratio of major religions being followed in London is: Christianity has been followed by 58.23% of the total population. The second highest religion being followed in London is no religion, i.e. atheist. The third biggest population of London, in accordance with their religion, is Muslims, who make up 12.39% of the proportion. The remaining religions being followed are Hinduism, Judaism, Sikhism, Buddhism, etc.

Source: Population UK (2020).

3 Size of electorate and turn out (1889–1964)

Table A6 Inner London 1889–1964 electorate, turnout and number of seats
(Not including the City of London–two seats).

Parliamentary				LCC				Boroughs			
Year	*Electorate*	*T. Out*	*Seats*	*Year*	*Electorate*	*Turnout*	*Seats*	*Year*	*Electorate*	*Turnout*	*Seats*
1900	566,557	69	57	1901	710,163	37.7	118	1900	683,471	45.4	1,362
1906	589,394	80	57	1904	725,574	45.7	118	1903	705,725	47.0	1,362
1910	622,332	88	57	1907	840,575	55.5	118	1906	815,247	47.8	1,362
1910	622,332	79	57	1910	795,230	51.0	118	1909	771,154	50.0	1,362
1915	683,319	–	–	1913	791,858	52.2	118	1912	777,827	44.1	1,362
1918	1,936,099	45	60	1915	826,628[a]	–	–	1919	1,662,736	28.5	1,362
1922	2,083,124	66	60	1919	1,601,995	16.6	124	1922	1,825,869	35.4	1,362
1923	2,125,971	65	60	1922	1,817,883	36.8	124	1925	1,918,112	41.2	1,366
1924	2,210,872	60	60	1925	1,914,915	30.6	124	1928	1,920,835	32.2	1,385
1929	2,922,440	71	60	1928	1,945,777	35.6	124	1931	2,071,777	31.1	1,385
1931	2,952,724	66	60	1931	2,106,330	27.8	124	1934	2,043,341	34.1	1,385
1935	2,870,930	62	60	1934	2,080,323	33.5	124	1937	2,030,680	35.2	1,376
1945	2,004,874	68	60	1937	2,054,971	43.4	124	1945	2,115,305	35.1	1,374
1950	2,436,545	79	43	1946	2,205,623	26.4	124	1949	2,531,630	38.3	1,376
1951	2,449,385	78	43	1949	2,542,750	40.7	129	1953	2,443,665	39.5	1,356
1955	2,449,315	78	42	1952	2,460,715	43.4	129	1956	2,379,235	30.7	1,356
1959	2,368,207	69	42	1955	2,401,255	32.4	126	1959	2,284,334	31.9	1,336
1964	2,269,600	70	42	1958	2,317,046	31.5	126	1962	2,192,828	32.1	1,336
				1961	2,224,479	36.4	126				

a   The LCC electorate in 1915 of 826,628 was made up of 682,493 male commoners and parliamentary electors, 134,523 women (spinsters and widows) and
9,612 persons who owned property of an annual value of 40 shillings.
Source: *London Statistics, Vol. 25 (1914–1915)* (LCC 1916).

Appendix 269

Table A7 Inner London: percentage of parliamentary electorate to population in 1901 and 1911

Parliamentary borough	Population 1911	Parliamentary division or undivided borough	Number of electors 1901	Number of electors 1911	% of electorate to population	Estimate of the population with the vote (X4)
Battersea &	229,793	Battersea	15,072	19,258	19.0	76%
Clapham		Clapham	17, 307	22,927	17.8	71.2%
Bethnal	128,378	Bethnal Green	7,908	7,876	12.5	50%
Green		N.E.	7,952	7,083	10.8	43.2%
		Bethnal Green S.W.				
Camberwell	282,162	Camberwell,	12,192	12,552	13.9	55.6%
		North	12,926	17,083	16.8	67.2%
		Dulwich	11,947	13,798	15.3	61.2%
		Peckham				
Chelsea	87,081	Chelsea	12,595	11,517	13.2	52.8%
City of	19,657	City of London	5,170	30,988	157.6	
London						
Deptford	109,446	Deptford	14,981	15,802	14.4	57.6%
Finsbury	142,955	Finsbury,	8,324	8,457	14.4	57.6%
		Central	5,670	5,155	15.7	62.8%
		Finsbury, East	10,625	8,541	16.6	66.4%
		Holborn				
Fulham	153,360	Fulham	17,381	22,051	14.4	57.6%
Greenwich	95,834	Greenwich	12,480	13,552	14.1	56.4%
Hackney	255,005	Hackney,	8,598	9,718	14.4	57.6%
		Central	11,703	12,618	14.9	59.6%
		Hackney, North	13,609	14,173	13.8	55.2%
		Hackney, South				
Hammersmith	121,254	Hammersmith	13,290	14,787	12.2	48.8%
Hampstead	85,922	Hampstead	14,568	12,392	14.4	57.6%
Islington	327,508	Islington, East	10,471	12,092	14.0	56%
		Islington, North	12,165	13,490	13.3	53.2%
		Islington, South	8,650	8,696	12.5	50%
		Islington, West	9,018	8,882	12.6	50.4%
Kensington	168,434	Kensington,	9,353	10,490	12.4	49.6%
		North	8,995	9,374	11.2	44.8%
		Kensington, South				
Lambeth	294,985	Brixton	10,611	11,858	15.6	62.4%
		Kennington	10,733	10,078	13.9	55.6%
		Lambeth, North	6,995	6,422	12.1	48.4%
		Norwood	11,502	14,956	16.0	64%
Lewisham	160,972	Lewisham	16,682	26,025	16.2	64.8%
Marylebone	117,245	Marylebone,	6,823	7,088	14.2	56.8%
		East	8,683	9,100	13.5	54%
		Marylebone, West				
Newington	117,124	Newington,	8,504	10,214	17.4	69.6%
		West	7,810	9,333	16.0	64%
		Walworth				

(Continued)

270   *Appendix*

Parliamentary borough	*Population 1911*	*Parliamentary division or undivided borough*	*Number of electors 1901*	*Number of electors 1911*	*% of electorate to population*	*Estimate of the population with the vote (X4)*
Paddington	127,141	Paddington, North	8,246	11,035	15.1	60.4%
		Paddington, South	5,755	6,595	12.2	48.8%
St George, Hanover Sq.	69,648	St George, Hanover Sq.	9,897	9,229	13.3	53.2%
St Pancras	218,674	St Pancras, East	7,247	9,523	16.6	66.4%
		St Pancras, North	7,493	9,955	17.1	68.4%
		St Pancras, South	5,701	5,504	12.1	48.4%
		St Pancras, West	7,321	8,684	15.1	60.4%
Shoreditch	110,930	Haggerston	6,732	7,069	13.1	52.4%
		Hoxton	7,904	7,665	13.4	53.6%
Southwark	201,467	Bermondsey	11,148	10,691	13.4	53.6%
		Rotherhithe	9,394	8,902	13.5	54%
		Southwark, West	8,077	8,308	15.0	60%
Strand	40,898	Strand	9,642	8,085	19.8	79.2%
Tower Hamlets	442,430	Bow and Bromley	11,006	10,669	12.3	49.2%
		Limehouse	6,706	6,374	12.2	48.8%
		Mile End	5,678	5,701	11.9	47.6%
		Poplar	10,210	9,519	12.6	50.4%
		St George	3,458	3,252	6.7	26.8%
		Stepney	5,746	4,606	7.3	29.2%
		Whitechapel	4,768	4,035	6.0	
Wandsworth	253,797	Wandsworth	22,150	39,821	15.7	62.8%
Westminster	47,360	Westminster	7,349	7,187	15.2	60.8%
Woolwich	121,408	Woolwich	15,079	19,275	15.9	63.6%
Totals	4,530,868			670,110	14.8	

Sources: Compiled from LCC Statistics; William Saunders, *A Digest of the Results of the Census of England and Wales in 1901* (London 1903).

Notes: In 1900, the only people entitled to vote in parliamentary elections were men over 21 who were ratepayers or independent lodgers and who had resided in one place for 12 months. It was also possible to be placed on the register in a second constituency as the occupier of private or business premises, and university graduates, too, had an extra chance to vote in the 12 university seats, including 2 in London. The number of the electorate was equal to 58% of the adult male population, but because of plural voting, the actual proportion of men with the franchise cannot have been much more than 53%. Registration procedures were cumbersome and, in some cases, whether a man got onto the register depended upon claims or objections made by local party organisations (Butler and Stokes, *Political Change in Britain*, p. 228).

The very high figure for the City of London is due to the presence of 6,395 livery voters and the smallness of the City residential population. The day population of the City was recorded as 362,742, while the night-time population was recorded as 19,657.

There were no fewer than 83 constituencies in which the population was upwards of 100,000 per member of parliament, most of them in the rapidly growing suburbs in London, as follows:

Table A8 Growth of the suburban electorates before 1914

Constituency	1881 Population	1911 Population	Change 1881–1911	1911 Number of electors
Wandsworth	66,792	253,759	+186,967	39,821
West Ham South	62,278	187,230	+124,952	27,310
Croydon	78,947	169,551	+90,604	28,397
Lewisham	71,702	160,963	+89,261	26,026
Fulham	114,811	153,319	+38,508	22,051
Romford	52,690	312,804	+260,114	55,951
Harrow	54,717	247,820	+193,103	38,865
Walthamstow	51,885	246,768	+194,883	42,029
Tottenham	46,456	186,619	+140,153	29,280
Enfield	54,153	180,069	+125,919	30,565
Wimbledon	15,947	160,289	+144,342	29,929
Ealing	15,766	158,125	+142,359	26,779

Source: Census 1881; Census of England and Wales 1911 – Vol III Parliamentary Areas Cd. 6343.

272 *Appendix*

Table A9 Comparison of electorate between 1915 and 1918

1915 — Inner London (57) Constituencies	Lodgers	Total	1918 — Inner London (59) Constituencies	Parliamentary			Local Government			Service Vote
				Men	Women	Total	Men	Women	Total	
Working class (24)	43,291	222,628	Working class (23)	399,832	271,504	671,336	287,153	272,443	559,596	157,706
Mixed class (15)	36,395	199,126	Mixed class (19)	388,615	275,925	664,540	253,774	277,693	531,467	145,353
Middle class (18)	31,565	261,565	Middle class (17)	313,613	234,236	547,849	212,273	230,615	442,888	117,861
Total Inner London 1915	111,251	683,319	Total Inner London 1918	1,102,060	781,665	1,883,725	753,200	780,751	1,533,951	420,920
Outer London (14)			Outer London (37)							
Total Outer London 1915	31,281	464,253	Total Outer London 1918	739,927	519,998	1,259,925	516,003	524,811	1,040,814	275,358
Total Greater London 1915	142,532	1,147,572	Total Greater London 1918	1,841,987	1,301,663	3,143,650	1,269,203	1,305,562	2,574,765	696,278
Total UK	444,656	8,357,648		12,913,166	8,479,156	21,392,322	8,689,015	8,515,438	17,204,153	3,900,135
Greater London %	32%	13%		14%	15%	15%	15%	15%	15%	18%

Notes

1 The total number of lodgers in inner London who had the vote in 1915 was estimated by the LCC to be 108,214.

2 The local government electorate for inner London in 1910 included 68,655 male commoners who were entitled to vote because they occupied lodgings of a clear annual value, if let unfurnished, of £10. This included, besides ordinary lodgers and boarders, young men over 21 years of age living at home.

3 It has not been possible to estimate from the census the total number of lodgers in London in 1915 in order to make a comparison between the numbers who did have the vote and those that did not.

Sources: compiled from Census Return Relating to Parliamentary Constituencies (February 1915) Cd. 120; Parliamentary and Local Government Electors (18 November 1918) Cd. 138; London Statistics, Vol. 25 (1914–1915) (LCC, 1916). p. 24; London Statistics, Vol. 20 (1909–1910) (LCC 1911), p. 18.

Appendix 273

Table A10 Inner London: Size of parliamentary electorate (male and female) 1918–1945

Year	Male	Female	Total	UK male %	UK female %
1918	1,151,522	806,533	1,958,055	60.4	39.6
1922	1,179,254	950,536	2,129,790	57.4	42.6
1923	1,198,151	970,952	2,169,103	57.3	42.7
1924	1,221,066	989,806	2,210,872	57.2	42.8
1929	1,329,949	1,592,491	2,922,440	47.3	52.7
1931	1,339,267	1,613,457	2,952,724	47.1	52.9
1935	1,303,292	1,567,638	2,870,930	47.2	52.8
1937	1,297,211	1,558,331	2,855,542		

Source: Compiled from LCC Statistics, vols. 39 & 40; Craig, *British Parliamentary Election Statistics 1918–1970.*

The division of the register into male and female was discontinued in 1938.

Table A11 Greater London 1964–2018 – electorate and turnout

Parliamentary				GLC/Assembly				Boroughs (32)			
Year	Electorate	T.Out	Seats	Year	Electorate	T.Out	Seats	Year	Electorate	T.Out	Seats
				GLC							
1966	5,414,118	72	103	1964	5,466,756	44	100	1964	5,481,013	36	1,859
1970	5,628,825	64	103	1967	5,319,023	41	100	1968	5,307,958	36	1,863
1974	5,300,452	75	92	1970	5,524,384	35	100	1971	5,473,860	39	1,863
1974	5,300,452	67	92	1973	5,313,470	37	92	1974	5,255,640	36	1,867
1979	5,147,135	72	92	1977	5,183,668	43	92	1978	5,155,593	43	1,908
1983	5,093,471	68	84	1981	5,086,997	44	92	1982	5,095,833	44	1,914
1987	5,111,379	71	84					1986	5,113,730	45	1,914
1992	4,876,604	74	74	*ILEA*	(Inner L.)	–	–	1990	4,960,826	48	1,914
1997		68	74	1986	1,728,604	44	58	1994	4,872,088	46	1,917
2001		55	74					1998	5,010,999	35	1,914
2005	5,049,694	58	73	*GLA*				2002	5,209,247	32	1,861
2010	5,276,910	64	73	2000	5,089,300	34	25	2006	5,340,657	38	1,861
2015	5,407,830	65	73	2004	5,197,792	37	25	2010	5,689,223	62	1,861
2017	5,459,427	70	73	2008	5,419,913	45	25	2014	5,878,824	39	1,851
				2012		38	25	2018	5,962,160	39	1,833
				2016	5,741,155	46	25				

Source: Compiled from London Data Store Elections.

274 *Appendix*

4 Parliamentary elections 1892–2017

Table A12 Labour results in parliamentary elections in London compared to the UK 1900–1970

Year	UK			Inner London			Outer London		
	Number of candidate	*% vote*	*MPs elected*	*Number of candidate*	*% vote*	*MPs elected*	*Number of candidates*	*% vote*	*MPs elected*
1900	15	1.3	2	1	0.8	0	1	7.0	0
1906	51	5.9	30	2	2.0	2	2	6.0	1
1910 (J)	78	7.6	40	1	1.5	1	1	5.0	1
1910 (D)	56	6.4	42	3	2.7	3	1	7.0	1
1918	361	20.8	57	29	13.0	2	25	20.0	2
1922	414	29.7	142	42	25.0	9	26	27.0	7
1923	427	30.7	191	48	38.0	22	35	35.0	15
1924	514	33.3	151	54	41.0	19	36	36.0	7
1929	569	37.1	287	58	44.0	36	36	39.0	18
1931	516	30.9	52	56	33.0	5	36	31.0	3
1935	552	38.0	154	60	45.0	22	36	43.0	11
1945	603	48.0	393	59	59.0	48	49	54.0	37
1950	617	46.1	315	43	51.0	34	49	46.0	23
1951	617	48.8	295	43	55.0	29	49	49.0	21
1955	620	46.4	277	43	54.0	28	50	47.0	22
1959	621	43.8	258	41	51.0	25	50	43.0	19
1964	628	44.1	317	41	53.0	32	50	43.0	21
1966	622	48.0	364	41	58.0	36	50	47.0	21
1970	625	43.1	288	41	55.0	33	50	46.0	26

Sources: Compiled from Harmer, *The Labour Party 1900–1998*, pp. 29–41; Craig, *General Election Results* (various).

Table A13 Labour results in parliamentary elections in London compared to the UK 1974–2017

Year	UK			Greater London		
	Number of candidates	*% vote*	*MPs elected*	*Number of candidates*	*% vote*	*MPs elected*
1974 (F)	623	37.2	301	92	40.0	52
1974 (O)	623	39.2	319	92	44.0	51
1979	623	36.9	269	92	40.0	42
1983	633	27.6	209	84	30.0	26
1987	633	30.8	229	*84*	*31.0*	*23*
1992	634	34.4	271	84	37.0	35
1997	639	43.2	418	74	50.0	57
2001	640	40.7	413	74	47.0	55
2005	627	35.2	348	73	39.0	44
2010	631	29.0	258	73	37.0	38
2015	631	30.4	232	73	44.0	45
2017	631	40.0	262	73	55.0	49
2019	631	32.2	202	73	48.1	49

Sources: Compiled from Harmer, *The Labour Party 1900–1998*, pp. 29–41; House of Commons, *General Election 2019*, Briefing Paper CBP 8749 (January 2020).

Appendix 275

5 Regional elections – LCC, GLC, London Assembly 1889–2016

Table A14 Results London County Council (LCC) 1889–1961

Year	Moderate municipal reform, conservative seats	%	Progressive, Liberal Seats	%	Labour seats	%	Total seats
1889	45	36.4	73	47.1	–	0.0	118
1892	35	29.7	83	52.3	–	0.0	118
1895	59	48.3	58	48.0	–	0.0	118
1898	48	39.8	70	49.2	–	0.0	118
1901	32	27.1	86	55.6	–	0.0	118
1904	35	28.8	82	51.5	1	1.7	118
1907	79	66.1	37	40.7	3	0.0	118
1910	60	50.8	55	41.9	2	2.5	118
1913	67	56.8	49	40.3	15	0.8	118
1919	68	54.8	40	24.3	16	12.1	124
1922	82	66.1	26	17.0	35	12.9	124
1925	83	66.9	6	9.4	42	28.2	124
1928	77	62.1	5	15.0	35	33.9	124
1931	83	66.9	6	5.7	69	28.2	124
1934	55	44.4	–	3.4	75	55.6	124
1937	49	39.5	–	1.2	90	60.5	124
1946	30	24.2	2	1.1	64	75.8	124
1949	64	49.6	1	1.3	92	49.6	129
1952	37	27.7	–	0.8	74	71.3	129
1955	52	41.3	–	1.4	101	58.7	126
1958	25	19.8	–	3.0	84	80.2	126
1961	42	33.3	–	6.0		66.7	126

Source: Adapted from Ken Young, *Local Politics and the Rise of Party.*

Table A15 GLC Election results 1964–1981

Date	Labour (%)	Conservative (%)	Liberal (%)
1964	44.6	39.8	10.4
1967	34.0	51.9	9.5
1970	38.8	50.8	6.2
1973	47.4	37.9	12.5
1977	32.4	52.5	7.8
1981	41.8	39.7	14.4

Source: Compiled from London Data Store.

276 *Appendix*

Table A16 Percentage share of vote London Assembly elections 2000–2020

Year	Con % & seats	Lab % & seats	Lib Dem % & seats	Green % & seats	Labour change
2000	29% (9)	30% (9)	15% (4)	11% (3)	N/A
2004	28% (9)	25% (7)	17% (5)	9% (2)	Down 2
2008	35% (11)	27% (8)	11% (3)	8% (2)	Up 1
2012	32% (9)	41% (12)	7% (2)	8% (2)	Up 4
2016	29% (8)	40% (12)	6% (1)	8% (2)	No change
2020	postponed				

Source: Compiled from London Data Store.

Table A17 Percentage share of the vote London Mayoral elections 2000–2020

(Second round percentages)

Year	Con	Lab
2000	27	Livingstone & Dobson 52
2004	44.6	55.4
2008	53.2	46.8
2012	44.0	48.5
2016	35.0	56.8
2020	Postponed	

Source: Adapted from House of Commons, *London Elections 2016* (CBP 7598 April 2016).

6 Metropolitan Borough council election results (1900–2018)

Table A18 Metropolitan Borough elections 1919–1937

Date	Labour		Municipal reform (conservatives)	Progressives (liberal)	Total votes	Total seats
	Votes	Seats	Votes	Votes		
1919	185,600	572	179,100	111,400	476,100	1,362
1922	210,700	259	342,300	48,700	601,700	1,362
1925	294,700	364	441,700	31,500	767,900	1,366
1928	253,700	459	284,700	45,600	587,900	1,376
1931	198,100	257	374,900	23,200	602,300	1,385
1934	332,900	729	300,100	17,200	654,800	1,386
1937	253,000	778	306,000	16,000	683,100	1,371

Source: Adapted from Donoughue and Jones, *Herbert Morrison*, p. 655.

Appendix 277

Table A19 Share of votes and seats in the London Boroughs 1900–1962

Year	Conservative		Labour		Liberal/ Alliance		Total seats	Labour seats	Number of councils/ labour councils
	% Vote	% Seats	% Vote	% Seats	% Vote	% Seats			
1900	43.8	59.7	0.6	0.1	37.5	33.9	1,362	0	28/0
1903	38.5	42.1	5.2	2.5	41.9	48.3	1,362	0	28/0
1906	51.5	74.0	9.7	2.4	31.2	19.3	1,362	0	28/0
1909	50.3	72.1	9.2	2.9	33.0	20.5	1,362	0	28/0
1912	49.9	74.0	11.0	3.5	31.8	18.9	1,362	0	28/0
1919	39.3	48.5	39.4	41.0	16.3	9.7	1,362	573	28/13
1922	58.2	78.7	35.3	19.0	3.0	1.9	1,362	262	28/6
1925	55.5	71.5	38.5	26.8	4.0	1.5	1,366	362	28/8
1928	48.9	62.8	43.1	32.6	5.0	2.6	1,385	458	28/8
1931	61.9	78.2	32.9	18.6	2.3	3.0	1,385	257	28/3
1934	45.5	46.9	50.8	52.6	1.1	0.0	1,386	729	28/15
1937	44.3	43.2	51.5	56.7	1.2	0.0	1,377	779	28/17
1945	34.7	22.9	56.4	75.4	1.3	0.0	1,377	1,040	28/23
1949	49.6	44.9	45.3	54.0	2.3	0.0	1,373	742	28/17
1953	44.1	35.2	53.1	64.7	1.8	0.0	1,356	876	28/19
1956	42.5	33.7	52.6	65.4	1.9	0.0	1,356	888	28/21
1959	44.4	35.7	50.1	64.0	2.9	0.0	1,336	853	28/19
1962	35.7	30.0	49.9	68.6	10.5	0.7	1,336	919	28/21

Source: Adapted from Ken Young, *Local Politics and the Rise of Party.*

Table A20 Percentage share of vote London Borough elections 1964–2018

Year	Conservative	Labour	Lib Dem	Other	Total seats	Labour change
1964					1,859	Up 193
1968	60.1	28.3	7.2	4.4	1,863	Down 762
1971	39.4	53.1	4.2	3.3	1,863	Up 871
1974	41.7	42.9	12.3	3.1	1,867	Down 131
1978	49.6	39.6	6.4	4.4	1,908	Down 208
1982	43.0	30.4	24.6	2.9	1,914	Down 101
1986	35.8	37.4	23.8	3.1	1,914	Up 176
1990	37.8	38.3	14.1	9.7	1,914	Down 32
1994	31.3	41.5	21.8	5.4	1,917	Up 119
1998	32.3	40.5	20.6	6.6	1,917	Up 6
2002	34.4	33.8	20.3	11.6	1,861	Down 184
2006	35.1	27.6	20.3	17.0	1,861	Down 181
2010	32.0	32.6	22.0	13.4	1,861	Up 190
2014	26.1	37.4	10.2	26.3	1,861	Up 185
2018	29.0	44.1	12.7	14.2	1,861	Up 60

Source: Compiled from London Data Store Election results.

278　*Appendix*

7　Referenda results (1998–2016)

Table A21　Referendum on Europe 2016; results for Greater London

| *Remain – 2,263,519 (59.9%)* | | | | *Leave 1,513,232 (40.1%)* | | | |
| *Inner London* | | | | *Outer London* | | | |
District	*Turn out*	*Remain %*	*Leave %*	*District*	*Turn out*	*Remain %*	*Leave %*
				Barking & Dagenham	63.8%	37.6%	62.4%
Camden	65.4%	74.9%	25.1%	Barnet	72.1%	62.2%	37.8%
City of London	73.5%	75.3%	24.7%	Bexley	65.0%	59.7%	40.3%
				Brent	65.0%	59.7%	40.3%
City of Westminster	64.9%	69.0%	31.0%	Bromley	78.8%	50.6%	49.4%
				Croydon	69.8%	54.3%	45.7%
				Ealing	70.0%	60.4%	39.6%
Greenwich	69.5%	55.6%	44.4%	Enfield	69.0%	55.8%	44.2%
Hackney	65.1%	78.5%	21.5%	Haringey	70.5%	75.6%	24.4%
Hammersmith & Fulham	69.9%	70.0%	30.0%	Harrow	72.2%	54.6%	45.4%
Islington	70.3%	75.2%	24.8%	Havering	76.0%	30.3%	69.7%
Kensington & Chelsea	65.9%	68.7%	31.3%	Hillingdon	68.9%	43.6%	56.4%
Lambeth	67.3%	78.6%	21.4%	Hounslow	69.7%	51.1%	48.9%
Lewisham	63.0%	69.9%	30.1%	Kingston Upon Thames	78.3%	61.6%	38.4%
				Merton	73.4%	62.9%	37.1%
				Newham	59.2%	52.8%	47.2%
Southwark	66.1%	72.8%	27.2%	Redbridge	67.5%	54.0%	46.0%
Tower Hamlets	64.5%	67.5%	32.5%	Richmond Upon Thames	82.0%	69.3%	30.7%
Wandsworth	71.9%	75.0%	25.0%	Sutton	76.0%	72.8%	27.2%
				Waltham Forest	66.6%	59.1%	40.9%
Average Inner London	**67.5**	**71.6**	**28.4**	**Average Outer London**	**74.4**	**49.4**	**48.6**

Source: Electoral Commission.

Bibliography

Primary sources

Manuscript collections

Bishops Gate Institute

Greater London Labour Party
London Cooperative Society

Black Cultural Archives, Brixton

Runnymead Trust

Croydon Archives

Ernest Wimble Scrap Book & Cuttings
Croydon Labour Party

Lambeth Archives

Papers of Charles Ford
Lambeth Central Labour Party
Lambeth Labour Group (1985–1986)
Norwood Labour Party
Norwood Conservative Association (1920–1925)
Vauxhall Liberal Association (1981–1988)

London Metropolitan Archives

London Labour Party – Executive Committee Minutes and papers
LCC Emergency Committee (1914–1915)

Modern Records Centre, University of Warwick

Croydon Trades Council
Lambeth Trades Council
London Trades Council

280 *Bibliography*

The People's History Museum, Manchester

National Labour Party

London School of Economics

Webb Papers
North Lambeth Labour Party
Donoghue and Jones back ground papers to biography of Herbert Morrison

Census

Census reports for London 1901–2011.
Census of England and Wales 1921. County of London. Workplaces in London and
    the Home Counties (1923).
Census reports for the Greater London Area – parliamentary constituency tables
    1966 to date
GLS Intelligence 2016-based ethnic group projections (November 2017).
GB Historical GIS/University of Portsmouth
ONS, Age Structure of London Boroughs, 2011.
www.visionofbritain.org.uk

Newspapers and periodicals

Brent Socialist
Common Sense Croydon Liberal Party
Contemporary Review
Croydon Advertiser
Croydon Labour Outlook. Journal of the Croydon Labour Party
Croydon News. Croydon Labour Party
Croydon Citizen (Labour Party)
Croydon Labour Journal Monthly (South Croydon LP)
Croydon Times
Daily Herald
Daily News
Daily Chronicle
Ealing Gazette
East London Observer
Independent
Justice
Labour Leader
Labour Organiser
Labour Weekly
The Labour Woman
London Daily News
London Labour Briefing
London Labour Party Circular
Marxism Today
New Society

New Life
New Statesman
Norwood News
The Times
The Guardian
Kentish Independent
Pall Mall Gazette
South London Press
West Indian World
West London Observer
Worker's Dreadnought

Secondary sources

Contemporary books, articles, pamphlets and reports

Alan Argent (ed.), *The Angels' Voice. A Magazine for Young Men in Brixton, 1910–1913* (London: London Record Society, 2016).

Charles Booth, *Inquiry into Life and Labour of the People of London* (London: MacMillan, 1886–1903).

Beatrix Campbell, 'Politics, Pyramids and People,' *Marxism Today* (December 1984).

Beatrix Campbell & Martin Jacques, 'Goodbye to the GLC,' *Marxism Today* (April 1986).

Tony Crossland, *The Future of Socialism* (London: Constable, 2006).

David Englander, *The Diary of Fred Knee* (Manchester: Society for the Study of Labour History, 1977).

Harry Gosling, *Up and Down Stream* (London: Spokesman Books, 2010).

Charles Hadfield & James MacColl, *Pilot Guide to Political London* (London: Pilot Press Ltd., 1945).

Percy Harris, *Forty Years In and Out of Parliament* (London: Melrose, 1947).

Ben Judah, *This is London* (London: Picador, 2016).

David Lammy, *Tribes How* (London: Constable, 2020).

William Lax, *Lax of Poplar* (London: Epworth Press, 1927).

Emanuel Litvinoff, *Journey through a Small Planet* (London: Robin Clarke, 1993).

Ken Livingstone, *If Voting Changed Anything, they'd Abolish It* (London: Fontana, 1987).

Ken Livingstone, *You Can't Say That* (London: Faber, 2011).

Hubert Llewellyn-Smith, *The New Survey of London Life and Labour*, Vols. 1–9 (London: P S King, 1931–1935).

LCC, Administrative County of London Development Plan (1951).

LCC, Administrative County of London Development Plan (1957).

LCC, Statistical Abstract for London 1939–1948 (1950).

Jack London, *People of the Abyss* (Teddington: Echo Library, 2007).

London Society of Compositors, Jubilee Souvenir 1848–1923 (London: Nabu Press, 1923).

John Major, *The Autobiography* (London: Harper Collins, 2010).

Mass Observation, *Puzzled People* (London: Faber, 2009).

Charles Masterman, *The Condition of England* (London: Faber, 2009).

282　*Bibliography*

Andrew Mearns, *The Bitter Cry of Outcast London* (London, New York: Humanities Press, 1883, republished in 1970).

Richard Mudie-Smith, *The Religious Life of London* (London: Nabu Press, 2010).

Malcolm Muggeridge, *Chronicles of Wasted Time* (London: Regent College, 2006).

Arthur Newton, *Years of Change: Autobiography of a Hackney Shoemaker* (London: Hackney WEA, 1974).

John O'Farrell, *Things Can Only Get Better: Eighteen Miserable Years in the Life of a Labour Supporter* (London: Black Swan, 1999).

Sylvia Pankhurst, *Home Front* (London: Hutchinson, 1932).

Alexander Patterson, *Across the Bridges or Life by the South Side Riverside* (London: Edward Arnold, 1915).

Maud Pember-Reeves, *Round About a Pound a Week* (London: Persephone Press, 2008).

Mike Phillips, *London Crossings: A Biography of Black Britain* (London: Continuum Group, 2001).

David Rosenberg, *The Battle for the East End: Jewish Responses to Fascism in the 1930s* (Nottingham: Five Leaves, 2011).

Andrew Rothstein, *The Hackney and Kingsland Branch of the SDF – 1903–1906* (Our History Pamphlet No. 19, 1960).

Stanley Rothwell, *Lambeth at War* (London: SE1 People's History, 1981).

Len Snow, *Signs of Co-operation in Brent and Harrow* (London: Brent & Harrow Cooperative Party, 2003).

Peter Tatchell, *The Battle for Bermondsey* (London: Gay Men's Press, 1983).

Robert Tressell, *The Ragged Trouser Philanthropists* (London: Franklin Classics, 2018).

Scholarly books

Peter Ackroyd, *London – the Biography* (London: Vintage, 2001).

Paul Addison, *Road to 1945: British Politics and the Second World War* (London: Pimlico, 1994).

Andrew Adonis & Stephen Pollard, *A Class Act: The Myth of Britain's Classless Society* (London: Hamish Hamilton, 1997).

Claire Ainsley, *The New Working Class* (Bristol: Policy Press, 2019).

Geoffrey Alderman, *British Elections – Myth and Reality* (London: Batsford, 1978).

Geoffrey Alderman, *London Jewery and London Politics* (London: Routledge, 1989).

Paul Allender, *What's Wrong with Labour?* (London: Merlin Press, 2001).

M K Aly, *Becoming Arab in London* (London: Pluto Press, 2015).

Rowland Atkinson, *Alpha City: How London Was Captured by the Super-Rich* (London: Verso, 2020).

Brian Barker, *Labour in London* (London: Routledge, 2018).

Anthony Barnett, *The Lure of Greatness* (London: Unbound, 2017).

Frank Bealey & Henry Pelling, *Labour and Politics 1900–1906* (London: Praeger Press, 1982).

Francis Beckett & Mark Seddon, *Jeremy Corbyn and the Strange Rebirth of Labour England* (London: Biteback Publishing, 2018).

Tony Bennett et al., *Culture, Class, Distinction* (London: Routledge, 2008).

M Benney, A P Gray & R H Pear, *How People Vote* (London: Routledge, 1956).

Stefan Berger, *The British Labour Party and the German Social Democrats 1900–1931* (Oxford: OUP, 1994).

Bibliography 283

John Bew, *Citizen Clem. A Biography of Attlee* (London: Riverun, 2016).

Clive Bloom, *Violent London* (London: Palgrave MacMillan, 2010).

Martin Body & Colin Fudge, *Local Socialism? Labour Councils and New Left Alternatives* (London: Basingstoke, 1984).

Janine Booth, *Guilty and Proud of it! Poplar Rebel Councillors and Guardians, 1919–1925* (London: Merlin Press, 2009).

Pierre Bourdieu, *Distinction* (London: Routledge, 2010).

Duncan Bowie, *Politics, Planning and Homes in a World City* (London: Routledge, 2010).

Duncan Bowie, *Reform and Revolt in the City of Dreaming Spires, Radical, Socialist and Communist Politics in the City of Oxford* (London: University of Westminster, 2018).

Noreen Branson, *Poplarism, 1919–1925: George Lansbury and the Councillor's Revolt* (London: Lawrence and Wishart, 1979).

Marc Brodie, *The Politics of the Poor, 1880–1914* (London: Clarendon Press, 2004).

Callum Brown, *The Death of Christian Britain* (London: Routledge, 2009).

Callum Brown, *Religion and Society in Twentieth Century Britain* (London: Routledge, 2006).

Sue Bruely, *Women in Britain since 1900* (London: MacMillan, 1999).

Nick Buck et al., *Working Capital: Life and Labour in Contemporary London* (London: Routledge, 2002).

Julia Bush, *Behind the Lines* (London: Merlin Press, 1984).

David Butler, *British General Election of 1951* (London: MacMillan, 1952).

David Butler, *British General Election of 1955* (London: Franck Cass, 1965).

David Butler & Donald Stokes, *Political Change in Britain* (London: MacMillan, 1969).

Tim Butler & Chris Hamnett, *Ethnicity, Class and Aspiration* (Bristol: Policy Press, 2011).

Tim Butler & Garry Robson, *London Calling: The Middle-Classes and the Remaking of Inner London* (London: Berg, 2003).

John Callaghan, *Interpreting the Labour Party* (Manchester: MUP, 2003).

Ben Campkin, *Remaking London* (London: Tauris, 2013).

David Cannadine, *The Rise and Fall of Class in Britain* (New York: Columbia University Press, 2000).

Centre for Contemporary Cultural Studies, *The Empire Strikes Back: Race and Racism in 1970s Britain* (London: Hutchinson, 1982).

John Carvel, *Citizen Ken* (London: Hogarth Press, 1987).

Terrence Chapman, *Caroline Ganley* (London: History and Social Action Publications, 2018).

Marc Clapson, *Suburban Century* (Oxford: Berg, 2003).

Peter Clarke, *Lancashire and the New Liberalism* (Cambridge: CUP, 2007).

Hugh Clegg, *Labour Relations in London Transport* (Oxford: Blackwell, 1950).

Fox Clegg & Thompson, *A History of British Trade Unions since 1889, Vol. 1* (Oxford: Clarendon Press, 1964).

Catherine A Cline, *Recruits to Labour* (New York: Syracuse University Press, 1963).

Alan Clinton, *The Trade Union Rank and File* (Manchester: MUP, 1986).

Ken Coates & Tony Topham, *The Making of the Labour Movement* (London: Spokesman Books, 1994).

Cynthia Cockburn, *The Local State* (London: Pluto Press, 1977).

284 *Bibliography*

Cynthia Cockburn, *Looking to London. Stories of War, Escape and Asylum* (London: Pluto Press, 2017).

G D H Cole, *The Coops and Labour* (London: LSE, 1946).

G D H Cole, *A History of the Labour Party since 1914* (London: Routledge, 1948).

Robert Colls, *Identity of England* (Oxford: OUP, 2002).

Chris Cook, *The Age of Alignment: Electoral Politics in Britain 1922–1929* (London: Palgrave MacMillan, 1975).

J T Coppock & H C Prince, *Greater London* (London: Faber & Faber, 1964).

Jeffery Cox, *The English Churches in a Secular Society: Lambeth 1870–1930* (Oxford: OUP, 1982).

M Cragoe & A Taylor (eds.), *London Politics, 1760–1914* (London: Palgrave Macmillan, 2005).

F W S Craig, *British Parliamentary Elections 1885–1918* (London: MacMillan, 1974).

F W S Craig, *British Parliamentary Elections 1918–1949* (London: Political Reference Publications, 1969).

F W S Craig, *British Parliamentary Elections 1950–1973* (Aldershot: Dartmouth, 1983).

Sean Creighton, *Radical Croydon 1860–1939* (London: Croydon Radical History Network, 1982).

Jonathan Davis & Rohan McWilliam, *Labour and the Left in the 1980s* (Manchester: MUP, 2018).

Sam Davies, *Liverpool Labour: Social and Political Influences on the Development of the Labour Party in Liverpool 1900–1939* (Newcastle-under-Lyme: Keele University Press, 1996).

Sam Davies & Bob Morley, *County Borough Elections in England and Wales*, Vol. 3 (London: Routledge, 2006).

Daniel N DeHanas, *London Youth, Religion and Politics: Engagement and Activism from Brixton to Brick Lane* (Oxford: OUP, 2016).

Geoff Dench, Kate Gavron & Michael Young, *The New East End. Kinship, Race and Conflict* (London: Profile Books, 2006).

D T Denver & Gordon Hands, *Issues and Controversies in British Electoral Behaviour* (London: Prentice Hall, 1992).

Fiona Devine et al., *Rethinking Class: Culture, Identities and Lifestyles* (Basingstoke: Palgrave, 2004).

Mark Donnelly, *Sixties Britain, Culture, Society and Politics* (London: Longman, 2005).

David Donnison & David Eversley, *London: Urban Patterns, Problems and Policies* (London: Heinemann, 1973).

Bernard Donoughue & G W Jones, *Herbert Morrison* (London: Littlehampton Book Services, 1973).

Danny Dorling, *Peak Inequality* (Bristol: Policy Press, 2018).

Danny Dorling & Bethan Thomas, *People and Places. The 21st-century Atlas of the UK* (Bristol: Policy Press, 2016).

Danny Dorling & Sally Tomlinson, *Rule Britannia* (London: Biteback Publishing, 2019).

R E Dowse, *Left in the Centre* (London: Longmans, 1966).

Michael Drayson, *Croydon* (Portsmouth: University of Portsmouth School of Architecture, 2001).

Bibliography   285

H J Dyos, *Victorian Suburb* (Leicester: Leicester University Press, 1986).

David Edgerton, *The Rise and Fall of the British Nation. A Twentieth Century History* (London: Allen Lane, 2018).

Geoff Eley & Keith Nield, *The Future of Class in History: What's Left of the Social* (Michigan: University of Michigan, 2007).

Gregory Elliott, *Labourism and the English Genius* (London: Verso, 1993).

Jackson W Eric, *A Short History of the LCC* (London: Longmans, 1965).

Geoffrey Evans & Anand Menon, *Brexit and British Politics* (Cambridge: Polity Press, 2017).

Geoffrey Evans & James Tilley, *The New Politics of Class* (Oxford: OUP, 2017).

David Feldman & G S Jones, *Metropolis London: Histories and Representations since 1800* (London: Routledge, 1989).

Geoffrey G Field, *Blood, Sweat and Toil* (Oxford: OUP, 2011).

Steven Fielding, *Class and Ethnicity: Irish Catholics in England, 1880–1939* (Buckingham: McGaw Hill, 1992).

Steven Fielding (ed.), *'England Arise': The Labour Party and Popular Politics in the 1940s* (Manchester: MUP: 1995).

Steven Fielding, *The Labour Party. Continuity and Change in the Making of 'New' Labour* (London: Palgrave, 2002).

Michael Foot, *Aneurin Bevan* (London: Faber & Faber, 2009).

Francis Fukuyama, *Identity. Contemporary Identity Politics and the Struggle for Recognition* (London: Profile Books, 2019).

Jean Gaffin & David Thoms, *Caring and Sharing: A Centenary History of the Co-operative Women's Guild* (London: Holyoake Books, 1993).

Tom Gallaher, *Glasgow: The Uneasy Peace* (Manchester: MUP, 1987).

Joel Garreau, *Edge City. Life on the New Frontier* (London: Anchor Books, 1980).

Ian Geary & Adrian Pabst (eds.), *Blue Labour* (London: Tauris, 2015).

John B Gent (ed.), *Croydon – The Story of a Hundred Years* (London: Croydon Natural History and Scientific Society, 1979).

Lindsey German & John Rees, *A People's History of London* (London: Verso, 2012).

Justin Gest, *The White Working Class* (Oxford: OUP, 2018).

Ruth Glass, *London: Aspects of Change* (London: McGibbon & Kee, 1964).

John Goldthorpe et al., *The Affluent Worker in the Class Structure* (Cambridge: CUP, 1969).

David Goodhart, *The Road to Somewhere. The New Tribes Shaping British Politics* (London: Penguin, 2017).

Sue Goss, *Local Labour and Local Government – A Study of Changing Interests, Politics and Policy in Southwark from 1919 to 1982* (Edinburgh: Edinburgh University Press, 1988).

Clare Griffiths et al., *Class, Culture and Politics* (Oxford: OUP, 2011).

Jonathan Haidt, *The Righteous Mind. Why Good People Are Divided by Politics and Religion* (London: Penguin, 2013).

Sir Peter Hall, *Cities in Civilisation* (London: Pantheon Books, 1998).

Sir Peter Hall, *London: 2001* (London: Routledge, 1989).

Sir Peter Hall, *London Voices, London Lives* (Bristol: Policy Press, 2007).

P G Hall, *Industries of London since 1861* (London: Hutchinson, 1962).

Stuart Hall, *Familiar Stranger* (London: Allen Lane, 2017).

Stuart Hall, *The Hard Road to Renewal: Thatcherism and the Crisis of the Left* (London: Verso, 1988).

286 *Bibliography*

Chris Hamnett, *Unequal City* (London: Routledge, 2003).

Simon Hannah, *A Party with Socialists in It* (London: Pluto Press, 2018).

June Hannam, *Feminism* (London: Routledge, 2006).

David Harvey, *The Urban Experience* (Oxford: Blackwell, 1989).

David Harvey, *The Ways of the World* (London: Profile, 2017).

Dianne Hayter, *Fightback! Labour's Traditional Right in the 1970s and 1980s* (Manchester: MUP, 1985).

Anthony Heath et al., *The Political Integration of Ethnic Minorities in Britain* (Oxford: OUP, 2013).

Richard Heffernan & Mike Marqusee, *Defeat from the Jaws of Victory* (London: Verso, 1992).

James Hinton, *The First Shop Stewards Movement* (London: Allen & Unwin, 1973).

James Hinton, *Labour and Socialism* (Boston: University of Massachusetts Press, 1983)

Eric Hobsbawn, *Age of Extremes* (London: Michael Joseph, 1984).

Eric Hobsbawn, *On History* (London: Lawrence & Wishart, 1997).

Karin Hofmeester, *Jewish Workers and the Labour Movement, 1870–1914* (London: Routledge, 2004).

David Howell, *British Workers and the Independent Labour Party, 1888–1906* (London: Palgrave Macmillan, 1983).

Rupa Huq, *On the Edge. The Contested Cultures of English Suburbia* (London: Lawrence & Wishart, 2013).

Paul Husselbee & Lesley Ballard, *Free Churches and Society* (London: Continuum, 2012).

Sarah Jackson & Rosemary Taylor, *East London Suffragettes* (Stroud: History Press, 2014).

Martin Jacques & Francis Mulhern, *The Forward March of Labour Halted* (London: Verso, 1981).

Mark Jenkins, *Bevanism: Labour's High Tide* (London: Spokesman, 2012).

Ben Jones, *The Working-Class in Mid-Century England* (Manchester: MUP, 2012).

Gareth Stedman Jones, *Outcast London*: (London: Verso, 2013).

Owen Jones, *Chavs* (London: Verso, 2012).

Eric Kaufman, *White Shift. Populism, Immigration and the Future of the White Majority* (London: Penguin, 2018).

Dennis Kavanagh, *The Reordering of British Politics* (Oxford: OUP, 1998).

Bryan Keith-Lucas, *The English Local Government Franchise* (Oxford: Blackwell, 1952).

Paul Keleman, *The British Left and Zionism. History of a Divorce* (Manchester: MUP, 2012),

Anne J Kershen (ed.), *London the Promised Land Revisited* (London: Ashgate, 2015).

Anthony J King, *Global Cities. Post-Imperialism and the Internationalisation of London* (London: Routledge, 1990).

David Kogan, *Protest and Power. The Battle for the Labour Party* (London: Bloomsbury Reader, 2019).

Stephen Koss, *Nonconformity in Modern British Politics* (London: Shoestring, 1975).

David Kynaston, *Modernity Britain 1957–1962* (London: Bloomsbury, 2015).

Bill Lancaster & Tony Mason, *Life and Labour in a Twentieth Century City: The Experience of Coventry* (Coventry: Cryfield Press, 1986).

Stewart Lansley, Sue Goss & Christian Wolmar, *Councils in Conflict* (London: Palgrave Macmillan, 1989).

Bibliography   287

Scott Lash & John Urry, *Economies of Signs and Space* (London: Sage, 1994).

John Lawrence, *Me, Me, Me: The Search for Community in Post War England* (Oxford: OUP, 2019).

Adam Lent, *British Social Movements since 1945* (London: AIAA, 2001).

Jo Littler, *Against Meritocracy: Culture, Power and Myths of Mobility* (London: Routledge, 2017).

John Lloyd, *Light and Liberty* (London: Weidenfeld & Nicholson, 1990).

Stuart Macintryre, *A Proletarian Science, Marxism in Britain 1917–1933* (London: Lawrence & Wishart, 1986).

David Marquand, *The Progressive Dilemma* (London: Weidenfeld & Nicholson, 1989).

John Marriott, *The Culture of Labourism* (Edinburgh: Edinburgh University Press, 1991)

John Marriott, *Beyond the Tower* (New Haven: Yale University Press, 2012).

J E Martin, *Greater London: An Industrial Geography* (London: Harper Collins, 1966).

Jane Martin, Peter Sunley & Ron Wills, *Union Retreat and the Regions: The Shrinking Landscape of Organized Labour* (London: Routledge, 1996).

Doreen Massey, *World City* (London: Polity, 2007).

Declan McHugh, *Labour in the City: The Development of the Labour Party in Manchester 1918–31* (Manchester: MUP, 2007).

Peter McInnes & Paula Sparkes, *Croydon at Work* (London: Croydon Chamber of Commerce, 1991).

R McKenzie & A Silver, *Angels in Marble: The Working-class in Urban England* (London: Heineman, 1968).

Ross McKibbin, *Evolution of the Labour Party* (Oxford: Clarendon, 1984).

Ross McKibbin, *The Ideologies of Class* (Oxford: OUP, 1994).

Ross McKibbin, *Parties and People* (Oxford: OUP, 2010).

Hugh McLeod, *Class and Religion in the Late Victorian City* (London: Archon Books, 1984).

Keir Milburn, *Generation Left* (London: Polity Press, 2019).

Ralph Miliband, *Parliamentary Socialism* (London: Merlin Press, 2009).

Lewis Minkin, *The Contentious Alliance: Trade Unions and the Labour Party* (Edinburgh: Edinburgh University Press, 1992).

Anna Minton, *Big Capital, Who Is London For?* (London: Penguin, 2017).

Jim Moher, *Stepping on White Corns* (London: JGM Books, 2007).

H Keatley Moore (ed.), *Croydon and the Great War* (London: Naval & Military Press, 2006).

Kevin Morgan, Gideon Cohen & Andrew Flinn, *Communists and British Society 1920–1991* (London: Rivers Oram Press, 2007).

Kenneth O Morgan, *Consensus and Disunity* (Oxford: OUP, 1986).

Kenneth O Morgan, *Labour in Power* (Oxford: OUP, 1985).

Kenneth O Morgan & Jane Morgan, *Portrait of a Progressive* (Oxford: OUP, 1980).

Terence Morris, *The Criminal Area* (London: Routledge, 2013).

Ferdinand Mount, *Mind the Gap* (London: Short Books, 2010).

Pippa Norris, *British By-Elections* (Oxford: OUP, 1990).

Pippa Norris, *Electoral Change since 1945* (London: Wiley, 1996).

Pippa Norris & Neil Gavin, *Britain Votes* 1997 (Oxford: OUP, 1998).

ONS, *Ethnicity in the 1991 Census* (London: HMSO, 1996).

288 *Bibliography*

Leo Panitch & Colin Leys, *Searching for Socialism. The Project of the Labour New Left from Benn to Corbyn* (London: Verso, 2020).

Frank Parkin, *Middle Class Radicalism* (Manchester: MUP, 1968).

G Parry, G Moyer & N Day, *Political Participation in Britain* (Cambridge: CUP, 1992).

Sheila Patterson, *Dark Strangers* (Bloomington: Indiana University Press, 1964).

Henry Pelling, *Social Origins of British Elections, 1885–1910* (London: MacMillan, 1967).

Kennetta Perry, *London is the Place for Me* (Oxford: OUP, 2016).

Gordon Phillips, *The Rise of the Labour Party, 1893–1931* (London: Routledge, 1992).

Thomas Picketty, *Capital and Ideology* (Cambridge: Harvard University Press, 2020).

Roy Porter, *London: A Social History* (London: Penguin, 2000).

Martin Pugh, *Making of Modern British Politics* (London: Wiley, 2009).

Martin Pugh, *Speak for Britain* (London: Vintage, 2011).

John Ramsden, *An Appetite for Power* (London: Harper Collins, 1999).

Daniel Renshaw, *Socialism and Diasporic 'Other'* (Liverpool: Liverpool University Press, 2018).

J Reynolds & K Laybourn, *Labour Heartland: A History of the Labour Party in West Yorkshire* (Bradford: Bradford University Press, 1987).

Gerald Rhodes, *The Government of London* (London: Routledge, 1973).

Rita Rhodes, *An Arsenal for Labour: The RACS and Politics 1896–1996* (London: Holyoake Books, 1999).

Richard Rogers & Mark Fisher, *A New London* (London: Penguin, 1992).

David Rosenberg, *Rebel Footprints; A Guide to Uncovering London's Radical History* (London: Pluto Press, 2015).

W D Rubinstein, *Capitalism, Culture and Decline in Britain, 1750–1990* (London: Routledge, 2015).

S R Ruck & Gerald Rhodes, *The Government of Greater London* (London: Allen & Unwin, 1970).

Walter G Runciman, *Relative Deprivation and Social Justice* (Berkeley: University of California Press, 1966).

Michael Savage, *Dynamics of Working-Class Politics* (Cambridge: CUP, 2009).

Michael Savage, *Social Class in the Twenty First Century* (London: Pelican, 2015).

Jonathan Schneer, *London 1900: The Imperial Metropolis* (New Haven: Yale University Press, 2001).

G R Searle, *The Liberal Party. Triumph and Disintegration* (London: MacMillan, 1992).

Patrick Seyd, *The Rise and Fall of the Labour Left* (London: Palgrave, 1987).

Patrick Seyd & Paul Whiteley, *Labour's Grass Roots* (Oxford: OUP, 2003).

L J Sharpe, *A Metropolis Votes* (London: LSE, 1962).

Eric Shaw, *Discipline and Discord in the Labour Party* (Manchester: MUP, 1998).

Eric Shaw, *The Labour Party since 1945* (London: Wiley, 1996).

John Shepherd, *George Lansbury* (Oxford: OUP, 2004).

Stan Shipley, *Club Life and Socialism in Mid-Victorian London* (Oxford: History Workshop Pamphlet, 1971).

Kalbir Shukra, *The Changing Pattern of Black Politics in Britain* (London: Pluto Press, 1998).

Bibliography 289

Roger Silverstone (ed.), *Visions of Suburbia* (London: Routledge, 1997).

Michael Squires, *Saklatava: A Political Biography* (London: Lawrence and Wishart, 1990).

Guy Standing, *The Precariat. The New Dangerous Class* (London: Bloomsbury, 2014).

Penny Summerfield, *Women Workers in the Second World War* (London: Routledge, 2012).

A J Sutcliffe (ed.), *Metropolis 1890–1940* (London: Mansell, University of Chicago, 1984).

Florence Sutcliffe-Braithwaite, *Class, Politics and the Decline of Deference* (Oxford: OUP, 2019).

Marvin Swartz, *The Union of Democratic Control in British Politics during the First World War* (Oxford: OUP, 1971).

Duncan Tanner, *Labour's First Century* (Cambridge: CUP, 2007).

Duncan Tanner, *Political Change and the Labour Party 1900–1918* (Cambridge: CUP, 1990).

Graham Taylor, *Ada Salter. Pioneer of Ethical Socialism* (London: Lawrence & Wishart, 2016).

Richard Taylor & Nigel Young, *Campaigns for Peace. British Peace Movements in the Twentieth Century* (Manchester: MUP, 1987).

Willie Thompson, *The Long Death of British Labourism* (London: Pluto Press, 1993).

Edward P Thompson, *The Making of the English Working Class* (London: Penguin, 1991).

Paul Thompson, *Socialists, Liberals and Labour* (London: Routledge, 1967).

Andrew Thorpe, *A History of the Labour Party* (London: Palgrave, 2008).

Andrew Thorpe, *The Parties at War* (Oxford: OUP, 2009).

Michael Tichelar, *The Failure of Land Reform. The Triumph of Private Property* (Abingdon: Routledge, 2019).

Peter Townsend, *Poverty in the UK* (London: Penguin, 1979).

Tony Travers & George Jones, *The New Government of London* (London: Joseph Rowntree Foundation, 1997).

J E Turner, *Labour's Doorstep Politics in London* (London: MacMillan, 1978).

John Turner, *British Politics and the Great War* (New Haven: Yale University Press, 1992).

Roger Undy, *Change in the Trade Unions* (London: Hutchinson, 1981).

Alexander Vasudevan, *The Autonomous City. A History of Urban Squatting* (London: Verso, 2017).

Hilary Wainwright, *Labour – A Tale of Two Parties* (London: Hogarth Press, 1987).

Bernard Waites, *A Class Society at War 1914–1918* (London: Berg, 1992).

Kenneth D Wald, *Crosses on the Ballot* (Princeton, 2016).

Edwin Walford & Jeremy Morris, *The Growth of 'New London' in Suburban Middlesex – 1918–1945* (London: Edwin Mellen Press, 2007).

David Walsh, *Making Angels in Marble: The Conservatives, the Early Industrial Working-class and Attempts at Political Incorporation* (London: Breviary Stuff Publications, 2012).

Daniel Weinbren, *Generating Socialism. Recollections of Life in the Labour Party* (Stroud: Sutton Publishing, 1997).

Jonathan Wheatley, *The Changing Shape of Politics: Rethinking Left and Right in a New Britain* (London: Palgrave MacMillan, 2019).

290   *Bibliography*

Jerry White, *Campbell Bunk. The Worst Street in North London between the War* (London: Pimlico, 2003).

Jerry White, *London in the Twentieth Century* (London: Vintage, 2008).

Jerry White, *Zepppelin Nights. London and the First World* War (London: Bodley Head, 2014).

Paul Whiteley, Harold Clarke, David Sanders & Marianne Stewart, *Affluence, Austerity and Electoral Change in Britain* (Cambridge: CUP, 2013).

Peter Willmott & Michael Young, *Family and Kinship in East London* (London: Routledge, 2011).

Clair Wills, *Lovers and Strangers. An Immigration History of Post-War Britain* (London: Allen Lane, 2017).

John F Wilson, Anthony Webster & Rachel Vorberg-Rugh, *Building Co-operation* (Oxford: OUP, 2013).

Alex Windscheffel, *Popular Conservatism in Imperial London* (London: Royal Historical Society, 2007).

Jay Winter, *Socialism and the Challenge of War* (London: Routledge, 2014).

Matthew Worley (ed.), *Labour's Grass Roots: Essays on the Activities of Local Labour Parties and Members 1918–1945* (London: Ashgate, 2005).

Matthew Worley, *Labour Inside the Gate* (London: I B Tauris, 2009).

Ken Young, *Local Politics and the Rise of Party* (Leicester: Leicester University Press, 1975).

Ins Zweiniger-Bargielowska, *Women in Twentieth Century Britain* (New York, Abingdon: Routledge, 2001).

Scholarly articles, research papers, reports and book chapters

Claire Ainsley, 'Winning Back the Working Class,' *IPPR Progressive Review*, 25, 3 (2018).

Sally Alexander, 'A New Civilisation? London Surveyed 1928–1940s,' *History Workshop Journal*, 64, 1 (2007).

Archbishop of Canterbury, *Faith in the City* (London: Church House, 1985).

Lukas Audickas, '*Membership of UK Political Parties*,' House of Commons Briefing Paper, SNO5125 2018.

Lukas Audickas, *UK Election Statistics: 1918–2018*, House of Commons Research Paper, CBP 7529 (2020).

Andrew August, 'A Culture of Consolation? Rethinking Politics in Working-class London, 1870–1914,' *Historical Research*, 74, 184 (2001).

Les Back et al., 'New Labour's White Heart: Politics, Multiculturalism and the Return of Assimilation,' *Political Quarterly*, 73, 4 (2002).

L Bailey & O Baston, *'For the Many.' Understanding and Uniting Labour's Core Supporters* (London: Fabian Society, 2018).

Dudley Baines & Paul Johnson, 'In Search of the 'Traditional' Working Class: Social Mobility and Occupational Continuity in Interwar London,' *Economic History Review*, 52, 4 (1999).

Laura Balderstone, 'Semi-detached Britain? Reviewing Suburban Engagement in Twentieth Century Society,' *Urban History*, 41, 1 (2014).

Tim Bale, Paul Webb & Monica Poletti, *Grass Roots. Britain's Party Members* (London: Mile End Institute/QMC, 2018).

Bibliography 291

John Barnes, Bob Colnutt & Patrick Malone, 'London: Docklands and the State,' in Patrick Malone (ed.), *City, Capital and Water* (London: Routledge, 2014).

Jeff Bartley & Ian Gordon, 'London at the Polls. The 1981 GLC Election Results,' *The London Journal*, 8, 1 (1982).

Lewis Bastion, 'Rising Damp in the Suburbs. Or 'Whatever Happened to the Villa Tory?,' *Political Quarterly*, 90, 1 (2019).

Laura Beers, 'Education or Manipulation? Labour, Democracy and the Popular Press in Interwar Britain,' *Journal of British Studies*, 48, 1 (2009).

Mark Benny & Phyllis Geiss, 'Social Class and Politics in Greenwich,' *British Journal of Sociology*, 1, 4 (1950).

Stefan Berger, 'Herbert Morrison's London Labour Party in the Inter War Years and the SPD.' *European Review of History*, 12, 2 (2005).

Craig Berry, 'Class, Place and Values: Labour's Lost Tribe,' *Renewal*, 26, 4 (2018).

Mark Bevir, 'The Labour Church Movement 1891–1902,' *Journal of British Studies*, 38, 2 (1999).

Paul Bickley & Nathan Mladin, *Religious London: Faith in a Global City* (London: Theos, 2020).

L E I Black, '"Still at the Penny-Farthing Stage in a Jet Propelled Era": Branch Life in 1950s Socialism,' *Labour History Review*, 65, 2 (2000).

Amy Black & Stephen Brooke, 'The Labour Party, Women and the Problem of Gender, 1951–1966,' *Journal of British Studies*, 36 (1997).

Jo Blanden & Stephen Machin, *Recent Changes in Intergenerational Mobility: Report of the Sutton Trust* (2007).

Neal Blewett, 'The Franchise in the United Kingdom 1885–1918,' *Past and Present*, 32 (1965).

Paul Bloomfield, 'Labour's Liberalism: Gay Rights and Video Nasties,' in Jonathan Davis & Rohan McWilliam (eds.), *Labour and the Left in the 1980s* (Manchester: MUP, 2018).

Marc Brodie, 'Free Trade and Cheap Theatres; Sources of Politics for the Nineteenth Century London Poor,' *Social History*, 28, 3 (2003).

Marc Brodie, 'Voting in the Victorian and Edwardian East End of London,' *Parliamentary History*, 23, 2 (2004).

Stephen Brooke, 'Labour and 'The Nation' after 1945,' in Jon Lawrence & Miles Taylor (ed.), *Party, State and Society* (Aldershot: Scolar Press, 1997), pp. 153–175.

Kenneth D Brown, 'London and the Historical Reputation of John Burns,' *London Journal*, 2, 2 (1976), pp. 226–238.

Robin Bunce, 'Race Today Cannot Fail': Black Radicalism in the Long 1980s,' in Jonathan Davis & Rohan McWilliam (eds.), *Labour and the Left in the 1980s* (Manchester: MUP, 2018).

Susannah Bunce, 'Pursuing Urban Commons: Politics and Alliances in Community Land Trust Activism in East London,' *Antipode*, 48, 1 (2016).

Julia Bush, 'East London Jews and the First World War,' *London Journal*, 6, 2 (1980).

Tim Butler, '"People Like us": the Gentrification of Hackney in the 1980s,' in T Butler & M Rustin (eds.), *Rising in the East* (London: Lawrence and Wishart, 1996).

292 *Bibliography*

Tim Butler & Chris Hamnett, 'Walking Backwards to the Future – Waking Up to Class and Gentrification in London,' *Urban Policy and Research*, 27, 3 (2009).

Tim Butler, Chris Hamnett & Mark Ramsden, 'Inward and Upward: Marking Out Social Class Change in London, 1981–2001,' *Urban Studies* 45, 1 (2008).

John Callaghan, 'Ross McKibbin: Class Cultures, the Trade Unions and the Labour Party,' in John Callaghan (ed.), *Interpreting the Labour Party* (Manchester: MUP, 2003).

Rosie Campbell, 'The Average Voter Is a Woman: Sex and Gender Differences,' in Phil Cowley & Robert Ford (eds.), *Sex, Lies and Politics* (London: Biteback Publishing, 2019).

Harold Carter, 'Building the Divided City: Race, Class and Social Housing in Southwark, 1945–1995,' *London Journal*, 33, 2 (2013).

Peter Catterall, 'Morality and Politics: The Free Churches and the Labour Party between the Wars,' *Historical Journal*, 36, 3 (1993).

Centre for Labour and Social Studies, *The Facts and Fixes: Class* (London: Centre for Labour and Social Studies, November 2019).

Centre for Towns, *The Aging of our Towns* (London, 2020).

Michael Childs, 'Labour Grows Up: The Electoral System, Political Generations and British Politics 1890–1929,' *Twentieth Century British History*, 6, 2 (1995).

M Clapson, 'Localism, the London Labour Party and the LCC between the Wars,' in A Saint (ed.), *Politics and the People of London* (London: Hambledon Press, 1989).

Gloria Clifton, 'Members and Officers of the LCC, 1998–1965,' in A Saint (ed.), *Politics and People of London* (London: Hambledon, 1989).

Kevin R Cox, 'Suburbia and Voting Behaviour in the London Metropolitan Area,' *Annals of the Association of American Geographers*, 58, 1 (1968).

R C W Cox, 'Across the Road: Contrast in Urban Development in South Croydon,' *Croydon Natural History and Scientific Society Proceedings*, 13 (1959–1965).

David M Craig, 'High Politics and the New Political History,' *Historical Journal*, 53, 2 (2010).

Ivor Crewe, 'The Labour Party and the Electorate,' in Dennis Kavanagh (ed.), *The Politics of the Labour Party* (London: Routledge, 2012).

James Cronin, 'Coping with Labour, 1918–1926,' in J Cronin & J Schneer (eds.), *Social Conflict and the Political Order* (New Brunswick: Ruthers University Press, 1982).

Gary Cross, 'The Suburban Weekend. Perspectives on a Vanishing Twentieth Century Dream,' in Roger Silverstone (ed.), *Visions of Suburbia* (London: Routledge, 1997).

Jon Cruddas, 'The Left's New Urbanism,' *Political Quarterly*, 90, 1 (2019).

Niall Cunningham & Mike Savage, 'An Intensifying and Elite City: New Geographies of Social Class and Inequality in Contemporary London,' *City*, 21, 1 (2017).

John Curtice, 'Political Sociology, 1945–92,' in Peter Catterall (ed.), *Understanding Post-war British Society* (London: Routledge, 1994).

Sam Davies & Bob Morley, 'Electoral Turnout in County Borough Elections, 1919–1938,' *Labour History Review*, 71, 2 (2006).

John Davis, 'Community and the Labour Left in 1970s London,' in Chris Williams & Andrew Edwards (eds.), *The Art of the Possible* (Manchester: MUP, 2015).

John Davis, 'From GLC to GLA: London Politics from Then to Now,' in Joe Kerr & Andrew Gibson (eds.), *London from Punk to Blair* (London: Reaction Books, 2012), pp. 97–105.

Bibliography 293

John Davis, 'Radical Clubs and London Politics, 1870–1900,' in David Feldman & G S Jones (eds.), *Metropolis London: Histories and Representations since 1800* (London: Routledge, 1989).

John Davis, 'The London Cabbie and the Rise of Essex Man,' in Clare Griffiths et al. (eds.), *Classes, Culture and Politics* (Oxford: OUP, 2011).

Alan Deacon & Eric Briggs, 'Local Democracy and Central Policy: The Issue of Pauper Votes in the 1920s,' *Policy and Politics*, 2, 4 (1974).

Department of Education and Science, *Minority Ethnic Pupils in Maintained Schools* (London: HMSO, 1999).

Danny Dorling, 'Dying Quietly: English Suburbs and the Stiff Upper Lip,' *Political Quarterly*, 90, 1 (2019).

C Dwyer, D Gilbert & B Shah, 'Faith and Suburbia: Secularisation, Modernity and the Changing Geographies of Religion in London's Suburbs,' *Transactions of the Institute of British Geographers*, 38, 3 (2013).

H J Dyos, 'Greater and Greater London: Notes on Metropolis and Provinces in the Nineteenth and Twentieth Centuries,' in J S Bromley & E H Kossmann (eds.), *Britain and the Netherlands*, Vol. 4 (Hague: M Nijhoff, 1971).

Geoffrey Evans & Jonathan Mellon, 'Identity, Awareness and Political Attitudes: Why Are We Still Working-class?,' *British Social Attitudes: The 33rd Report* (2016).

Clive D Field, 'Faith in the Metropolis: Opinion Polls and Christianity in Post-War London,' *The London Journal*, 24, 1 (1999).

Steven Fielding, 'Brotherhood and the Brothers: Responses to 'coloured' Immigration in the British Labour Party c. 1951–1965,' *Journal of Political Ideologies*, 3, 1 (1998).

Steven Fielding, 'Labourism in the 1940s,' *Twentieth Century British History*, 3, 2 (1992).

Steven Fielding, 'What did 'the People' Want? The Meaning of the 1945 General Election,' *Historical Journal*, 35, 3 (1992).

Steven Fielding & Andrew Geddes, 'The British Labour Party and 'ethnic entryism': Participation, Integration and the Party Context,' *Journal of Ethnic and Migration Studies*, 24, 1 (1998).

Stephen Fisher, 'Racism at the Ballot Box: Ethnic Minority Candidates,' in Phil Cowley & Robert Ford (eds.), *Sex, Lies and Politics* (London: Biteback Publishing, 2019).

Stuart Fox, 'Youthquake? The Mystery of the Missing Young Voters,' in Phil Cowley & Robert Ford (eds.), *Sex, Lies and Politics* (London: Biteback Publishing, 2019).

Martin Francis, 'Labour and Gender,' in Tanner (ed.), *Labour's First Century* (Cambridge: CUP, 2007).

Laura Gardiner et al., 'Painting the Towns Blue: Demography, Economy and Living Standards in the Political Geographies Emerging from the 2019 General Election' (Resolution Foundation, 12 February 2020).

Peter Ghosh, 'The Guv'nor: The Place of Ross McKibbin in the Writing of British History,' in Clare Griffiths et al. (eds.), *Classes, Cultures and Politics* (Oxford: OUP, 2011).

D Gilbert, C Dwyer & N Ahmed, 'Ethnic and Religious Diversity in the Politics of Suburban London,' *Political Quarterly*, 90, 1 (2019).

David Gilbert & Rebecca Preston, '"Stop being so English": Suburban Modernity and National Identity in the Twentieth Century,' in D Gilbert (ed.), *Geographies of British Modernity* (Oxford: Blackwell, 2003).

294   *Bibliography*

James Gillespie, 'Poplarism and Proletarianism: Unemployment and Labour Politics in London, 1918–34' in D M Feldman & G Stedman Jones (eds.), *Metropolis London* (London: Routledge, 1989).

Stefan Goebel & Jerry White, 'London and the First World War,' *London Journal,* 41, 3 (2016).

Matthew Goodwin & Oliver Heath, *Low Income Voters, the 2019 General Election and the Future of British Politics* (Joseph Rowntree Foundation, 23 June 2020).

Pamela Graves, 'An Experiment in Women-Centred Socialism: Labour Women in Britain,' in H Gruber & P Graves (eds.), *Women and Socialism, Socialism and Women. Europe between the Two World Wars* (Oxford: Berghahn Books, 1998).

Greater London Authority, *Poverty in London, 2019* (London: GLA, 2020).

P G Hall, 'Industrial London' in J T Coppock & H C Prince (eds.), *Greater London* (London: Faber & Faber, 1964).

Sir Peter Hall, 'London Voices 1957–2007,' *City*, 12, 1 (2008).

Chris Hamnett, 'Gentrification and the Middle-class Remaking of Inner London, 1961–2001,' *Urban Studies*, 40, 12 (2003).

Chris Hamnett, 'London's Turning: the London Effect,' *Marxism Today*, July 1990.

Chris Hamnett & Tim Butler, 'Reclassifying London: A Growing Middle Class and Increasing Inequality,' *City*, 17, 2 (2013).

June Hannam, 'Women and Labour Politics,' in Mathew Worley (ed.), *The Foundations of the British Labour Party* (London: Routledge, 2016).

June Hannam, 'Women as Paid Organisers and Propogandists for the British Labour Party Between the Wars,' *International and Labour Working-Class History*, 77, 1 (2010).

Harry Harmer, 'The Failure of the Communists: the National Unemployed Workers Movement, 1921–1939,' in Andrew Thorpe (ed.), *The Failure of Political Extremism in Interwar Britain* (Liverpool: Liverpool University Press, 2005).

Michael Hart, 'The Liberals, the War and the Franchise,' *English Historical Review*, XCVII, CCCLXXXV (1982).

Nicky Hart, 'Gender and the Rise and Fall of Class Politics,' *New Left Review*, 175, 1 (1989).

David Harvey, 'The Right to the City,' *New Left Review*, 53 (2008).

Owen Hatherley, 'The Government of London,' *New Left Review*, 122 (March–April 2020).

Dianne Hayter, *The Labour Party: Crisis and Prospects* (London: Fabian Society, 1977).

Anthony Heath, 'Ethnic Minority Voters at the Ballot Box,' in O Khan & K Sveinsson (eds.), *Race and Elections* (London: Runnymead Trust, 2015).

Anthony Heath, 'Why Ethnic Minorities Vote Labour: Group Norms,' in P Cowley & R Ford (eds.), *Sex, Lies and the Ballot Box* (London: Biteback, 2014).

Oliver Heath, 'A Growing Class Divide: MPS and Voters,' in P Cowley & R Ford (eds.), *Sex, Lies and the Ballot Box* (London: Biteback, 2014).

Kathleen Heneham, 'Pick Up the Pace: The Slowdown in Educational Attainment Growth and Its Widespread Effects' (London: Resolution Foundation, 18 March 2019).

John Hindell, 'Trade Union Membership,' *Planning*, 28, 463 (July 1962).

James Hinton, 'Women and the Labour Vote, 1945–50,' *Labour History Review*, 57, 3 (1992).

Eric Hobsbawn, 'Labour in the Great City,' *New Left Review*, 1, 116 (1987).

Bibliography 295

Eric Hobsbawn, 'The Making of the Working-Class 1870–1914,' in Eric Hobsbawm (ed.), *Worlds of Labour* (London: Weidenfeld & Nicolson, 1984).

Eric Hobsbawn, 'Marx and History,' *New Left Review*, 1, 143 (1984).

Eric Hobsbawm, 'The Nineteenth Century London Labour Market,' in Eric Hobsbawm (ed.), *Worlds of Labour* (London: Weidenfeld & Nicolson, 1984).

Lester Holloway, *Where Are all the BME Councillors?* (Runnymede Trust, 15 June 2017).

Nancy Holman & Andrew Thornley, 'The Reversal of Strategic Planning in London: The Boris Effect with a Focus on Sustainability,' *Recherche*, 11 (2011).

Janet Howarth, 'Class and Cultures in England after 1951: The Case of Working-Class Women,' in Clare Griffiths et al. (eds.), *Class, Culture and Politics* (Oxford: OUP, 2011).

Karen Hunt, 'The Politics of Food and Women's Neighbourhood Activism in First World War Britain,' *International Labour and Working-Class History*, 77 (2010).

Rupa Huq, 'Postcards from the Edge? Setting the Suburban Scene,' *Political Quarterly*, 90, 1 (2019).

Christopher H Husbands, 'East End Racism 1900–1980,' *London Journal*, 8, 1 (1982).

John Hutchinson, 'Diaspora Dilemmas and Shifting Allegiances: The Irish in London between Nationalism, Catholicism and Labourism (1900–1922),' *Studies in Ethnicity and Nationalism*, 10, 1 (2010).

David Jarvis, 'Mrs Maggs and Betty. The Conservative Appeal to Women Voters in the 1920s,' *Twentieth Century British History*, 5, 2 (1994).

Tom Jeffery, 'The Suburban Nation. Politics and Class in Lewisham,' in D M Feldman & G Stedman Jones (eds.), *Metroplois London* (London: Routledge, 1989).

William Jennings & Jerry Stoker, 'Tilting towards the Cosmopolitan Axis? Political Change in England and the 2017 General Election,' *Political Quarterly*, 88, 2 (2017).

Joy Johnson, 'Perfect Political Storm,' *Political Quarterly*, 3, 79 (2008).

Ron Johnstone et al., 'House Price Increases and Higher Density Housing Occupation: The Response of Non-white Households in London, 2001–2011,' *International Journal of Housing Policy*, 16, 3 (2016).

R J Johnston, D J Rossiter & C J Pattie, *Three Classifications of Great Britain's New Parliamentary Constituencies* (Colchester: University of Essex Department of Government, 1977).

Gareth Stedman Jones, 'Working-Culture and Working-Class Politics in London, 1870–1900,' *Journal of Social History*, 7, 4 (1974).

Peter Joyce, 'The Liberal Party and the Popular Front: An Assessment of the Arguments over Progressive Unity in the 1930s,' *Journal of Liberal History*, 28 (2000).

Paul Keleman, 'Zionism and the British Labour Party: 1917–1939,' *Social History*, 21, 1 (1996).

Omar Khan, *One Nation Boris? Not for Black or Asian Londoners* (London: Runnymede Trust, 21 July 2019).

Helen Kim, '"We're Just Like Everyone Else! Rethinking the Cultural Politics of London Asian Urban Music Scene,' *European Journal of Cultural Studies*, 20, 2 (2017).

Michael Kullmann, 'Notting Hill Hustings,' *New Left Review*, 1 (1960).

Labour Together, *Election Review 2019* (June 2020).

The Lambeth Inner Area Study: Changes in Socio-Economic Structure (DOE, 1975).

296 Bibliography

Jon Lawrence, 'The British Sense of Class,' *Journal of Contemporary History*, 35, 2 (2000).

Jon Lawrence, 'Movement Politics, the Electoral Machine and the "masses": Lessons from the Early Labour Party,' *Renewal*, 24, 3 (2016).

Jon Lawrence, 'Political History,' in S Berger, H Feldner & K Passmore (eds.), *Writing History: Theory and Practice* (London, 2010).

Jon Lawrence & M Taylor, 'Electoral Sociology and the Historians,' in Jon Lawrence & Miles Taylor (eds.), *Party, State and Society* (Aldershot: Scolar Press, 1997).

Loretta Lees, 'The Urban Injustices of New Labour's "New Urban renewal": The Case of the Aylesbury Estate in London,' *Antipode*, 46, 4 (2014).

David M Levinson, 'The Orderliness Hypothesis. The Correlation of Rail and Housing Development in London,' *Journal of Transport History*, 29, 1 (2008).

Fred Lindop, "Racism and the Working Class: Strikes in Support of Enoch Powell in 1968," *Labour History Review*, 66, 1 (Spring 2001).

Jane Martin, 'Engendering City Politics and Educational Thought: Elite Women and the London Labour Party, 1914–1965,' *Paedogogica Historica*, 44, 54 (2008).

Linda McDowell et al., 'Precarious Work and Economic Migration: Emerging Immigrant Divisions of Labour in Greater London's Service Sector,' *International Journal of Urban and Regional Research*, 32, 1 (2009).

Rebecca McKeee, 'Signed, Sealed and Delivered…Testing Politicians' Responsiveness to Voters,' in Phil Cowley & Robert Ford (eds.), *Sex, Lies and Politics* (London: Biteback Publishing, 2019).

Donald McNeil, 'Livingstone's London: Left Politics and the World City,' *Regional Studies*, 36, 1 (2002).

S Majima & M Savage, 'Contesting Affluence,' *Contemporary British History*, 22, 4 (2008).

Ross McKibbin, 'The Franchise Factor in the Rise of Labour,' *English Historical Review*, 91, 361 (1976).

John Marriott, 'The Political Modernism of East London,' in T Butler & M Rustin (eds.), *Rising in the East* (London: Lawrence and Wishart, 1996).

Nicole Martin, 'A Demographic Time Bomb: The Right and Ethnic Diversity,' in Phil Cowley & Robert Ford (eds.), *Sex, Lies and Politics* (London: Biteback Publishing, 2019).

Nicole Martin, 'Ethnic Minority Voters in the UK 2015 General Election: A Breakthrough for the Conservative Party?' *Electoral Studies*, 57 (2019).

N Martin & O Kkan, *Ethnic Minorities at the 2017 British General Election* (London: Runnymede Trust, February 2019).

T Mason & P Thompson, '"Reflections on a revolution?": The Political Mood in Wartime Britain,' in N Tiratsoo (ed.), *The Attlee Years* (London: Continuum, 1991).

Doreen Massey, 'The World we're in: An Interview with Ken Livingstone,' *Soundings*, 36 (Summer 2007).

Stuart Middleton, 'Affluence' and the Left in Britain, c.1958–1974,' *English Historical Review*, 129, 536 (2014).

Milner Holland Report on London Housing (1965) Cmd. 2605.

Kenneth O Morgan, 'The Boer War and the Media (1899–1902),' *Twentieth Century British History*, 13, 1 (2002).

Jeremy Morris, *The Nonconformist Experience in Croydon* (Croydon: Croydon Natural History & Scientific Society, 1992).

Bibliography 297

Jeremy Morris, 'Secularisation and Religious Experience,' *Historical Journal*, 55, 1 (2012).

M Muroki & P Cowley, 'Getting Better Slowly. Ethnicity, Gender and Party in London's Local Government,' *Political Quarterly*, 90, 1 (2019).

Katrina Navickas, 'What Happened to Class?,' *Social History*, 36, 2 (2011).

Simon Naylor & James Ryan, 'The Mosque in the Suburbs: Negotiating Religion and Ethnicity in South London,' *Social and Cultural Geography*, 3, 1 (2002).

Pippa Norris, 'Elections and Public Opinion,' in A Seldon & D Kavanagh (eds.), *The Blair Effect 2001–5* (Cambridge: CUP, 2005).

James M Nott, '"The Plague Spots of London": William Joyson-Hicks, the Conservative Party, and the Campaign against London's Nightclubs, 1924–29,' in Clare Griffiths et al. (eds.), *Classes, Cultures and Politics* (Oxford: OUP, 2011).

Avner Offer, 'British Manual Workers: From Producers to Consumers c. 1950–2000,' *Contemporary British History*, 22, 4 (2008).

Teresa Olcott, 'Dead Centre: 'The Womens's Trade Union Movement in London, 1874–1914,' *London Journal*, 2, 1 (1976).

P Panayi, 'Cosmopolis: London's Ethnic Minorities,' in J Kerr & A Gibson (eds.), *London from Punk to Blair* (London: Reaktion, 2003).

Charles Pattie & Ron Johnston, 'A Low Turnout Landslide: Abstention at the British General Election of 1997,' *Political Studies*, 49 (2001).

Daisey Payling, '"Socialist Republic of South Yorkshire': Grassroots Activism and Left-Wing Solidarity in 1980s Sheffield,' *Twentieth Century British History*, 25, 4 (2014).

Sarah Perrigo, 'Women and Change in the Labour Party 1979–1995,' *Parliamentary Affairs*, 49, 1 (1996).

Thomas Picketty, '"Brahmin Left" vs "Merchant Right". Rising Inequality and the Changing Structure of Political Conflict,' (Wid.word Working Paper Series No. 2018/7, March 2018).

Ben Pimlott, 'The Socialist League: Intellectuals and the Labour Left in the 1930s,' *Journal of Contemporary History*, 6, 3 (1971).

Martin Pugh, '"Class Traitors": Conservative Recruits to Labour 1900–1930,' *English Historical Review*, CXIII, 450 (1998).

Martin Pugh, 'The Rise of Labour and the Political Culture of Conservatism 1890–1945,' *History*, 87, 288 (2002).

Paul Readman,'The Conservative Party, Patriotism and British Politics,' *Journal of British Studies*, 40, 1 (2001).

Alastair J Reid, 'Class and Politics in the Work of Henry Pelling,' in John Callaghan (ed.), *Interpreting the Labour Party* (Manchester: MUP, 2003).

Neil Riddell, 'The Catholic Church and the Labour Party, 1918–1931,' *Twentieth Century British History*, 8, 2 (1997).

Matthew Roberts, 'Popular Conservatism in Britain, 1832–1914,' *Parliamentary History*, 26, 3 (2007).

N Robertson, 'A Union of Forces Marching in the Same Direction: The Relationship between the Co-op and Labour Parties 1918–39,' in M Worley (ed.), *Foundations of the British Labour Party Parties* (London: Ashgate, 2009).

Emily Robinson, Camilla Schofield, Florence Sutcliffe-Braithwaite & Natalie Tomlinson, 'Telling Stories about Post-war Britain: Popular Individualism and the 'Crisis' of the 1970s,' *Twentieth Century British History*, 28, 2 (2017).

Garry Robson & Tim Butler, 'Coming to Terms with London: Middle-Class Communities in a Global City,' *International Journal of Urban and Regional Research*, 25, 1 (March 2001).

298   *Bibliography*

Gillian Rose, 'Locality-Studies and Waged Labour: An Historical Critique,' *Transactions of the Institute of British Geographers,* New Series, 14, 3 (1989).

Caroline Rowan, 'Women in the Labour Party, 1906–1920.' *Feminist Review,* No. 12 (1982).

Gwyn Rowley, 'The Greater London Council Elections of 1964 and 1967: A Study in Electoral Geography,' *Transactions of the Institute of British Geographers,* 53 (1971).

Andrew Saint, '"Spread the People": The LCC's Dispersal Policy, 1889–1965,' in A Saint (ed.), *Politics and the People of London* (London: Hambledon Press, 1989).

Raphael Samuel, 'Empire Stories: the Imperial and the Domestic,' in *Island Stories,* Vol. 2 (London: Verso, 1998).

Raphael Samuel, 'The Lost World of British Communism,' *New Left Review,* 154 (1958).

Michael Savage, 'Understanding Political Alignments in Contemporary Britain: Do Localities Matter?,' *Political Geography Quarterly,* 6, 1 (1987).

Michael Savage, 'Urban History and Social Class: Two Paradigms,' *Urban History,* 20, 1 (1993).

Michael Savage et al., 'Ordinary, Ambivalent and Defensive Class Identities in the North-West of England' *Sociology,* 35, 4 (2001).

John Saville, 'The Ideology of Labourism,' *Socialist Register* (1967).

Lord Scarman, *The Scarman Report* (London: Penguin, 1981).

Peter Scott & Peter Walsh, 'Patterns and Determinants of Manufacturing Plant Location in Interwar London,' *Economic History Review,* 57, 1 (2004).

A W Singham, 'Immigration and the Election,' in D Butler & A King (eds.), *The British General Election of 1964* (London: MacMillan, 1965).

D Snoussi & L Mompelat, *'We are Ghosts'. Race, Class and Institutional Prejudice* (Runnymede Trust, 2019).

Maria Sobolewska, 'Is Labour Losing the Ethnic Minority Vote?,' *New Statesman* (5 January, 2015).

C T Stannage, 'The East Fulham By-election,' *Historical Journal,* 14, 1 (1971).

Christopher Stevens, 'The Electoral Sociology of Modern Britain Reconsidered,' *Contemporary British History,* 13, 1 (1999).

Richard Stevens, 'Containing Radicalism: The TUC Organisation Department and Trades Councils, 1928–1953,' *Labour History Review,* 62, I (1997).

Gerry Stoker, 'Inner-city Policy in Britain,' *Urban Affairs Review,* 32, 3 (1997).

Patrick Sturgis et al., 'Ethnic Diversity, Segregation and Social Cohesion of Neighbourhoods in London,' *Ethnic and Racial Studies,* 37, 8 (2014).

Duncan Tanner, 'Elections, Statistics, and the Rise of the Labour Party,' *Historical Journal,* 34, 4 (1991).

Duncan Tanner, 'Gender, Civic Culture and Politics in South Wales: Explaining Labour Municipal Policy, 1918–39,' in Matthew Worley (ed.), *Labour's Grass Roots* (Aldershot: Ashgate, 2005).

Duncan Tanner, 'Labour and Its Membership,' in D Tanner (ed.), *Labour's First Century* (Cambridge: CUP, 2007).

Duncan Tanner, 'The Parliamentary Electoral System, the Fourth Reform Act and the Rise of Labour in England and Wales,' *Historical Research,* 56, 134 (1983).

Alan Taylor, 'The Effect of Electoral Pacts on the Decline of the Liberal Party,' *British Journal of Political Science,* 3, 2 (1973).

Pat Thane, 'The Impact of Mass Democracy on British Political Culture, 1918–1939,' in J Gottlieb & R Toye (eds.), *The Aftermath of Suffrage* (London: Palgrave MacMillan, 2013).

Pat Thane, 'The Women of the British Labour Party and Feminism, 1900–1945,' in Harold L Smith (ed.), *British Feminism in the Twentieth Century* (London: Edward Elgar, 1989).

Brinley Thomas, 'The Movement of Labour into South-East England, 1920–32,' *Economica*, 1, 2 (1934).

Paul Thompson, 'Liberals, Radicals and Labour in London 1880–1900,' *Past & Present*, 27, 1 (1964).

Andrew Thorpe, 'The Membership of the Communist Party of Great Britain, 1920–1945,' *Historical Journal*, 43, 3 (2000).

Michael Thrasher et al., 'BAME Candidates in Local Elections in Britain,' *Parliamentary Affairs*, 66, 2 (2013).

James Tilley, '"We Don't Do God"? Religion and Party Choice in Britain,' *British Journal of Political Science*, 45 (2014).

Adam Tinson et al., *London's Poverty Profile* (New Policy Institute, 2017).

Nick Tiratsoo, 'Labour and the Electorate,' in D Tanner (ed.), *Labour's First Century* (Cambridge: CUP, 2007).

Nick Tiratsoo, 'Popular Politics, Affluence and the Labour Party in the 1950s,' in A Gorst (ed.), *Contemporary British History* (London: Institute of Contemporary British History, 1991).

Nigel Todd, 'Labour Women: A Study of Women in the Bexley Branch of the British Labour Party,' *Journal of Contemporary History*, 8, 2 (1973).

Jim Tomlinson, 'De-industrialisation: Strengths and Weaknesses as a Key Concept for Understanding Post-war British History,' *Urban History* (May 2019).

John Turner, 'The Labour Vote and the Franchise after 1918,' in P Denley & D Hopkin (eds.), *History and Computing* (Manchester: MUP, 1987).

John Turner, 'Sex, Age and the Labour Vote in the 1920s,' in Peter Denley & Deian Hopkin (eds.), *History and Computing*, Vol. 2 (Manchester: MUP, 1989).

Satham Virdee & Brendan McGeever, 'Racism, Crisis, Brexit,' *Ethnic and Racial Studies*, 41, 10 (2018).

R Alan Walks, 'City-Suburban Electoral Polarisation in GB, 1950–2001,' *Transactions of the Institute of British Geographers*, 30, 4 (December 2005).

Michael Ward, *Municipal Socialism. The London Labour Party at County Hall 1934–81* (London: Wandsworth Community Publications, 1981).

S Waterman & B Kosmin, 'Residential Patterns and Processes: A Study of Jews in Three London Boroughs,' *Transactions of the British Geographical Society*, 13, 1 (1988).

Chris Waters, 'Progressives, Puritans and the Cultural Politics of the Council, 1889–1914' in A Saint (ed.), *Politics and the People of London* (London: Hambledon Press, 1989).

Paul Watt, 'The Only Class in Town? Gentrification and the Middle-Class Colonisation of the City and the Urban Imagination,' *International Journal of Urban and Regional Research*, 32, 1 (2008).

Paul Watt, '"It's not for us": Regeneration, the 2012 Olympics and the Gentrification of East London,' *City*, 17, 1 (2013).

Paul Watt, 'Respectability, Roughness and 'Race'. Neighbourhood Place Images and the Making of Working-Class Distinctions in London,' *International Journal of Urban and Regional Research*, 30, 4 (2006).

R J Webber, *Parliamentary Constituencies: A Socio-economic Classification* (London: OPCS, 1978).

Daniel Weinbren, 'Building Communities, Constructing Identities,' *London Journal*, 23, 1 (1998).

300 *Bibliography*

Daniel Weinbren, 'Labour Representation in Woolwich,' *Labour History Review*, 59, 3 (1994).

Daniel Weinbren, 'Sociable Capital: London's Labour Parties, 1918–1945' in M Worley (ed.), *Labour's Grass Roots* (Aldershot: Ashgate, 2005).

J H Westergaard, 'The Structure of Greater London,' in R Glass (ed.), *London: Aspects of Change* (London: MacGibbon, 1964).

Richard Whiting, 'Affluence and Industrial Relations in Post-War Britain,' *Contemporary British History*, 22, 4 (2008).

Paul Whitely, 'The National Front Vote in the 1977 GLC Elections,' *British Journal of Political Science*, 9, 3 (1979).

Paul Whiteley, 'Where Have All the Members Gone?,' *Parliamentary Affairs*, 62, 2 (2009).

Paul Whiteley et al., 'Oh Jeremy Corbyn! Why Did Labour Party Membership Soar after the 2015 General Election?,' *British Journal of Politics and International Relations*, 21, 1 (2019).

Jane Wills, 'The Geography of Community and Political Organisation in London Today,' *Political Geography*, 31 (2012).

Jane Wills, 'Making Class Politics Possible: Organising Contract Cleaners in London,' *International Journal of Urban and Regional Research*, 32, 2 (2008).

Peter Wilmott & Michael Young, 'Social Class and Geography,' in D Donnison & D Everley (eds.), *London: Urban Patterns, Problems, and Policies* (London: Heinemann, 1973).

Alex Windscheffel, '"In Darkest Lambeth": Henry Morton Stanley and the Imperial Politics of London Unionism,' in M Cragoe & A Taylor (eds.), *London Politics, 1760–1914* (London: Palgrave Macmillan, 2005).

Jonathan Wood, 'Socialist Outlook and Socialist Fellowship: The Labour Left, Trotskyist Entrism and the Cold War,' *Labour Heritage Bulletin*, Summer 2019.

Jamie Woodcock, 'Precarious Workers in London: New Forms of Organisation and the City,' *City*, 18, 6 (2014).

David M Young, 'Social Democratic Federation Membership in London,' *Historical Research*, 78, 201 (2005).

Jonathan Zeitlin, 'Craft Control and the Division of Labour: Engineers and Compositors in Britain 1890–1930,' *Cambridge Journal of Economics*, 3, 3 (1979).

Unpublished theses and manuscripts

Theses

Hugh Atkinson, 'The Rise and Fall of the London New Urban Left in London Labour Politics 1976–1987' (Ph.D., South Bank University, 1995).

R C W Cox, 'Urban Development and Redevelopment in Croydon, 1835–1940' (Leicester: University of Leicester, Ph.D., 1970).

James Gillespie, 'Economic and Political Change in the East End of London during the 1920s' (Cambridge: University of Cambridge, Ph.D., 1984).

Barbara Humphries, 'The Origins and Development of the Labour Movement in West London, 1918–1970' (Reading: University of Reading, Ph.D., 2021).

Arthur Marwick, 'The ILP 1918–1932' (Oxford: University of Oxford, B. Litt. 1960).

Bibliography 301

Richard Passmore, 'The Response of Labour-controlled Local Authorities to Major Changes in Housing Policy, 1971–1983' (London: University of London, Ph.D., 2015).

Gillian Rose, 'Locality, Politics and Culture: Poplar in the 1920s' (London: London University Ph.D., 1989).

Michael Tichelar, 'Labour Politics in Croydon, 1880–1914' (London: Thames Polytechnic BA Dissertation 1975) – Deposited in the Croydon Archives.

Heidi Topman, 'A Study of the Rise and Decline of Selected Labour Halls in the Greater London Area, 1918–1979' (Ph.D. University of Kingston, 2006).

Manuscripts

Cyril Pearce, The Anti-war Movement in Croydon 1914–1918 (Croydon Archives).

F G West, The Beginnings of Labour in Croydon. The Pioneers, 1890–1918 (Croydon Archives).

Index

Abercrombie, Patrick 48, 65
Abbott, Dianne 229, 239
abortion 213
acton 140
Acts of Parliament: Aliens Act
(1905) 219; British Nationality Act
(1948) 106, 221; Commonwealth
Immigration Act (1962) 106, 221,
227; Equal Pay Act (1970) 217;
Equality Act (2010) 231; Housing
Finance Act, (1972) 60, 149, 196;
Local Government Act (1985) 265;
Local Government & Planning Act
(1980) 63; London Government Act
(1899) 264; London Government Act
(1963) 264–5; Military Services Act
(1916) 111; Qualification of Women
Act (1987) 136; Representation of
the People's Act (1918) 18, 127; Trade
Board Act (1909) 109; Trades Dispute
and Trade Union Act (1927) 181
Addison, Christopher 32
affluence 10, 55, 57, 132, 215
Amalgamated Engineering Union
(AEU) 95–6, 100, 139
Amalgamated Society of Carpenters and
Joiners 108
Amalgamated Society of Railway
Servants 108, 137
Amalgamated Society of Watermen
25, 138
Ambrose, Robert 37, 232
Anderson, W. C. 111
Anti-Nazi League 220
anti-semitism 14, 86, 239–42
apathy, political 37, 55, 94, 100–2, 129,
152–5
Arab population 220
Atkin, Sharon 228

Attlee, Clement 25, 55, 188, 191
austerity 85, 88, 248, 251, 254

Baldwin, Stanley 181, 246, 259
Balfour Declaration 239–40
Bangladeshi community 126, 220
Banks, Tony 147
Barking 53
Barlow report 6
Barnet 241
Baron's Court 52
Battersea 24, 33, 39, 45, 83, 116, 118, 189
Beacontree Estate 46, 104
Bellos, Linda 199
Benn, John Sir 136, 139
Benn, Tony 68, 136, 197, 200, 228, 248
Berger, Luciania 241
Berlin 5
Bermondsey 22, 30, 32, 45, 49, 51, 61,
83, 109, 120–1, 180, 197
Bethnal Green 26, 32–3, 38, 53, 80, 173
Bevan, Aneurin 169
Beveridge Report 49
Bevin, Ernest 187
Bexley 215
Bhownaggree, Mancherjee, Sir 173
Birth control 210, 213
Bishop, William 135
black coated proletariat 30, 43, 68, 95,
102, 129, 177, 246
black churches 232, 237–9
black electorate 64, 73, 78–80, 126, 145,
151, 203, 230, 257
Black Lives Matter 232
black population 265–9
black power 227
black sections 207, 225–232
black socialist society 229
Blair, Tony 75, 150, 199, 205, 260

304   *Index*

Blatchford, Robert 239
Blitz 104–5, 125
blue labour 201
Boateng, Paul 229
Boer War 6, 137, 173
Bow & Bromley 25
Bow & Poplar 211
Bourdieu, Pierre 118
Bowerman, Charles 100
Bradford 225
Brent 27, 34, 64–5, 70, 118
Brent North 82
Briant, Frank 139
British Nationalist Party 122, 249
British Socialist Party 26, 37, 177, 188
British Union of Fascists 220
Brixton 26, 53, 74, 99, 105, 114, 117, 134
Brockway, Fenner 220, 226
Brockwell Park 99
Bromley 22
Brotherhood Church 175, 233, 237
Brown, Gordon 76, 231
Burns, John 11, 24, 103
Busmen Rank and File Movement 190

cab drivers 111
cable street 220, 235
Callaghan, James 58
Camberwell 26, 32
Campaign Against Racist
    Discrimination (CARD) 220, 227
Campaign for Labour Party Democracy
    (CLPD) 197, 200
Campaign for Nuclear Disarmament
    (CND) 52, 59, 195, 203
Campbell Bunk 103
Cardiff 106, 221
Catholic Church 168, 200, 213, 219,
    232–3, 236–7
Census 41, 43
Centre for Contemporary Cultural
    Studies 227
Chamberlain, Joseph 259
Chamberlain, Ronald 192, 194
Charitable organisations 28, 245
Chartism 101, 131, 233
Chelsea 19, 45, 70, 155
Christian socialism 192
Church of England 174, 233–4
City of London 19, 62, 77, 260, 264
civil servants 181
Clapham 26, 50–1, 114, 149
Class *see* social class

Clause four 180, 195
Clay Cross, Derbyshire 60, 196
Clerkenwell 65
Cobbett, William 6
Commonwealth Party 192
Communist Party of Great Britain
    (CPGB) 29, 35, 45, 168–9, 185–92,
    250, 260
community identity *see* neighbourhood
    identity
Community Land Trusts 253
conscientious objection 179
conservatism, popular 23, 25–6, 30
conservative party 18, 19, 24, 45, 68, 78,
    191–2, 215
conscription 111
constituency classifications 65,
    129–31, 147
cooperative movement 34, 209, 247
Cooperative Party 34, 188
Corbett, Freda 216
Corbyn, Jeremy 11, 13, 67, 85, 156, 170,
    201, 241
Coseage, Percival, 179
Covent Garden 62
Cressingham Gardens, Lambeth 75, 253
Cripps, Stafford 169, 191
Crooks, Will 11, 36, 103, 110, 177
Crossland, Anthony 55, 169
Crossman, Richard 169
Croydon 18, 22, 27, 64–5, 66–8, 70,
    82; electorate (1915–1918) 140;
    housing 107–8; suburban expansion
    of 107–114, 117; trade union
    organisation 108, 110–12
Croydon Central 72
Croydon East 143
Croydon Labour Party 175–6
Croydon Liberal Party 142
Croydon North 114
Croydon North West 57, 198
Croydon South 66, 72, 82–3, 112, 143
Croydon Trades & Labour Council 113,
    175–6
Crystal Palace 107
Cruddas, John 152

Dagenham 21, 28, 40, 53, 152, 217
Dale, John 136
Dartford, Kent 83, 123
Dawson, Agnes 209
de-alignment (class) 12, 124, 132,
    147, 249

Index 305

de-industrialisation 12, 58, 66, 98, 114–18
demographic changes 59, 62, 64, 74, 258, 267
Deptford 25–6, 31, 45, 100
Disraeli, Benjamin 68
Dobson, Frank 56
Dock Labour Scheme 63
Docks 21, 27, 30, 47, 63, 123
Doulton Pottery Factory 105
Dubs, Alf 118
Dulwich & West Norwood 65, 115, 148

Ealing 9
East Fulham 39
East Ham 37
Edge City 83, 117
Edmonton 30, 38
educational attainment 59, 83, 89, 117, 126, 152
election agents 180, 186
election results, metropolitan borough councils 276–7
election results, parliamentary *see* General Elections
election results, regional (LCC, GLC, Assembly) 275–6
elections, boards of guardians 30, 33
elections, school boards (1900) 135
elections, turnout 7, 29, 37, 84, 87, 145, 249, 273
electoral registers 25, 30, 38, 141
Eltham 83, 122
equality legislation 57, 73, 206, 219, 250
ethnic minorities *see* black electorate, black population, black sections, race

Fabian Society 72, 172, 175
Fabians 4, 22, 24, 31, 127
Faith in the City 225, 237
family allowances 210, 213
feminism 57, 59, 170, 203, 208, 243, 247
feminism, second wave 210, 218
Financial crash (2008) 77, 151, 248, 252
Finchley 48, 232, 241
Finsbury 26, 173
Flapper Vote 40
Foot, Michael 169, 197
Ford, Charles 137
Franchise 3, 9, 18, 24–5, 29, 31, 37–8, 129, 139
Fraser, John 199–200
Fulham 31, 51, 140

Galloway, George 79
Gambling 26
Ganley, Caroline 34, 216
Gants Hill 122
Gas Workers Union 174
Gay rights 243
Geldhart, Rev. E M 234
gender 208–219; *see also* feminism; women's sections; Women's Cooperative Guild; Women's Labour League
general elections: (1900) 137; (1906) 134–5, 138; (1910) 25, 133, 139, 157; (1918) 36, 139, 158; (1929) 2, 17, 140, 159; (1935) 142, 160; (1945) 2, 3, 10, 49, 143, 153, 161; (1964) 145; (1966) 162;(1974 February) 147, 163; (1979) 147, 164; (1997) 2, 4, 70, 148, 165;(2001) 71; (2005) 71; (2010) 71; (2015) 10, 67, 71;(2017) 4, 6, 7, 13, 67, 149–50, 166, 219, 241; (2019) 4, 5, 6, 7, 13, 14, 67, 71, 78, 155, 241
general election results 274–5
General Strike (1926) 33, 35, 95, 98, 169, 181, 246
Generation Rent 80, 148, 254
gentrification 56, 60–1, 75, 114–18, 223
Gladstone–MacDonald Pact (1904) 176
Glass, Ruth 6, 61
Glennie, William 139
globalisation 80, 248
Golders Green 232
Goldsmith, Zac 258
Gosling, Harry 25, 110, 138, 178
Gould, Ayrton 139
Grayson, Victor 128
Greater London Area, definition 264–5
Greater London Council (GLC) 4, 10, 30, 45, 54, 64, 76, 206, 247, 265
Green Belt 4, 46, 76
Green Party 149, 249
Greenwich 31, 32, 50, 57, 122
Greenwich Election Survey (1950) 50
Grenfell Tower Fire 85
Griffiths, Peter 226
Gulf War 199

Hackney 9, 39, 53, 62, 64–5, 74; industry, 99, 101–2
Hall, Peter, Sir 7, 74, 118–9, 125, 230
Hall, Stuart 206, 222
Hammersmith 39, 46, 52, 140
Hampstead 45, 155

306   *Index*

Hardie, Keir 24, 121, 137, 172
Haringey 253
Harris, Percy 140
Harrison, James 52
Harrow 48
Hayes 66
Hayter, Dianne 198
Hattersley, Roy 228
Healey, Gerald 196
Henderson, Arthur 37
Hendon, 113, 232
Herbert Commission (1960) 60
Hoey, Kate 229
Hollamby, Edward 75
Holland, Stuart 229
Homophobia 207
Hounslow 69, 78
Housing 59, 74, 76, 82, 96, 116, 148,
   224–5, 247, 250
Howell, George 173
Hughes, Simon 61, 197
Hyndman, Henry 172, 239

identity politics 11, 55, 57, 206–244, 255
Ilford 70, 122, 232
immigration 5, 22, 63, 70, 96, 145, 226
immigration controls 219
imperialism 19–28
Independent Labour Party (ILP) 11, 24,
   26–7, 31, 96, 168, 188–90, 203, 250
inequality 9, 69, 77, 80–4, 88, 132, 151–4,
   252, 257
Inner City policy 98–106, 223
Inner London Education Authority
   (ILEA) 10, 45
Iraq War 71, 170, 202, 220, 248
Iremonger, Charles 135, 173
Irish 24, 37, 52, 219, 236
Iron Founders Society 135, 173
Isaacs, George 33, 100
Islam 238–9, 242
Isle of Dogs 64, 74, 116
Islington 38, 46, 53, 62, 74, 102, 140

Jewish ghetto 233–5
Jewish migration 235
Jews, 20, 37, 99, 115, 168, 175, 190, 219
Johnson, Boris 11, 71, 76, 81, 85, 257
Jones, Jack 11, 36
Joseph, Keith 52
Joyce, William 53

Kennington 99, 104, 114, 134
Kensington 19, 25, 51, 70, 85, 87, 155

Khan, Sadiq 1, 11, 67, 77, 81, 201, 231,
   257
Kinnock, Neil 198, 229
Knee, Fred 31, 100
Knight, Ted 147, 169, 194, 196–7,
   199, 239

Labour Aristocracy 134
Labour Church Movement 176
Labour Party Constitution (1918) 180,
   210
Labour Party black membership 230
Labour Party membership 31, 78–9, 150,
   180–6, 191–3, 201–2, 209, 247
Labour Party organisation 55, 193
Labour Party, prospects 256
Labour Representation Committee
   (LRC 1900) 172, 204
Labour Solidarity Campaign 198
Labour Together (Report 2020) 6
labourism 8, 10, 54, 60, 69, 96, 131,
   138–40, 171, 204
Lambeth 9, 30, 32–3, 60, 64, 98–106,
   219–231; black population
   106–7, 220–24; social structure
   115–17; voting and social class
   133–8; socialism 172–4; trade union
   organisation 100–1, 105, 109
Lambeth Central 149, 193–4
Lambeth Council 75, 135, 196, 199
Lambeth Inner Area Study 223
Lambeth Trades Council 135, 172–3, 177
Lambeth Walk 104–5
Lammy, David 126, 244
Lancashire 68
Land reform 27, 74, 136, 178
Lansbury, George 1, 11, 23, 28, 33, 37,
   174, 188, 190, 211
Lansman, John 200
Lawrence, Susan 212
Lax, William 235, 237
law centres 59
Lea Valley 21, 30, 66
League of Nations 36
Leicester 235
Leyton 30
Lewisham 30, 192
Liberal Democrats 34, 57, 86, 149, 199
Liberal Party 4, 19, 24, 26, 31–2, 35, 140,
   171, 181
Liddle, Roger 198
Limehouse 202
Lipton, Marcus 192, 229
Liverpool 2, 87, 97, 106, 137, 167, 197

Living Wage Campaign 252–3
Livingstone, Ken 11, 54–5, 59, 68, 76, 81, 147, 194, 196, 239–40
local government 47, 95, 168, 170, 195–6, 202, 247–9
locality-studies 94, 96–8, 128, 167
Lock, William 174
Lodgers 25, 38, 40, 141
London: de-industrialisation 4, 12, 58, 98, 114–8; East End 3, 21, 24–5, 30, 35–6, 47, 53–4, 66; labour market 22, 27, 41–2, 64; migration 221–4; population 265; problem of 5; social structure 82–88; World City 1
London Cooperative Society 34, 188, 192
London County Council (LCC) 3, 18, 22, 25, 30, 34, 46, 246, 264
London Docklands Development Corporation 63
London Labour Briefing, 206, 240
London Labour Party 24, 29, 53, 60, 63, 95, 181, 185
London Passenger Transport Board 47
London School of Economics 50
London Society of Compositors (LSC) 100, 108, 187–8
London Trades Council 26, 41, 185, 190
London & Provincial Union of Licensed Vehicle Workers 111
Loony Left 56, 207
Low, Sidney 18–19

MacDonald, Ramsay 1, 17, 128, 259
McDonnell, John 11
Mafeking 21, 137
Major, John 83, 146
Manchester 2, 87, 97, 137, 167
Mandelson, Peter 198
Marxism 96–8, 137, 170–1
Marxism Today 61
Massey, Doreen 68
Masterman, Charles 18–19
Maternity rights 210
Mendelsohn, Vivien 195
Men's League for Women's Suffrage 211
Meritocracy 80–1, 88
MetropolitanRadical Federation 22
Middlesex 21, 193, 202
Miliband, Ed 204
Miliband, Ralph 96, 171, 195
Militant Tendency 198, 201, 225
Milner Holland Report 225
Momentum 5, 67, 170, 200–5

Morrison, Herbert 11, 29, 30–1, 33, 39, 46, 99, 146, 186, 190
Mosley, Oswald 35, 52–3, 220
Muddie-Smith, Richard 234
Muggeridge, Henry 175–6, 179
Muggeridge, Malcolm 179
Municipal Reform Party 18, 46, 135–6, 173, 236, 249
Music halls 103, 109

Nandy, Lisa 259
Naoroji, Dadabhai 173
Napiers 105
Naruyan, Rudy 147, 229
National Federation of Women Workers 212
National Front 53, 196, 229
National Union of Clerks 43, 212
National Union of Fascists 223
National Union of Police & Prison Officers 136
National Union of Railway Men (NUR) 188
National Union of Teachers (NUT) 227
Neighbourhood identity 94–7, 102, 118–24, 224, 250, 259
New Labour 12, 45, 55, 70, 170, 200, 248
New Left 4, 10, 45, 54–5, 60, 168, 170, 194–206
New Liberalism 26, 47, 57, 68
New Political History 97, 167, 171–2
New Survey of London Life and Labour 3, 103
New Unionism 24, 101, 109, 172
New York 1, 5, 8, 76
Newham 53, 63, 74, 121
Non-conformism 2, 3, 24, 207, 233–4, 236
Non-Conscription Fellowship 179
North Kensington 52
Northern Ireland 68
North Lambeth 100–3, 109, 118, 135, 173, 177
Norwood 26, 109, 134–5
Norwood Conservative Association 214
Norwood Labour Party 192, 194, 198–9
Notting Hill Gate 52, 125, 222
Nottingham 106, 221, 228

Olympic Games (2012) 76
One Member One Vote (OMOV) 199
Operation Swamp 81, 224
Osamor, Martha 229
Oxford 167

308 *Index*

Paddington 26
Patterson, Sheila 221
Poale Zion 233, 236
Palestine 232, 239
Pankhurst, Sylvia 28, 36, 112, 168, 211
Paris 2, 5, 65
Parliamentary elections *see* general
  elections
Patriotism 95, 242–3, 247, 255
Peace and disarmament 36, 179–80,
  204, 246
Penge 211
Pentecostal churches 126, 129, 208, 238
People's Front 169, 189
Phillips, Marion 212
Picketty, Thomas 207, 255
Pitt, David 220, 227
Plaid Cymru 68
Poll Tax 198–9
Poor Law 23, 29–30, 33, 46, 172, 250
Poplar 1, 3, 25, 29, 36, 45, 65
Poplar Labour Party 97, 196
Poplarism 30, 35, 60
Population 40, 62, 78, 265–6, 269
Populism 1, 207, 260
Port of London Authority 47
Porter, Shirley 116
poverty 4, 27, 42, 62, 75, 154, 239,
  245–8, 250
Powell, Enoch 53, 146, 219
Precariat 10, 63, 69, 77, 248, 252
Preston 41, 93, 97, 128
Proffitt, Russell 228
Progressives 22, 26, 36, 47, 101, 138,
  181, 245
Progressive Alliance 18–28, 31–2, 57,
  178, 245, 249
Protestants 219, 236
Purley 107, 142

Quakers 174, 179
Quelch, Harry 172

Race 219–232
racism 9, 226–7, 240, 249–50
Rachmanism 13, 222, 225
rate capping 45, 170, 197, 248
rate-equalisation 12, 35, 59–60, 246
ratepayers associations 113, 140–1, 179,
  246, 256
Rayner, Angela 259
rearmament 66, 95, 247, 255
Redbridge 122
Referendum (2016) 71, 149, 278

regeneration 74–81, 114–8, 253
relative deprivation 8, 249
religion 12, 117, 126, 129, 232–39
residuum *see* social class
Revolutionary Communist Party 194
Richmond 48
Right to Buy 59, 116, 148
Right to the City Movement 253
Riots 9, 125, 222–4, 227
Rogers, George 52, 219
Rosebury, Lord 11
Royal Arsenal Cooperative Society
  (RACS) 34, 65, 146, 180, 188, 192, 202
Ruskin Labour Church 233

Saklatvala, Shapurji 118, 189
Salter, Ada 11
Salter, Alfred 11, 191
Scarman Report 224
School Board elections 172
Scottish National Party 68, 259
Sealey, Phil 225
secularisation 233–4
service vote 37, 272
settlement movement 23, 25
sheffield 55, 206
Shoreditch 25
Silvertown 21, 30
Slum Vote 12, 250
Smethwick 226
Smith, Frank 137, 177
social class: definition 7–10, 20, 77,
  80–1, 127–133, 251–6; labour vote by
  class 153; "new working class" 155,
  248, 251, 255; polarisation 61, 125,
  224, 250; residiuum 18, 27, 40, 63,
  87; white working-class 2, 87–9, 132,
  151, 155–6, 207, 220, 241–3, 256, 259;
  working-class Tories 102
social cohesion 254
Social democracy, definition 46–7, 126
Social Democratic Federation (SDF) 22,
  26, 37, 96, 168, 172, 174–5
Social Democratic Party (SDP) 4, 32, 56,
  61, 146, 197
Social Democratic Party (Germany) 170,
  186, 203, 246
Social liberalism 207, 239, 242–3, 254–5
Social mobility 8, 77, 81, 151, 260
socialism 167–205
socialism, ethical 174–6, 195
Socialist Labour League 195
Socialist League 22, 169, 175, 181, 191
Socialist Sunday School 176

Index 309

Somers, Annie 212
South Kensington 51
Southall 66
Southwark 22, 38, 63, 120, 226
Spanish Civil War 169, 214
Spatial-mobility 98, 124
Stand Up to Racism Movement 220
Stanley, Henry, Morton 136
Starmer, Keir 2, 11, 241, 259
Stepney 102, 235
St. Helier Estate (LCC) 46, 104
Stimpson, David 197
Stockwell 99, 106
Stranks, Sidney 179
Strauss, George 169, 191
Streatham 65, 114–6, 148–9
Streatham Labour Party 194
Streatham Liberal Association 198
suburbanisation 12, 18–19, 26, 83, 85, 98, 152, 256–7
Summerskill, Edith 216
Sweden 70

Tanner, Jack 111
Tariff Reform 135
Tatchell, Peter 61, 120, 198, 207
Thorne, Will 36
Thornton Heath 142, 210
Tillett, Ben 108, 179
Tilley, John 229
Tokyo 1
Tottenham 30, 38, 42, 264
Tower Hamlets 23, 26, 32, 35, 38, 63, 78, 253
Trade Union Congress (TUC) 29, 35, 186
Trade union membership 33, 41, 62–3, 95, 115–6
Trade Unions 9, 12, 22–3, 27, 57, 62, 95–7
Trades councils 28, 109, 169, 172, 180, 187, 190
Transport & General Workers Union (T&GWU) 58, 95, 106, 109, 138, 187, 252
Tressell, Robert 101
Trotskyism 169–70, 194, 196, 201, 203, 250
Tulse Hill 104
Twain, Mark 54
Twelves, Joan 198–9

Union of Democratic Control 179
Union of Post Office Workers 185
Unite Union 252
Urban Priority Areas 225

Vauxhall 65, 82, 114–6, 148–9
Vauxhall By-election (1987) 229
Vienna 2, 66
Vietnam War 59, 195, 247

Waddon, Croydon 107, 111, 142, 177
Wainwright, Hilary 196
Wales 68, 94, 113
Walthamstow 18, 42, 45
Walworth 22
Wandsworth 26, 42, 120
Waterloo 100, 102
Webb, Beatrice 23, 29
Wembley 27, 107, 113
Westminster 45, 85, 99
West Ham 3, 18, 22–4, 35, 45, 264
West Norwood 99
Whitechapel 37, 63, 232, 235
Willesden 27, 42, 66, 107, 113
Williams, Thomas 139
Wilmott and Young 84, 94, 125
Windrush Scandal 231
Wilson, Harold 146
Women organisers 212, 214, 218
Women's Advisory Committee 212–4
Women's Cooperative Guild (WCG) 28, 34, 210–11
Women's Labour League 97, 111, 208–9, 211
Women's Liberation Movement 210, 218
Women's Publicity Planning Association 215
Women's Sections 35, 209–19
Women's Trade Union League 108
Women's Unit GLC 209
Woodcraft Folk 187
Woods, Diedre 61, 198
Woolwich 3, 21, 25, 93, 202
Woolwich Arsenal 28, 65, 110
Working Men's Clubs 100, 175, 233

Youth culture 253

Zionism 232–5, 239–42

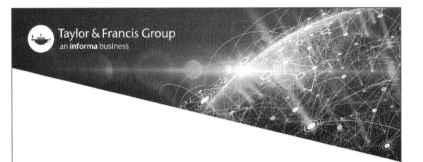

Printed in the United States
By Bookmasters